D0554533

ROTH FAMILY FOUNDATION

Music in America Imprint

Michael P. Roth

and Sukey Garcetti

have endowed this

imprint to honor the

memory of their parents,

Julia and Harry Roth,

whose deep love of music

they wish to share

with others.

The publisher gratefully acknowledges the generous contribution to this book provided by the Music in America Endowment Fund of the University of California Press Foundation, which is supported by a major gift from Sukey and Gil Garcetti, Michael Roth, and the Roth Family Foundation.

Making Music in Los Angeles

Making Music in Los Angeles

Transforming the Popular

CATHERINE PARSONS SMITH

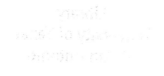

University of California Press

BERKELEY   LOS ANGELES   LONDON

University of California Press, one of the most distinguished university presses in the United States, enriches lives around the world by advancing scholarship in the humanities, social sciences, and natural sciences. Its activities are supported by the UC Press Foundation and by philanthropic contributions from individuals and institutions. For more information, visit www.ucpress.edu.

The following chapters were previously published in different form and appear courtesy of their original publishers: a portion of chapter 3 as "Making Music in Los Angeles: The E. C. Bagley Collection," *Coranto: Journal of the Friends of the USC Libraries,* no. 26 (1992): 56–70; chapter 4 as " 'Popular Prices Will Prevail': Setting the Social Role of European-Based Concert Music," *Selected Reports in Ethnomusicology* 10 (1994): 206–21 (Los Angeles issue), used by permission of the Department of Ethnomusicology Publications, University of California, U.C. Regents; chapter 8 as " 'Something of Good for the Future': The People's Orchestra of 1912–1913," *Nineteenth-Century Music* 16, no. 2 (1992): 147–61, copyright 1992–1993 by The Regents of the University of California; and chapter 10 as "Founding the Hollywood Bowl," *American Music* 11 (1993): 206–43, courtesy of University of Illinois Press.

University of California Press
Berkeley and Los Angeles, California

University of California Press, Ltd.
London, England

Library of Congress Cataloging-in-Publication Data
Smith, Catherine Parsons.
    Making music in Los Angeles : transforming the popular / Catherine Parsons Smith.
        p.   cm.
    Includes bibliographical references (p.) and index.
    ISBN 978-0-520-25139-7 (cloth : alk. paper)
        1. Music—Social aspects—California—Los Angeles—History—20th century.   2. Music—Social aspects—California—Los Angeles—History—19th century.   I. Title.
ML3917.U6S65   2007
780.9794'94—dc22   2006036207

Manufactured in the United States of America

16   15   14   13   12   11   10   09   08   07
10   9   8   7   6   5   4   3   2   1

This book is printed on New Leaf EcoBook 50, a 100% recycled fiber of which 50% is de-inked post-consumer waste, processed chlorine-free. EcoBook 50 is acid-free and meets the minimum requirements of ANSI/ASTM D5634-01 *(Permanence of Paper).*♾

Contents

Illustrations

TABLES

Preface and Acknowledgments

Making Music in Los Angeles evolved through a series of productive accidents and timely detours. Inspired by the wave of feminist discovery that had filtered into the field of musicology by the late 1970s, I found myself tracking the biography of a little-known American composer of opera, Mary Carr Moore. My quest led to Los Angeles, where some rather simple questions presented themselves: Why had "my" composer actually *chosen* to go there, to a city long ridiculed as not really much of a city at all? More to the point, why did she choose to *stay* there through the last half of a long and productive creative career, in a place long rumored to be utterly lacking in musical interest? I had long accepted what I now call the "musical vacuum" theory about music in Los Angeles. Moore's career forced me to reexamine my assumptions about her choice and started me thinking more carefully about the role of music and music making in the lives of Los Angelenos, in the lives of other Americans, and, by extension, even—especially—in our lives today.

I soon learned that there was much more to the city's musical life than the usually recognized handful of canonic high spots, such as the founding of the Philharmonic in 1919 and the arrival of the composer-émigrés from Hitler in the 1930s. Everywhere I looked, there was more material that raised more questions. As I discovered, my composer was just one of numerous journeyman composers who survived very nicely, most of them independent of the film colony, finding sufficient audiences and students and supporters to thrive, however modestly, in what was for many of them a kind of artistic Eden.[1] When I finished the Moore project, I was just discovering Los Angeles and the culture on whose shoulders she and her contemporaries stood.

A number of stories emerged as I worked backward, looking for an appropriate starting point for my new topic. Early on, there was a seminal contest over how concerts by visiting artists would be presented. There was the People's Orchestra, whose short and highly politicized career is now forgotten, because it was carefully ignored by the now-dominant *Los Angeles Times*. There were the contesting interests that, miraculously, gave the city the Hollywood Bowl as a permanent institution. There was a series of defining opera productions. There was the conundrum of the city's leading impresario, a self-promoting and tenacious individual who did not always attract universal admiration. After 1920, there was the puzzle of "new" music, welcomed early on and, after a few years, vigorously resisted. And finally, there was the Federal Music Project, whose strengths and weaknesses more or less reflected the position of music making and music makers at the end of my period. Coaxing out these accounts, and others, proved a long-term challenge.

My investigations continued intermittently, long after the biography of Moore was completed. Presently, my study came to include the decades from the arrival of the Santa Fe Railroad in the late 1880s up until the start of World War II. It encompasses the period of political Progressivism and, as it emerges, musical progressivism, along with their aftermath, that is, the emergence of the modern, with its own strengths and vulnerabilities that echo in our own time. All the while, the complexities of individual involvement in music making and in the overall cultural fabric of the community grew more obvious. Almost certainly more such stories remain unidentified and untold—very likely as many music-making stories as there were communities and generations—just in this one city. In these pages, it seems, I have just begun to count the ways that we, like those long-ago Los Angeles characters, have come to love and struggle with music as an essential means of communication and self-expression.

The stories are unique, but their underlying messages are not. In Los Angeles, as elsewhere, music inevitably reflects the wider cultural fabric and even influences it. As I attempted to understand some of these inflections, I marveled at the wealth of music making that kept turning up and at the passionate engagement it regularly attracted among all who involved themselves, whatever the manner of their participation. The feminist origins of my engagement with music making in Los Angeles have surely affected the outcome of this study, both my various discoveries and my ways of interpreting them, although by now the influences are more indirect, entangled with other themes and considerations.

.   .   .

Several opportunities over a considerable period have enabled me to pursue this project to its completion. Sabbatical leaves from the University of Nevada, Reno, and two fellowships from the National Endowment for the Humanities all made this project possible and contributed materially to my exploration of what is basically a new area of study. Shorter fellowships from the Andrew Mellon Foundation Fund at the Huntington Library, the New York Times Foundation, and the Institute for the Federal Theatre Project at George Mason University, along with several travel grants from the Graduate School and the Department of Music at UNR, allowed research on specific topics.

Many individuals have helped me discover and interpret the wealth of Los Angeles music history explored here. Their expertise has been invaluable, and I thank them for sharing it with me. I am especially grateful to the staff at the California State Library in Sacramento, the University of California at Los Angeles (both the Young Research Library and the Music Library), the University of California at Berkeley (both the Bancroft Library and the Music Library), California State University Long Beach, Cambria Master Recordings and Archives, the Honnold/Mudd Library of the Claremont Colleges, the Getty Library, the Hollywood Bowl Museum, the Huntington Library, the Library of Congress, Los Angeles City Archives, George Mason University (Fenwick Library), Los Angeles Music Center Archives, Los Angeles Philharmonic Archives, Los Angeles Public Library, National Archives and Records Administration, New York Public Library for the Performing Arts, San Francisco Public Library, Southwest Museum, Syracuse University (Arents Library), University of Arkansas at Fayetteville Library, University of Melbourne (Grainger Museum), University of Southern California (Archival Research Center), University of Texas at Austin (Harry Ransom Humanities Research Library), Yale University (Beinecke Library), and my home library at the University of Nevada, Reno. Innumerable discussions with colleagues at UNR (both in music and in several other departments) and in the Society for American Music, the American Musicological Society, and the Conferences on Feminist Theory and Music, held biennially since 1989, have stimulated and challenged my thinking. Several individuals made their private collections available and lent their personal expertise, and I thank them. Lance Bowling at Cambria Master Recordings and Archives of Lomita, California, has been particularly helpful; his Cambria label plans to issue an audio CD of sounds from pre–World War II Los Angeles in support of this volume. Ralph E. Shaffer helped with accessing materials not easily available otherwise. In addition, I am particularly grateful to Paul Charosh, John Koegel, Leta Miller, Gayle Murchison, David

Nicholls, Cindy Richardson, Wayne Shirley, Marge Sill, and several others for their careful reading of all or substantial portions of the manuscript at various stages and for the valuable suggestions that resulted. The editors at the University of California Press and a whole series of anonymous readers there have contributed materially to the shaping of the volume as well as the preparation of the manuscript. Family members and friends have heard much more about this project than they might have chosen for themselves; I thank them profoundly for their tolerance and patience, their consistent support, and their many useful suggestions. In the end, though, I am responsible for the topics chosen, the opinions expressed, and the conclusions drawn in this book.

Chapters 3, 4, 8, and 10 originally appeared in different form in scholarly journals and are used here with permission. Earlier versions of these and several other chapters were read as papers to the Society for American Music, the American Musicological Society, and elsewhere.

I also acknowledge with thanks a subvention from the Society for American Music, which defrayed most of the author's expenses for manuscript preparation.

1 Music Making as Popular Practice

Los Angeles is regularly reported as having had little to offer in the way of music—"culturally unfocused" in one recent, relatively tolerant formulation—until émigrés from Hitler's Germany began to find their way there in the mid-1930s.[1] Yet in 1910 more musicians and music teachers were working there, in proportion to its total population, than in any other city in the United States. In fact, almost half again as many professional music makers addressed the demand for music teachers, church soloists, bandsmen, theater musicians, and other paid music makers per capita than in New York City, then the center of the entertainment industry in America.[2] Even if the U.S. Census figures (summarized in two appendices here) are less than precise, it is clear that, long before canned and digitized music of all descriptions could be had virtually anywhere for little more than the touch of a finger, a lot of music making took place, involving a lot of people. More than that, the presence of music was so fully taken for granted, so commonplace as a way of life, that later observers thought its abundance scarcely worth comment. Music making was truly popular.

This widespread practice of music as a popular activity changed over the three decades before and after that 1910 Census, just as other aspects of the culture changed, resulting in the "transformation" referred to in my title. By following that changing practice in this one city, over that half century and more, this book lays bare some unexpected elements bridging two style periods in music (late romantic versus modernist for concert music) that are often, for the United States, considered separate and almost independent of each other. On one hand, the book sketches a part of the essential background against which the musics of commercial mass culture blossomed in the twentieth century. On the other, it suggests some previously unexplored, even deliberately ignored, connections (and disconnections) between the practice of American musical romanticism (sometimes labeled the "genteel" tradition) and the seemingly abrupt emergence of musical modernism in the 1920s. Although these two periods have been described in terms of stylistic differences in the music, it turns out that the gaps between them reflect changing ideas and practices about class, gender, age, and ethnicity as well. Those gaps, as we also discover, were repeatedly contested in music as elsewhere, though in often fragmented and indirect ways.

As is already clear, I use *popular* here in its earlier sense of widely prevalent forms of engagement with music, rather than in the later sense of music's most commercially profitable (as well as widely prevalent) genres. At the start of my period, the term was appropriate to much music that we no longer consider popular. In fact, a lot of the music making (and music makers) traced in this book became less visible when the term *popular music* came to imply primarily the music of commercial mass culture. Some music of that older sense of popular has disappeared, and some of it came to be considered "elite," partly for its increasingly rigid class associations, partly because its survival depended on some form of special investment or some other cultural formation, as opposed to commercial mass culture. Because of this focus, the book might be thought of as describing a special case of the "antimodern."[3] In music, though, the situation has its own complexities, for that now largely submerged earlier practice did much to shape the terms under which much later public music making took place. It becomes clearer than ever in these pages that apparently straightforward acts of music making carried wider social and political freight than the notes on the page might suggest and that the complexities of the process were far greater than music critics noted at the time or even than recent cultural critics have argued.[4]

This, then, is a social history. Even though much of it deals with what is now called concert music, it rarely deals directly with the notes or the sounds. Instead, it centers on the extensive web of listeners, patrons, teachers, students, and entrepreneurs, as well as performers and composers, all of whom I include in the term *music makers*. It celebrates the involvement of a large portion of the population, even before commercial mass culture and new forms of mechanical or electronic reproduction gained more than a toehold.[5] The European-based concert and opera traditions, right along with the practices of domestic, theatrical, ceremonial, religious, and many other kinds of music, all had widespread currency in Los Angeles—as elsewhere in the United States—as common means of self-expression and communication, among men as well as women, and across a wide range of ethnic and racial identities.[6] Most of the music making discussed here comes from these traditions and practices.

I treat a wide range of music makers, women as well as men, for no single individual or group could embody so widespread and varied a practice. The organization of public music making is also very important to my study. Yet I have deliberately chosen to avoid focusing on such criteria as success in importing the most famous virtuosi to give public concerts, or the music of commercial mass culture, or the primacy of the mid-twentieth-century aesthetic of high modernism, as other authors have done.[7] (All of these criteria come up, but so do many other things less often discussed. On the same principle, I have not placed the Los Angeles Philharmonic Orchestra (1919–), for long the lynchpin of the city's concert music establishment, in its customary front-and-center position.) Often-drawn distinctions such as amateur-versus-professional or public-versus-private are likewise downplayed or, occasionally, challenged. All of the four types of activities proposed by Michael Broyles as necessary to the formation of a concert music establishment—the development of musical organizations including performing groups, the construction of concert venues, the emergence of patrons, and the education of an audience—are among the activities reported here. Yet they are present in far less tidy categories and with far more overlapping and mixed motivations than those neat categories might imply; even then they are not the whole story, for commercial presenters and their various economic interests played an essential role, too.[8] In practice, that means that the individuals I discuss were performing musicians as well as variously patrons, entrepreneurs, and other musical activists. Some can fit into more than one of these categories. Social class, gender conventions, racial and ethnic identities, business interests, and political leanings shaped the manner of their participation as much as did individual talent and personal inclination.

This is a regional study as well as a social history, unusual because it does not focus on a specific genre or performing organization, as many studies centered on individual cities do.[9] For Los Angeles, the only works with wide historical aspirations until recently have been Henry W. Splitter's "Music in Los Angeles," covering Anglo concert life and theater circa 1850–1900, and Howard Swan's 1952 *Music in the Southwest*, which traces the history of concert music in the city almost entirely through the eyes of one impresario.[10] As a regionally based social history, this book takes us in directions in which, given the constraints of their one-volume format, the several excellent overviews of American music cannot go, for their size limitations prevent them from offering more than broad-stroked accounts of regional differences.[11] The West Coast perspective of this book is, in fact, a rare one for an investigation of Progressive-era music making or the advent of musical modernism in the United States. The choice of Los Angeles, with its early geographic isolation, its roots as a Mexican mission settlement, and its relatively late development as an Anglo city, may even seem quixotic for such a study. Yet, within limits, Los Angeles can be taken as a case history for medium-sized U.S. cities, especially those in the heartland and the far west. Minneapolis, Denver, Portland (Oregon), and Oakland (California), for example, all reported large proportions of musicians and music teachers in those tantalizing 1910 Census figures in appendix B, table 10; as with many other cities, they too organized community choruses, symphonies, and concert series, all with their own stories.

There is some justice in choosing Los Angeles as an example for the Progressive era, though, for the city was a hotbed of political and social progressivism. (Most dramatically, California's late vote for Bull Moose candidate Theodore Roosevelt tilted the presidential election of 1912—the first election in which California women voted—away from the dominant Republican Party to Democrat Woodrow Wilson.) Actually, public music making became directly entangled with Progressive politics; that entanglement is an important part of this story. There is also irony in choosing Los Angeles, for the city eventually became one of the major world centers for the new entertainment technologies (especially the movies, but also recording and television) that radically changed the practice of music making in the course of the twentieth century. These new practices, though spawned in part from the Progressive-era music culture, ultimately dwarfed much of that culture. I defer here to the substantial bibliography that already exists on the new media, for the several general studies of Southern California history are largely silent about the music making discussed here, although it played so important a role in the culture.[12]

Another irony, given Los Angeles' more recent racial, ethnic, and linguistic diversity, is important here. In 1890, one-fourth of the city's population was foreign-born, at first glance a large proportion but nevertheless small by comparison with San Francisco, Chicago, or New York. Even the residents who identified themselves in the U.S. Census as Mexican, always more numerous than in most other U.S. cities, remained a relatively small minority, though one with more influence than the suspiciously low census numbers suggest. (The city had, after all, begun as a part of Mexico, and the cultural memory of this origin has never been lost.) During the years of the spectacular growth described here, most of the city's new residents were already U.S. citizens, coming from elsewhere in the country rather than from abroad, giving the city a rather unusual degree of middle-class homogeneity.

It may come as a surprise that the broad transformation in the practice and experience of music such as is exposed here can be traced through a social history that focuses on any one city, let alone this one. Surprisingly, the concept of transformation emerged in the course of what began as a regional study, with no real idea that it would become the book's main theme. Coupled with the emphasis on music making as an everyday activity, the regional approach has another, related aspect. It has been pointed out with respect to literature that regional studies allow women more visibility and more agency than has been the case for more broadly based surveys.[13] Thus, the feminist tilt present here (in this case by initial authorial intent) has been closely tied to the regional approach all along; it has also become a catalyst, an essential element for understanding the dynamics of cultural transformation.

In all U.S. cities, women were always much more numerous among music makers than they were among the most famous musicians of the age, and Los Angeles had a significantly higher proportion of female residents than was the case for other western cities.[14] Women made up 60 percent of the musicians and music teachers who serviced the city's music makers in the 1910 Census and 61 percent of the total population. (See table 8 in appendix B.) Locally as well as nationally, performing musicians tended to be male and foreign-born, whereas teachers of music were more likely to be female and U.S.-born. (The tendency for women and men with special talent and strong interest in music to follow different career paths is dramatized here, part of my insistence on including both in most of the stories told.) The high proportion of women engaged in public music making, much of which turned out to be teaching, led some critics to express concern over the "feminization" of a profession long considered dangerously unmasculine for U.S.-born white males, even after the ratio of women to men was reversed in the 1920s.[15]

There is, further, a class distinction about music making relative to the sexes, for music makers in this time period were only beginning to emerge from the cultural assumption that the music professions were not appropriate for U.S.-born males, for whom almost any profession or trade would presumably be more "manly" as well as more stable financially, but that music making was, for middle-class women, a desirable domestic skill. As opportunities arose to make music outside the home, women of a certain class and level of achievement were better situated to pursue them than they were to take up many other occupations. In addition, the woman-dominated audience that had developed for many music events, and indeed the separate "women's sphere," remained important even after the Nineteenth Amendment gave women the vote in 1920, as the thriving women's club culture of the following two decades attests. Forms of music making mainly associated with the women's sphere rapidly lost their formal audiences after 1945 and have by now largely disappeared. It seems important to acknowledge these points as playing a major role in several of the music-centered projects described here.

The relatively short period covered here—just over a half century—lends a certain Aristotelian unity of time as well as place to this story. Concert organizing, so large a factor in this narrative, developed over a considerably longer period in cities older than Los Angeles. Almost from the start in this case, the newer media were beginning to challenge or augment the older practices of concert giving, live theater, music printing, piano sales, and do-it-yourself home music making, as means for the dissemination of music. The older practices rubbed up against developing new technologies with increasing frequency, especially from the time of World War I. In addition to these factors, contemporary, largely external but influential changes in the organization of the entertainment industry were impacting public music making and changing the lives of working musicians.[16] Moreover, the rapid population growth that took place nationwide (mainly through immigration) was carried to an extreme in LA, lending its own twist to the narrative. While the overall population of the United States tripled in the half century between 1880 and 1930, Los Angeles grew by a factor of 100, from a town of 11,000 to a metropolis of 1.2 million. (See appendix A for more of the numbers.) Up until 1930, the city's population at least doubled in every decade but one. This meant that local institutional history was carried by relatively few people, and traditions of music making were frequently readapted to the new geographical situation or reinterpreted by the continuing supply of new residents.[17] Thus, as critic Julian Johnson remarked in 1909, Los Angeles was by no means a "settled city" with "settled musical interests."[18]

The Progressive era in U.S. history encompassed the closing of the western frontier, the Spanish-American War, and World War I. Higher real income and shorter hours for workers combined with the new technologies of sound recording, motion pictures, and (eventually) radio to draw forth an entirely new cluster of industries, collectively dubbed commercial mass entertainment, and even new kinds of music.[19] The new industrial and commercial monopolies generated a labor movement in their wake.[20] Along with immigration, increased ethnic diversity, and the women's rights movement, these changes (and more) generated public discussion, most visibly among educated, U.S.-born white men, about who we were as a nation and what we should become. Both the changes and the discussions had broad implications for music making, which became especially clear in the debates precipitated by Antonín Dvořák's sojourn in the United States in the 1890s.[21] In the various pronouncements of the participants in that debate, the rapid development of commercial mass culture and the major role played by music in it were acknowledged only indirectly. The increasing polarization of commercially successful (i.e., "popular" music, in the later sense, as opposed to "elite" music) was not acknowledged either. Specific racial and ethnic contributions are subsumed at one end of this polarization, unrecognized in print but widely understood nonetheless. African American contributions were ignored, and European, particularly Germanic influences, decried as participants in the discussion fumbled toward the invention of a characteristically "American" tradition in music. In Los Angeles, the discussions about "American" music bore their most visible fruit in the production of the American opera *Fairyland*, but they also were part of the background that generated other experiments, such as the People's Orchestra.) The particular size and makeup of Los Angeles' immigrant populations, shown in appendix A, was another factor that affected the changing status of music making in the early twentieth century.

. . .

This investigation of the popular (widely prevalent) in Progressive-era music takes several specific forms, including explorations of events, organizations, and individuals, as it exposes these underlying, extramusical themes. The several stages in the transformation of my title are marked here by descriptions of the visits of three traveling opera companies (selected from many.) Each appeared under very different and very revealing circumstances. At the start, opera was popular entertainment in both senses, with visits from a half dozen companies in most years; therefore, I begin part I with the spectacular 1887 visit of the pretentious National Opera Company and its anomalous reception in Los Angeles as a highly successful popular entertainment. (The company's visit to Los Angeles is routinely omitted from accounts of its history, making this moment the first of several surprises here.)[22]

I continue with discussions of the careers of several individuals. In addition to any claim they have to historical importance or previous neglect, they are chosen to demonstrate the range of personal involvement to be found among individuals caught up in this culture of music making. I take up such disparate figures as Charles Leland "Lee" Bagley, journeyman clarinet player and durable union activist, and Lynden Ellsworth Behymer, the city's best-known impresario, whose role was rather different from what has been commonly thought. I describe a selection of early public events for which working musicians provided music. Among performers, I concentrate on Harley Hamilton, respected violinist, teacher, and conductor, and Edna Foy, aspiring violinist and long-time concertmaster of the Los Angeles Women's Orchestra. Public concerts were often organized by the musicians themselves or by early theater operators and music dealers, such as Henry C. Wyatt (hereafter H. C. or Harry C. Wyatt) and Frederick W. Blanchard (hereafter F. W. or Fred W. Blanchard). Some of these individuals—most prominently Behymer, who surfaces several times—remained active and influential for decades. In addition to the wider cultural implications of music making, I want to establish what making music meant to each of these individuals and how it helped define and was defined by their roles in the culture. They remind us that, no matter how mediated by cultural circumstances, music making can bring forth powerful, sometimes unexpected and contradictory individual responses; these can be emotional, sensual, rational, intellectual, kinesthetic, or any of these in combination, and they can change with changing conditions.

Part II addresses the period circa 1905–22, when musical progressivism reached its high point and its ideology was most fully articulated. Its major operatic event, the heavily promoted local production of a new "American" opera, Horatio Parker's ill-fated *Fairyland* (1915), actually followed several other Progressive-era landmarks spread over several years. Its predecessors included the construction of what came to be known as Philharmonic Auditorium, with its specific church connection as a lasting reminder of deeply held convictions about the moral and ethical power of music, common across the political spectrum; the short and conflicted career of the People's Orchestra (another discovery); and the events leading up to the founding of the Symphonies under the Stars at the Hollywood Bowl, by far the most successful and long-lasting product of progressive music making and ideology in Los Angeles. Their organizers and patrons, among them Clara Bradley Burdette, Charles Farwell Edson, Artie Mason Carter, and (once more) Fred W. Blanchard, are perhaps an even more varied lot than the individuals who appear in part I.

In part III, I take up the transition from the Progressive to the modern and the "ultramodern," thus addressing aesthetic issues more directly along with cultural changes. Performers and composers (Olga Steeb, Dane Rudhyar, Harold Bruce Forsythe, William Grant Still, and more) take the stage somewhat more frequently here. Back-to-back visits of two competing opera companies in 1925 dramatize the demise of opera as a widely popular event and its entrenchment as an elite, class-affirming happening. Where visiting opera companies large and small had once been a staple of the much smaller city's theatrical life, now two weeks of large-scale opera were too much, even though the city's population was ten times larger. Other changes are juxtaposed with the simultaneous social ascent and accompanying ossification of opera. For one, a potent echo of the New Negro movement resonated in the Los Angeles of the 1920s.

The repertoire of traveling virtuosi and the large opera companies may have grown static, but the "ultramodern" arrived anyway, leading to a new aesthetic polarization between the old and the new in concert music as well as to a new relationship between the sexes in matters musical. Contrary to received tradition, experimental, often dissonant ultramodernist music was at first welcomed in Los Angeles, although the welcome deteriorated rapidly after 1926. The welcome reminds us forcefully of the early identification of the ultramodern with mysticism and the occult, as well as its association with the dangerously foreign "other." (This story, told in chapter 13, has been so well obliterated that even the founders of the Evenings on the Roof series a decade later were unaware of it. They believed that they had introduced ultramodernism to Los Angeles themselves.)

The career of the Federal Music Project, a part of the Depression era's Works Progress/Work Projects Administration (WPA in both cases) (1935–42), serves as a postscript, both summing up the role of music making through the Progressive era and setting the scene for the music making of a later generation. The FMP's Los Angeles version included an effort to reinvent opera as a community-based ensemble event and restore its popular aspect in a new way. Although that project ran aground in a sea of mismanagement, the changes it helped set in motion became significant in later decades.

Differences in the cultural values associated with different genres make the stories diverse for bands, orchestras, opera, choruses, and other music media, but they share some elements in common. Tensions were pervasive and continuing over the ways performances were organized and promoted. A range of commercial aspirations and more-or-less altruistic interests was always present, with seemingly endless variations and anomalies. Sometimes the divisions fell along lines separating political Progressives (with some Democrats and socialists as musical allies) from more orthodox Republicans. Most often, the issues involved who the audiences should be, including the construction (literal and figurative) of venues and the setting of ticket prices, as well as what features of performance and repertoire were considered most desirable. Gender, too, became an underlying theme, for women were more likely to claim the high ground of altruism and to act under the old banner of music, particularly concert music, as a secular religion. It is no accident that women were so powerfully involved in the idealistic ventures described in part II or that the disillusionment with ultramodernism that becomes so clear in part III was tied to the decoupling of dissonant-sounding and experimental music from religious mysticism. Indeed, it was in the 1920s that the role of L. E. Behymer as impresario became a negative one, discouraging new musical enterprises and in the process shunting women toward what was fast becoming a ghettolike women's club culture, despite such successes as the low-budget opera reading clubs.

Throughout, the distinction between the popular and the elite in music making was unstable, its inflections dependent on both the date and, in part, the position of the observer as well as the genre. As becomes clear, opera, once a major, self-supporting element of popular culture, struggled to survive as new forms of popular culture, particularly the movies but also vaudeville, emerged to shove it aside. (Signs of its rebirth were still rare at the end of the period discussed in this book.) It is one of the ironies that the symphony orchestra and its literature, which had so fully captured the imagination and intelligence of so many well-trained musicians of goodwill, became so thoroughly entrenched in opera's elitist role, dependent by the end of World War I for its audiences and its very survival on the patronage of the white middle and upper classes. Fortunately, a constructive, if quiet, cross-fertilization has always occurred among the relatively elite operatic and symphonic repertoires and the genres we think of as more commercially oriented or less musically literate, if only because no music making, and none of its makers, exists in a cultural vacuum.

For all my claims of inclusiveness, I acknowledge several omissions as well. Mexicans colonized the Los Angeles area several generations before the coming of the Anglos; their continuing and diverse presence has always been significant, even at those moments when their numbers were relatively small in proportion to the whole population. In treating that influence only in passing here, I defer to the already large body of scholarship on the Mexican presence and influence in Southern California.[23] Likewise, I have not addressed in any detail the growing importance of the Hollywood movie colony, the technological changes in music making, or the coming of the émigrés from Hitler. Each of these topics would have provided many more excellent stories and greater insight; together they would have extended this book to several more volumes.

It is not surprising that a city's music making carried these complex and incomplete cultural narratives in the Progressive era, a period when concert music and opera were marginalized as elite, white, confusingly gendered fragments of a much larger amusement industry. It is also not surprising that many persons strongly resisted the pigeonholing of concert music as an elite form of entertainment, with a relatively narrow audience, and that women played a large role as resisters. In fact, resistance to the elitist aspect that came with the commodification of concert life remained a major factor in Los Angeles' music history.

Some of what is described here survives now in such unexpected places as school music programs and remains prestigious for an ever-smaller circle. Yet it is little known or understood by most of those who make their music largely by newer means. The accounts here combine to reveal the wide range of music-making interests, activities, and values that lie beneath that remarkable census figure from 1910 and, in doing so, offer some insight about the changing role of music making in the city and the nation. Always, in Los Angeles as elsewhere, the basic issue in the Progressive era and afterward was about the ownership of music. The resulting struggles often echoed and even influenced pervasive battles about economic organization, class, gender, ethnicity, and race. Who would call the tunes, who would perform them, who would hear them, and what would be the context in which they would be heard? How did the widely popular in concert music and opera come to blossom in the era of political Progressivism, then find itself transformed a few decades later, unreasonably burdened with restrictive, class- and gender-related associations, yet prepared, on some level, for a rebirth? This book addresses those questions.

PART I

Music for the "People"

2 "The Largest and Most Enthusiastic Audience That Ever Has Assembled in the City"

The National Opera Company of 1887

The city of Los Angeles began as a Spanish mission, founded by a party of thirty-one ethnically diverse Mexican citizens, in 1791. The community that grew up around it remained small, diverse, isolated, and generally left to its own devices long after Mexico became an independent country and the missions were secularized and effectively abandoned. When Anglos began arriving in the 1840s and a takeover threatened from the north, Pio Pico, then governor of the Mexican province of Alta California, asked histrionically, "Shall we remain supine, while these daring strangers are overrunning our fertile plains, and gradually outnumbering and displacing us?"[1] The inability of the Mexican government to respond, because pressed by its losses in the Mexican War, made a nonanswer pretty much inevitable; as a result, Los Angeles joined the more Anglo-dominated northern part of California to become part of the United States in 1848. Like their more northerly compatriots, the Spanish-speaking Californios of the Los Angeles basin, who had only recently displaced the local Native Americans, were themselves displaced, left to assimilate as they might into the new culture. Later Anglo arrivals, most prominently Charles Lummis, cherished a sentimental fondness for the lost frontier culture, exoticizing it through mission-style architecture, a run of Chamber of Commerce–inspired fiestas, and an extensive folklore around the mythical "days of the dons."[2]

For most of the 1880s, the city-to-be remained an isolated frontier town on the far side of the already-storied Wild West. In a note for the 1880 Census, Mayor J. R. Toberman reported that half of the city's six square miles was planted in orchards and vineyards, which served as its parks. Its water supply came from the Los Angeles River, an uncertain source; street sweepings and dead animals were buried, spread, or dumped in the often dry riverbed downstream from the town. He also claimed two theaters seating about six hundred people each and several smaller rooms used for concerts and lectures. These catered variously to German- and Spanish-speakers, both of whom were abundant, as well as Anglos.[3] One venue was Turn-verein Hall, opened in 1872; another was the Teatro Alarcón, opened in 1878 in the Terán Building on Upper Main Street.[4] Already, visiting opera companies, albeit small ones, were an integral part of Los Angeles theatrical life, taking their place as a thriving popular entertainment with a widespread audience.[5] For example, in 1875, when the city's population was well under ten thousand, two small troupes came from San Francisco, offering popular operatic scenes. Sig. Marra's Grand Opera Company offered excerpts from *Don Pasquale* (Gaetano Donizetti, 1843) and *Il Trovatore* (Verdi, 1853); the Inez Fabbri Company offered excerpts from *Linda di Chamounix* (Donizetti, 1842), *Norma* (Vincenzo Bellini, 1831), *Der Freischütz* (Carl Maria von Weber, 1821), and *La Traviata* (Verdi, 1853). Both companies found it profitable to make return visits.[6] Considerable church music was also presented; late in the 1870s, local performers were to be heard at the "Unitarian Thursdays," initiated by Caroline Severance, and in other public and semipublic locations.

The celebrated Adelina Patti, perhaps the most famous diva of the nineteenth century, performed in Mott's (renamed Armory) Hall, the largest indoor performing space available, in 1886. Her visit helped inspire some serious theater building. The O. W. Child's Grand Opera House, seating a modest five hundred, opened in 1884, and the larger Los Angeles Theater opened four years later. In between, in 1887, Hazard's Pavilion, a much larger hall without permanent seating, went up. All three new venues hosted entertainments mainly intended for English-speaking audiences, marking the cultural shift brought by the city's rapid growth. Small opera troupes, all self-supporting, all offering cut-down versions of operas and operettas, expanded their visits in the course of the 1880s. Relative to the population, they played to good-sized audiences, usually at prices that ranged from twenty-five cents to a dollar. Shortly before the Grand Opera House opened, the Campanini Operatic Company had offered a program with operatic excerpts. At the Grand Opera House, the Bijou, Pyke, and the Emma Abbott English opera companies, all were well enough received to pay return visits, shifting to the larger Los Angeles Theater on their return. The Abbott company, which had first visited in 1885, offered *La Traviata*, *Lucrezia Borgia* (Donizetti, 1833), *The Mikado* (Gilbert and Sullivan, 1885), *Martha* (Friedrich von Flotow, 1847), *Il Trovatore*, *Mignon* (Ambroise Thomas, 1866), *La Sonnambula* (Bellini, 1831), *The Bohemian Girl* (Michael W. Balfe, 1843), *Faust* (Charles Gounod, 1859), *Linda di*

Figure 1. Third Street, Los Angeles, 1885. Day's Music Store is on the left. Courtesy of Cambria Master Recordings and Archives.

Chamounix, Crispino e la comare (Federico and Luigi Ricci, 1850), and *The Carnival of Venice* (Errico Petrella, 1851). When the Carlton Opera Company came for the first time, it played *Manon* (Jules Massenet, 1884), *Erminie* (Edward Jakobowski, 1885), and one other, then added *Fra Diavolo* (Daniel Auber, 1830) and *The Drum Major's Daughter* (Jacques Offenbach, 1879) for a second run.

The first transcontinental railroad, completed in 1869, had terminated hundreds of miles to the north, in San Francisco. Another line, a branch of the Southern Pacific, soon ran south from San Francisco to Veracruz, Mexico, providing Los Angeles with indirect rail links to both countries. When a second line was completed in 1886, this one leading directly from Kansas City to Los Angeles, the city's already-rapid growth accelerated. Competition from the new Atchison, Topeka, and Santa Fe drove cross-country fares down sharply and opened the city to the massive overland immigration that became its hallmark.

· · ·

Almost as soon as it was physically possible, an opera company that was designed to alter the role of opera as a favorite popular entertainment appeared on the scene. The National Opera Company, directed by the famous Theodore Thomas, was spectacularly different in overall size, aesthetic pretensions, and ticket prices from others that visited both before and after.[7] It required its own train (reportedly thirty-one cars) to haul its extensive costumes, scenery, and its 305 members, including a large orchestra, ballet, and chorus. (Most companies numbered a handful and depended on whatever local musicians constituted the orchestra at each stop.) Founded a year earlier as the American Opera Company, by Jeannette Thurber of New York, the giant company's stated purpose was to raise the standards of operatic performance around the country and domesticate large-scale operatic performances as self-consciously "American" by including Americans in the casts and singing in English.[8] The paying public would thus have access to the elite version of opera, not often available outside New York. The hoped-for result would be the provision of more elaborate and "authentic" (i.e., more complete) performances with full forces, presented as works of art with their own integrity for a nationwide public rather than as entertainments freely adapted to local circumstances.

In its second season, the big company traveled to San Francisco, then a much larger, richer, and more cosmopolitan city than LA. Its visit to Los Angeles was an afterthought at that time, and it remains so, for it is consistently omitted from later accounts of the company's career.[9] Despite its lofty aspirations and extravagant size, the company was expected to pay its own expenses on the road, just as the smaller companies did. In San Francisco, its audiences were disappointingly small, as apparently had been the case elsewhere. There was open time as a result, creating the possibility of an added engagement. Even so, the company's managers demanded the enormous guarantee of twenty thousand dollars—or so the LA papers reported—before it would risk playing to this smaller market to the south.

Otto Weyse, identified as a wealthy German wine merchant, was said to have posted the guarantee, probably acting in concert with other wealthy individuals. The Southern California backers tried a different approach from San Francisco's. They spurned the almost-new Grand Opera House, still the only structure in town equipped for visiting theatrical companies, partly because its owners demanded a higher rent than usual, partly because it seated only five hundred. Instead, they elected to rent Hazard's Pavilion, which had opened just two weeks earlier with a flower show (the first of many locally generated events there). The presence of Hazard's allowed the local promoters to try for a much larger audience than the formal Grand Opera

AMERICAN OPERA

BY THE

National Opera Company

Hazard's Pavilion,

Los Angeles, Cal.

Five Performances of

GRAND OPERA IN ENGLISH

BEGINNING MAY 16th, 1887.

225 Post Street—Dodge Brothers—San Francisco—4-15-87

Figure 2. National Opera Company program book, inside cover, May 1887. Two performances were added to the original five in response to the program's enthusiastic reception. Courtesy of Cambria Master Recordings and Archives.

Figure 3. Hazard's Pavilion, 1887–1904, site of conventions, exhibitions, major opera productions, and, in its last years, prizefights. Philharmonic Auditorium replaced it on the same site. Courtesy of Cambria Master Recordings and Archives.

House could accommodate. The new hall quickly acquired a temporary stage and approximately four thousand seats, some of them nothing more than redwood planks on temporary risers.

. . .

To give a better idea of what a huge undertaking this project was for this small and remote town, I digress long enough to describe the other commercial entertainment offered at the same time—in May 1887—as advertised (or otherwise covered) in the city's daily papers. Apart from a few locally organized fundraisers, theatrical competition with the big company came from events scheduled at the Grand Opera House. Earlier in May, Baird's Minstrels had played there for a few days, and Mr. and Mrs. George S. Knight had played *Over the Garden Wall* (Willis and Herman, 1885) and *Rudolph, Baron von Hollenstein* (Howard and Belasco, 1887) on alternate evenings, leavened by one matinee consisting of *Otto, a German* (Marsden, 1878). (Both companies had played in New York City and elsewhere, taking

Figure 4. Hazard's Pavilion interior, circa 1900. SECURITY PACIFIC COLLECTION/Los Angeles Public Library.

advantage of the popularity of dialect-based comedy.) During the opera's weeklong visit, Professor A. E. Carpenter offered "scenes in psychology and mesmerism . . . wonderful, amusing, instructive," also at the Grand Opera House.[10]

More serious competition came from the local Turf Club, which offered its second annual horse-racing meet, four afternoons at Agricultural Park (now Exposition Park), probably also the location for professional baseball games. The daily trotting and running events drew coverage as extensive as the big opera company, although reports on who attended and the finery of the women present (probably few in number at the racetrack) were absent from newspaper accounts. The Turf Club's ads included "Good Music" among its (clearly secondary) supporting attractions.[11] Closer in, at Main and Nineteenth, Washington Gardens, already a well-established pleasure garden and later an amusement park, offered an ostrich farm ("40 ostriches on display at all times"), a zoo, and regular concerts by Meine's military band and Doh's orchestra, well-known local groups.[12] Somewhere in between, a "Great Cyclorama" of the Battle of Gettysburg was open in the daytime and evenings. (Cycloramas were a popular form of spectacle before the advent of movies.) The ad concluded with directions: "Take the South Main-street cars to the immense Pavilion especially erected to exhibit this decisive battle of the late civil war." The National Opera Company's visit promised to eclipse all previous public events, certainly including those described in the ads.

Although they had had little advance notice of the National Opera's coming, all of the local newspapers carried enthusiastic promotional stories and plot summaries before each performance, then reviewed both the performance and the audience. With one accord, the normally competitive papers reported the whole week as a major social happening and a "high-class" music event, making a fuss over the splendor of the ladies' attire and printing long lists of the more prominent locals and out-of-towners from Pasadena and elsewhere who came for the performances. The prominent *Tribune, Herald,* and *Evening Express* all carried similar front-page accounts.[13] (So did the now-ubiquitous *Times,* at that point a minor sheet with a knack for attracting adverse libel judgments.) Although the reported numbers are contradictory, it is clear that the attendance was very large, especially considering the modest population of the area.

Newspaper reporting of the company's third performance, Charles Gounod's very popular *Faust,* illustrates the company's critical reception in more detail. The *Evening Express* called it a "grand performance. . . . A vast audience filled every seat in the great hall. . . . Not less than 4000 were present. . . . Much more pleasing to the popular ear than the music of Wagner."[14] The *Tribune,* which claimed the largest circulation in the city, stressed the popular, merely "tuneful" nature of Gounod's music and carefully distinguished between those listeners who were and were not musically "educated."

> The largest and most enthusiastic audience that ever has assembled in the city of Los Angeles greeted the National opera company last evening. Every seat in the vast auditorium was filled, and the aisles and lobbies were packed. Well did the performance justify the size of the audience. The opera of *Faust* is one of the most tuneful and bright in the company's repertoire. Gounod, while not a master of composition, as was his acknowledged ideal, Gluck, is yet a master of the art of composing music that pleases the ear of the people (by the people meaning these who have not been educated to understand and appreciate the more subtle movements of musical action). His opera of *Faust* is perhaps his best work. The cast last evening was fully adequate to the correct interpretation of this master piece, and the mise en scene was gorgeous in the extreme; indeed, it may be doubted that any production has ever been more elaborate.

The *Tribune* critic noted the production of *Faust* by the Abbott company two years earlier and remarked that Emma Juch, the Marguerite, lacked the appropriate "girl-like appearance of innocence and trusting love" of others who had sung the role, that she had not "enough mezzo-soprano quality" to handle the low notes, also that her acting lacked "the virile energy" of Emma Abbott. Nevertheless, he agreed that she infused "a deal of sympathetic earnestness," that "her voice is sweet and strong," and "her . . . moderate conception of the character fully disarmed any critical comparisons. She was enthusiastically applauded."[15]

In addition to its other coverage, the *Times* supplied a wonderfully Darwinian account of the history of music as it had evolved through the ages, leading directly to this particular week of opera: "In the [National] Opera Company we find the consummation of what Jubal in the world's younger days reached toward so eagerly with untaught hand; what the Egyptian, in his pride of power and pleasure, so longed to attain; what Greece hewed the way for, and with ready ear was listening for down the line of ages. Let us rejoice in our triumph and be glad. All the ages have been at work to give us what we now enjoy."[16] The company's initial repertoire had included *Lakmé* (Leo Delibes, 1883), *Lohengrin* (Wagner, 1853), *Faust*, *The Merry Wives of Windsor* (Otto Nicolai, 1849, here as a matinee), and *Aïda* (Verdi, 1871). The response to the first two operas was so enthusiastic that on Wednesday evening the management announced two added performances, a double bill of Delibes' ballet *Coppelia* (1870) and Victor Masse's *The Marriage of Jeannette* (1853), for Friday evening. (Flotow's *Martha* was substituted at the last moment for the ballet.) They also added a grand finale for Saturday evening, Anton Rubinstein's monumental *Nero* (1879). It is worth noting that none of these operas was as much as forty years old, and the grand finale less than ten. Thus this enormously successful run consisted entirely of what would be considered today contemporary works, in sharp contrast to the later practice of large opera companies.

Even allowing for the inconsistent and very likely exaggerated reports, the attendance figures are staggering for so small a city, whether for popular events or not. Some newspaper reports have the large house full for every performance except for the ill-fated Friday evening double bill. Some were silent on attendance at the matinee, raising a question about how full the house was that afternoon. The most conservative figures come from the *Express*, which reported only twenty-five hundred on opening night. For *Faust*, however, "a vast audience filled every seat in the great hall. . . . Not less than 4000 were present." For *Aïda*, "some say 3700 people were gathered." *Martha* drew the "lightest house," and the audience for *Nero* was the largest "except for *Faust*."[17] (The report for Tuesday's *Lohengrin* is missing, and no numbers are given for the matinee.) The *Tribune's* numbers were higher. It seems reasonable to guess that for the seven performances, the total audience numbered on the order of twenty thousand and may well have been more. The city's total population (including the very young and the very old) would not reach fifty thousand for another three years (or one hundred thousand if the surrounding towns are included). While it is true that some of the audience came from Pasadena and other neighboring towns and that some people attended more than once, the response to the National Opera Company indicates that its visit to Los Angeles was a grand community happening.[18] At least half the town's adult population was "elite" for the week, if the claims to such status for opera are to be taken seriously.

Clearly the role of opera—how its class association was to be viewed—was in a state of flux. The *Times* compared the National Opera Company's money-losing run in San Francisco with its performance in Los Angeles, one of the few places where it prospered, in these terms:

> The [San Francisco] city papers attribute this fact to the high prices at which tickets were sold, which excluded virtually the great middle-class of well-to-do people, who, while they have enough upon which to live in comfort, have not enough to pay three and four dollars for as many hours amusement. There is doubtless something in this. These high prices result in exclusiveness, shutting out that large class in the community who are able to pay only a fair price for being entertained, but whose combined contributions would make a much better showing than the larger sums paid by the wealthy. Many people thus deprived of attending are people of musical taste and fine culture—people who would be as appreciative listeners as could be desired. It would be no loss to any operatic company if their schedule of prices were placed within the reach of this class in every community. The time is coming when the wisdom of such a course will be more fully appreciated.[19]

Nevertheless, as the *Herald* reported, the audience "willingly paid prices for seats four times greater than the ordinary rate charged for first-class entertainments." From this the paper inferred "an aesthetic taste and culture on the part of our people which argues that we possess more dilettanti to the square foot than any other city in the Union."[20] The company's Los Angeles success resulted from the local decision to stage it in the largest available venue—a decision that clarifies opera's continuing role as popular entertainment, with a large public following.

Theodore Thomas later wrote in his scrapbook for this tour: "Travel with opera from April 10th, going to San Francisco, ended tour in Buffalo June 15th, 1887. Of all experiences in my life, this was the most trying."[21] While he may have been responding to specific problems with management, budgets, and productions, the comment may also relate to the far greater complexity of "improving" the taste of Americans for opera than for symphony, the challenge he mainly addressed during his long career. Certainly there were specific local challenges; adapting the scenery to the informal conditions of Hazard's Pavilion, which had no permanent stage, was just one. Even so, it is regrettable that Thomas apparently had nothing to say about the company's remarkable reception in Los Angeles. Thomas's elite opera company with popular aspirations drew an audience so large that it has to be seen as distinctly popular. At other times and places (and a generation later in Los Angeles), presenters of opera battled for the allegiance of high society and paid only lip service to the general public. Although the authoritative *New Grove* reports that the National Opera Company "failed dismally," it was anything but a failure in Los Angeles.[22] There, for one glorious week in 1887, newspaper hype or not, the elite, the popular, and even the commercially successful were unequivocally one and the same.

3 "A Precarious Means of Living"

Early Working Musicians and Their Jobs

"Music is to some a luxury, to others a necessity. . . . it is a business which feels the touch of financial depression more than others and has therefore at times furnished a precarious means of living to some of its votaries."[1] With this pronouncement, Charles Leland ("Lee") Bagley began his "History of the Band and Orchestra Business in Los Angeles," a project whose fruits appeared serially between 1924 and 1937 in the *Overture*, the monthly magazine published by Local 47, the white musicians' union in Los Angeles. Decade by decade starting with 1850 and year by year after he became active as a performer around 1890, Bagley proceeded to describe "individual musicians, bands, orchestras and things done by them . . . all theatres and other places of entertainment and amusement . . . , for these furnish most of the work done by musicians . . . teachers of instruments and to the instruments used in early times. . . . It will develop that some of the wealthiest and most prominent citizens of the community were a generation or two ago, conspicuous figures in the field of music."[2] His chronicle is laden with factual detail for which other documentation no longer exists. In his extended account, which goes through 1920, Bagley reveals only a little about himself but a lot about one stream of the city's musical life—the way working instrumental musicians practiced their trade.

Bagley's career was at first that of a journeyman musician; later he studied law and became a long-time union functionary on both the local and national levels.[3] Born in Iowa, Lee Bagley came to Santa Ana in Southern California as a teenager. He became a photographer's apprentice and by 1890 was playing clarinet and cornet in the town's Silver Cornet Band.[4] When he began to play professionally, he went first to Pasadena and then, in 1893, to Los Angeles. He played in the old Los Angeles Symphony Orchestra throughout its life span, from 1898 to 1920; in addition, he was a member

Figure 5.   Douglas Military Band. Courtesy of University of Southern California, on behalf of the USC Specialized Libraries and Archival Collections.

of the house band at the Mason Opera House (a commercial theater, despite
its name) for twenty-five years from the time it opened in 1903. Like most
working musicians in Los Angeles early on, his second, "day" job (in his case
as a photograph retoucher) was a matter of financial necessity.[5]

   In Bagley's Los Angeles, bands were very popular, performing at many
events, indoors and out. Early on, the Douglas Military Band, sometimes
called the Meine Brothers' Band, was the most prominent of several bands
that played, especially at outdoor events, year round. Anton Birklein, later
the proprietor of a music store, served as contractor. Birklein used an ad hoc
method of contacting the musicians (most already downtown, because they
held day jobs) to advise them of performance dates:

> Musicians' headquarters since 1882 had been at the cigar store of W. F.
> Ball, 110 S. Spring St. In 1893 it was still the rendezvous and at the
> noon hour daily, one could meet the principal musicians of the city
> there. Anton Birklein had long made the place headquarters for the
> Douglas Band and his method of engaging men was unique. Just inside
> the door and on the jamb thereof was screwed an ordinary slate of large
> dimensions with a slate pencil hanging down attached to a string. When
> an engagement was secured he wrote down at the top of the slate the

time and place of the function with such instructions about uniforms, [music] stands and other things as were necessary and then followed a list of the men he desired to employ with the instruments of each designated. The men would come and signify their acceptance by marking a cross after their respective names. If a man on the list could not accept the work he wrote the fact and another name was substituted. The slate continued to do duty until Birklein retired from the business fifteen years or more thereafter. Many times have I placed on it the "X" after my name, and to "watch the slate" was an everyday habit among all of us.[6]

An early union price list, published in 1895, lists the categories of events for which music was often provided, suggesting how widespread and varied their performances were:

UNION LIST OF MUSICIANS' JOBS (1895)

Grand Opera, Opera Buffa, Operettas, Spectacular Performances, etc.

Concerts, Oratorios, etc.

Weddings

Church Music

Theaters, Concert Halls, etc.

Stage Bands

Minstrels (necessary wardrobe to be furnished)

Dancing

Holidays

Picnics and Excursions

Escort

General Celebrations

Parades and Serenades

Political Meetings

Funerals

Public Parks, Gardens, etc.

Band Wagons

Fairs

Circuses and Menageries

Encampments

Private Houses

Entertainments

Banquets and Dinners at Hotels

Dancing Schools

Rehearsals (not already provided for)

Business Openings

Horse and Bicycle Races

Summer Resorts; etc.

> Scale for a single evening performance, five dollars, including one re-
> hearsal. An engagement lasting three nights or more, $2.50/performance,
> with $2 for an added matinee.[7]

Two large public events that would have fallen somewhere in these categories are described more fully here as examples of how musicians worked
in the larger community and of public music making.

LA FIESTA DE LOS ANGELES

The city's already well-established history as a Mecca for health seekers and
a center for new religious denominations was an aspect of its reputation that
commentators often treated with a certain wry humor, but the producers of
La Fiesta—the local Merchants and Manufacturers Association—took their
event and the image they sought for the city very seriously indeed.[8] The
city's business establishment adopted La Fiesta to cultivate the faux-
Spanish "days of the dons" image it sought to project, that is, for local color
and perhaps even to distract attention from the concentration of Mexicans
in low-income jobs. At the same time, La Fiesta served as a demonstration
of patriotism, linking the city with the East and Midwest. Program books
from the annual Fiesta give the flavor of this locally generated event,
which, in its early years, extended over several days and drew widespread
participation and large audiences for its parades, balls, concerts, and other
events. Surviving program books from 1894, 1897, and 1903 illustrate its
changing contents and its unchanging focus on the cultural and climatic
wonders of Los Angeles. The 1894 cover features banners for the region's
counties (Los Angeles, San Bernardino, Riverside, Orange, Ventura, and San
Diego) in one corner. Three female angels with trumpets serve as the fore-
ground for a silhouette of the city's (still quite modest) downtown skyline.
The festival began on Tuesday, April 10, with a reception at Sixth Street
(later Fiesta) Park and a parade, starting at 1 P.M. A performance of "La Fiesta March" by the band, fanfares, a welcoming ode or two sung by the
United Male Vocalists of the City, and speeches started things off. The pa-

rade was lengthy, with bicycle outriders, platoons of police, heralds, and several bands. The floats, with their escorts, are worth listing, along with making the observation that the names of participants rarely match ethnically or racially themed floats. Leading off with the requisite historical and Spanish-theme floats, the parade reveals very extensive community participation:

LIST OF FLOATS IN LA FIESTA PARADE, 1894

Car of the Angeles—Spanish Cavaliers

Prehistoric California—Aztec Indians

Landing of Cabrillo—Cavaliers

The Old Missions—sixteen Monks

Prairie Schooner—Vaqueros

Early Mining Days—Miners with a pack train of fourteen burros

Irrigation

Boom Band Wagon with Band, the Boom Float, Boomers in Carriages

The Busted Boom Float

Solid Prosperity

Products

Los Angeles

Ship of State

Turnverein Germania

Knights of Pythias

Royal Arcanum

Maccabees

Foresters—Knights of Honor

Italian Benevolent Society

Legion Française

Sailors Union from San Pedro

San Diego

Pomona

Santa Monica

Mercantile display

Oriental—Chinese

Los Angeles Business College

Chamber of Commerce

Meyberg Bros.

Bob Kern

Hamburger & Sons

Colored People

Burbank Theater

Los Angeles Stoneward Co.

Maier & Zobelin

(Others not reported)

The following evening, Carnival Night, began with another parade, this one illuminated, featuring many of the same organizations and floats with more added. The bands, not identified in the first day's list, included the Los Angeles Military Band, the Seventh Regiment Drum and Bugle Corps in Mask, the LA Cadet Band, and the Musso Brothers' Band. Engravings of several floats, too faded to reproduce here, are supplied. One was labeled "Prosperity in Sunshine," featuring a large bag decorated with a dollar sign sitting atop a flag-draped box and attached with streamers, whose ends were held by an encircling group of women and men. The "Prehistoric Float" featured a half dozen Native Americans dancing in elaborate feathered head-dresses and buckskin, with a wigwam at one end. Another figure, a woman, labored with a mortar and pestle; a large boulder and a few pine trees decorated the other end.

Thursday was Children's Day, with blocks of students from Los Angeles High School and other area high schools as well as thirty-three grade schools; "cadets" (i.e., students) from Los Angeles Normal School (a teacher-training institution, a forerunner of UCLA) brought up the rear. The paraders listed in the program book add up to several thousand participants. On Friday, Floral Military Day, yet another afternoon parade was followed up by the First Grand Ball of the Fiesta, at Hazard's Pavilion. Unlike the parades, this was an ostentatiously selective social occasion: "Tickets to the Ball can only be purchased by those holding invitations, the latter may be obtained upon application to the Social Committee at their rooms. . . . No invitation is required for those desiring to purchase spectator's tickets. Ball and spectator tickets are on sale at Box office windows of Music Hall."

A formal program opened the evening's proceedings, with music, a reception given by the "patronesses" listed in the program, the entrance of the Fiesta queen (soprano Mamie Perry, a local favorite) and her court, and a grand march of the Maskers.[9] From eight to eleven, "no guest will be permitted upon the floor who is not in costume and mask." General dancing of the unmasked began at eleven. The printed program of dances in those days before ragtime includes waltzes, two-steps, and marches, almost all selections available nationally on cylinder recordings from the same time and later familiar as "pops."[10] Perry and the patronesses are almost the only women to be recognized in the entire printed program; the extensive organization of committees responsible for the overall event was all male. The names of several musicians appear in the program: conductor and pianist Adolf Willhartitz, critic H. T. Kubel, tenor Charles Modini-Wood, and theater manager H. C. Wyatt are all listed as members of the sponsoring Merchants and Manufacturers Association.[11]

Three years later the Fiesta remained an elaborate affair. A series of woodcuts of the floral-based floats appears in the 1897 program book. Classical, operatic, and fairy-tale references abound: "Morning Glory—Aurora," "Night Blooming Cereus—Queen of the Night," "Lady Slipper—Cinderella," "The White Rose—House of York," "Pansy—Midsummer Night's Dream," "Marguerite—Faust," "Pond Lily—Iolanthe," "Papyrus—Cleopatra," and "Laurel—Olympic Games" are among them. All these floats paled next to "An Evening with the Aborigines," which consisted of eight dances, as annotated in the list below:

"AN EVENING WITH THE ABORIGINES" (1897)

1. Drouth Dance, by 100 Mission Indians, a peculiar religious ceremony.

2. Native Songs, by a strong chorus of maidens and squaws

3. Folk-Lore Tales, by the various chiefs of the different tribes

4. The Thrilling Fire Dance, by 30 male and female Indians.

    NOTE—This is the most wonderful dance ever seen by civilized eyes. The Indians literally extinguish a well-developed fire of flames and coals by dancing upon them with their naked feet and rolling over the burning coals with their almost nude bodies. Nothing in modern times is half so realistic.

5. Dance by Indian Maidens, to music from the primitive instruments of the San Luiserinos

6. Dance of the Balloon Man. This Indian inflates himself with air until he is distended to many times his natural size. This is a phenomenon which physicians are unable to explain.

7. Ceremonial dances, by all the Indians of different tribes to music furnished by a chorus of maidens and squaws.

8. Medicine Men Dances, in native costumes, a wild and weird dance.[12]

The Fiesta planners thus merged Greek mythology, references to popular opera, Shakespeare, and Native American exoticism into their celebration of the city's Mexican-Spanish roots, all for the benefit of Anglo tourists and potential new residents. (For the record, it is highly unlikely that Native Americans were much involved in this representation, since their numbers had dwindled sharply with the coming of first the Spanish and later the Anglos. As counted in the censuses for 1890 and 1900, their numbers were far lower than the number of persons said to be participating in La Fiesta as Native Americans.)

There was more, of course. A Grand Fiesta Concert was offered by the Music Committee at Hazard's Pavilion, with the Grand Fiesta Chorus and Orchestra directed by Mr. L. F. Gottschalk and solos from the visiting Mme Johnstone-Bishop, soprano. If the sponsors had hoped that the concert would serve as a capstone event, showing the supremacy of European culture amid all the daytime exoticism, they were nevertheless dismayed that it did not pay for itself. This explanation was offered:

> The concert was an artistic success, first-class in every particular. The committee does not consider it to be in any way a reproach that it was not more successful from a financial point of view. The low price of the tickets and the fine character of the performance rendered, made it impossible for the one to pay the price of the other. The house was filled almost to overflowing and the public showed its appreciation and enjoyment, which was all that was to be desired or expected. The committee, which consisted of C. M. Wood, Harley E. Hamilton and J. A. Osgood, are entitled to high praise and sincere congratulations.[13]

The next year, there was an attempt at a concert that would pay for itself and even serve as a fundraiser. This time the orchestra was jettisoned in favor of a large band, a patriotic theme was emphasized, and speeches were added: "The largest band ever formed in this city—consisting of 45 musicians and a chorus of 200 voices—will be especially notable in this concert, which was originally designed as a part of La Fiesta entertainment and was retained as a means for providing funds for patriotic purposes." Even so, the concert failed to draw well, despite the "fervor of patriotism which swayed the audience."[14]

FAUST AND FIREWORKS

Gounod's *Faust* was first heard in Los Angeles in 1885; two years later, in a more sumptuous production, it would be the National Opera Company's biggest draw. The opera's enormous popularity was crudely exploited a decade later (in 1897) when the title, sections of the plot (enacted in pantomime), and selections from the music (played here by a "wheezy band") were used to frame an outdoor entertainment venture at Fiesta Park. "Grand Spectacular Production, 'Faust,'" trumpets the "Exclusive Official Program," which provides a brief summary of the action labeled "Story of 'Faust.'" The evening's entertainment began recognizably enough, with Faust in his study, making his bargain with Mephistopheles and, shortly, encountering Marguerite. "The garden scene with its electric flower bed" follows, and then Marguerite's brother returns from war. At that point the story, which has already skipped over several elements present in Gounod's opera, is suspended while a new character (the "Duke de Mores") is introduced and a series of "specialty" acts interpolated: a high wire act, two "Refined European Grotesque Pantomines *[sic]*," chariot races, trapeze artists, a fire-eater, a ballet, a "German Bravo March and Drill," and a fireworks display. Faust and company return briefly in time for his "electric duel scene" with Valentine. Here is the summary of what happens next:

> Mephisto gloats over the ruin he has wrought, and being assailed for
> his treachery by the now remorseful Faust, he turns in bitter scorn and
> denunciation and climbing to the Brocken Heights at the back and cen-
> ter of the stage, Mephisto calls up the Evil Spirits, and all the gruesome
> inhabitants of his realms, and a weird scene [follows,] to be terminated
> finally by the edict of damnation of the village and its inhabitants. The
> form of Mephisto is seen at the back amid a rain of fire and smoke,
> while the houses fall and crash in amid flames, and evident signs of de-
> struction [appear] on all sides. The villagers in terror rush madly from
> the scene, and a fine display of fireworks closes the show.[15]

Three to five performances weekly were promised, in contrast to the single staged performance of the "authentic" opera by the National Opera Company a decade earlier. What of Gounod's music was performed by the forces led by Professor Coomber, the musical director, we can't know, any more than we can be sure of the fates of Marguerite and Faust in this version. If the *Times'* tepid review and the rapidity with which this production disappeared from view are

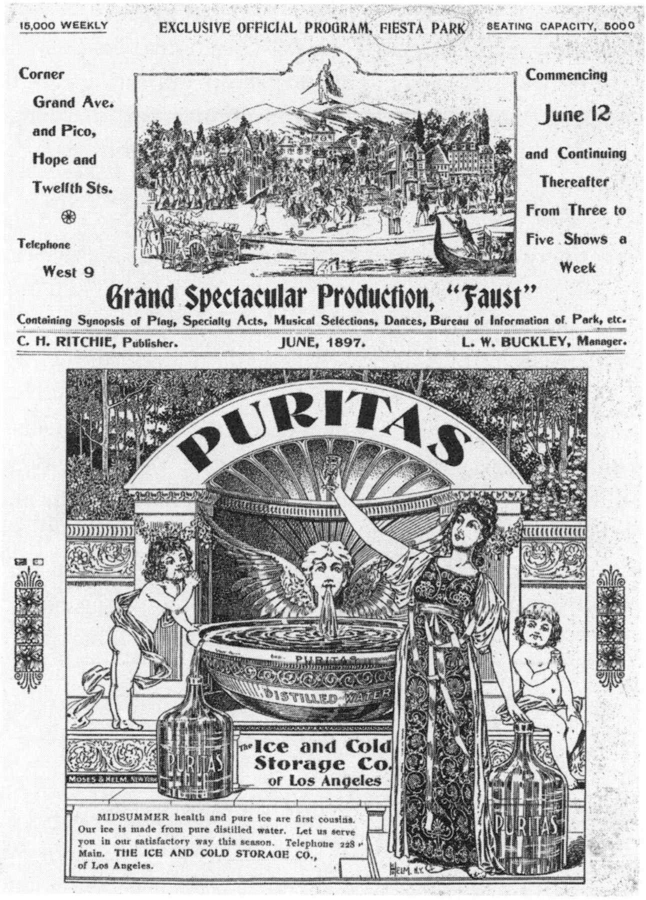

Figure 6. Program, outdoor *Faust* with added entertainments at Fiesta Park, June 1897, with ad. Courtesy of Cambria Master Recordings and Archives.

any indications, it did not last very long. The Faust story did not adapt to an amusement park setting, in spite of the interpolations.[16]

The presenters of this spectacle were at pains to offer a version of the opera's very popular seduction scene, which takes place in Marguerite's backyard garden. That flower bed was important enough as part of the story not only to be preserved but also to become an important site for the "electrical" lighting effects described in the synopsis. (Electrical effects were frequently advertised as elements of vaudeville and other theatrical performances in these years, which were also the early years of experimentation with motion pictures.) The theme of flowers had local resonance; it picks up on the flower show that had opened Hazard's Pavilion a decade earlier. Flowers in midwinter were an icon of local boosterism, outlasting even the Faust theme. Later Fiestas, which drew less community participation, concentrated on floral exhibits and very probably used fewer musicians.

.   .   .

Bagley's experience as a performer began, and for some time remained, with bands. Their size and performance quality was variable. When John Philip Sousa, at the head of the U.S. Marine Band, paid the first of many sold-out visits to Los Angeles in 1892, Bagley was greatly impressed: "Mr. Sousa was even then compared favorably with . . . great conductors, though he was but a little over 35 years old. As for my own opinion, I had never heard so large a band before, and it was the best in the world."[17] When the opportunity arose, Bagley also became an enthusiast of symphonic music and of the movement to bring it to local audiences. His reports on early efforts to create professional orchestral concerts in Los Angeles are therefore especially valuable, notwithstanding some disagreement over which attempt deserved to be called the first. For example, he dismissed Adolf Willhartitz's pioneering "Philharmonic" concert of 1888, later claimed by Howard Swan as the city's first concert of symphonic music, probably because many of its performers were "amateurs" (i.e., unpaid), and the program included choral music and soloists performing alone.[18]

Several other attempts at organizing a professional orchestra proved abortive. In March 1892, an orchestra of twenty men under conductor Dion Romandy, director of the house orchestra at the Palace Saloon, offered a Sunday evening concert, intended as the first of a series. The series seems never to have reached a second performance. Romandy's group was very well received when it played at a reception for the winter graduating class at Los Angeles High School at about the same time: "They had the Hungarian Orchestra, or Romandy's Orchestra. Oh! They play perfectly lovely. Romandy is absolutely grand with a violin in his hand. He has not played very much in concerts or anything like that so people do not know how grand he is. They used to play in the 'Palace' Saloon in the Wilson Block, but now they have given that up. In the orchestra are Romandy and another violinist, a clarinet and Stanzione, with the grandest flute I ever heard in my life."[19]

Theater orchestras were more prestigious than the Palace Saloon, but Romandy seemed on his way to overcoming that handicap. Bagley, who by then was committed to the professionalization of music performance, commented, "Then as now there were enthusiastic musicians who thought they could give public concerts to paying business. But alas, the individual citizen though always anxious for music, when asked for financial support, is seldom sufficiently interested to pay for it."[20]

That same summer, the thirty-piece Orchestra Society Lute gave two concerts under the direction of Ludomir Tomaszewicz, a nephew of the famous actress Helena Modjeska.[21] In the fall, A. J. Stamm organized another Philharmonic of forty musicians; Bagley believed that this was the city's first "real" symphony, apparently because the musicians were paid. Part of this group played for an otherwise undocumented production of Weber's *Der Freischütz* that December, very likely a few scenes in a concert version, perhaps to highlight Mamie Perry, the leading local soprano, and her husband, tenor Charles Modini-Wood. The full orchestra presented a season of four concerts starting in January 1893, but there was no second season. Bagley lists the membership of this short-lived orchestra as well as its programs, which included music by Felix Mendelssohn, Rossini, Wagner, Edmund Kretschmer, Thomas, Johann Strauss, Rubinstein, and Giacomo Meyerbeer. He joined it for its third concert: "[Stamm] was the first conductor of major quality and ability under whom I played, and he had the friendship of the whole local profession. . . . I was in a heaven of delight, having never played with so large an orchestra before and I could conceive of nothing better."[22] Writing in 1927, when Stamm (born in 1850) was still alive and well, Bagley expressed the hope that this pioneer organizer would one day be invited to conduct the still-new, full-time Los Angeles Philharmonic, which by then had enjoyed eight years of unprecedented financial support from its principal patron, William Andrews Clark, Jr.[23] That act of healing between the old and the new never took place.

In addition to paying its members, Stamm's Philharmonic represented a new departure in the orchestral sound heard in Los Angeles. It was the first group to abandon the old high pitch used in bands (and commonly employed by the brass and wind players when they joined the strings), thereby taking on a more truly symphonic sound and taking an innovative forward step: "Up to the advent of the Philharmonic Orchestra organized by A. J. Stamm high pitch only was used in Los Angeles. The Philharmonic began work with low pitch 435-A and Mr. Stamm bought some of the necessary instruments at that pitch which were lacking. It was then that I acquired a set of low pitch clarinets—the first I believe that were owned by any local resident performer on that instrument." The resultant relatively dark and mellow sound may account for the *Times'* critic's remark, as quoted by Bagley: "'He strings a little overweigh the reeds and brass instruments.'"[24]

Bagley played in the first concert of the Los Angeles Symphony in February 1898. The new group was built on the original Philharmonic's failed efforts. This time, Bagley's account is far less starry-eyed, for he had become a union official concerned about securing incomes for his colleagues:

> It had no financial backers and the plan was to first pay expenses and then divide equally among the musicians whatever sum remained. I played the concert and received as my share fifty cents. . . . I have not attempted to give the personnel of the orchestra for the reason that, so far as I can ascertain, no authentic lists exist. It was made up largely, however of the same men who played with A. J. Stamm in the Philharmonic during 1893–1894. We cannot justly compare the programs played with that of our modern symphony orchestras, because it is to be remembered that this organization was deficient particularly in oboes, bassoons and French horns.[25]

The Symphony's performance level was not very high at first, and some problems persisted; the reservations expressed in 1915 by conductor Alfred Hertz as he prepared to conduct the premiere of Horatio Parker's *Fairyland* indicate that some of these problems were never entirely solved.

Bagley follows the Symphony through its twenty-three-year history. After Harley Hamilton retired from conducting both the Symphony and the Women's Orchestra in 1914, he was succeeded by Adolf Tandler, violinist and leader of the locally acclaimed Brahms Quintet.[26] A letter in the Bagley Collection refers to Tandler's reign as one that was heavily "intrigued," though no details are provided. The Symphony's demise followed the season 1919–20.[27] For that one season, the Symphony attempted to compete directly with the newly organized Philharmonic, initiated and single-handedly supported by Clark in response to his frustration over the Symphony's persistent shortcomings. (Clark had first offered support to the Symphony, but his offer carried a demand for artistic control, which the board, and probably Tandler, was unwilling to accept.) Bagley believed that the Symphony board, faced with much greater deficits than it was willing to meet, manufactured a conflict with the union as an excuse to retire from the field.[28] He also gave the Symphony credit for performing, at what turned out to be its last concert, a program entirely of music by Los Angeles composers: H. W. R. Strong, Nicola Novelli, Hans Linne, Harley Hamilton, Henry Schoenefeld, Carrie Jacobs Bond, Charles Wakefield Cadman, and Fannie Charles Dillon.[29] Not until the Federal Music Project of the 1930s was there another concert program devoted entirely to symphonic music by Los Angeles composers.

The Symphony's failure was frustrating for others besides Bagley and

Clark. The relatively new *Pacific Coast Musician* ran an angry editorial under the headline "WEALTH VERSUS SYMPHONY IN LOS ANGELES: SIX HUNDRED MILLIONAIRES AND SEMI-MILLIONAIRES IN LOS ANGELES: AMPLE WEALTH TO BUILD SYMPHONY HALLS AND ENDOW ORCHESTRAS."[30] Decisions by several among these millionaires not to step forward with more support may be taken as affirming Bagley's observation of "intrigued" orchestral politics. Lingering bad feelings over the Symphony's fate were a factor in the relatively slow acceptance of the Philharmonic in later years; Tandler, who resurfaces in this narrative from time to time, always carried political baggage with him from that very public wreckage.

Bagley was also a participant at what he believed was the first incursion of ragtime into Los Angeles theatrical life. This momentous event took place at the Los Angeles Theater, during a production by the Frawley Company, in the summer of 1900:

> At the particular period "ragtime," the potent forerunner of modern "jazz," was beginning to hold a great deal of attention. "Ragging" was considered an attractive as well as comical feat, but not within the capability of all musicians. In the last performance of "With Flying Colors," a sensational English melodrama, there is a scene where British soldiers go on board ship enroute to a war in foreign parts. The wind, brass and drums, W. H. Mead, C. L. Bagley, J. L. Edmiston, P. F. Heibel and Robert W. Burns, were required to be on the stage at this point and play "The British Grenadier" as a cadence for the marching troops. After we had started that stirring air, Burns began "ragging" it and the rest of us did likewise. It was pandemonium. The actors (some of them English) laughed so they could scarcely say their lines, and we had to endure only the disapprobation of the "heavy," Mr. Harrington Reynolds, himself a Briton of a type now almost extinct. His frowns did no good, however, and we finished as we began in a maze of cacophonous syncopation. I never heard the "British Grenadier" in that rhythm before or since.[31]

Unfortunately, there is no evidence as to when black musicians in Los Angeles began ragging, though it was probably at about the same time.[32]

The first attempt at organizing a musicians' union in Los Angeles was made in 1888. Harley Hamilton, who later organized the Los Angeles Women's Orchestra and would presently become the first conductor of the Los Angeles Symphony, was elected as the first president of Local 19, National League of Musicians. Bagley was part of the next and more successful effort to organize, in 1894. There was little doubt about the need. In one colorful incident from 1892, newspapers reported that the Hungarian Ladies' Band had skipped town, and that the operator of the Palace Saloon, where they had worked, would charge their leader with embezzlement. Bagley commented, "From my recollection of reputations at that time I would venture to say it was more likely that the orchestra left because Schurtz [the bandleader] did not pay them."[33]

Bagley's beloved profession had changed radically by the time he left the local's presidency in 1922 and began to contemplate writing his "History." Military bands were "in a state of depression," reduced from their earlier abundance of appearances to weekly concerts at Lincoln Park, Venice, Ocean Park, Long Beach, and Catalina Island. (They persisted for a very long time in that format, however.) Traveling musical theater companies were dying out; the long-standing restaurant-saloon-cafés with orchestras and entertainment and even frequent work at parties, weddings, receptions, and churches, were likewise fast disappearing. These losses were more than offset by the booming vaudeville houses and the growing numbers of silent film theaters, all of which employed more musicians than ever; in addition, touring "name" jazz bands were beginning to become popular. It was, in fact, "the day of opportunity for the orchestral player . . . salaries went upward and material prosperity was well distributed within the profession."[34] Business for musicians was so good that the new Philharmonic could hold its musicians only by paying a regular weekly salary, a large step up from the per-service pay policy that had left the old Symphony struggling to keep its musicians. By 1920 the Los Angeles local had grown from the 108 men and 6 women listed in its first directory (1895) to more than 3,000, making it the fourth largest in the country.

The changes were so great that Bagley himself is portrayed as obsolete in an account of the Los Angeles local's explosive growth, presented in the San Francisco (Local 6) union's journal:

> For many years the currents of union administration have revolved about the remarkable personality of C. L. Bagley, who is doubtless known to most of you. This very capable officer has, year after year, whenever he has consented to become a candidate, outdistanced all his opponents by large and complimentary majorities. This year he was defeated by Harry Moore for [American] Federation [of Musicians] Delegate and was re-elected to the presidency only by a scanty majority of 22 votes. To my mind this is significant of the growth of a feeling of restlessness—of impatience with the old order of things. Local 47, rank and file, wants its own headquarters. It needs a Business Agent terribly. It needs a campaign of advertising such as was so successful in Local 6. It needs many things which the old guard deems impolitic or extravagant. It ought to have a newspaper, too—only heaven help the man that

runs it. So with this bulging growth in members and with these healthy signs of the times, I feel that this young giant of the Southwest is capable of astonishing things in the near future.[35]

In 1931, when nationally the union was faced with severe technological and economic setbacks, Bagley returned to the national American Federation of Musicians' governing board and became a vice president once again. This time he held the office for twenty-eight years, until 1959.[36] At the time he was elected, Joseph N. Weber (also a clarinetist and a one-time member of Romandy's Hungarian Ladies Orchestra in a Los Angeles restaurant) had served as president for thirty years. In 1940, the much younger James C. Petrillo, leader of the Chicago local, became president. Thus, Bagley continued his long-running activity as the leading representative of one of the largest and wealthiest locals in the federation.

The last installment of Bagley's narrative appeared in 1937, at a point when the fortunes of working musicians had sadly fallen after decades of growth. The comfortable, glossy format of the *Overture*, with photos, advertisements, and space for the lengthy obituary notices Bagley often wrote for the old-time musicians, was replaced by a stripped-down version that carried long lists of unemployed union members suspended or dropped for nonpayment of dues. The end of the silent film era, around 1930, capped by the Great Depression, dealt the profession a devastating double blow, which even the booming sound film industry and the Federal Music Project could not cushion. Even so, in 1936 Bagley reported the membership of Local 47 as 4,100, and of Local 767 (the segregated black local) as 150.[37] Again, after World War II, the pages of the *Overture* were filled with the names of even more members who had left the profession and did not return. Presently the postwar prosperity spread again to the profession and its union; that was the situation when Bagley finally retired from his long-standing service as legal counsel to Local 47 and as a vice president of the federation.

The success of the musicians' union in the early decades of the twentieth century owed much to the new opportunities that resulted from the explosion of commercial mass culture, first, vaudeville and, later, silent movies. In Los Angeles, where the *Times'* virulently anti-union posture took its toll, the successes of Locals 47 and 767 stood out. Bagley was a major figure in laying the groundwork for the growth of Local 47 and the separate, very unequal existence of Local 767. His "History" chronicles the professionalization of public, instrumental music making—one important part of the overall music scene.

．　．　．

One must add here some of the things that Bagley's account does not touch because of its single-minded focus on the work of paid instrumental performers. The Los Angeles Musicians Mutual Protective Association, as Local 47 was called, included women as members from the start, but their number was small, because the number of women working as instrumental performers was small. (They were clustered in the restaurant jobs, which were less stable than the theater orchestras.) Their numbers grew with the increasing opportunities for all musicians, but women did not take leadership roles in the local until much later in the twentieth century. Their role was much larger in the Southern California Music Teachers Association, a group that organized after the turn of the century, for which the record is much less complete. Bagley's union history does not hint at the substantial number of singers who worked in churches and theaters. Also, as already stated, African American musicians were not accepted as members. The much smaller Local 767 developed around 1920 from a separate booking operation run by the Spikes Brothers and did not merge with Local 47 until 1953.

The women and men who made music in public but considered themselves amateurs are also not included in Bagley's history. In particular, singers and choral groups were never part of the union and are therefore omitted from Bagley's chronicle. From late in the 1880s, large mixed choruses were assembled, often as a part of summer Chautauquas, at first by music store operator Charles E. Day, later a member of the school board, and then by F. A. Bacon, who came to Los Angeles to teach at the University of Southern California.[38] These choruses were the source for the Los Angeles Oratorio Society, later conducted by John Smallman, who succeeded Bacon as choir director at the First Congregational Church in 1918. The ethnic German presence in Los Angeles was signaled by the prominence of Turnverein/Turner Hall and several large single-sex choral societies, including the Apollo Club and the long-lived Ellis Club (the oldest, founded in 1888) for men, as well as the Women's Lyric Club (founded 1889).[39]

4 "Popular Prices Will Prevail"
Competing and Cooperating Impresarios

Theater operators and music store owners presented an increasing number of musical events in the 1890s, both concerts by traveling virtuosi and performances by local groups and individuals. A lively competition for audiences, involving different approaches and personalities, began to emerge among these presenters only in 1899. Six years later, the competition had subsided, leaving in its wake the pattern of organized concert giving recognizable as typical for much of the twentieth century.

Traveling entertainers, theatrical troupes, and musicians had visited from earlier times, but substantial theaters had gone up only in the 1880s. In the 1890s, a third theater, the Burbank, joined the Grand Opera House (reinvented in 1895 as the Orpheum, a vaudeville palace) and the Los Angeles Theater as the major commercial houses. By the end of the decade, the Los Angeles Theater no longer remained dark in the summer. A run of box office records at the Huntington Library documents the changing fare and rising attendance. While the occasional minstrel show still appeared, drawing consistently but not often filling the house, touring companies playing hit Broadway productions now attracted far larger audiences.[1] Locally, choral societies, orchestras, and chamber music ensembles were organized in the late '80s and '90s. Characteristically they offered two or three concerts per season, usually without any thought of professional management beyond their leader-organizers, who often doubled as church choir directors or private music teachers or both. Large special events still took place at Hazard's Pavilion, and smaller local concerts were held at Simpson's Auditorium (a Methodist church) and other, smaller spaces.

In early 1899, when the concert-giving competition began, the Burbank presented the Wakefield Andrews Opera Company, whose offerings included the double bill of *Cavalleria rusticana* (Pietro Mascagni, 1890) and

43

Trial by Jury (Gilbert and Sullivan, 1875). At the Orpheum, the all-black ragtime opera *Clorindy* (1898), conducted by its composer, Will Marion Cook, appeared among the vaudeville acts.[2] Among other music events in the first part of 1899, Blanche Rogers (later Lott) and other local artists offered the Lott-Krauss series of three well-respected chamber music concerts.[3] The Los Angeles Symphony was in its second season. Other concerts were offered by C. S. De Lano's Guitar, Banjo, and Mandolin Club (part of an annual season of ten concerts); by Harry Barnhart, basso (of whom more below); and by the University of Southern California's Glee, Mandolin, Banjo and Guitar Club.[4] The several music store operators, who sold both sheet music and musical instruments as well as the latest in recordings and phonographs, were prominent members of the music scene. Among them A. G. Bartlett, the longest established, had recently helped the University of Southern California organize its first music curriculum (a money maker for the university for several decades to come), and Anton Birklein continued his activity in organizing bands for outdoor functions. Charles E. Day doubled as a choir director. Though both theater and music store operators were important in developing public and private music making, they brought contrasting backgrounds and styles to their concert organizing, as becomes clear from these sketches of Harry C. Wyatt, long the manager of the Los Angeles Theater, and Fred W. Blanchard, owner of Blanchard's Music Company.

The oldest among the major players in this period of entrepreneurial competition, Wyatt had been a drummer boy in the Confederate army and had, so it was said, lost his left arm during Pickett's Charge, at Gettysburg on July 3, 1863. Twenty-one years later he was the manager (and probably an actor) in a minstrel troupe that appeared in Los Angeles. He stayed on, becoming manager of Child's Grand Opera House in 1886. Two years later he moved to the management of the larger, newly opened Los Angeles Theater, where he remained for fifteen years.

Lee Bagley, ever the musicians' advocate, admired Wyatt's professionalism, writing (in caps) that "HE ALWAYS PAID" the house musicians, sometimes pawning some large diamonds so he could meet his payroll.[5] Besides the indirect comment on the vagaries of other employers, Bagley's remark is indicative of his respect for Wyatt's steady influence and integrity. As business grew, Wyatt developed agreements with theaters in other Southern California towns. Presently he could schedule events in Pasadena, San Bernardino, San Diego, and elsewhere in addition to his home theater, a useful setup in order to attract touring companies with high expenses and large guarantees, and useful as the entrepreneurial competition developed

Figure 7. Harry C. Wyatt, lessee and manager, Los Angeles Theater. Courtesy of University of Southern California, on behalf of the USC Specialized Libraries and Archival Collections.

among aspiring concert promoters. (In Los Angeles, Wyatt could also book events at New Turner Hall as early as 1888 and, after it opened in 1887, Hazard's Pavilion.) Another hallmark of his practice, common to the theater business, was to advertise heavily. All the local papers regularly carried ads for theaters and amusement parks on their front pages; Wyatt's were usually at the top. (He also placed signs on trolley cars and billboards on downtown buildings and used walkers carrying sandwich boards.) According to surviving expense records, his advertising budgets often exceeded his payroll for the pit orchestra.[6]

Wyatt remained at the Los Angeles Theater when it was purchased around 1896 by William H. Perry, owner of the local gas company. One of Perry's interests was to provide an occasional venue for his daughter,

Mamie Perry, the soprano, and for her husband, tenor Charles Modini-Wood.[7] Major changes elsewhere in the theater business eventually limited Wyatt's control. Three years after Perry's purchase, Wyatt was required by the Orpheum's new ownership not to offer "low-end" attractions that might compete with their regular vaudeville shows, restricting the broad-based audience appeal of his offerings.[8] When the New York–based theatrical syndicate (deprecatingly labeled the "theater trusts" in the local papers) gained control over local theater bookings after 1900, it became more difficult for Wyatt to present the local events (often society-generated fundraisers) that had provided appropriately "safe" venues for local performers. Perry sold the Los Angeles Theater in 1902 and invested in the new and larger Mason Opera House, opened the following year. Wyatt moved to the new house, which he managed until his death in 1910.[9]

The range of events that took place under Wyatt's management before he made peace with the syndicate and gave up control of his house is worth noting. English-language opera troupes and minstrel shows were staples from the start; an assortment of local orchestra concerts appeared, starting with A. J. Stamm's Philharmonic in 1893. In the last three months of 1897, he scheduled the Del Conte Italian Opera Company, coming from Mexico City, the Grau Opera Company from New York, and Veriscope reproductions (an early, not very satisfactory, motion picture format) of the famous Corbett-Fitzsimmons fight, held earlier in the year in Carson City, Nevada. (Soon all three theaters were meeting the competition from the new one-reel movie parlors by adding some form of moving pictures to their regular fare.)

The two-week visit (extended from one) brought a major operatic "first" to Los Angeles. The Del Contes offered a rich Italian repertoire: six by Verdi (*Un ballo in maschera, La Traviata, Il Trovatore, Ernani, Rigoletto, Otello*); Ponchielli's *La Giaconda;* Donizetti's *Lucia di Lammermoor* and *La Favorita;* the twin bill of *Cavalleria rusticana* and *I Pagliacci* (Mascagni and Leoncavallo); and the U.S. premiere of what soon became one of the most popular of all operas, Puccini's *La Bohème.*[10] The operas were presented in Italian, still unusual for most touring companies and heretofore a marker for elite, "high-end" operatic attractions rather than more popular ones. The Del Contes did not do as well as the National Opera Company had done a decade earlier or as well as more recent English-language companies such as the Bostonians. The city's population was, of course, at least twice what it had been in 1887, but the nature of theatrical entertainment had changed. Box office receipts indicate that the Del Conte's run was quite decent for the New Los Angeles Theater at that time, though the house was not filled. As for many other attractions, the theatergoing public turned out in only moderate numbers on week nights but showed up in force for the Saturday night production of *Il Trovatore,* still one of the most popular operas in the repertoire, and then of *Cavalleria rusticana* and *I Pagliacci* the following week.[11] The Italian company drew as well as several of the dramatic events on the calendar before and after its visit.

Newspaper publicity said that the company had come by rail via Mexico City rather than from some other U.S. city. The company reportedly chose this route because political problems made it impossible for it to play in Havana, as had been planned. The orchestra was described as "31 . . . professors from the National Conservatory of the City of Mexico."[12] In addition, the coverage emphasized the "otherness" of the troupe's Italian-Latino ethnic identity. The *Los Angeles Herald* reported of the premiere performance of *La Bohème* that there were 523 people in the audience, less than half the theater's capacity: "The opera [company] did not attract the people of wealth. Italian and Mexican citizens were conspicuous in the audience throughout the engagement, but the bon-ton of American society sought its pleasure elsewhere."[13] The Del Contes were, by this account, apparently not elite enough to attract major support as a social event, nor were they able to attract the usual popular, Anglo-dominated theater audience that had kept other traveling companies in business over the years.

Two years later, a visit by the less pretentious Lambardi Grand Opera Company attracted large audiences for a run of several weeks. *La Bohème* now drew an overflow audience, and the company's stay was extended twice. (Despite its reported success, a final return run in August resulted in financial difficulties that required a complicated bailout, described below.) This time the weekly *Western Graphic* noted with approbation the behavior of the ethnic (minority) presence in the crowd: "It was noticeable that the cheers and bravos came from those auditors whose dark complexions indicated the warm southern blood that is impulsive and hearty."[14]

For some of these events, Wyatt had collaborators. One was his treasurer and concessionaire in charge of ushers, programs, and opera glasses, L. E. Behymer, who had already become a reliable lieutenant. Others were music store owners, who sometimes helped post financial guarantees. Principal among these was Fred W. Blanchard.[15] The musically trained son of an industrialist father, Blanchard was born in Millbury, Massachusetts (near Worcester). He graduated from Boston Latin School and traveled and studied abroad before going to Los Angeles in 1886. At first he opened a music business in partnership with James T. Fitzgerald, who had bought out Charles E. Day. They added a small recital space, Blanchard-Fitzgerald Hall, in their store in 1896, but the partnership soon broke up. (There were clear differences in personal style; Fitzgerald was a far more flamboyant figure.) In 1900, Blanchard opened the much grander Blanchard Music and Art Building, with studio space for 150 musicians and artists, an art gallery, and a larger recital hall, where he sponsored recital series by local chamber music groups.[16] When Blanchard Hall opened its fourth-floor art gallery and all its studios with a large reception, the local *Western Graphic* produced a thirty-two-page special edition devoted to music and art in Southern California. Its anonymous society columnist reported that Blanchard and Fitzgerald were the two individuals most responsible for the city's flourishing concert life, even though they no longer spoke to each other.

Though Blanchard remains a rather shadowy, self-effacing figure, his name appears frequently over the next two decades. Blanchard held in common with the other business people his entrepreneurial success. His long dedication to bringing art and music to the people (including his customers and tenants), always at "popular prices," made him strongly sympathetic to the community music movement and some other later developments. Blanchard helped form the original Municipal Art Committee in 1904 and was responsible for its becoming an official, city-sponsored body. In addition to promoting concerts and operating his studio building and recital hall, he kept the Symphony going for several years after Behymer had abandoned it, played a major role in bringing the "$10,000 Prize Opera" to Los Angeles in 1915, and stepped into the presidency of the Hollywood Bowl at a key moment in its early history.[17]

. . .

The first six months of 1899 was a period of more or less open competition and occasional cooperation among concert presenters. The principal music events, and their sponsors, were as follows:

> James T. Fitzgerald, music store owner and, later, backer of Merle Armitage's career as an impresario, in Los Angeles since 1891, published the *Fitzgerald Bulletin*, a flyer promoting six visiting "attractions" that included the Kneisel Quartet, pianist Emil Sauer, and the immensely popular John Philip Sousa with his band.[18]

> Frederick W. Blanchard presented pianist Moriz Rosenthal to open the new, eight-hundred-seat Blanchard Hall in his new Music and Art Building, which provided studio space for artists and music teachers. Blanchard also presented at least one concert in a lyceum course offered by the Epworth League of Methodist Youth at the YMCA.[19]

Figure 8.   Frederick W. Blanchard. Courtesy of Cambria Master
Recordings and Archives.

At the Los Angeles Theater, manager H. C. Wyatt presented the Lambardi Grand Opera Company in Italian repertory; the Bostonians
playing Victor Herbert and De Koven; Black Patti's Troubadours; and
Hi Henry's Minstrels, among other events. (All were returning after
successful earlier visits under Wyatt's management.)

In a major cooperative venture, Wyatt and Blanchard offered the large
Ellis Grand Opera Company, featuring soprano Nellie Melba, conductor Walter Damrosch, and the New York Symphony Orchestra, in
two performances at Hazard's Pavilion, still the city's one large mul-
tipurpose auditorium. This effort to bring elite, high-priced opera to
Los Angeles was less than successful in this short end-of-century period of uncertain class identity for opera. Even with Melba as its fea-

tured star, its performances of *Faust* and *Carmen* were not well attended, and the company left in a flurry of claims about who lost how much on the venture.

L. E. Behymer, theatrical publicist, program publisher, ticket seller ("assistant treasurer") for the Los Angeles Theater, and a hard-working and reliable employee of H. C. Wyatt, offered Ian McLaren, a popular lecturer of the time, not his first venture as an impresario.

Two among these presenters stepped up their activities sharply in the following seasons. Music store owner Blanchard scheduled many local artists and a few touring ones in his recital hall. In the fall of 1901 he arranged his first "Star Entertainment Course" of ten lectures and concerts, largely booked through eastern agents, especially the Redpath Lyceum Bureau in Boston.[20] Tickets were sold by the Women's Guild of the Independent Church of Christ. The ten events were sold for one dollar and included a concert by the local Congregational Orchestra of thirty-five amateur musicians (adults and students) under William H. Mead; the Enoch Arden Concert Company of Washington, D.C.; and the Leonora Jackson Grand Concert Company, whose featured soloist was a well-known violinist.

This course sold out so quickly that Blanchard added a second, "Imperial," course, underwritten by an organization of University of Southern California alumni, and a third, "People's" course, this one sponsored by the Ladies' Aid Society of the First Methodist Church. Each was a series of ten events, priced at one dollar for the series; each had as its primary audience the members of its sponsoring organizations, two of them church-related. The People's Course included the Los Angeles Women's Orchestra under Harley Hamilton; the Throop Institute (later California Institute of Technology) Mandolin and Guitar Club; and the Chicago Symphony Orchestra.[21]

Behymer countered Blanchard's activity aggressively with two big-budget events, offering the Grau Metropolitan Opera Company, in a return engagement for Melba and Damrosch, and the Eduard Strauss Concert Orchestra. Behymer, who did not arrange a church-affiliated sponsorship, advertised his events intensively in the local press and asked much higher ticket prices. The next season, 1902, he followed Blanchard's lead, offering his first concert series package.[22]

The competition between Blanchard and Behymer was based on very different approaches to their presentations, both aesthetic and practical. Blanchard intended his concerts for an audience that started with the church- and university-based groups for whom his series were initially organized, then expanded to include the relatively high proportion of the city's population that were customers (or potential customers) for the city's music stores: teachers and students of music; amateur and professional musicians. As a Progressive activist for the arts in the city's everyday life, he acted on the belief—one that is still imbued as part of the European concert music tradition and one that he likely acquired as part of his own musical training—in the inherent educational and ethical, even religious, value of "serious" music. His conviction that such music should be universally accessible is reflected in his concert ads, which frequently contained the rubric "popular prices will prevail." As a practical matter, this usually meant that there were plenty of seats available for twenty-five cents, if not always for ten, and the most expensive seats often went for no more than fifty cents.[23] Although he brought in traveling virtuosi, he also sponsored local artists, such as the Lott-Krauss chamber concerts and, later, the Brahms Quintet, in the small concert hall he had built for that purpose.

. . .

The contest between Blanchard and Behymer reached its peak in 1904. The most visible part of the battle from our perspective was not the concerts by visiting virtuosi but rather a duel between rival mixed choruses. By helping to organize and back these competing choruses, the two entrepreneurs sought to win the loyalty of the city's musicians, teachers, and amateur music makers, who formed the heart of the local audience for concert music. Although only single-sex choral societies had been able to establish any continuity in Los Angeles up to that time, mixed choral singing was close to the hearts of musicians in the community and close to the peak of an implicit hierarchy among performing groups. In tackling Blanchard here, Behymer took very seriously the local critic who wrote of the city's weakness in "the very highest sphere of musical exploitation . . . the combination of large mixed chorus, organ and orchestra."[24]

Blanchard managed the Los Angeles Choral Society, conducted by Harry Barnhart; Behymer backed the Los Angeles Oratorio Society, under Julius Jahn. In May 1904, the quadrennial national convention of the Methodist Episcopal Church attracted between three thousand and five thousand delegates to Los Angeles. Two months beforehand, Blanchard announced a series of eight events, spread over the three weeks of the convention, for one dollar, "the only authorized course": seven lectures and a concert by a chorus of six hundred under Barnhart, along with a "Philharmonic Orchestra" of sixty musicians, actually members of the Symphony, conducted by its concertmaster. (The Symphony did not appear under its own name or with its regular conductor, because Behymer, who was by then its manager, did not allow it.) Several weeks later, Behymer trumped Blanchard when he announced his own "Great Philharmonic Course," three musical events for three dollars, including soprano Marcella Sembrich, the Symphony (in this case, under its own name and with its regular conductor, Harley Hamilton, for Behymer, as its manager, could authorize this), and his 150-voice Oratorio Society.[25] Sembrich was scheduled to appear one day before the Blanchard-Barnhart extravaganza. Both entrepreneurs suffered financially when a train wreck—or a strike, depending on which paper one reads—delayed the arrival of most of the delegates beyond the dates of the first two concerts. But Blanchard and Barnhart's "Conference Chorus" presently won the praise of the unfriendly *Times* with a repeat performance: "The Conference Chorus gave its final concert last evening. . . . Few finer things have been presented here by a choral organization of any sort than 'Babylon's Wave,' [Gounod] as it was sung last night. Barnhart had his vocalists exactly under the sway of his baton, and out of the great unwieldy group he got real pianissimos, crescendos that rose on a graduated scale for evenness, and strenuous climacteric chords that were of surprising strength."[26]

Blanchard came out slightly ahead on this one. A duel of *Messiah*s followed in the fall. The Blanchard and Barnhart performance was scheduled for Hazard's Pavilion, and "popular prices" meant, in this case, 50 cents to $1. Behymer and Jahn's group performed in the much smaller Simpson's, with prices between 50 cents and $1.50. In December, Behymer took the offensive, announcing that "in the first place, amateurish attempts will be avoided" by his group. Blanchard countered with a fatal and unnecessary defensiveness, remarking his chorus's steady improvement and "judicious pruning" of voices.[27] Despite having the superior conductor, Blanchard made no published reply to Behymer's claim that "there have been more applications for good things musically, as well as medium and bad attractions, than ever before in the history of music in this city . . . anything playing under the name of Manager Behymer this season will bear the stamp of the best in music."[28] One critic afterward confirmed the politicized nature of this contest, writing in the *Graphic:* "In commenting upon the various musical events of the past few months professional critical opinion has run to such violently opposite extremes that one can scarce find a resting place for the foot of common-sense, everyday fact. For instance, one writer lauded the [Blanchard-Barnhart] *Messiah* to the seventh heaven, while another pretty well consigned it to the nethermost hell. Mr. Jahn's venture in the same field met a like fate."[29]

After one more round in the spring of 1905, when Barnhart's *Creation* (backed by Blanchard) apparently outdid Jahn's *Elijah* (backed by Behymer) by a substantial margin, both choruses faded from sight.[30] Blanchard abandoned the impresario field and went abroad for a year. When he returned, it was to concentrate on his prosperous music store and his role as sponsor of local events, champion of music and art as tools for community self-improvement, and occasional silent partner in Behymer's concert promotions. Behymer took over Blanchard's summer Chautauqua bookings at Venice Beach in addition to his winter events, thereby consolidating his pre-eminent position in offering visiting concert attractions in Los Angeles for the next four decades.

The choral competition left baggage that still lingered a few years later, when new Progressive-style music initiatives were contemplated (in this case a festival). *Times* critic Julian Johnson summed it up when he wrote, "But—believe one who has observed for the past seven years!—if there are any more half-baked, spite-ridden chorus or alleged festival schemes of personal elevation, or clique-promotion, the festival and chorus idea will be effectually killed in Southern California for many, many seasons to come."[31] (Johnson favored the encouragement of strong local performers over the importation and promotion of expensive traveling virtuosi, a position that may have led to his departure from the *Times*.) Indeed, the personal and political animosities that were a by-product of this misplaced competition did remain, perhaps never fully dissipating among its participants, including its numerous choristers. Even the city's continuing growth, which meant that a rapidly increasing proportion of the potential concert audience would soon be unaware of and indifferent to the individual histories of the various concert promoters, could not fully dilute the aftereffects.[32]

Through his lyceum series, Blanchard introduced the subscription concert series to Los Angeles. To book the several series he introduced, he dealt with the national Redpath Lyceum Bureau and took a local partner to administer them. One of his publicity promotions read, "The marked demand for seats at 'popular-priced' entertainments this season has been greater than ever, and the Star, Imperial and People's courses, blocked out months in advance, have been readily taken to by the local public."[33] Behymer's approach, on the other hand, was launched from his background in the commercial theater as press agent and concession operator. Unlike Blanchard, he was unencumbered by the peculiar ethical freight built into formal music training. Shut out of the possibility of managing a commercial theater and not owning a retail business, he sought other opportunities in the world of entertainment; one of these was concert promotion. To that end, he took on the management of the Symphony and the new Los Angeles Oratorio Society. He became manager of Hazard's Pavilion and Simpson's Auditorium, probably acquiring them from his mentor, Wyatt; he also began to promote concerts by visiting virtuosi who had earlier appeared under the older management.

·   ·   ·

Public concerts were very closely associated with commercial theater when the competition began. It was inevitable, and quite irrelevant to the ugly choral competition, that developments in commercial theater would have a tremendous influence on concert giving, well beyond Behymer's creative appropriation of commercial marketing techniques or their application to Barnhart versus Jahn as choral directors. The explosive growth of commercial mass entertainment in the years of this competition was ensuring that public concerts would have to develop a new relationship to what amounted to a new "amusement" industry. Vaudeville had first appeared in Los Angeles late in 1894, and the first kinetoscope parlor opened in 1896. The opening of Tally's Electric Theatre in 1902 and the Mason Opera House in 1903 heralded the start of a decade of theater building and the proliferation of vaudeville and burlesque as well as silent movies and other forms of commercial entertainment.[34] As in other cities, the audience for these new "cheap amusements" was not so much drawn from the older middle class, although "high-end" theater was also growing, as it was mainly new, consisting of workers who were just beginning to have leisure time because of their slightly shortened workday, coupled with increased real income.

Given these developments, the relative positions of the two major competitors here shifted in those critical years. Blanchard had reaped the earlier advantage from his position as a music store operator who cultivated music teachers and their students as customers for his business; he continued to view his concert-giving activities as a service to his clientele as well as a way to improve the community. Behymer made a virtue of his nonmusical background and presented himself in another way, in the stereotypically masculine role of entrepreneur and would-be monopolist, with concerts by visiting virtuosi among the amusement products he offered, his position gained ground in parallel with the changes in the nature of public entertainment.

Arthur Farwell's presence in Los Angeles, along with his lecture to the Friday Morning Club just as rehearsals for the competing *Messiah* performances were getting into high gear in November 1904, reminds us that these were the years when the first American music movement blossomed, partly in response to the expansion of commercial entertainment. One of the LA newspapers quoted a member of Farwell's audience: "We are trying to develop a definite American musical art, which shall be indicative of the character of us in the same way that German music is of Germany, and Russian music is of Russia, and Bohemian music is of Bohemia."[35] Acceptance of European visiting virtuosi (however they were presented) meant acceptance of their European repertory, which raised the issues of nationalism and prejudice against the foreign-born that have sometimes made the symphony orchestra problematic as an elitist institution in America. Even though Farwell's presentation included music derived from Indian and African American, as well as Yankee, sources, and even though his collaboration with Charles Lummis in making field recordings for *Spanish Songs of Old California,* seems a harmless enough exercise in regionalist self-identification, they raise the question of musical nationalism and its relationship to the peculiarities of Los Angeles' population mix as subtexts of this competition among impresarios.[36]

While it lasted, this competition brought a rich variety of public performances to Los Angeles. One may certainly speculate about how it might have come out had the relatively well-heeled Blanchard been as ambitious, persistent, and media-savvy as his rival, or had the other music store operators taken more aggressive roles in the competition, but that is to ignore the profound cultural and economic changes that were taking place at the same time. Even so, Behymer's victory was never quite total. For one, James T. Fitzgerald, Blanchard's former partner, never reconciled himself to Behymer's dominance. Fitzgerald retained control of John Philip Sousa's popular and profitable annual visits and later, in the 1920s, encouraged Merle Armitage to compete with Behymer with his Auditorium Artists series. Yet it is clear that the competition of impresarios described here sets the scene for many of the events that followed. As for Behymer, his role and his efforts to maintain the position he had won will form the meat of another chapter.

5 Amateurs, Professionals, and Symphonies

Harley Hamilton and Edna Foy

Two early participants in symphonic music making present sharply contrasting experiences, shaped by differences in background, class, and gender as well as individual ability. Harley Hamilton, a violinist, first came to Los Angeles while touring with a minstrel company. Active as a teacher as well as a performer, he became prominent as the conductor of the first local symphony orchestra that was able to sustain itself for more than a few performances. One of Hamilton's many students, Edna Foy, played a major role in the formation and evolution of the Los Angeles Women's Orchestra. Besides telling us much about one kind of organized music making, the ins and outs of Hamilton's and Foy's overlapping careers show that the distinction between "professional" and "amateur" was not based entirely on the presence or absence of financial remuneration, nor was it determined solely by ability. Even the sources on which this chapter is based reinforce these differences; Hamilton is traced mainly through published records, while Foy can be followed mainly through private correspondence.

Hamilton's upbringing in a utopian religious community enabled a successful career for him in music at a time when U.S.-born males were rarely prominent in that profession. Foy was encouraged by her prosperous parents to develop her skill as a violinist. In the end, she could not pay the high personal price—or, probably, the economic price—that crossing into the world of paid music making would have cost her. In this she exemplifies many middle-class and upper-middle-class women who worked hard to qualify themselves for careers that they could pursue only in a limited fashion, if at all. In a period of increasing professionalization of many services (most obviously seen here in the growth of the musicians' union), women were often shunted into the category of "amateur," devaluing their contribution to the profession. Some later women in this position became patrons

56

Figure 9.   Harley Hamilton, organizer and first conductor of the LA Women's Orchestra and the LA Symphony. This item is reproduced by permission of The Huntington Library, San Marino, California, from the Foy Family Papers.

of music (for example, Artie Mason Carter and Florence Atherton Irish at the Hollywood Bowl, Bessie Bartlett Frankel at the Philharmonic); some found related work (e.g., Isabel Morse Jones as *Times* music critic, 1925–47).[1] Some combined careers as highly professional performers and studio teachers, developing substantial regional and local reputations (Blanche Rogers Lott, Olga Steeb, and Paloma Schramm, all pianists, the last also as a movie actress; Otie Chew as a violinist). Earlier on, Mamie Perry, a soprano, had her career foreclosed by her father's convictions about women on the stage; she sang in church and elsewhere, always without pay. Foy, a violinist, was barred from playing in a professional symphony orchestra, not by her parents, but by the orchestra's all-male membership, and was thus the first woman in Los Angeles that we know of who met this orchestral glass ceiling, one that remained in place through the period covered by this book.[2]

.   .   .

Harley Hamilton did not leave an archive or a written memoir, so we must rely heavily on published reports of his music-making activities and mentions in a few letters. Bagley reports that he arrived in June 1883 and soon became choir director at the Presbyterian church, where he sang tenor and led the congregation's hymn singing with his cornet. Trained as a printer as well as a musician, he set up a small press in the church attic (where he also lived) and printed the minister's weekly sermons. He directed the amateur and student Semi-Tropic or Good Templars Band but was fired from that position for substituting in the Club Theater band, that is, for taking a one-night paying job considered inappropriate for a church musician. More positively, he formed the Haydn Quintette Club, an instrumental group, which concertized successfully in the area.[3] At some point he left town (perhaps after losing his band job), returning in August or September 1887 and resuming his musical activities. He led the orchestra at Hazard's Pavilion for the Pyke Opera Company's visit and the Webster Brady Show. Before long, he was leading the house orchestra at the new Los Angeles Theater. He attracted a following among the prominent; his students included a daughter of Harrison Gray Otis (editor of the *Times*) as well as Edna Foy. When William H. Mead formed an amateur orchestra (the Los Angeles Orchestral Society) of townspeople and students at the Congregational church, Hamilton was its first conductor.

By 1892 he had started gathering his students on Saturday mornings to play together, forming them into a small orchestra. He encouraged them to organize string quartets and coached them at least occasionally. We may guess that he played in Adolf Willhartitz's early Philharmonic; we know that he served as concertmaster, soloist, and occasional conductor of A. J. Stamm's abortive Philharmonic of 1893–94. In that same season, he organized the more long-lasting LA Women's Orchestra. Four years later, he brought local theater musicians and bandsmen together to form the Los Angeles Symphony Orchestra. By 1907 he had begun to go abroad in the summers; critic Julian Johnson reported a year later that both Hamilton and the orchestra had substantially improved the quality of their offerings.[4] In 1909, when the city fathers decided to support outdoor band concerts, he conducted those too.[5] By the time he resigned from both of these orchestras in 1913 with little public explanation beyond a hint of advancing deafness, he had provided a steady hand in developing the city's symphonic music making over a quarter of a century.[6] Some of the city's wealthier amateur musicians treated him and his wife to a trip to Europe after his last concert; when they returned, according to the *Graphic*, "Harley Hamilton was given two hearty greetings in public last week in addition to hundreds in private. The first was at the Gamut Club, where his associates gave him a very glad hand on his return from Europe, and the second was at the symphony rehearsal, where the orchestra gave its founder and for sixteen years its leader a fanfare—the only time this honor has been paid anyone by this orchestra."[7]

Hamilton's contribution is unusual for several reasons. Virtually all symphony conductors in American cities in those years were born abroad and largely trained there; Hamilton, by contrast, was born in upstate New York and trained mostly in the United States. (It is quite likely that his U.S. birth made him more acceptable to Los Angeles audiences at that time.) Moreover, no other symphony conductor in America maintained an affiliation with a women's orchestra throughout his primary conducting career. The mix of directing both the Women's Orchestra and the Symphony is also confounding, for it appears to involve both "amateur" and "professional" musicians. (He was not paid for his work with the Symphony at the start, and any remuneration he received for the Women's Orchestra consisted of dues paid by its members.)[8] One wonders, How did he manage to acquire his expertise as a violinist and conductor in the first place, then win the support of the many foreign-born musicians who played for him at a time when professional music making was considered the province of foreign-born males? Why did he organize the Women's Orchestra and then stay with it so long, even after the all-male Symphony was launched?

The answers almost surely lie in his background. Hamilton was born and raised in the Oneida Community, in New York, the most prosperous and long-lasting of the numerous utopian Christian communities that sprang up in the early part of the nineteenth century. At its peak, in Hamilton's youth, Oneida had about three hundred members. Notorious because of its practice of "complex marriage" and its later experiment in eugenics ("stirpiculture"), the community encouraged all its members, women and men, to take a turn at all the community's tasks, reducing the sharp distinctions often made between men's and women's work elsewhere in American society.[9] Child rearing was treated as a community responsibility once the children were weaned. Literacy and learning of all kinds were encouraged. The community published its own newsletter and other materials. Moreover, there was a theater on the Oneida property; dramatics and music, including at one point an orchestra of twenty-two members and a quintet, played large roles in the community's life.[10] The evidence is that these factors played an important role in Hamilton's young life.

Harley Hamilton's parents, Susan C. Williams Hamilton and Henry W. Burnham, joined the Oneida Community in 1848; Harley was born in 1861. His mother died of tuberculosis three years later. A year before her death, he was adopted by his mother's second husband, Erasmus H. Hamilton, the leader of the colony. The formal agreement, dated March 8, 1863, transfers to Hamilton "all the rights of a Father. This transfer shall be considered a discharge of Mr. Burnham from the ordinary duties of a Father so long as Mr. Hamilton performs those duties. Mr. Hamilton engages to do for Harley whatever he would be bound to do if he were his real Father. When Harley shall be old enough to think and act for himself, he shall be at liberty to take the name of either his real or his adopted Father."[11]

Given his adoptive father's prominence in the community, it seems likely that Harley was able to take full advantage of the considerable educational opportunity offered, including his training as a violinist and a printer. The community owned property in Wallingford (Connecticut) and Brooklyn (New York); it could easily have sent Harley to Brooklyn and abroad for more study, and apparently it did. A sketch in the *Los Angeles Evening Express,* part of a comprehensive series, "Musicians of Los Angeles," reports that he was "a graduate of the New York College of Music, a student of the violin under Mollenhauer, Listemann and Sauret, with a large orchestral experience in England and in eastern Cities."[12] He could hardly have carried out his study with those European artists or achieved the position in LA that he did without such training.

The Oneida Community broke up in 1881. At that point Hamilton, along with Horatio Noyes, another member of his string quartet, joined Warners Minstrel Troupe and presumably began the career as a traveling musician that led him to Los Angeles.[13] He maintained his connection with the community to some extent. Edward Inslee, an older member of the community, joined him as a violinist when he first came to Los Angeles.[14] Much later, after the death of his first wife in 1926, Hamilton traveled to Kenwood, Ontario, where some former community members lived, to marry Winifred Herrick, very likely a descendant of another member of the community.

Hamilton came away from all this with an unusual acculturation about gender, work, and music, in addition to his training as a musician. He had grown up where teaching and learning were a community responsibility, extending to women as well as men. Music making held a central place at Oneida for both sexes. This forms a sharp contrast with the usual attitude of disdain for "piano-thumping young ladies" to be found repeatedly, for example, in the pages of *Dwight's Journal of Music,* published over about the same time span as that in which the Oneida Community flourished.[15] Music did not become a common profession for U.S.-born American males until well after the time Hamilton came to Los Angeles. More commonly, music was considered part of "women's sphere," a suitable domestic accomplishment for women but suspect as an effeminate occupation for men. I believe that Hamilton's acculturation made it seem natural to organize the Women's Orchestra and continue with it as long as he was able. Organizing men into an orchestra with a season of six to ten concerts on a cooperative or pay-per-service basis in contrast with organizing women into another orchestra with a season of two or three concerts on a club basis, in which the members actually paid for the privilege of playing, is certainly an example of a separate and distinctly unequal arrangement. It was much better than offering no opportunities at all for women, though, and, to his credit, Hamilton took on the responsibility of creating that opportunity and keeping it open for two decades.

Despite their less than perfect solution, both Hamilton and, as we will see, Foy did their best to confound the stereotype of competent symphonic playing as limited to males only. More than a decade after the Symphony refused to accept a woman as a member, critic Alfred Metzger reported on a concert by the Women's Orchestra: "Unlike the usual amateur orchestra the Women's Orchestra is exceptionally strong in the brass section and let me tell you they play, too, and they play IN TUNE—this is the most wonderful part of it. In order to emphasize the musical value of this feat I must repeat that every instrument is played by a woman."[16]

We have nothing from Hamilton about the rejection of his student Edna Foy by the Symphony. Clearly he acceded to it, but what he thought about it and whether it originated with him or with the orchestra's members are not known. Perhaps Hamilton's own view can be inferred from the fact that the two orchestras joined forces for his farewell concert: "Combining forces, the Symphony Orchestra and the Woman's Orchestra presented an excellent program last week, as a testimonial to Harley Hamilton, the conductor of both. The program was lighter than the customary offerings of the Symphony. There were ninety-five players on the stage and after their years under the same conductor, it was little wonder that good results were obtained at short notice."[17]

My speculation about the influence of Hamilton's upbringing on his career suggests a mutually beneficial connection between the qualities he brought to his task and the city's unique features as a location for music making, namely, the large numbers of musicians and music teachers per unit population, the large proportion of women in the music teaching professions, and the unusually high proportion of women and U.S.-born whites in the general population.

.   .   .

Edna Foy grew up in Los Angeles as a female member of a well-established family. That circumstance, along with the nature of the record about her experience, gives us a view of the area's musical life that contrasts sharply with the pictures yielded by the archives from Bagley the union musician, Behymer the impresario, and Burdette the clubwoman-financier-philanthropist (the last two to appear in the following two chapters). Unlike the other informants, Foy was educated in Los Angeles. Like Bagley, Foy aspired to be a musician. Unlike him and the working men (and the occasional woman) about whom he wrote, she was definitively blocked from that career path by her sex. Social constraints may have discouraged her are well.[18] Unlike Behymer, she was trained as a musician, and she was probably never dependent on music making (her own or others') for her livelihood. In contrast to the public images Bagley and Behymer constructed from materials they collected as adults, the evidence on Foy and her siblings emerges mainly from the private sphere, most of it from correspondence within the family. When Foy or any of her five sisters traveled, they wrote letters to the others; many of these are preserved. Moreover, the Foy record encompasses Edna's years of apprenticeship, starting in her teens; it reveals much about how she and her family experienced music as a part of their everyday lives.

Foy was one of the few Anglo residents of Los Angeles of her time who had actually been born in Southern California. Her father, Samuel Calvert Foy, came west to San Francisco in 1852 and, two years later, to Los Angeles, where he established a business, described in this newspaper ad: "Samuel C. Foy. 1854. 1883. The Oldest Business House in Los Angeles. Mfr and Dealer in Harness, Saddles, Whips, Horse Collars, Tents, Wagon Covers etc. Fly-Nets, Lap-Robes, Dusters, Horse Brushes and Curry Comb. Harness, Saddle and Sole Leather. Silver-Inlaid Spanish Bits and Spurs."[19]

In 1860, the elder Foy married sixteen-year-old Lucinda Macy, whose family had migrated to Los Angeles in 1852. Edna was the seventh of ten children born between 1860 and 1883, the fourth to survive beyond infancy (three of the four boys died very early), and the third of the six sisters. Of these, her two older sisters, Mary (1862–1962) and Cora (1870–1920), shared Edna's interests most fully and play the largest roles in the surviving correspondence.[20]

Reports within the family describe the life of this privileged Anglo clan.

Figure 10.   Edna Foy, later concertmaster of the LA Women's Orchestra. This item is reproduced by permission of The Huntington Library, San Marino, California, from the Foy Family Papers.

Music was a regular feature of Edna's surroundings even in the summer. Until the early 1890s, when Edna was in her teens, the family joined other families on the beach at Santa Monica for several months in the summer, living in tents erected annually on fixed wooden platforms.[21] Her father rode the Big Red trolley cars daily to look after his business in town. Entertainments were simple. In a letter to her older sister Cora, Edna describes a visit by the navy cruiser *Charleston* in late July 1891. An extra train brought more tourists from the city, and the ship's searchlights created an impressive display. The ship's lifeboats brought the tourists ashore on the beach, as she reported, leaving some to make an unexpected wet landing. At about the same time, her younger sister Alma wrote to Cora, "They have free concerts every afternoon up on the beach. The actors are, a lady who sings, a man who plays the piano, and two boys that act on the trapeze, but on Sundays they have a man fixed up as a Dutchman that makes all the noises of instruments, and a man dressed as a donkey, that sings and dances."[22] The following year, Cora wrote to Edna from San Diego, describing a reenactment of the landing of Father Cabrillo and the establishment of the San Diego mission. Indian dances in the morning were followed by the landing, a parade, and an oration at the plaza.[23]

Later on, Edna spent parts of her summers with extended family at Camp Indolence, a private mountain retreat near San Bernardino. By this time she had begun to study violin, first at age twelve with Robert Paulson (who did not remain long in LA) and then with Harley Hamilton. A little later, she describes evening practice sessions at the campfire: "I have been practicing a good deal the last few days. In fact your few encouraging words in your letter spurred me on a bit. They all think I play beautifully and I have to keep thinking of how little I am thought of in Los Angeles, and how much less in bigger places, to keep from getting conceited. . . . My favorite time for practicing seems to be after dark. . . . I often stay playing by the fire long after every one has turned in. It is so much nicer then, than in the day time, and easier to practice."[24]

Edna's letters to Cora reveal the growing seriousness of her music study: "I am taking violin lessons now too. Every Wednesday morning I get excused from school at recess and come home and take my lesson. Mr. Hamilton has put me back to work on Kreutzer's studies again. They are very difficult. I think I'll stop school Christmas and not go for a year or so. Mr. Hamilton says that I'm just at the stage when I ought to make a very hard study of my violin and that two years of study now will be better for me than in a few years."

Her music making was closely connected with social activities:

> Oh, I must tell you about our new musical & literary club of 20 girls about my age. Every one can do something. We meet twice a month. Every other Saturday, from 2 o'clock until four. And maybe you don't think we give some good programs. We have about 10 lady patronesses. The following are some: Mrs. Dan Stevens, Miss Packard of the High School, Miss Agnes McLean, Mrs. C. Modini Wood, Mrs. Pomeroy & Mrs. Crowder. How's that for style? We meet at the houses of the different members, take turns at making the souvenir programs. I made them for the last meeting. They were real cute. I'll send you one perhaps if you won't lose it or crush it.[25]

Edna signed this one "Sissie Edna, The celebrated violinist of America," suggesting an aspiration never fulfilled.[26] Soon afterward, she wrote to Cora again, this time to announce that she and her friend Adele, who was doing well with voice lessons, were forming an ensemble; when Cora returned from Oakland (where she had been studying elocution for some months) she might be their accompanist. "We'll be the famous 'Trio,'" Edna wrote.[27]

Early in 1892, Edna carried through her intention of dropping out of school in order to practice. A month later she reported on her new regimen, along with some performances. Most interesting, she wrote: "Every Saturday morning I spend at Mr. Hamilton's studio. There are about 13 of his pupils come every Saturday morning and we play orchestral music. He is going to give a recital in about 6 weeks, he thinks. We play lovely music together."[28] She duly reported on the recital, at which the students played individually and as an ensemble.

> The recital was last eve. and was a *howling* success.
> It was entirely violin music and no one but Mr. Hamilton's pupils took part.
> . . . It took place in the Lecture room of the First Congregational Church. Corner 6th & Hill Sts. The pupils did most of the inviting and we had a packed house I tell you. Mr. Hamilton has more advanced pupils now than he ever had. There were nine solos. All quite different, relieved by numbers by the orchestra. I invited about 30 people. I was next to the last number on the programme and it was the first time in ever so long that I was what you might call nervous. My piece was not so difficult as one or two others but I made quite a hit. It is a Scotch fantasie, "The Keel Row." . . . Everybody was pleased and I received so many compliments & I could hardly carry them [the flowers] home.[29]

The *Los Angeles Capital* records another recital several years later, when Edna played music by Beethoven, Vieuxtemps, and Spohr, the last a duo with her teacher.[30] Mr. Hamilton's ensemble class, formed from his students and presently expanded, turned out to be one of the seeds that developed into the Los Angeles Women's Orchestra.

As already mentioned, Hamilton had already been conducting an amateur orchestra. A program in the Foy family papers describes a concert by the Los Angeles Orchestral Society on June 30, 1890, at the First Congregational Church. Five of the thirty-six musicians are listed as "Miss"; Edna Foy is among the second violins. This orchestra was made up of students and adult amateur musicians, some prominent for other activities, including Hancock Banning, cornet, and Charles E. Pemberton as leader of the second violin section.[31] It was organized on a club basis; its members paid twelve dollars per year to cover expenses.

Another probable seed leading toward the formation of the Women's Orchestra appears in a performance led by Edna in 1893: "The programme was interspersed with orchestral numbers and songs by a double quartet, composed of Mrs. Richardson, the Misses Amy Knewing, Eva Young, Olive La Berge, Messrs. J. L. Whitaker, Charles Morton, G. Brookman and Munton. The orchestra which was led by Miss Edna Foy, violin, included Messrs. Harry Wood, Julius Stamm, Loring Brook, Harry Knoll, Arthur Wood, Julius Bierlich and S. H. Pierce."[32]

Foy's parents were progressive in encouraging their daughters to pursue their interests and develop their skills. Both Mary and Cora studied in the Bay Area, living with relatives while they attended classes; Mary studied literature at the University of California, and Cora studied elocution. Edna, her sisters, and their friends attended the theater fairly often. They also liked to go to baseball games at Washington Gardens on Ladies' Days, when it was appropriate for women to attend.[33] Victorian restraints around ladyhood played a large role in the sisters' lives, however. Their mother was particularly concerned about her next older sister, Cora, who after her study in Oakland spent extended periods with relatives in Northern California: "I fear you are too free in your behavior and do not maintain your dignity as much as you should and that Aunt Nan would not like to tell you, so I do. Do not indulge in too much freedom when with your friends for they might criticize severely looking backward. Of course I write as your letter affects me. If I were there I might have nothing to say against it, but reserve & dignity is a good watchword for a young lady away from home. Mind just what I advise."[34] Cora, who was both the percussionist and long-time president of the Women's Orchestra, considered at one point whether it was appropriate for her to take money for her readings; some of Cora's correspondence with her mother and with her friend and teacher Marion Short, who had a brief career in New York, addresses this matter.[35] Her mother wrote, "Of course we have no objection to your reciting for a consideration."[36]

Once the Women's Orchestra was organized, Edna took her responsibility as concertmaster seriously, trying to help along the less experienced or skilled musicians:

> *Elijah* will come off in about a month or 6 weeks and we girls have our hands full I tell you. I have no doubts but what the girls can play the thing in a very creditable way, but the rehearsals have not been as well attended as they should be, and it has worried me terribly. I still maintain that a full orchestra (amateur) is the most difficult thing to keep running smoothly devoid of worry. It is an impossibility! . . .
>
> I am going to have the girls up on next Saturday afternoon to study a little bit outside of the playing. Intend having some one read Upton's,

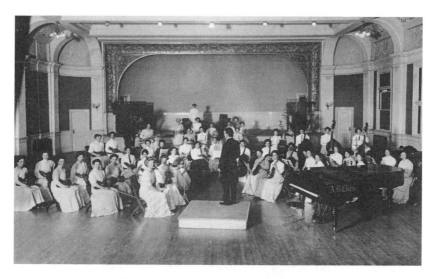

Figure 11.   Los Angeles Women's Orchestra, Harley Hamilton, conductor; Edna Foy is probably concertmaster and is seated in front and to the left of the conductor. This item is reproduced by permission of The Huntington Library, San Marino, California, from the Foy Family Papers.

origin of the oratorio, another his sketch of *Elijah* and some one else Mendelssohn's life.[37]

In addition, she rehearsed regularly with a string quartet and a piano-violin-cello trio.

A lengthy *Los Angeles Express* account of A. J. Stamm's Philharmonic concert the following winter (February 12, 1894) raises the question whether Edna played in that orchestra; the absence of any letter mentioning her participation and her later experience tells us that she did not. When there was another attempt to organize a professional symphony in the fall of 1897, though, Foy sought to join. Here she encountered her glass ceiling, for she was not permitted to become a member of the new Los Angeles Symphony Orchestra, which was to serve as the city's professional symphony for the next two decades. The rejection was made worse because Harley Hamilton, its conductor, was her teacher. Moreover, he had organized and conducted the amateur Orchestral Society and later the Women's Orchestra, in both of which she had played for several years. As concertmaster of the latter, she was the best violin student Hamilton had produced. It seems highly unlikely that she was unqualified to join the orchestra or that there were enough competent violinists to fill the section without her.

Hamilton, who was preeminent among the working string players in the theater orchestras that made up the new group's string section, had encouraged her at every turn, and she apparently did not hold him responsible for her rejection.[38]

As compensation, she was invited to play a solo with the orchestra. Three letters tell this story. The first two are from Edna:

> I appreciate the honor. I suppose Mr. Hamilton thought he would have to do something to appease my wrath at not being allowed to play *in* the orchestra.
>
> It is my first trial with orchestral accompaniment and I do hope I won't disgrace myself. I don't feel a bit nervous about it somehow. It will be in about three weeks.[39]

Once the rehearsals began, she reported again:

> I am so relieved and happy that I must vent my feelings on you. With fear and trembling, I went to the Symphony rehearsal this morning dreading the first rehearsal more than the concert. Mrs. Cook and Miss Irwin (reporters) were there. The men were very nice, and although there were quite a number that did not play they all stayed till mine was finished, and the whole tribe applauded when I had finished.
>
> Now I am not a bit afraid as I have three more rehearsals with them. They played it very well for the first time and my own part went surprisingly well. Mr. West, one of the 1st violins, and leader of the orchestra at the Burbank, had put his violin away and had gone, as I thought, but when I began playing here he came back. When I had finished he told me that it was fine etc. which coming from some one who I did not know was gratifying. Birklein complimented me very highly as did . . . a number of others. Tis my private opinion that Kubel does not approve of my being the soloist. He is such an old crank.[40]
>
> But I intend showing them that I *can play* at this concert. I fully expect a hard criticism from Kubel. He gave Perry an awful dig not long ago on this same piece. So I mean to work especially on my harmonics.[41]

Mama Foy reported the performance, including a brush with stage fright, to Mary, her eldest daughter, who was studying literature at Berkeley:

> Edna acquitted herself to the satisfaction of the largest audience that the concerts have had. . . . Edna says she did not do as well as she thought she would. In the starting out, before she had gone 20 bars she found she was missing a few notes and was nearly paralyzed but did not show it. The *Herald* laid it on the orchestra accompaniment, but she recovered and from then on she did not miss a note, but grew better and bet-

ter. Mr. Hamilton said that it was nothing as against all the grand work she did.[42]

Kubel, whose criticism she had feared, gave her a short paragraph in an otherwise lengthy review, possibly taking the route of damning with faint praise, though he actually wrote about her performance rather than following the common practice of commenting only on the costumes of female performers: "Miss Edna Foy, the solo violiniste of the concert, gave an artistic rendering of Leonard's *Souvenir de Bade*, with the support of the orchestra. Miss Foy's tone production was good, as it always is, and her number received a well-deserved encore, to which she responded with Carl Bohm's 'Legende,' also accompanied by the orchestra."[43]

One way or another, Foy reached the conclusion from this experience that she needed more study. Her family sent her to London, dispatching her sister Mary, thirteen years her senior, to serve as chaperone while she furthered her own studies in literature and art. After some months during which an unspecified finger injury prevented Edna from practicing, she was able to audition for Émile Sauret, a well-established disciple of Eugène Ysaÿe who had concertized years earlier in Los Angeles, probably recommended by Harley Hamilton; Sauret in turn sent her to one of his students, Frederik Christian Frederiksen.[44] Eventually she found herself in a residence for single women, enrolled in theory classes and a student orchestra as part of a diploma program at the Royal Academy of Music.[45] Much of her concert going consisted of attending musicales at large houses in London. She describes in some detail a shared solo recital in Stratford. She also describes teaching the two-step to many dance partners at various social events.[46] One unlabeled clipping reports her progress to her hometown following: "Miss Edna Foy's many admirers will be glad to know that she is making satisfactory progress at the London Conservatory of Music. The promising young violinist had a good deal to unlearn, which is always a painful process, literally so in the case of the violin. . . . D." The sisters spent a full three years abroad (some of the time Cora was with them) before their father's terminal illness called them all home.[47]

After Edna's return to Southern California, the record becomes much scarcer. She continued to be involved in chamber music performances, some of which she organized.[48] A flurry of correspondence and clippings from 1907 show Edna writing to Cora repeatedly about the orchestra's personnel and national publicity for the group. Cora is quoted as making the orchestra's amateur club status a matter of pride:

This Women's Symphony orchestra of Los Angeles is absolutely unique, not only in LA, not only in the US, but in the world. No such organization has ever been held together in any other city. It was tried in Boston, New York and San Francisco, but these enterprises failed. There have been orchestras on the road composed wholly of women, but they were drawn from every part of the Union and were on salary.

Our orchestra is composed wholly of amateurs—by that I mean those who study music for the love of it, and receive no compensation but the satisfaction they derive from the study. . . .

We don't give music in public until we are prepared, but we study it in its highest forms. . . . In any other kind of club a woman can join and shirk work; in an orchestra it is impossible. Come to our practice any Tuesday and you will find every woman blowing, sawing or pounding with all her might.[49]

Foy's marriage in 1909 to the German-born architect Otto H. Neher was the occasion for a family rift, apparently over the suitability of the match. The rift, never healed, was followed by a further division over the settlement of her father's estate the following year.[50] At one point, Edna returned Christmas presents that family members had sent to her but not to her new spouse.

Most of Foy's work as a musician came through (unpaid) club activities, some of which she herself created. Edna reported an early "row with the union" in 1895, presumably over an unpaid performance that was seen as unfair competition with working musicians.[51] The older, relatively easy crossover between the public and domestic spheres in music making was yielding to a more formal organization involving increased professionalization. Clubs—volunteer organizations of individuals with similar interests, often but not always organized on gender lines—formed the model around which much of the city's music activity was organized.[52] Neither the Women's Orchestra, which Edna and her sister Cora helped organize and run for much of its first decades, nor any of its predecessors is an exception. Perhaps the most interesting feature of the Foy record is the way in which her student activities and organizations, many of them involving both girls and boys, dovetailed into mainly all-female adult clubs as the boys grew up and left the domestic sphere behind them.

Yet, had she chosen to follow it, there was an alternate path available, at least for a time. Letters from Cora's friend Gertrude Barrett describe a career as an oboist in professional women's orchestras, successively in San Bernardino, Santa Cruz, and, finally, with Caroline Nichol's Fadettes, based in Boston, an organization that played in vaudeville theaters in New York and Montreal, among other places. These opportunities ended near the start of World War I, as movies began the long process of displacing vaudeville; by 1915, Barrett had returned to Los Angeles and the Women's Orchestra.[53] Another example, not in music, lay closer to home. Foy's eldest sister, Mary, who, like Cora, remained single, had served as librarian of the city's first public library in 1880, taught school, and managed the family's real estate holdings.[54] Thus, a (somewhat limited) independent, professional role was a possibility, had Edna chosen to pursue it.

Though Edna lived for another half century, there is little more in the record. A few letters to her mother survive, posted from western vacation spots that were a part of the middle- and upper-class Southern California lifestyle, such as Yosemite, the Grand Canyon, Idylwild, and Big Bear Lake.[55] Edna's resentment toward Mary, an ardent Democrat and suffragist who was the most vocal family member in disapproving of her marriage, may have influenced her decision to oppose the vote for women, granted in California in 1911.[56] She continued to report musical events to Cora, who by early 1920 was in an Arizona sanitorium, desperately ill with tuberculosis.[57] As late as 1922 and again in 1924, Edna is shown, with violin in hand, as president of the orchestra, although she had already surrendered the concertmaster's chair to the younger Bessie Erb-Fuhrer.[58] Then she vanishes from even the private records of the Foy family, possibly incapacitated by mental illness. After Neher's death in 1960 (at age eighty-one), Edna lived in Camarillo, California, with a cousin. She died in a nursing home in Pedley, Riverside County, in 1971, at the age of ninety-six, having long outlived her involvement as a performer and orchestral advocate.

·   ·   ·

By the time Edna gave up her concertmaster's chair, the Women's Orchestra, begun with such optimism, had become entrenched as a ladies' preserve, part of an elite social establishment. It continued as an unpaid, so-called amateur group, limiting its relevance in the 1920s, the one decade of near-full employment for musicians in the twentieth century. There was a struggle over this issue. In the late 1920s, some of the members formed a voluntary organization whose purpose was to support the orchestra. These women were content to continue their passionate and generally expert participation, reaping personal satisfaction from their involvement as they always had, despite the changes around them. Those who desired to work professionally probably drifted away, at least for a time. In 1931, as the Depression gathered steam, a small group, many of them former Women's Orchestra members, formed a string orchestra and gave at least one concert under the baton of Bessie Chapin, a violinist who had subbed at least once for conductor Henry Schoenefeld. And a few years later, some hint of controversy may be inferred from critic Isabel Morse Jones's blast in the *Times:* "With experience, the Women's Symphony Orchestra . . . is making musical progress and becoming very much less personal and emotional about it. . . . This question of impersonality is an important one in every organization in which women figure, and music is no exception. Women's ensembles have to do much better than other groups in order to succeed for there is a decided prejudice against them all along the way. The emotional habits of women have something to do with this."[59]

This comment is the more remarkable because Jones herself had been a member of the orchestra's violin section. Once, the orchestra had been intended to show that women were capable of a high performance level in music. Though Edna Foy was not among them, some women had eventually been able to move beyond it. The orchestra remained and continued to fulfill a role, even as its former member now turned to blame the victim. It remained for the Federal Music Project (1935–42) to begin providing, within months of this comment, the experience that opened the ranks of professional orchestras to women and their principal chairs to U.S.-born white men. Racial minorities were forced to wait even longer.

6 "Our Awe Struck Vision"

A Prominent Impresario Reconsidered

Like many others who came to California to seek their fortunes, Lynden Ellsworth Behymer reinvented himself not once but several times in the course of his life. This would be a matter of merely antiquarian interest, except that Behymer's career became a public one for which he made greatly exaggerated claims. He repeatedly took credit for single-handedly inventing Los Angeles' concert life almost from the moment of his own arrival there in 1886, then for single-handedly nurturing it for decades afterward. He did this, as he later insisted, by bringing all of the major concert artists and opera companies that appeared there for half a century. Despite a certain skepticism from musicologists, his inventions have assumed the status of a creation myth for Los Angeles concert life, distorting our understanding of that rich history in several ways.[1]

The Behymer myth has obscured his own (real) achievements and those of many others. It has led to a too-narrow focus by historians of Southern California's music history, diverting attention from much other music making and from numerous significant, formative moments in the city's cultural life. Fortunately for us, in the course of his long career he amassed a very large collection of memorabilia, which he donated to the Huntington Library. His collection documents the city's commercial theater history and a sizable chunk of its music history from the mid-1880s, revealing much that otherwise might have been lost, including most of the documentation I have used to show some of his own later fabrications.

Robert Stevenson, a thorough and prolific scholar of Southern California's music history, has chosen to address Behymer's myth by ignoring him and it entirely. Behymer is purposefully omitted, for example, from Stevenson's excellent article on Los Angeles in *The New Grove Dictionary of American Music*, the standard music encyclopedia for the United States.[2] Stevenson's approach serves as an antidote to the central position Behymer holds in Howard Swan's older *Music in the Southwest*, whose chapters on Los Angeles musical life are organized around Behymer's long career.[3] I have chosen to tackle his myth directly as a way to access some other narratives about the city's concert life. One important outcome of my approach is that it reveals Behymer's real contribution, whether for good or ill; he served as the agent through whom concert music, especially performances by traveling virtuosi, was commodified—and later frozen in place—in Los Angeles.

Behymer has already appeared in chapter 4, "'Popular Prices Will Prevail'"—a rubric he detested—where his emergence as the dominant Southern California impresario is documented. Here I address his earlier years in Los Angeles—the most contested part of his career—and his path during and beyond his competition with F. W. Blanchard, including some of his "low-end" ventures. Then I turn to his later career and samples of the more questionable fabrications by which he sought to retain his influence. These will begin to explain how he achieved (and later abused) his aura of musical czar of Los Angeles, with enough power that the advocates of modern music who organized the Evenings on the Roof concert series in the late 1930s could state explicitly that one of their major motivations was to subvert his authority by breaking up his "monopoly" on the city's concert life.[4]

·　　·　　·

Behymer arrived in Los Angeles in 1886 at the age of twenty-three with his wife, Minette ("Nettie") Sparks Behymer, a former schoolteacher who was involved in his business enterprises from the beginning, and the first of their three children.[5] He was a personable fellow with the gift of gab and an enthusiasm for books, two qualities probably encouraged because of the limitations on his physical activity imposed by one substantially shortened leg, the result of childhood polio. (Swan refers to him several times as "the little manager.") He had little or no training in music and claimed no skill as a musician; his knowledge of the theater, to which he was drawn much more than he was to music, was also relatively limited at the start.

The yarn he told about how he happened to come to Los Angeles in the first place demonstrates the method he used to devise his later fabrications. In the early 1880s, he was one of three partners in a failed general store in Highmore, Hyde County, Dakota Territory (adjacent to the Rosebud Sioux reservation in what is now the state of South Dakota). The *Hyde County Bulletin* reported the failure this way:

> Our quiet town was startled, Monday morning, by the rumor that the firm of Behymer, Brace & Sparks had assigned [i.e., been taken over by

its creditors]. Inquiry corroborated the rumor and soon everyone knew of the fact and were more than surprised thereby. The firm had been doing the largest grocery business in the town and was considered upon a substantial footing, but numerous large and unfortunate purchases have lead [*sic*] to the above named result. Since the assignment numerous attachments have been made and much litigation is likely to follow. It is a hard blow to the town as well as the boys and in their difficulty they have the sympathy of us all.[6]

Presently the Behymers took advantage of the newly opened Santa Fe Railroad and immigrated to Los Angeles.

For his later Southern California audiences, Behymer coined a more apocalyptic story, namely, that his business had been destroyed by a "cyclone." For good measure, he added that he had been "1884–86, State Commissioner Hyde county, Dakota."[7] Two months after he lost the business, a tornado struck the town of Sauk Rapids, Minnesota, a few hundred miles to the east of Highmore, inflicting major damage. The *Hyde County Bulletin* carried the real tornado story, reporting twenty-five deaths and the destruction of a store.[8] Loss by tornado made a better story than confessing to a business failure, so Behymer appropriated the Minnesota tornado into his own history. In the same way, he later incorporated musical events from 1887 and subsequently into his own autobiography. (In Los Angeles, Nettie, who would not have forgotten the business failure, kept close track of his entrepreneurial adventures, managing his box office for almost five decades.)[9]

The period from the time of his arrival in 1886 until 1899, when the competition of impresarios began, is the most problematic in terms of conflicting, probably unresolvable, claims about Behymer's career. Los Angeles city directories give no hint of Behymer's activity as an impresario before 1901, fifteen years after his arrival and almost that long after he later claimed to have been speculating in concert promotion. Well before the 1901 listing, Behymer was working on the edges of the theater business with modest but clear success, however. His early jobs as salesman, first of lumber and then of books, might be thought of as parallel to the day jobs held by professional musicians in those years, for example, Harley Hamilton as a printer or Lee Bagley as a photo retoucher. (Neither of them thought to misrepresent the early part of their careers, however.)

BEHYMER BY THE DIRECTORIES

1886—not listed

1887—salesman

1888, '89—salesman, Los Angeles Storage Commission and Lumber Company

1891—travelingman, Stoll & Thayer

1892—travelingman

1900—publisher's agent

1901, '02, '03—treasurer Los Angeles theater, manager Symphony Orchestra and subscription books [a new home address, 1902 Carondelet St., listed at this point]

1904, '05—treasurer Mason Opera House and manager Musical and Lyceum Attractions, LA Symphony Orchestra and LA Choral Society [separate listing under the Lyceum and Musical Bureau includes J. F. Allen, manager, Harry Bell, secretary, and Nettie S. Behymer, treasurer]

1907—president Great Western Lyceum and Musical Bureau, president L. E. Behymer Lyceum and Musical Bureau, manager LA Symphony Orchestra and LA Choral Society[10]

Behymer is said to have gotten his start in the theater business by scalping tickets at the Grand Opera House. According to Swan's account, Behymer hired high school boys to stand in line in the mornings when general admission balcony tickets went on sale. Behymer resold these at a profit in the evening. Probably in response to complaints in the press, the theater manager made a deal with him; before long, he had a similar deal with the management of the Los Angeles Theater.[11]

After a while Behymer also managed the box office, handled the concessions, and published playbills for the two local theaters, turning a profit by selling advertising space in the playbills. (He used the unsold space to promote his own book sales.) When the Burbank, the town's third theater, opened, he got that concession contract too. He was able to quietly dip his toe into the promotion business, seemingly for the first time, in late 1893, when he wrote to Nettie, "Mr. Lehman [manager of the Grand Opera House] and I are going into partnership. In fact, already have done so on a new theatrical deal. I am to play General Lew Wallace [author of *Ben-Hur* and a popular lecturer] here in the spring, on a $350 guarantee. I am working in conjunction with Major Pond of New York City and Col. J. F. Boagg of San Francisco."[12] That may be about when he joined the Chamber of Commerce and the Merchants and Manufacturers Association, serving on the businessmen's committees that organized La Fiesta and, after several years, landing more program-printing contracts.[13]

Six years later, he signaled his aspirations by going out of his way to publicize his role in another venture. Writing in April 1899, the anonymous author of "Around the Theaters," a regular column in the *Los Angeles Capital*, ridiculed Behymer's then-new claim:

> Other great showmen speak meanly of our city, but there is a gleam of light in this o'erclouding sky, and for this let us rejoice and give thanks. A new Napoleon of the show business has been among us and we knew it not. Last Sunday came the first hint of his dawning greatness. Charles Frohman, you know, always "presents" John Drew, or Maude Adams, or Annie Russell, and the rest of the bloomin' lot. Now Ian McLaren is coming to town and guess who is to "present" him to our awe struck vision? Guess the name of this budding Barnum under whose managerial patronage the canny Scotsman comes. Can't guess? Well then:
>
> "Len Behymer presents Ian McLaren," etc., etc. Len's impecunious friends in the newspaper business, who, reading this, will at once begin to borrow money of him, are requested to come early and not to shove or crowd.[14]

At this point, Behymer was definitely not viewed as an architect of the arts. The year before, he had been passed over for manager when the Burbank Theater undertook a reorganization. The younger, more theatrically experienced and talented Oliver Morosco was brought from San Francisco for the job.[15] At that point, Behymer must have realized that he needed more varied experience to supplement his press agent–salesman image if he were to move up in the entertainment business. He quickly became the manager of both Simpson's Auditorium (a church that was a venue for chamber music and choral concerts) and Hazard's Pavilion, neither of which had previously had manager-promoters.

H. C. Wyatt, his boss at the Los Angeles Theater, also gave him some new opportunities. One involved managing artists and repertoire on the road. When the Lambardi Grand Opera Company threatened to disband after its run at the Los Angeles Theater in 1899, leaving its debts and its contentious singers behind, Behymer was given the challenge of shepherding it eastward and seeing that it earned enough to pay off its obligations. He wrote back of the remarkable hold Verdi's opera *Il Trovatore* held on the population in various cities and towns on the route of the Santa Fe Railroad, reinforcing our understanding that opera remained an important part of the popular culture: "The songbirds are doing nobly tonight. Famous old 'Il Trovatore.' . . . That is all they want through the one-night stands. We have two casts now made up, so we can sing 'Il Trovatore' every night if they want it. With the city people, it is different. 'Carmen' is the first cry, 'Rigoletto' next. 'Faust,' 'Aida,' 'Norma' are on a par. But in all the operas, there is nothing sweeter than the dear old 'Miserere' scene in the last Act."[16] Up to this time, most of his experience had been in the front of the house, taking care of the audience. Now he had responsibility for the back of the house (i.e., the actual production) as well, including practice at handling touchy performers under challenging circumstances.

One opportunity Behymer saw and took advantage of had to do with black entertainers. He occasionally acted as manager of a smaller side theater (the Music Hall) when several visiting African American artists appeared, for example, Sissieretta Jones, the "Black Patti," and the Nashville Students, both in December 1897. A few years later, he had a hand in organizing a quartet of black artists and helping them obtain lyceum bookings; three were California singers (Pauline Powell Burns, Juvia Beatrice Roan, and James A. Logan); the fourth was Richard B. Harrison (1864–1935, later famous for creating the role of de Lawd in *The Green Pastures*).[17] Behymer did not see fit to include these efforts on his later bragging lists.

A major business lesson Behymer gleaned from his apprenticeship with Wyatt was to invest heavily in promotion. Theater managers consistently bought front-page newspaper advertising for the events they scheduled; in addition, they put up billboards and indulged in other promotions. Behymer applied this practice to the concerts he presented. This and the higher fees he was willing to pay for famous names were probably his most important innovations. The generous advertising budgets helped him win friends among local newspaper publishers. They probably helped him place the blizzard of promotional stories he diligently supplied, filling—and even expanding—the local papers' space for coverage of music as well as theater. They bore other, more overtly political fruit as well. Along in 1902, Behymer began to get editorial support from the archconservative publisher of the *Los Angeles Times*, Harrison Gray Otis. The idiosyncratic Otis took a dim view of all things labeled "progressive," including Behymer's then-rival in the concert promotion business, F. W. Blanchard. It is probably not entirely coincidental that Behymer's later claims became the semiofficial myth for the entire development of classical music in Los Angeles in parallel with Otis's eventual triumph over all competing dailies, especially the Progressive-leaning *Express*.[18]

. . .

Behymer's activities in 1900 and 1901 are of special interest here, because, like his work with black entertainers, they show him seeking to find a secure place in the entertainment business wherever it might present itself. That meant dabbling in various "low-end" enterprises at the same time as his concert promotions. When he went east in the summer of 1900, he had two separate objectives. He intended to close deals with the Grau Metropolitan Opera Company and a traveling virtuoso or two for the following winter. In addition, he planned visits to amusement parks around the country. En route, he sent dispatches to his home newspapers that reflected his newfound enthusiasm for the profits to be had from this resurgent form of public entertainment:

> The [Chicago] chutes run 17,000 to 25,000 admissions a day to the grounds and fully 50 per cent of these ride the chutes, which make an average of 25,000 to 40,000 at 10 cents a head. The place is clean and neat; no skin games, no drinking, no rowdyism. All are asking about the new one at Los Angeles. I have studied chutes from one end to the other. Can talk chutes in rag-time, and am so thoroughly saturated with chutes that I really think it is going to be an awfully good thing for LA. Most of the income stays right in your own city and is distributed among all classes of people. I looked into their operation thoroughly in St. Louis, Milwaukee and Chicago and particularly from an amusement standpoint, their concessions, their music, their entertainment and safety, and I conclude that it is a splendid addition to Los Angeles amusement enterprises.[19]

In passing, he added that Sarah Bernhardt would be coming to Los Angeles, along with the Alice Nielson Opera Company and the Grau Metropolitan Opera Company. Behymer saw nothing unusual about reporting these two kinds of amusements in one dispatch; they were all part of the same entertainment industry, each appealing to the same public in his home city. After all, at about the same time at least one observer had remarked of the vaudeville house in Los Angeles: "The Orpheum furnishes good wholesome amusements at the minimum of expense. The management deserves more than passing commendation in their care in pruning away any words or acts that might offend the finest sensibilities of their patrons, who include the best families of our city. I have been informed more than once by the performers on the Orpheum stage that no where is the vaudeville audience made up of so fine a quality of people, so nicely dressed and appreciative of pure, clean entertainment."[20]

His visits to amusement parks served as preparation for a new venture. In February 1901, he negotiated a contract to operate nickel arcade picture-show machines and some other new mechanical amusements at the old

Washington Gardens, still located south of downtown, at Nineteenth (now Washington Boulevard) and Main. Fourteen years earlier, when the National Opera Company had created a sensation, the Gardens had featured an ostrich farm, with band concerts on Thursdays and Sundays. Now refurbished by new owners, its offerings were radically expanded; some newly constructed chutes had become its main attraction.[21]

The terms of Behymer's one-year contract with Chutes Park/Washington Gardens are laid out in this letter:

February 1st, 1901

LE Behymer Esq
Dear Sir:

In regard to the following concessions, will state that this company will grant to you the exclusive privilege of what is known as the "Futurescope," "Vitascope" and "Graphoscope" and certain "nickel in the slot machines," on the following basis; to wit; you to receive 75% of the gross receipt of each and every one of the above named concessions less 75% of the salary of such cashiers as may be necessary to operate the same (this company to appoint these such cashiers) and this company to receive 25% of the total gross receipts of the above named concessions and to bear 25% of said cashier's wages; also, the exclusive privilege of what is known as the "Soft Ball," "Babies," "Archery," "Revolving Barrels," "Filipino Javelins," "Baseball Throwing," "Multiscope," and "Phonograph" concessions, together with certain nickel in the slot machines, on the following basis, to wit., you to receive 60% of the gross receipts of each and every one of said concessions, less 60% of the wages of such cashiers as may be necessary to operate the same (this company to appoint these such cashiers) and the company to receive 49% of the total gross receipts of such concessions and to bear 49% of the total gross receipts of such concessions and to bear 40% of said cashiers wages. . . .

> Los Angeles County Improvement Co. [signed] by James E. Salmagi, President.
> I accept the foregoing propositions [signed]. L. E. Behymer

The letterhead on which this is written indicates that Behymer's part of the operation was still a small part of the whole, for the Los Angeles County Improvement Company, operators of Washington Gardens, claimed to offer

> the most complete and extensive amusement park in the world: Shooting the Chutes, Vaudeville Theatre, Roller Coaster, Athletic Grounds,

Base Ball Grounds, Foot Ball Grounds, Japanese Village, Japanese Tea Garden, Performing Animals, Noah's Ark "Zoo," Natatorium, Bowling Alleys, Shooting Gallery, Children's Play Ground, Pony and Goat Carts, Bicycle Race Track, Pony & Foot Race Tracks, Merry-Go-Rounds, Monkey & Snake Houses, Restaurant and Cafes, Casino, Maze, Panorama, Electric Fountain, Search Lights, Cinder Race Track, Miniature Steam Railroad, Riding Elephant, Riding Camel.[22]

Like his bosses at Washington Gardens, Behymer saw opportunities in the new technology and in the new modes of popular entertainment. How long he operated these concessions and when he left them is not documented in his collection. However, in 1904 he was still paying five dollars a month to the city to license "picture machine advertising," also offering band concerts there three times a week for an admission fee of ten cents a head.[23]

Behymer also had a connection with Fiesta Park, a venue for professional sports. It is quite likely that he had something to do with professional baseball games (then considered disreputable) played there, for in 1905 he is reported as saying, "I make money on some of the minor amusements which I manage, occasionally—baseball games and such. I use that to make up the deficit in my grand opera receipts," adding the patronizing remark that the local music lovers didn't know enough to know who the big-name musicians were until he told them.[24]

The use of Hazard's Pavilion for prizefights while Behymer was its manager created consternation among some "respectable" downtown business and church people and was damaging to Behymer as a concert presenter.[25] Relatively little information about his sports promotions exists in the Behymer collection, but there is enough to demonstrate his involvement in them at some level. One 1897 program for a "Carnival of Sport," probably a track meet, survives.[26] In a much later interview (in 1933) he boasted about fights staged at Hazard's Pavilion by the Century Athletic Club. The fighters included Jack Johnson, Jack Jeffries, and Kid McCoy. "Reputable men supported us and were our friends. They came to the fights by the hundreds. Many a time we have had a crowd of between 4000 and 5000."[27] (The details in such later claims may be no more precise than his claims about his early concert giving.) Contemporary documentation exists for another event at the Los Angeles Theatre, however. A treasurer's statement signed by Behymer records the gate for a "benefit boxing contest for San Francisco [earthquake and fire] Sufferers," dated Tuesday, April 24, 1906.

TREASURER'S STATEMENT FOR BOXING MATCH, APRIL 24, 1906

12 box seats @ $10	$120.00
222 seats @ $5.00	$1110.00
712 seats @ $2	$1424.00
Cash at the door	$38.65
Flowers sold by girls	$50.
Total	$2742.65

Signed, L. E. Behymer, Treasurer.[28]

The event was not a sellout, but it did well. If Behymer was a regular backer of prizefights, that part of his life was not publicized and probably grew less important to his financial well-being as his career developed. One of his later assistants remembered him near the end of his life as preferring to watch a wrestling match over a concert he was sponsoring.[29]

Meanwhile, Behymer's concert promotions were not without problems. When the Symphony began its run in 1898, Behymer was present, but only in the capacity of managing the box office and the concessions as part of his regular duties at the Los Angeles Theater. He became more fully involved only after the Symphony had survived for several seasons and had found at least one guarantor. At that point, it became clear that serving as its manager would offer greater access to the "high-class" subscribers he was learning to cultivate for what would become his primary attractions. His managerial debut was not entirely auspicious: "It is a pity the management of the Los Angeles theater did not provide better facilities for handling the big attendance. The crush in the entrance foyer was terrific, and as only one door was open, with one man taking tickets, the delay in gaining admission was not only disappointing in that many had to miss the first number, but the personal discomfort in the waiting patrons was great."[30] One hopes that he developed some competence at orchestral management in his years with the Symphony. We know that he left the Symphony's management at least two years before its demise, then moved to the new and much better financed Philharmonic when it was organized in 1919.[31] He left the Philharmonic management after three years, though he continued to maintain an office in the Philharmonic Auditorium building for the rest of his life.

Behymer was especially proud of having presented the touring Grau Metropolitan Opera Company production of Wagner's *Parsifal* in 1901, an engagement finalized during his trip east the previous August. Alfred Hertz, the conductor, remembered that performance for a different reason, however:

One of the most amusing incidents, now that I look back on it, occurred in Los Angeles. When I started the Prelude of *Parsifal*, the neutral gray curtain which we took to be the regular curtain but which proved to be the asbestos, slowly went up and, horror of horrors it uncovered an advertising curtain the entire height of which displayed one huge bottle on which was printed in enormous letters, "HUNJADY JANOS, THE BEST PURGENT IN THE WORLD."

I do not know if people laughed; I only know that I for one could not laugh. In vain was I weighing in my mind while I continued to conduct the orchestra in that sublime Prelude, what I could do. However, I came at length to the conclusion that the damage had been done. That there was nothing to do but for me to go through with it.[32]

Whether this was an example of incompetence or a practical joke remains unknown, nor is it clear from Hertz's account who was responsible. Published in a San Francisco newspaper, the incident served to reinforce the image of Los Angeles' ineptitude relative to "high" culture. Behymer had to learn the hard way that his promotions required detailed and continuing attention if they were to succeed.

Behymer's simultaneous invasion of the concert management field and his various "low-end" ventures, especially the prizefights, generated a class-related issue involving gender roles and public "morality." In the public rivalry with F. W. Blanchard that was taking place at the same time, Behymer was challenging a person who held the cultural high ground. Blanchard's concert promotions were designed—and perceived by the public—as a service to his customers and to the city rather than as money-making enterprises, a stance more acceptable to the middle-class women who figured large among his customers and among concert audiences. Behymer was left to present himself as the little guy trying to gain a foothold against the "theater trusts." There was very likely some question among his potential concert ticket buyers whether anyone other than the actual performers ought to make money from musical events. To make things worse, he had unwisely fostered several public and destructive choral competitions, as discussed earlier, as part of his rivalry with Blanchard.

By the time Blanchard retreated from the field of public concert giving in 1905, Behymer had learned to downplay, or perhaps actually abandoned, his low-end promotions. The closure of old Hazard's Pavilion punctuated this move definitively, for it eliminated the main venue used for prizefights. (For a time, Behymer was even shut out of the management of the new Temple (later Philharmonic) Auditorium, a reason he was still pushing for a new civic auditorium several years later.)[33] To cement his new position as the leading presenter of concerts and operas and nurture the social role that went with it, he organized the all-male Gamut Club in 1904 and encouraged interested women to organize the supporting Dominant Club.[34] Behymer needed to make peace with the (male) rivals he had recently vanquished in the impresario business, for he would continue to depend on their financial backing.

Before long, the Gamut Club's membership was extended "to include men of various arts, professions and businesses, the requirements for membership being simply that the applicant be a man of education and well recommended."[35] George A. Dobinson, a teacher of elocution and an amateur musician, thoughtfully provided the men with a clubhouse. Monthly dinner meetings, including occasional "ladies' nights," provided the setting for concerts by the members and impromptu entertainments for (and by) visiting virtuosi, as well as discussions about the growth of the music profession and musical activity in the city. Blanchard was a prominent member, and so was Charles Farwell Edson (of whom more later), a singer and voice teacher whose first effort as a musical organizer was to broaden and extend the Gamut Club's membership.[36]

To reinforce his public commitment to visiting virtuosi and opera companies after 1900, Behymer began to emphasize the high-end aspects of his work. Thus, the announcement of his 1905 concert season carried this disclaimer: "The Great Philharmonic Course this season is appealing to the better class of the amusement public, the class who take seriously the best in music and literature, and Manager Behymer has at last realized that the Los Angeles public desire only the best."[37]

His dawning awareness of the distinction between the concert audience on one hand and his amusement park fans on the other may explain why it was Behymer-the-nonmusician who pushed his events as "high-class" attractions and why he learned to use, even to flaunt, the rhetoric of exclusion, morality, and duty in his promotion of concerts in Los Angeles. The application of this rhetoric and the constant reference to "high-class attractions" confirm Behymer's careful cultivation of class distinctions (once he understood them) among these audiences for his various offerings after he came to control the major touring musical attractions.

· · ·

As early as 1905 and '06, Behymer was already spinning his image as a promoter, boasting about his "nerve" in offering large guarantees for visiting virtuosi, to Frank Searight of the *Los Angeles Record* and expanding on this for Alfred Metzger, the unsuspecting editor of the Oakland-based *Pacific Coast Musical Review*. (Following San Francisco's devastating 1906 earthquake and fire, Metzger took refuge in Southern California for a couple of years.) Metzger wrote, "The rapid development of musical culture in Southern California is largely due to the untiring efforts of L. E. Behymer, who has not shunned any expense, nor has he ever been timid to risk pecuniary loss when he could obtain for his territory an artist whom he thought his public ought to hear."[38]

Elaborations on this hype came later on, when Behymer claimed more and more credit for any noteworthy historical theatrical and musical events that had taken place when he happened to be around and that he may or may not have been marginally involved with, starting with Adelina Patti's 1886 concert and the visit by the National Opera Company a year later. More and more, he conveniently "forgot" the pioneers on whose shoulders he stood, Wyatt and Blanchard among them.

The specific claims that exaggerate Behymer's influence, making it hard to straighten out the facts of the matter, begin in earnest around 1910, with Robert Grau's *The Business Man and the Amusement World*. They continue with M. B. Leavitt's *Fifty Years in Theatrical Management* (1912) and a series of interviews with Behymer published in the *Los Angeles Evening Express*, beginning in December of the same year.[39] In Grau, for example, he is credited with providing local management for the U.S. premiere of Puccini's opera *La Bohème* (the entry, which gives no date, claims the wrong company and the wrong venue) and also credited with having helped to organize and even to underwrite the Los Angeles Symphony from the beginning, something about which he was uncharacteristically silent at the time.[40]

A list prepared for a Gamut Club celebration in 1924 forms another step in the myth-making process. It contains numerous errors of fact about the period before 1900, the years of Behymer's apprenticeship. Even the dates are incorrect. Behymer's name does not appear as presenter or sponsor in connection with any of these events at the time they took place, except for the last one on the list. (In a few cases, the attraction did return at a later date under Behymer's management. That is true for Patti, who returned in 1904, and Paderewski, who gave several concerts in 1907–8, for which contracts exist in Behymer's papers. Here the correct dates are listed, along with the guarantors, sponsors, or impresarios of record.)

"THIRTY-FIVE YEARS OF ARTISTIC SERVICE"

(Behymer's claims of service made at Gamut Club dinner, November 5, 1924)[41]

Presentations according to Behymer's claims:	*Actual presenter/guarantor and dates (information from contemporary sources):*
National Grand Opera Company, Dec. 13–19, 1887[42] Venue: Hazard's Pavilion	National Opera Company, May 16–21, 1887 Managers: McLain and Lehman Guarantor: Otto G. Weyse
Henry M. Stanley (lecturer), Jan. 10, 1888 Venue: Hazard's Pavilion	Mar. 21, 1891 Manager: H. C. Wyatt
Adelina Patti (in concert), Feb. 3, 1888 Venue: Armory/Mott's Hall	Jan. 20, 1887 Guarantor: Walter S. Maxwell
Booth and Barrett, Feb. 27– Mar. 4, 1888 Venue: Grand Opera House	Dates correct Manager: H. C. Wyatt
Emma Abbott Grand Opera Co., Dec. 24–30, 1888 Venue: Grand Opera House	Dec. 30, 1886–Jan. 8, 1887 Managers: McLain and Lehman
Emma Juch Grand Opera Co., Jan. 7–13, 1890 Venue: Grand Opera House	Juch English Opera Company, Jan. 29–Feb. 3, 1889 Managers: McLain and Lehman Program pub. by Myer Siegel
Bostonian Lyric Opera Co., Feb. 20–26, 1890 Venue: Grand Opera House	The Bostonians, May 6–15, 1889 Manager: H. C. Wyatt
Sarah Bernhardt and Company, Sept. 14, 1891 Venue: Grand Opera House	Date correct Managers: Wyatt and Conant
Ignace Jan Paderewski, Feb. 7, 1896 Venue: Grand Opera House	Date correct Manager: H. C. Wyatt Program publisher: L. E. Behymer

Melba Grand Opera Company,
    Apr. 25–27, 1898
Venue: Los Angeles Theater

Dates correct; Nellie Melba,
    featured soprano of Damrosch-
    Ellis Grand Opera Association
Managers: H. C. Wyatt and
    F. W. Blanchard

Grau Metropolitan Grand
    Opera Co., Mar. 10–12, 1901
Venue: Hazard's Pavilion

Nov. 9–10, 1900
Manager: L. E. Behymer

Behymer chose to lead off his list with the National Opera Company, though it was not the earliest on the list, because it was the best-remembered of these events among his 1924 audience.

By 1938, when Behymer doctored a program for a concert given by Paderewski in 1896, more than forty years earlier, adding "L. E. Behymer presents" at the top, Behymer's misrepresentations had become routine.[43] Figure 12 shows the program as it originally appeared, surrounded by the ads that had adorned the original program. Next to it is the doctored version, set on a backing of newsprint, trimmed with pinking shears, on which the name "Bach" is suggested. "L. E. Behymer presents" is inserted into the old program. To be sure, Behymer had sold tickets and printed the programs for Paderewski's first appearance in Los Angeles. But the presenters of this 1896 concert, the ones who signed the contracts and took the financial risks, were Behymer's long-time mentor, theater manager Harry C. Wyatt, and his long-time business and political rival (and sometime silent partner), Frederick W. Blanchard.

Behymer claimed more generally that, early on, he developed a chain of theaters in Southern California so that he could assure more than a single booking for many of his events. When he booked such events as the Eduard Strauss Concert Orchestra at Hazard's Pavilion and in Pasadena, San Bernardino, and San Diego in late December 1900, though, he was taking advantage of a chain booking system already developed by his mentor and colleague, H. C. Wyatt, who at this point managed or had agreements with a number of theaters in Southern California. By the prosperous 1920s, Behymer had developed a similar practice over a fairly wide territory in the Southwest, providing opportunities for regional artists, though at much lower fees than the international stars commanded, in smaller cities such as Fresno and Reno as well as Phoenix. He was never able to break into the business in more cosmopolitan San Francisco, where Will L. Greenbaum provided local management, or in much

Figure 12. An L. E. Behymer self-promotion. The original program of an 1896 piano recital by Ignacy Paderewski is shown be-
side a reproduction as it appears in a 1938 Shrine Auditorium
program for Paderewski's farewell concert. "1896" and "L. E. BE-
HYMER presents" are inserted in the original program. The ads
that surrounded the program in the original are replaced by
more recent newsprint trimmed with pinking shears and containing the words *Bach, Salzburg, violinist,* and so forth. Programs courtesy of Cambria Master Recordings and Archives.

smaller Seattle, where a strong women's club controlled the bookings of
traveling virtuosi.

• • •

Behymer saw most of the initiatives in concert giving described in part II of
this book as challenges to his hegemony as an impresario. His opposition to
programs aimed at increasing the popular appeal of symphonic music is obvious from his reluctance to expand the Symphony's season or add pop concerts, his opposition to the People's Orchestra of 1912–13, and his pointed
lack of interest in helping get the Hollywood Bowl concerts under way.[44] His

bogus claims tended to become more brazen as each of these new initiatives (and a few others besides) appeared. In fact, very little amounted to a serious threat to his position, for his foot dragging managed to discourage or seriously handicap new programs. One major threat came in 1922 from J. T. Fitzgerald, the music store operator who had continued to present Sousa's very popular band and a few other events. Fitzgerald formed a partnership with Merle Armitage with the intent of challenging Behymer, and Armitage's Auditorium Artists series continued for several years before Armitage found greener pastures elsewhere.[45] Another threat is described in chapter 11.

From circa 1922, after he left the management of the Philharmonic, until his death in 1947, long after his early colleagues and competitors had retired from the scene or died, Behymer hung on to regional control of his many touring artists. His contribution became less constructive as he grew out of touch with the changing musical and theatrical scene. A few months before the stock market crash in 1929, for example, he lost substantially on the Los Angeles Repertory Theater, a new project. He wrote to Nettie, who was often his business partner:

> Next winter you can run the shows and concerts. . . . I am finished. My ambition, faith in clubs and the people gone. I guess I have outlived my usefulness and have lost my cunning. . . .
> I wanted to do things for the city and the world and be useful—I have stumbled and that's the end.[46]

In his concert promotions, Behymer had always been closely identified with the traveling virtuosi and the limited repertoire they offered. The lack of music in his own background, which had helped him early on, became more and more problematic, for he had little creativity of his own to keep him abreast of artistic trends. (By contrast, Merle Armitage, for all the ridicule heaped on him recently by Kevin Starr, had his creative interests as a designer and writer to stimulate him.)[47] Very few of the half million people in Los Angeles in 1920 had been among the fifty thousand of 1890 or even the hundred thousand of 1900 who had known Behymer as "the little press agent." How were they to know or care that such a senior, respected figure did not remember everything accurately or that he was fudging his facts? Yet despite this, or perhaps even because he lacked the peculiar snobbery that sometimes goes with music training, he continued to sponsor concerts by African Americans, though he never boasted about them.

Behymer's relationship to the Federal Music Project, documented in a folder of letters at the Huntington Library, provides a sorry latter-day post-

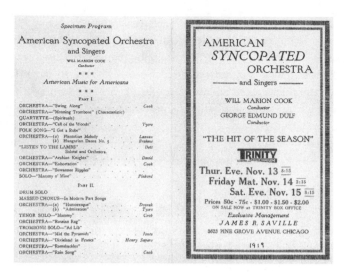

Figure 13.   Program, American Syncopated Orchestra, Trinity
Auditorium, Los Angeles, November 13–15, 1919, presented lo-
cally by L. E. Behymer, who had quietly presented many African
American artists. Courtesy of Cambria Master Recordings and
Archives.

script to his story. By the time of the project, his posture of defending the
institutions from which he profited spilled over into the frankly venal. Taking care of people he could no longer employ or help with his own money,
even at the expense of a federal program he liked to criticize for its bureau-
cratic waste, was just another such opening.[48]

·   ·   ·

The historical assumption of Behymer's utter hegemony over the art of
music in Los Angeles has been fostered, then, by several elements, beginning with Behymer's own long-term diligence as a press agent and his tireless promotions of any events in which he had an interest. He never fully
overcame the anomaly created by his early, simultaneous cultivation of
"high-" and "low-end" amusements. When I interviewed one of his grand-
children in the early 1990s, she asked rather anxiously, "Was my grandfa-
ther a crook?" My answer then was, probably not. With considerably more
evidence, that opinion stands, although the episode with the Federal Music
Project pushes the envelope. I do not hold the prizefights against him; indeed, his work with black entertainers now seems a plus, though it was

probably not seen that way at the time. Nevertheless, a certain undertone lingered on over the years, a suggestion that he was something of a charlatan. His likely preference for the low-end sporting entertainments he had sponsored early in his career could not be entirely masked, lending an air of phoniness to his protestations about the quality and importance of the visiting virtuosi, whose fame he sought to appropriate. The later misrepresentations of his early career have served to intensify the questions.

Once the uncertainties are identified and the inaccuracies planted by Behymer himself are straightened out, the nature of his contribution becomes far more interesting than the myth he created. Behymer and his contemporaries functioned at a cultural crossroads that is only now being documented. His formative years in the theatrical business were just at the time when, in the form of vaudeville and "picture shows," large-scale commercial mass culture first saw the light of day in Los Angeles. It is also when what we now think of as "classical" music became an anchor of a newly emerging elite, "highbrow" culture, functioning in a niche market instead of as a fixture in an older, long-standing popular culture. The emergence of commercial mass culture led to a more pronounced cultural hierarchy that exaggerated previous, already understood distinctions. What Behymer did was to apply the methods and principles he had learned in his years of ticket selling, usher organizing, press agentry, and general business management in Los Angeles' handful of commercial theaters to the presentation of music events for the elite. He didn't set out to do that, of course. Lacking the quasi-religious view of concert music that is part of the training every classical musician still receives, he was able to respond to the new circumstances more directly and pragmatically. This same lack brought him a great deal of criticism, some of it I think unjust, by his opponents in the music establishment, who wanted music to be a popular art whose value lay in its moral freight, rather than a commercial art.

Behymer's mythical position as the Moses of Los Angeles music is worth unraveling and reconstituting, as I have done here, for several reasons. Los Angeles' musical life in the Progressive era, circa 1890–1920, was enormously rich and far too varied to have been dominated by any one individual. Behymer, and others who have followed, claimed it was a musical desert more because of exclusionary definitions of music than because there was no music making. He achieved his position of primacy in concert presenting considerably later than he claimed, building on the substantial foundations laid by other theatrical and musical pioneers. Through a process of trial and error, he became a competent concert manager, though one with a rather limited perspective who outlasted his usefulness. Yet, to be a successful presenter of music events and a successful press agent in his own behalf, over so long and interesting a period, was a major achievement. It is unfortunate that Behymer thought he had to embroider on this history in order to secure his own position in it.

PART II

Progressive-Era Musical Idealism

7 The "True Temple of Art"

Philharmonic Auditorium and
Progressive Ideology

The Progressive movement developed in parallel with the growth of professional music making in Southern California; its political arm actually embraced—marginally, anyway—public music making as one of its values. It is no accident that, at the same time that Los Angeles was becoming a hotbed of political Progressivism, the city's many musicians and advocates for concert music and opera endowed their art with an essential, constructive ethical power that enhanced its value and justified its cultivation as a civic asset. A quasi-religious, ethical value was intrinsic to both. Musicians, mostly male, were by then found routinely in theaters, hotels, restaurants, churches, parks, and even in private homes. Many more music teachers, mostly female, were found in numerous private conservatories such as the Von Stein Academy (which claimed as many as 700 private students before it vanished on the eve of World War I), in the 150 studios (for both musicians and artists) housed in the Blanchard Music and Art Building, and in other studios and private homes. Clubs, most often segregated by race, gender, ethnicity, and (more loosely) class, and racially segregated churches provided large and appreciative audiences for performances of art music, most often given by local musicians. In all fairness, one must stress that music and the other arts were peripheral to Progressivism as a political movement. Nevertheless, *California Outlook,* the movement's local magazine, argued its social utility in articles such as "The Influence of Good Art and Literature on Character": "It should be the aim of all good citizens to foster the love of art, and to bring its benign influence to bear upon the whole people; to diminish and neutralize the exhibition of what is coarse and vulgar, and develop by every possible means the taste for the beautiful."[1]

The Jane Addams Chorus, formed to greet Progressive presidential candidate Theodore Roosevelt when he appeared in Los Angeles in 1912, exemplifies the view of music held by Southern Californians, including Progressives. "Never has a more inspiring and elevating idea been introduced into American politics than that embraced in the organization of the Jane Addams Chorus," the *Outlook* announced. A thousand white-clad women, including a hundred African Americans, were to march to the front of the auditorium to greet the candidate with song. The newly enfranchised women and the music they provided were expected to improve the tone of politics:

> Music is always a refining influence—the right kind of music! And the songs of the Jane Addams Chorus are precisely the right kind—the old songs of the hearths and hearts of the American people, the national airs, the soul-songs of a great country.
>
> These women sing for us the anthems of the North, the melodies of the South, the hymns of the East and the ballads of the West. No note of rag-time is sounded, no cheap appeal is attempted. Their music has the dignity of that which is genuine, the sweetness of that which is pure.[2]

The first real success of musical progressivism—here with a small *p*, embodying these long-held idealistic but fatally narrow views in a new and formative way—came almost a decade before Teddy Roosevelt's famous Bull Moose campaign.

Surveys of American music rarely fail to point out the widespread nineteenth-century sense of music as a secular religion, often reinforcing their points by quoting from Boston-based John Sullivan Dwight, who told the Harvard Musical Association in 1841 that the purpose of music was "to hallow pleasure, and to naturalize religion." Dwight reiterated that position for another four decades, mainly in the pages of his journal.[3] Los Angeles musicians, especially teachers of music, were very much a part of the same tradition. For example, the influential pianist and teacher Thilo Becker produced a collection of aphorisms for his students that includes these:

> Music— / Sublime authority of / God.
> The gates of music / are guarded / by the Holy Spirit.
> Music / relates man to God / when man / relates God to music.
> Production of Tone / is not a mechanical process. / Tone is born of
>   God, / or not at all.[4]

Becker imparted these views along with his knowledge of technique and the literature of the piano to some outstanding students who carried on the tradition; Paloma Schramm, Blanche Rogers Lott, Lester Donahue, and Olga Steeb all had substantial regional careers as soloists, chamber musicians, and teachers.

Later on, in 1919, Walter Henry Rothwell, the first conductor of the new Philharmonic, prepared an elaborate Christmas greeting for the orchestra's founder in the midst of their first season; the members of the orchestra signed it as well. Part of the text is worth quoting here:

> Now, more than ever, when men's faiths have been tried and a new feeling for tolerance and brotherhood is sweeping the world, it is natural that men should turn with renewed fervor, to the oldest and most communal of the arts. . . .
>
> By conferring this princely gift on the City of Los Angeles, you are erecting a structure, not only for musicians, but an edifice in which every member of the community can come to worship and be healed. It is not merely our hope, but our faith that this will indeed become a True Temple of Art.
>
> In voicing these scattered sentiments, I feel I am expressing far more than my personal beliefs; the enthusiasm of the community is, after all, the deepest and surest response.[5]

That belief system and the business and social organization that subscribed to it explain how it was that Temple Auditorium became a major feature of the city's downtown from the moment it opened in 1906 until it was torn down in the 1980s. In fact, it formed one cornerstone of the Progressive movement, which blossomed in the late nineteenth and early twentieth centuries, finding one of its strongest centers in Los Angeles.[6]

•   •   •

Music was never a primary interest for Clara Bradley (Wheeler Baker) Burdette.[7] Nevertheless, she set in motion a profound change in the city's musical life and pushed it through to completion. In the decisive burst of activity described here—a relatively small chapter in her long career as philanthropist and activist in other areas—she achieved what years of hype and bluster from L. E. Behymer were never able to match. Burdette led the successful campaign to build the concert hall/opera house that would house the city's "major" large-scale performances for much of the next six decades. Her actions, literally set in (reinforced) concrete, show how closely concert music and opera were thought of as a secular religion, capable of uplifting any community. This concept was routinely set in opposition to commercial, so-called popular entertainment. The contrast, and the implied class distinctions that were a part of it, became stronger as commercial entertainments grew and prospered.

Burdette brought unusual qualifications to the project. She had acquired considerable personal wealth, some of it in the form of downtown real es-

Figure 14.   Philharmonic (formerly Temple) Auditorium, 1906–67. Courtesy of Cambria Master Recordings and Archives.

tate, in the course of being twice widowed. In 1899 she married Robert Jones Burdette (1844–1914), a successful humorist-lecturer recently turned Baptist minister. She organized the California Federation of Women's Clubs and became its first president in 1900; later she became first vice president of the National Federation. In these positions she traveled independently of her husband and spoke to women's organizations quite widely. A year before the sequence of events began that resulted in the Temple Auditorium project, she was the subject of a highly gendered front-page attack on her women's club, feminist activism in the *Los Angeles Evening Express,* which serves to remind us of the obstacles that women, even wealthy white women, had to address if their public activities attracted attention. Some excerpts from the *Express* article:

MRS. BURDETTE ILL
FEARS EXPRESSED THAT SHE MAY NOT RECOVER FROM ATTACK
OF CONGESTION OF BRAIN
DUE TO MENTAL ANGUISH
HER SICKNESS IS ATTRIBUTED TO AMBITION TO BECOME
PRESIDENT OF GENERAL FEDERATION. . . .

Lying there in her beautiful home, surrounded by many luxuries and attended by loving friends, the prominent club woman tosses in her delirium and suffers from an illness brought on, it is believed, by her unhappiness over club matters. . . .

When Mrs. Burdette first became identified with club life in Los Angeles she gained favor rapidly with women of this city. She was a bright, vivacious speaker of charming tact. So well was she liked that when the State Federation of Women's clubs was organized she was made its first president and there was no dissenting voice. Then it was, so the story goes, that ambition seized upon her. . . . it is possible that her ambition may cost her life.[8]

Charged with unladylike ambition, Burdette was put in an impossible position in which almost any reply reinforced the editor's criticism. Convention seems to have demanded that the (male) editor responsible should be confronted by a male and that any private response from the editor directed to Burdette come from another woman. Thus, it was Rev. Burdette who appeared the following morning at the newspaper office to voice his own objections and deliver his wife's written reply. In answer, the editor then caused his wife, not herself a newspaper employee, to send a letter to Mrs. Burdette explaining that the whole thing was a misunderstanding. To follow this up, the editor wrote a lengthy letter to Rev. Burdette; its burden was that the story had been blown out of proportion.

The incident shows that it was no easy thing for a "lady" of Burdette's generation to go against the old convention that her name should appear in the public press only three times, to report no more than her birth, marriage, and death. The attack drew a storm of criticism from various women's organizations; it also affected the way Burdette represented herself afterward. Burdette found it necessary to explain and defend her long-standing career as a public speaker, claiming then and many times afterward that she traveled with her husband "to make a home for him wherever he went."[9] After such a public controversy, it is something of an irony that her key role in the building of Temple Auditorium was so little noticed in the press. The greater irony is that the attack in the *Express* carried an obvious political element, for the *Express* generally championed the cause of Progressive reform. Clara Burdette's position as a stockholder in the rival, archconservative *Times* made her a target, and explains the *Times'* one-page response, despite her work as a club organizer and an advocate of women's rights. The status of women was still low on the list of public issues that motivated Los Angeles' reform movement.

A few months after this contretemps, a group of the city's most prominent businessmen, led by Charles H. Barker (president of the city's largest department store), began public discussion of the problem of urban decay. Hazard's Pavilion, built in 1886, when the city's population was scarcely one-tenth as large, and still the only suitable home to large visiting opera companies and concerts, was Exhibit A. Its use for prizefights, definitely a lower-class form of entertainment, was judged offensive and seen as a sign of urban decline. "Everyone acquainted with Los Angeles knew that 'Hazard's Pavilion,' while it had in the past been the scene of great religious, political and musical gatherings, and had been transformed into a thing of beauty by Flower Festivals and Military Balls, . . . did not at this time bear 'an odor of sanctity' in the community. Its varied career was at an end."[10] At the same time, the large downtown Congregational and Methodist congregations were about to abandon the area.[11] The time seemed ripe to tackle the incipient urban decay and help the city's troubled Baptist denomination, as Burdette later wrote, by organizing a new congregation, to be located, of course, in the central business district, where there had not previously been a Baptist church.

According to Clara Burdette's own account of the project, *The Rainbow and the Pot of Gold* (1907), "During 1902–3 the Baptists of Los Angeles seemed to be testing the power of the spirit by leading an internal life that expressed itself externally as unsettled, unhappy and inharmonious."[12] Interest in the new church was strong, and by the time a public meeting was announced, Rev. Burdette had already been approached and had agreed to become its pastor. At an organizational meeting attended by 258 Baptists, the new congregation voted to incorporate and to hire the Rev. Burdette. It agreed to rent the vacant First Congregational Church (seating twelve hundred) as its temporary home.[13]

Successful from the start, the congregation soon outgrew even this large initial space. In October 1904 it bypassed Simpson's Auditorium (also available) and leased the much larger Hazard's Pavilion, bringing a definitive end to the prizefights as well as securing a much larger meeting place than had first been contemplated. A tongue-in-cheek, page-one headline tells the story: "Solar Plexus by Preacher. Sunny Burdette Knocks Out the Prize Fights. Single Blow without Glove . . . Hazard's Pavilion Leased for Temple

Church."[14] The lease would begin eight days after a scheduled prizefight already contracted for and last a year. The building would be renamed Temple Auditorium. C. R. Harris, another prominent businessman and a member of the new congregation's board of trustees, was quoted in the same article as saying, "All contracts had been carefully scrutinized and they were prepared to carry them all out. They will continue to rent the pavilion for such purposes as their judgment may dictate and high-class entertainments will find it open to them as it has been heretofore." Robert Burdette's success at attracting a congregation was also reported. The new congregation had already doubled in size, packing their initial meeting space and making an expansion necessary. The very large capacity of Hazard's Pavilion, which could seat at least three thousand, set an ambitious goal for church attendance. "By this rental and the final purchase of this property, the Temple Church had done what the city authorities had not been able or willing to do, closed the place for public prize fights in the heart of Los Angeles. The women are thoroughly cleansing and refitting this building that was to be re-named 'Temple Auditorium,' the 'dead past' was left to 'bury its dead.'"[15] Right away the new Baptist congregation began to look for a suitable site for its own permanent building. Because she was the minister's wife and had her own money, Clara Burdette was appointed to the committee assigned to seek the best possible downtown location. Both she and Barker traveled to other cities to investigate possible models for their new structure and for how to finance it.

It was probably Mrs. Burdette who persuaded them to choose a long-term solution based on the well-established model of the Tremont Temple in Boston, by then already in its third incarnation as a large, centrally located auditorium used for public lectures as well as for Baptist church services, with many floors of office space above it.[16] The new downtown congregation agreed with the recommendation, which was to purchase Hazard's, tear it down, and put their new structure on the same site. Acting as chair of the congregation's building committee, Clara Burdette stepped forward as the lease was to be renewed, unhesitatingly putting down ten thousand dollars of her own money for an option to buy the building and the land under it outright.[17] This report from the *Times* does not mention Mrs. Burdette's role:

> However, under the inspiration of their leader, the members determined to do something worthy of themselves and worthy of the progressive city of which they are a part. The plan for the erection of a Baptist Temple, costing $1,000,000, designed to combine an up-to-date church building with a business block, and including a vast auditorium

of which the city is in great need, to be rented just as they now propose to rent Hazard's Pavilion, was taken up, and is now so far along that Mr. Burdette and his congregation confidently expect to announce the success of the undertaking by the time their year's lease has expired on the pavilion.[18]

The proposal to build what came to be called the "Theater Beautiful," designed to accommodate the needs of the "City Beautiful," offer downtown office space, and serve a large Baptist congregation forty Sundays a year, required the formation of the separate Auditorium Corporation and outside financing. Burdette herself set out to secure the necessary capital for what had become both a business and a religious venture. Although she was now president of the California Federation of Women's Clubs, was accustomed to managing her own considerable business affairs, and had met (on a social basis) many of the eastern bankers and financiers she proposed to canvas, she had not previously tackled a project that required her to approach these bankers and financiers in their business roles.

We know about Clara Burdette's campaign through her letters to Robert. The letters reveal the difficulty she faced as a woman trying to do business on Wall Street, even business with so large a philanthropic ingredient:

[New York] Wed. night. [April 26,] 1905 . . . I am doing my last "do" for the Baptists. Spent the entire morning down on Wall and Broad and Broadway. Nothing doing.

[Boston] Fri Apr 28th, 1905, . . . the business I was on there was different from anything I ever went on before and I found it did not "go" for a woman to be prowling around Wall and Broad street alone. I lost self-respect every minute I was there and I made up my mind that I couldn't afford it even for the new Auditorium.[19]

One way or another, financing was arranged, even though she had failed to attract any investors in New York. With a speed that seems remarkable today, the old building came down and a very different new one opened in its place just fifteen months later.

The all-purpose Hazard's Pavilion, in its last year renamed Temple Auditorium, had been the only large hall in Los Angeles for almost two decades after it was built. Hazard's was where Melba sang, where the National Opera Company and later the Grau Metropolitan Opera Company played, and where John Philip Sousa conducted his famous concert band on his annual visits. Early on, it had been nicknamed the "Flower Bower," because it had opened with a flower show, the first of many fundraisers sponsored by various women's clubs, that one for a boardinghouse for working women. It had also housed early citrus festivals and automobile shows before it came to its later use as a site for prizefights.[20]

The new hall was intended to make "high-class" events (i.e., those deemed consistent with the mission of the Baptist church) available at popular prices. (These events included political conventions as well as concerts, operas, and lectures, but not prizefights or the "wrong" kind of music.) As a church, the building was dedicated on July 29, 1906; as a concert hall, it opened on November 9 with a production of Verdi's *Aïda* by the Lambardi Grand Opera Company, a low-budget company with low ticket prices (i.e., "dollar opera") and strong popular appeal. It continued its function as a popular location when it was renamed Clune's Auditorium in 1914 and began to offer the new feature-length silent movies, which were thereby accepted as high-class events. (The racist masterpiece *The Birth of a Nation*, featuring a continuous accompaniment by Carli Elinor's house orchestra, was thus considered "high-class" and ran there in 1915, drawing a lonely protest from the NAACP.) For a few years, the auditorium was also the home of the Los Angeles Symphony and the People's Orchestra, as well as assorted visiting virtuosi and opera companies. In 1920, William Andrews Clark, Jr., bought out the lease for his one-year-old Philharmonic Orchestra, closing down the movies and permanently renaming it Philharmonic Auditorium. Although large-scale opera companies moved to the newer Shrine Auditorium in 1925 (and briefly to Olympic Auditorium as well), the renamed Philharmonic Auditorium remained the central Los Angeles venue for symphony concerts and visiting virtuosi until it was abandoned after the Music Center opened in 1964. Behymer was pointedly excluded from its management at the start. Eventually he was forgiven for his prizefights, became its manager, and maintained his office there until his death in 1947. Throughout, it remained a Baptist church—a Baptist church that had its home in a profitable downtown real estate development, as Burdette called it, "a mercantile building with a human soul."

That a church congregation would take on the task of providing an auditorium with stage facilities large enough to house the touring Metropolitan Opera Company as well as the Philharmonic, where high-class events would be welcome in perpetuity, is a strong reflection of the pervasive view that concert music—and opera as well, despite its sometimes steamy plots—carried an intrinsic value that brought moral uplift to the congregation's auditors. This arrangement is also evidence that church activities involving music went far beyond hiring organists, choir directors, soloists, and instrumental musicians for regular services. Often thought of as a secular religion, in this case and others "the right kind of music" was viewed as entirely compatible with formally organized Protestant religion. This view was not new with Temple/Clune's/Philharmonic Auditorium but was widely shared and backed up by both private and institutional actions, especially by music dealers (the most visible commercial arm of the nineteenth-century music tradition) and church congregations. In one sense, it was simply an extension of the long-standing practice of housing concerts in churches, as had been done in the Methodists' smaller Simpson's Auditorium for some years.[21] By the time Howard Swan wrote in 1952, he saw this arrangement as rather quaint, but it persisted for another dozen years.

For years after the "Theater Beautiful" opened, Behymer pushed the idea of a single-purpose concert hall complex, one with no church connection, without success. Los Angeles owed its principal concert room for most of the twentieth century to Clara Bradley Burdette, a church-based entrepreneur, suffragist, philanthropist, university trustee, long-time officer of the National Federation of Women's Clubs, and someone who had attended theater and concert performances in Los Angeles since the 1880s, despite her occasional doubts about the morality of the theater, even of Shakespeare. Neither the *Express,* which had once ridiculed her for her activism, nor the *Times,* in which she owned stock, nor the other papers saw fit to cover this aspect of her career. Burdette, who outdid both Behymer and his other competitors in the matter of Temple Auditorium, is, of course, as little known now as the rest.

·   ·   ·

The biggest success of musical progressivism, at least in Los Angeles, remained for the post–World War I period, after political Progressivism had virtually disappeared in Southern California. The music profession prospered in the 1920s as never before or since. Popular symphony concerts became abundant. Orchestras routinely accompanied silent films at large theaters such as Grauman's, where weekly Sunday-morning symphony concerts were offered, starting in 1920. Summer seasons of popular-priced symphony concerts in the Hollywood Bowl began in 1922 and continue today. The efforts by Edson, Blanchard, and others to secure public aid for music to supplement private funding mostly failed but, even so, provided a precedent for more successful legislation later. (The content of Edson's bills in the California State Legislature is quite similar to later, more successful legislation.) The arts played a highly visible—and controversial—role in the Works Progress Administration of the 1930s, when such WPA agencies as the Federal Music Project, the Federal Theatre Project, the Federal Art Proj-

ect, and the Federal Writers' Project were all funded by the federal government. Inexpensive or free concerts of all kinds were given by the hundreds
in Los Angeles alone by the Federal Music Project, starting in late 1935. The
Progressive movement did indeed extend to the arts, providing a model for
the reforms of the New Deal a generation later in the arts as it did in other
areas.

Before any of these long-term successes, musical progressivism experienced two ambitious, splendid failures, both described here—the People's
Orchestra and the production of the "$10,000 Prize Opera," Horatio
Parker's *Fairyland*. Both of its enduring successes had to do with concert
venues: Philharmonic Auditorium, for one, and the Hollywood Bowl, which
survives to this day.

8 "Something of Good for the Future"

The People's Orchestra of 1912–1913

In the years immediately before World War I, "people's" orchestras and concert series were organized in several American cities.[1] Although each of these has its own story, some common themes and common motivations unite them. Established symphony orchestras catered to elite, upper-class audiences; they featured relatively high ticket prices and a repertoire built around the nineteenth-century German-Austrian symphonic literature. In the same period, the new commercial mass entertainment industry prospered, its markets seemingly boundless. People's orchestras and concerts attempted to bridge the rapidly growing gap between elite and mass entertainment. In doing so, they raised questions about whether the European symphonic tradition could be adapted to regional or national needs to create a concert practice with wide public appeal, perhaps even developing characteristics recognizably "American." The early twentieth-century struggles over this aesthetic question carried wider political, social, and economic overtones, even serving in some sense as a surrogate for them. The movement for progressive economic and political reform, the women's movement, and concern over integrating the mass of new immigrants into American life created the context in which the people's music ventures were carried out. The short career of the People's Orchestra of Los Angeles demonstrates how these issues arose and were addressed in one specific case.

Two items from the *Los Angeles Evening Express* of Friday, November 1, 1912, set the stage. They appeared on the eve of a presidential election complicated by the third-party candidacy of Theodore Roosevelt. The first reported a speech that echoed the progressive newspaper's editorial position on the election:

The republicans say, "Let Taft rule," the democrats say, "Let Wilson rule" . . . but the Progressive party and Colonel Theodore Roosevelt say, "Let the people rule." With the Progressive party . . . it is a question of human rights as against special privilege, the putting of government back into the hands of the people, so they may rule themselves. . . . When you go to the polls don't register your vote for the past; register it for what we may bring about of good for the future.

The second story appeared a few pages farther back in the same paper:

MUSIC TEACHERS WILL PLAN SUNDAY CONCERTS:
FIFTY-PIECE ORCHESTRA TO BE ENGAGED FOR POPULAR SERIES

A feature of the programs, which will be given weekly, will be the rendition each time of a number by an American composer and in this Los Angeles writers are especially invited to submit work for consideration.[2]

The first story quotes Katherine Philips Edson, one of the inner circle in Hiram Johnson's Progressive Republican state administration in Sacramento, from an address to an audience of newly enfranchised women at the Friday Morning Club in Los Angeles.[3] The second reports the activity of her spouse, Charles Farwell Edson, a singer, voice teacher, local champion of American music, and Progressive visionary of sorts.[4] The two news items are connected in ways that go well beyond the happenstance of the Edsons' prominence as individuals or their personal relationship. Some hint of the orchestra's idealistic, essentially political, purpose is given in the *Express*'s review of the first concert, which called it the "first large, tangible expression" of "a civic idea that has the musical uplift of the community for its aim."[5] The People's Orchestra, the developments that led to it, and its demise make up one incident in the struggle to invent a viable cultural context for symphonic music in America.

· · ·

At the November meeting reported in the *Express*, the Southern California Music Teachers Association (SCMTA) voted to sponsor six weekly concerts. It hired Edson (its president) as manager and fundraiser. Eduardo Lebegott, a well-known figure in Los Angeles from his appearances with the touring Lambardi Grand Opera Company, had already been hired as conductor.[6] "Public-spirited" members of the Los Angeles Symphony were recruited at the scale of five dollars for one concert and two or three rehearsals, a low rate allowed the new orchestra as a "patriotic concession" from the union.[7]

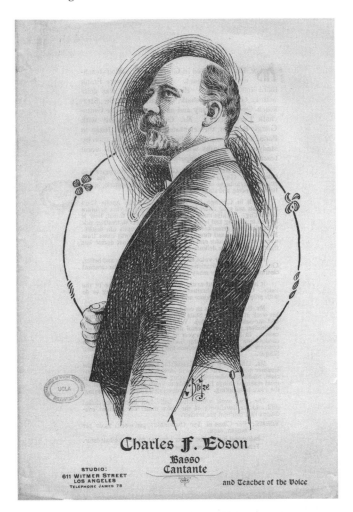

Charles F. Edson
Basso
Cantante

STUDIO:
611 WITMER STREET
LOS ANGELES
TELEPHONE JAMES 78

and Teacher of the Voice

Figure 15.   Charles Farwell Edson, president of the Southern
California Music Teachers Association when it sponsored the
People's Orchestra in 1912–13. Drawing from Katherine Philips
Edson Papers (Collection 235), Department of Special Collec-
tions, Charles E. Young Research Library, University of Califor-
nia, Los Angeles.

At first, the People's Orchestra was successful in attracting private financial backing, building an audience, and giving well-reviewed performances. Among the most prominent early donors was Anita Baldwin, well-
known as a horse breeder but also a sometime singer and composer, who
gave one thousand dollars. Charles Modini-Wood, formerly comanager of

the Los Angeles Theater, gave a library of orchestral music valued at eight hundred dollars. The Sunday afternoon concert time was chosen so that working people and students could attend. Attendance grew rapidly, judging from the public report that the first three concerts drew audiences of 500, 1,100, and then 1,800. When the MTA board met on January 20, 1913, it was reported that after the first two concerts, the next eight had generated an average paid attendance of 1,662.

The orchestra's repertoire reveals a programming policy that featured what its backers later called "intermediate classics."[8] As promised, the concerts included works by composers residing in Los Angeles. In addition, there were arias or concerto movements featuring local performers as soloists, also opera overtures, orchestral suites, and other short works by late romantic European composers. The orchestra's first program, on November 10, is typical: the overture to Wagner's *Tannhäuser;* a suite by Massenet; "Reverie for Strings," by Charles E. Pemberton (a member of the orchestra and an early faculty member at USC); and the "Dance of the Hours," from *La Gioconda.* The soprano soloist, Mrs. Willis H. Tiffany, sang Santuzza's aria from *Cavalleria rusticana* and "I Dreamt I Dwelt in Marble Halls" from *The Bohemian Girl.* All but Pemberton's piece were well known to concert audiences; Mrs. Tiffany's two arias were operatic favorites.

The initial performance was received enthusiastically, especially by the progressive *Express:*

PEOPLE'S CONCERT SERIES BEGINS WITH SUCCESS:
ORCHESTRA OF FIFTY PIECES GIVES PROGRAM THAT PLEASES
AUDIENCE

The People's orchestra . . . demonstrated beyond cavil yesterday afternoon that it is worthy of the most substantial public support. . . .

The playing of the men, under Eduardo Lebegott's baton, and with Julius Bierlich as concert master, was of the sort to deserve warmest praise. This was largely possible because of the personnel of the orchestra, which included men who have for years played together in the symphony concerts. Mr. Lebegott is a director who brings the magnetism of energetic, temperamental youth as well as experience and exceptional musical talent to his aid.[9]

The People's Orchestra gave thirty weekly concerts before suspending operations for the summer in June. It resumed performances in September, expiring the following January, after giving either forty-nine or fifty concerts during its life of one and a half seasons. Its musical achievement was substantial, although in hindsight one can see that hints of problems to come were visible almost from the start. The concerts were allowed to continue for several weeks beyond the initial experimental six concerts without any evaluation, although a graduated scale for ticket prices (25 cents, 35 cents, and 50 cents rather than the flat 25 cents) was adopted at that point. Edson had to be prodded to give away complementary tickets to "schools, factories, and laundries" as part of a campaign to attract a new and more democratic audience.[10]

The intent to attract a new audience for orchestral music is reflected by the heavy emphasis on operatic music, whose popular appeal remained strong. The most performed composers in the orchestra's repertoire were Wagner and Verdi (respectively, thirty and twenty-four performances), with Saint-Saëns, Massenet, Mendelssohn, Victor Herbert, Grieg, and Rossini in a group behind them. Excerpts from *Tannhäuser* and *Lohengrin*, Wagner's unequivocally successful early operas, led the overall popularity list. The most popular single works were Ponchielli's "Dance of the Hours" from *La Gioconda* (five); the overtures to *Tannhäuser* (five), the overtures to Rossini's *Semiramide* (four) and Verdi's *La Forza del destino* (four); Grieg's *Peer Gynt* suite (four); Lacombe's "Spring Morning Serenade" (four); and Morton F. Mason's Concert Overture in F. Brahms's *Tragic* overture was criticized as too heavy, but "Siegfried's Death and Funeral March," from Wagner's *Götterdämmerung*, appeared three times. Beethoven and Mozart were represented by overtures; Mozart's Clarinet Concerto, chosen by a soloist, was seen as exotic and referred to in the *Express* as "an early German writing."

The SCMTA quickly endorsed Lebegott's plan to organize a chorus to supplement the orchestra and involve more people in the project. In the first season, the chorus took part in an all-Wagner program and another that featured excerpts from Mendelssohn's *Elijah*. Chorus and orchestra observed the centennial of Verdi's birth with two performances of his *Manzoni Requiem*, the first (October 12, 1913), a Los Angeles premiere for this spectacular and demanding work. *Messiah* was given, after Hans Linne had replaced Lebegott, at two of the orchestra's final programs (December 28, 1913, and January 4, 1914). The People's Chorus outlived the orchestra; Lebegott conducted a concert version of Saint-Saëns's opera *Samson et Dalila* a few months after the People's Orchestra's last concert. These ambitious choral-orchestral undertakings were an exception to the orchestra's usual practice of avoiding extended works. They were clearly perceived as a significant part of the SCMTA's "popular" mission, however, and they drew large audiences.

The orchestra adhered faithfully to its commitment to serve Los Angeles composers and performers. Below are listed thirty-one American composers whose music was performed, including twenty Los Angeles residents and three women. Some, such as Morton F. Mason, had heard their music performed elsewhere. Others, such as Fannie Charles Dillon, required help with orchestration and were stimulated by the presence of the orchestra to study that specialized art. (Despite the local emphasis, Victor Herbert was the most performed American, with eight performances.) Many members of the sponsoring organization, the SCMTA, appeared as soloists. No fewer than seventy-four soloists (forty-three women, thirty-one men) appeared in all. There were fifty-two singers (thirty-six women, sixteen men), seven pianists or organists (two women, five men), and fifteen other instrumentalists (five women, ten men).[11] Among those who drew the largest audiences were pianists Gertrude Cohen and Paloma Schramm. An asterisk indicates the composer was a Los Angeles resident.

MUSIC BY AMERICAN COMPOSERS PERFORMED BY THE PEOPLE'S ORCHESTRA OF LOS ANGELES

*Adams, Albert J. "The Holy City"

Brewer, John Hyatt. "An Autumn Sketch"

Brockway, Howard. *Sylvan Suite*

Cadman, Charles Wakefield. "Indian Song" (*later)

Chadwick, George W. *Overture: Euterpe; Symphonic Sketches* (two performances)

Cole, Rossetter G. *King Robert of Sicily*

*Dillon, Fannie Charles. *Symphonic Suite:* "Evening" and "The Cloud"; two songs

*Edson, Charles Farwell. "The Race Mother"

*Elliot, Verne. Suite from *Mission Play*

*Freebey, Grace Adele. "Oh Golden Sun"

Friml, Rudolph (*later). Suite for orchestra (not further identified)

*Grunn, Homer. *Marche héroïque;* "On the Mesa"; "Serenade"

Hadley, Henry. *In Bohemia* (three performances)

Herbert, Victor. "Al Fresco"; *American Fantasie; Irish Rhapsody* (three performances); *Natoma,* selections; *Pan-Americana; Serenade;* selections (two not further identified)

*Jannotta, Alfredo. "Alidor" (two performances) (not further identified)

*Koopman, Julius. *Songs of Home*

*Kopp, Rudolph. *Concert Overture* (two performances)

*Lebegott, Eduardo. *Semele:* "Intermezzo"; *Symphonic Prelude* (two performances); "Spring"; "When I Looked into Your Eyes"

*Linne, Hans. *Indian Suite* (two performances)

*Lucchesi, Riccardo. *Francesca da Rimini*

*Mason, Morton F. *Concert Overture in F* (four performances); *Overture in D Minor; Novelette*

*McCaughey, W. Dwight. *Hungarian Legends*

Nevin, Ethelbert. "Oh, That We Two Were Maying"; *Suite romantique* (three performances)

Parker, Horatio. Concerto for Organ, op. 55

Pasmore, Henry Bickford (resident of San Francisco). *Miles Standish*

*Pemberton, Charles E. "The Light That Failed"; *Reverie for Strings* (two performances)

*Ross, Gertrude. "Dawn on the Desert"

*Stevenson, Frederick. "Danse bretonne"

Strube, Gustav. "Puck"

*Tandler, Adolf. *Johanna* (two performances?); *Prohibited Music; Vision of Nymphs*

*Tourjee, Homer. "Sweetheart of All My Dreams"

Wilson, Mortimer (*later). *Scenes from My Youth* (two performances)[12]

.   .   .

The genesis of the People's Orchestra extended over several years and is closely tied to the course of political Progressivism in Southern California. After a first hint of local political activism in the arts appeared in 1903, when the yet unofficial Municipal Art Committee petitioned the LA City Council not to cut the trees in Sycamore Grove, "dear to all lovers of the beautiful," the pace quickened sharply. F. W. Blanchard's name appears frequently as an advocate. (The arts had previously been funded entirely from private sources, and so, very likely, had parks.)

In early 1908, Edson inaugurated a series of school concerts by giving a recital himself. The concerts, priced at one dollar for the series, featured such prominent local performers as the Arnold Krauss string quartet, pianist Blanche Rogers Lott, and the Orpheus Club, a men's chorus. His goal, announced first through the Gamut Club (founded a few years earlier by L. E. Behymer) and presently urged in the course of several visits from Arthur Farwell, was popular (as in widely prevalent), low-priced orchestra concerts for students and for the general public that could not attend the Symphony's regular weekday afternoon series. *Times* theater reporter Julian Johnson, who doubled as Los Angeles's music correspondent for the *Pacific Coast Musical Review*, confidently announced a few months later: "There is every reason to expect that such concerts soon will be a distinctive feature of Los Angeles life."[13]

But in the fall of 1908, the Symphony announced no pops concerts. By January, Johnson was asking: "What has come of all our music agitation of the early fall, of the proposed 'Pop' concerts by the Symphony orchestra? . . . So far, nothing is visible. We continue our musical performances just as before, neither more nor less of them, no difference in quality." As a cure, Johnson proposed that the Gamut Club take the lead in organizing the funding for a permanent symphony, to include a regular season, popular concerts, and an annual festival.[14] Although the city voted funds to support weekly outdoor band concerts, no funding, public or private, was forthcoming for popular orchestra concerts.[15] L. E. Behymer, manager of the Symphony and by then the city's most prominent impresario, added his voice for municipal funding of the arts at the progressive City Club in August 1909: "It was time that this city took up artistic things as a municipality and not leave the beautiful to be handled by private individuals."[16] But neither the Symphony (managed at that point by Behymer) nor the city undertook such concerts. By January 1911, Johnson could write that a year earlier, "we seemed to have gone backward. . . . local effort was apparently at a standstill . . . when even the symphony orchestra, around which cluster the ambitions of so many devoted men and women, was accepted as a thing of moderate interest." This season, however, "it was apparent . . . three months ago, that big music in Los Angeles was at last upon a sure footing . . . really going forward. . . . The one desire of local music-lovers now is to see the work of the symphony orchestra enlarged to veritable popular scope." Nevertheless, added patronage was not forthcoming, leaving a situation in which "we are giving no more concerts—six this year—than we did when the town had scarcely more than 50,000 inhabitants! The population has increased six times." Moreover, the orchestra's repertoire, which once had been quite varied, was now restricted to a more limited canon, for which at least a fixed audience and reliable if limited patronage were assured.

Let [conductor Harley] Hamilton modernize his programmes as much as the young blood would like to see him do, and you see the stand-patters and gray-beards whose thrifty dollars are really the foundation on which the orchestra rests rise in an indignant body against this artistic insurgency. Beethoven . . . is the symphonic word of the Almighty, and woe to the baton-wielder who would wander regularly to another source for his stick's text. But if we can increase the concerts; if we can give "pops," and even double the present outlay, making the six twelve, I am sure we shall have some programmes of great interest. Will it be done? If I did not feel sure that the new year did not hold some definite enlargement of the symphonic work of Los Angeles I should not have typed the foregoing paragraphs.[17]

Johnson's prediction went unfulfilled for almost two more years. The Symphony continued to stand pat rather than risk any change; thus, it passed from the relatively progressive institution it had been in its earlier years to a very conservative one that did not respond to the growing community's needs.

Having repeatedly failed to enlist the support of the Gamut Club for his program or even for a cautious bill "to promote education in literature, music and the fine arts, and making an appropriation therefore," which he had introduced in the 1909 California State Legislature, Edson undertook to organize a group that would endorse his projects.[18] Late in December 1910, he helped organize the Southern California Music Teachers Association, whose activist membership excluded businessmen but included many women both among its rank and file and on its governing board. From its first meeting, the new association announced its intention to "promote Public Concerts at popular prices for the general public and School Children in particular—to be given by Orchestras, Bands, Vocalists and instrumentalists, performing the best class of music: resulting in a general and wholesome Musical uplift and influence on citizenship."[19]

Municipal support for these concerts was sought from the first. In January 1911, the SCMTA endorsed Edson's bill for state recognition and support of the arts and, in addition, petitioned the city for ten thousand dollars "for the purpose of giving popular concerts in suitable auditoriums, preferably the High School Auditorium of the city at the price of 10, 15, and 25 cents admission." A few months later, the membership decided to seek twenty-five thousand dollars from the Finance Committee of the City Council, "to give concerts at the maximum price of 25c." In 1912, having failed several times to get the Symphony's participation in its program or to generate the public financial support it

Figure 16.   Jennie Winston, soprano and an organizer and
early officer of the Southern California Music Teachers Association. From *Who's Who in Music in California, 1920,* 113;
author's collection.

sought, the SCMTA decided to wait no longer; it proceeded on its own
with the People's Orchestra.

•   •   •

The Symphony's management (both Behymer and the board of directors)
seems to have viewed the People's Orchestra as a dangerous rival from
the outset. It was very likely Behymer's opposition, as well as the orchestra's identification with political Progressivism, that blocked the
Gamut Club from supporting it and even persuaded the conservative

Times to ignore it totally and continuously. But the Symphony's first and only conductor up to that point, Harley Hamilton, demonstrated his personal support by lending the new orchestra music from his own library. Hamilton seems to have surprised everyone when, in February, he announced his retirement, effective at the season's end. Whatever his reasons (as we've seen, he later went abroad to seek treatment for deafness), his departure, coupled with the success of the People's Orchestra, forced the Symphony's board into an agonizing reappraisal. There was serious discussion about whether the Symphony should retire from the field in favor of the People's Orchestra, which had already drained away some of its audience. When a delegation from the SCMTA attended a Symphony board meeting late in the spring, it reported, "There was but one thing clear that the Symphony board wanted and that was for the People's Orchestra to give up."[20] The SCMTA had already sent a confident reply offering cooperation but not capitulation:

> Our field is so specific and the demand is so great for just what we are doing, that we cannot consistently consider any co-operative arrangement that would in any way destroy our identity, which is our usefulness. . . .
>
> The public schools have responded as enthusiastically as have the parents and we find that it is not the giving of a few popular concerts that is going to satisfy the people, but regular and studiously selected programs, constructively educational and an opportunity to hear our own local musicians in a creditable environment.
>
> Naturally we have no desire to encroach upon your field, having a distinct place of our own, but we can, with the greatest warmth, maintain a reciprocal relation and our directors can co-operate in the selection and hiring of the orchestral body; the leasing of an Auditorium; the purchasing of scores; contracting for advertising space; arrangements for rehearsals—in fact our exchange of courtesies can be such that you may consider us as a necessary feeder for your audience, for, as a matter of fact, appreciation is inspired and developed by the intermediate classics well rendered.[21]

Very likely the pamphlet comparing orchestra budgets, given as the list below, was prepared in the course of these discussions.

COMPARATIVE ORCHESTRA STATEMENT (1913)

Cincinnati Orchestra—30 concerts—deficit of $57,000

Philadelphia Orchestra—30 concerts—deficit of $48,000

Minneapolis Orchestra—guarantee fund of $65,000 used annually

St. Paul Orchestra—14 concerts—deficit of $35,000

San Francisco Orchestra—30 concerts—deficit of $40,000

Kansas City Orchestral Association—8 concerts—deficit $7,361

	L.A. Symphony	L. A. People's Orchestra
	expenses, 6 concerts $10,715	30 concerts $16,961
Box office receipts	$6,726	$10,600
Deficit	$3,989	$6,361
Total attendance	8,374	44,636
Average attendance	1,396	1,488
Average price, single seat	80c	29c
Average members in orch	65	53
Number of works performed	30	154
Number of soloists heard	5	51
Number of works now in library	254	40
Value of equipment (music)	$3,200	$1,500

It is owing to the fine educational work of the Los Angeles Symphony Orchestra Association that the Music Teachers Association could apply business methods to the Peoples Orchestra and make such a success.[22]

In the fall, the SCMTA decided not to initiate its own capital campaign to avoid interfering with the Symphony's need to raise money. It took pains to spell out its understanding of the distinction between the two orchestras as clearly as possible:

The fact is that the Symphony and the People's Orchestra will occupy quite different fields. There is room for both of them, and there is no reason why they should conflict. . . .

The Symphony will interpret music, in its highest forms, and play to people whose tastes demand the masterpieces of classic composition. The People's Orchestra can, and if it follows its rule of last year, will strike up in a somewhat different key. It will play the people's music to the people, touching the more tuneful familiar classics frequently, but leaving the more technical, involved and difficult works of the masters to the treatment of the older organization.

[To quote] a local musician . . . "The Symphony, musically speaking, represents the university, and the People's Orchestra the high school."[23]

The Symphony, too, prepared for its new season; it had reorganized with a new conductor, Adolf Tandler. A major fundraising drive, designed to guarantee more concerts and six months' guaranteed weekly salary for the Symphony's musicians, was announced and quickly failed. The resolute rigidity of the Symphony's response was a case of business as usual that assured its own eventual failure a few years later.[24]

Over the summer, Edson had busied himself by preparing the "Comparative Orchestra Statement" (see the list above), intended to show that the People's Orchestra had generated a much lower deficit than the Symphony per concert, especially in relation to the total attendance. There is no evidence that he took any steps toward retiring the debt, which was in fact 50 percent larger that the Symphony's. Members of the SCMTA, who lacked Edson's seeming confidence that an appropriation from the city would bail them out, worried about their individual and collective liability. As early as June, Edson had offered to take personal responsibility for the orchestra's deficit.[25] Angered by the continuing criticism of his management, he offered his resignation in September, was reinstated by the SCMTA board in October, and once more pledged, late in November, to assume the orchestra's debts. By that time, the SCMTA had decided that Lebegott must offer "lighter" music in order to attract increased attendance, although they could not agree on what the term meant.[26] Edson pondered whether to add motion pictures to attract a larger audience. Lebegott, who, like the orchestra's musicians, had gone unpaid for some time, resigned rather than alter his programs. SCMTA members were advised by an attorney that, despite Edson's pledge, they were indeed liable for the orchestra's still-accumulating debts. To no one's surprise but Edson's, the city government refused to take over the orchestra's operation.[27] When a final performance of *Messiah* brought the orchestra's career to a halt in January, the musicians' union was threatening to sue the SCMTA membership for a thousand dollars of unpaid wages, only a part of the wreckage. At the end, Edson had no idea what was owed to whom or how to find the money. His own financial resources had never been strong enough to cover the deficit.

·   ·   ·

In its particulars, the sadly truncated saga of the People's Orchestra is unique to Los Angeles. The details of its Progressive political associations, the extraordinarily ambitious role of the Southern California Music Teachers Association, and the ineptitude of the project's principal champion are interesting but essentially local phenomena. Here I propose to speculate about the role played by the People's Orchestra of Los Angeles, and very likely also by the other people's orchestras that sprang up around the country, and what it, or they, might tell us about American music—or music in America—in the Progressive era.[28] The central issue had to do with fixing the social role to be played by European-based concert music, as it had been a decade earlier in the previously discussed competition of impresarios. For the Los Angeles Symphony Orchestra, the idea of a sacralized, elite concert tradition seems to have come to the United States along with the German romantic symphonic canon, part of the baggage brought by successive waves of German-speaking immigrants.[29] But how rigid would the sacralization be, and how select the "elite"? Could there be regional or national adaptations of the European tradition that would give it a wider appeal, making it more of a "music for the people," even "American"? These questions were still very much at issue in Los Angeles in 1912. The People's Orchestra is tangible evidence of resistance by a sizable, musically literate middle class to the appropriation of symphonic music by a narrow social elite. This discussion of the orchestra's role addresses this cluster of questions in terms of three distinct but interrelated layers: the relationships among various groups within the concert music tradition; the role of concert music as a part of the new entertainment industry; and the metaphor offered by the developing tradition of concert music for the society in which it functioned.

The first layer of this contest occurred within the music community itself. In Los Angeles, still a small and new city, there was a very high proportion of musicians and music teachers in the population, a reflection (and a source) of unusually widespread musical literacy. Both musicians and teachers, who were in many cases the same people, sought performance opportunities. Competition occurred between U.S.-born (mostly female) and foreign-born (mostly male) members of the profession, between resident and visiting artists. Centralization of concert bookings in the hands of commercial agents and concert managers fostered economic elitism, tending to devalue the work of local musicians and exclude them from the artistic elite regardless of their ability. L. E. Behymer, the principal agent for the commodification of concert music in Los Angeles, presented the Symphony in a few high-priced concerts, employing a handful of visiting virtuosi at high fees and high ticket prices and a few local artists at much lower fees. Moreover, his press agentry in behalf of his traveling "attractions" tended to pre-empt space allotted by the local press for all music events. Although other promoters, most of them music store operators such as Blanchard, sponsored local chamber groups, such as the Lott-Krauss Quartet and the Brahms Quintet, and promoted some other events outside the "commodification" circuit, many artists still went unheard. Thus, Mrs. Tiffany, the soloist at the orchestra's first concert, could say: "Every soloist loves to perform with an orchestra, and, up to now, few of us here in Los Angeles have had the chance to do so. The Symphony orchestra almost invariably has given its solos to

outside talent. One cannot blame the symphony people. They are local performers and have wanted to give something new at their concerts. But this
course has shut out Los Angeles vocalists and instrumentalists from having
a chance to appear with orchestra."[30] This situation invited the competition
of more concerts, offered in this case by the Southern California Music
Teachers Association with its lively, if short-lived, People's Orchestra.

This competition was made explicit in the summer of 1913, when impresario Behymer complained that too many concerts were given on the
West Coast and that ticket prices had been driven down too far for performers (and, incidentally, impresarios) to turn a profit. His complaint appeared on the front page of *Musical America*. It drew this editorial response:

THE LOS ANGELES PROBLEM

Very interesting is the circumstance reported in *Musical America* last
week of the difficulties encountered by the Los Angeles Symphony Orchestra in meeting the competition presented by a popular Sunday orchestra with low-priced seats. This circumstance represents, in fact, the
very crux of one of the biggest musical problems which is working itself
out in America to-day. . . . Many persons, perhaps, will feel that such a
condition as that in Los Angeles represents a falling away from high
ideals and high possibilities.

The fact is that it represents nothing of the kind. It represents an immense broadening of the base upon which America is going to build. . . .
Our musical life is in dire need of such an infusion of new blood and all
advances in this direction are to be welcomed.[31]

Musical America, then, came down firmly on the side of the SCMTA and
the People's Orchestra.

If the first layer of issues raised by the People's Orchestra lay within the
profession of music, the second dealt with the response by advocates of concert music to its marginalization within the newly developing entertainment
industry. The decades preceding the appearance of the People's Orchestra had
seen a move toward the sacralization of concert music in America, with a
concomitant stratification of both audiences and music. As commercial mass
culture emerged in the Progressive era, the process of stratification accelerated, stimulated by the prospect of new profits at the "low-priced" end of the
business. The new phenomenon was devised to satisfy a whole new market
made up of workers, many foreign-born, who, because of generally rising
wages and the widespread adoption of the shorter work hours, had time and
money to spend on recreation for the first time. Recreation's emerging entrepreneurs soon turned their attention toward the middle class, a potential

source of even greater profit. This process was marked in Los Angeles by the opening of Tally Brothers phonograph parlor in 1893, the conversion of the old Grand Opera House to the Orpheum, a vaudeville theater (1894), the addition of kinetoscope movies to the Orpheum's vaudeville bills and Tally's offerings (1896), the loss of control over its own bookings by the Los Angeles Theater to the New York–based theater trust (circa 1900), and the appearance of several elegant new theaters in the years when Edson and the SCMTA were campaigning for the Progressive cause of Sunday pops concerts.[32]

At each step in the process, formally organized middle-class participatory movements sprang up, both in reaction to the perceived threat from the working class and the foreign born and in competition with the newly commercialized entertainment establishment. Locally sponsored concert series, the little theater movement, the music clubs, the pageantry movement were all part of the reaction. Common themes of these localized, noncommercial movements were: reassertion of the underlying value of the arts for self-improvement and community uplift; participation of women as well as men in their organization and management; and domination by a white middle-class effort to encourage universal participation in the production of art, always on terms that meant accepting the values of the older establishment as it was even then defining itself.

Advocates of concert music fought against the absorption of their art by the new entertainment industry, for the their art's very existence. They stressed the educational, uplifting, sacralizing power of music. They expanded these claims—which, after all, date well back into the nineteenth century and even earlier—by asserting that the new commercial mass culture was inherently immoral and destructive to society. Racism and nativism are latent subtexts in these assertions. The progressive *California Outlook* spoke of "the right kind of music" as having a particularly uplifting and "American" effect, meaning that ragtime was to be excluded.[33] A report to the California State Legislature in early 1914 expanded on these claims:

> Crime and evil-doing arise from these public recreation places which are owned and operated privately. So we may run the whole gamut of recreation places privately owned, and we will see that such civic problems as crime, poverty and white slavery are born largely, if not wholly, from these hours of recreation ill-spent. . . . not only must the municipality provide and supervise recreation for the people, but also . . . it must instruct the people in the use of their leisure hours. The love of the finer pleasures, such as music, reading, folk dancing, pageantry, must be cultivated to take the place of the wilder pleasures, such as gambling, drinking, ragging, skating.

Of course, its recommendations included

> the establishment of public concerts and of low-priced opera, the pro-
> duction of music festivals, historical pageants, etc. . . . We are rich in the
> inheritance of the art expression of many peoples. It is possible for this
> coast, with all its natural resources and its type of population, to become
> to a budding new world what Greece was to the world of her day, if
> commercialism is not given the right of way.[34]

These assertions led to the third layer of meaning for the People's Orchestra, which deals with music making as a metaphor, even as a model, for
society in general. The Progressive era was a period of political reform, continuing industrialization, and massive immigration, mainly from central Europe, that was seen as a threat to the existing domination of American life by
its native-born, white, middle-class, culturally Protestant citizens. It was also,
as Eric Hobsbawm has pointed out, a period particularly rich in the invention of traditions designed to deal with these rapid, potentially destabilizing
changes. By "invented tradition," Hobsbawm means (as previously stated) "a
set of symbolic ritual practices that function to inculcate values and behavior patterns signifying continuity with the past."[35] Lawrence Levine, referring specifically to the emergence of elite "high" culture in nineteenth-
century America, speaks of invented tradition as extending far beyond the
merely political: "The creation of the institutions and criteria of high culture
was a primary means of social, intellectual, and aesthetic separation and selection."[36] In other words, symphony concerts were a part of the newly developing high culture; they were also a sorting device with an active role in
the social stratification that was inseparable from the stratification of culture.

Examples of invented traditions aimed at the stratification of Los Angeles musical life and its society are the all-male Gamut Club and the complementary all-female Dominant Club, formalizing a tradition of male
hegemony that was threatened by the growing number of women music
teachers, musicians, and patrons in the area.[37] The Symphony's self-
consciously exclusive Friday-afternoon concerts, promoted as the apex of an
artistic hierarchy, are another. The survival of this elite music establishment
was a model and metaphor for the developing stratification of Los Angeles
society into social classes, based on ethnicity as well as economic authority
and strongly inflected by gender. On the other hand, the People's Orchestra, with its local soloists and local composers, including women in both categories and even an occasional female musician in the ranks, represents an
attempt to challenge the hegemony of the older organization. Its regular incorporation of music by local composers represents another attempt to rein-

vent the orchestral tradition in less elitist fashion. Indeed, the first American music movement, as advocated by Dvořák and Arthur Farwell, can itself be seen in a societywide perspective as an attempt to reinvent the already-invented tradition of concert music in another, less exclusionary, way. For Los Angeles, the People's Orchestra was one of a series of attempts in the early part of the twentieth century to resist the use of symphonic music as a means of articulating class distinctions. In the obvious shortcomings of its claim to democracy, as in its surprisingly close approach to success, it may well reflect the city's—and the nation's—continuing political and social ambivalence.

To paraphrase Katherine Philips Edson's political speech, quoted at the start of this chapter, the People's Orchestra may well symbolize the Progressive movement's imperfect attempts to put "government [read, 'music'] back into the hands of the people . . . an attempt to bring about something of good for the future." Moreover, its history is a dramatic illustration of the operation of all the participants—performers, sponsors, audience, critics, even political activists with little apparent tie to these concerts—in constructing and assigning meanings to a particular form of music making at one particular time and place.

· · ·

The spectacular nature of its ending overshadowed the remarkable accomplishments of the People's Orchestra. It provided a place for many members of the SCMTA to play or sing in public; it performed a large quantity of music by composers living in America, most of them in Los Angeles; and it succeeded in reaching a wider audience than the Symphony had done. In the process, it attempted to dilute the elite image even then being constructed for symphony concerts, to strengthen the role of concert music as a form of public entertainment, and to provide a more generalized, widely appealing model of excellence for society in general.

Could it have succeeded? It might never have appeared at all had the Symphony's management chosen to risk a few popular concerts of its own or even second performances of its regular fare. One could argue that, once begun, the People's Orchestra came within one effective manager of making a lasting impact on Los Angeles's musical life. One can argue with more conviction that, having demonstrated its potential, its failure helped lay the foundation for one of the most successful popular concert series ever, one that was inaugurated a decade after the debut of the People's Orchestra, in its own characteristic outdoor location—the summer Symphonies under the Stars in the Hollywood Bowl.

9   Producing *Fairyland*, 1915

While Edson and the Southern California Music Teachers Association were otherwise occupied, another progressive musical project, even more obviously involving municipal pride and Progressive idealism, was in the works. San Francisco was making extensive preparations for the Panama-Pacific International Exposition, to be held in 1915. The PPIE would celebrate the completion of the Panama Canal and the rebuilding of the city following the disastrous earthquake and fire of 1906. San Diego would have a smaller exposition at the same time. What would Los Angeles have to offer when the world came to newly accessible California? The program book for the National Federation of Music Clubs convention of 1915, held in Los Angeles, gives an official version of the story:

> At a meeting of the Board of the National Federation of Musical [sic] Clubs, which was held about three years ago, Mrs. Jason Walker, Chairman of the American Music Committee, offered a suggestion that during the year 1915, when all the world would be coming to the Pacific Coast, some western city might be willing to offer a prize for an American Opera through the Federation and undertake the production of the opera as one of its attractions. Mrs. Walker and Mrs. David Allen Campbell, another member of the committee, came west to look over the situation and decided that LA would be the best city to undertake the proposition.
>   At first thought it was enough to stagger the most enthusiastic, but though it looked almost too big a thing to undertake, it was much too big a thing for Los Angeles to reject. Mr. F. W. Blanchard, who was the chairman of the committee and is President of the American Opera Association, which was later formed to carry out the plans, suggested that it would be too much of an effort to put forth unless it could be made to assume something of a permanent form and it was finally decided that

if the National Federation of Music Clubs would consent to hold every
alternate festival in this city, for as long a time as we were willing to
offer a prize and produce a new American opera, we would undertake
the work.

The sum of $10,000 was decided upon as the amount of the prize,
and it was awarded to Mr. Horatio Parker for his opera "Fairyland."
There were fifty-six entries and the judges were unanimously in favor
of this one. The envelopes containing the names of the competitors
were opened in the presence of a notary after the award had been made
and it was found that Mr. Parker was the successful contestant.

The raising of the prize money and the production of the opera was
in the hands of the American Opera Association of Los Angeles. . . .

The production of a prize opera, by the united efforts of musicians,
philanthropic citizens and different organizations, coming as a climax to
a week of concerts and recitals devoted exclusively to the works of
American composers, marks an epoch in the history of American music.[1]

An additional guarantee of forty thousand dollars would be required to
mount the production. The ubiquitous Fred W. Blanchard, who had quietly
distanced himself from the People's Orchestra, more especially from the
hapless Edson, helped Jamison prepare the bid that brought the convention
to Los Angeles. Now he turned his experience at building broad community
support to this project. A committee of fifty quickly incorporated itself as
the American Opera Association, with Blanchard as president. His one-time
business rival L. E. Behymer and Abbie Norton Jamison were among the officers. Individuals contributed to the guarantee fund as well as organizations
(most prominently the well-established singing societies) and music store
operators. Blanchard's successful record as a businessman had not been tar-
nished by the affair of the People's Orchestra; his requests to the LA City
Council and the County of Los Angeles for one thousand dollars each to
supplement these privately raised funds for the prize money were immediately approved.[2]

The idea of a competition for a new American opera was not new. In
1910, the Metropolitan Opera of New York had announced a similar competition for an opera by an American composer not previously performed,
resulting in the production of Horatio Parker's first opera, *Mona*, in March
1912. A second competition so soon after this and with a relatively short
lead time—composing an opera could easily consume three years of steady
work—was not necessarily the most practical idea. Few American musicians
had the necessary skills to compose a stageworthy full-length opera; those
who did had been able to get productions (generally abroad) and were unable to complete a new work in time for the deadline.

After *Mona*, Parker had kept up a correspondence with Alfred Hertz, who had conducted the Met's production and who would become a judge in the new competition and, eventually, the conductor of the new prizewinner. (The enterprising Hertz, then the principal conductor at the Met, was soon to become conductor of the San Francisco Symphony. In a few years he would be the first to conduct the Symphonies under the Stars at the Hollywood Bowl.) Late in 1912, after the Los Angeles competition had been organized, Parker-the-composer wrote to Hertz-the-conductor from Munich, where he was attending opera frequently. He was hoping for a second production of *Mona* and, apparently, working on a new operatic project of his own:

> I haven't seen or heard anything to make me more discontented with *Mona* than I have been all the time and I hope you too have some affection left for her after all your care and troubles last season. . . .
>
> I believe that if we had as many opera organizations in America as there are here it would go the rounds and perhaps please the serious part of the public. . . .
>
> Now, I have made sketches for a new one as different from *Mona* as anything can be. . . . I am going to keep it liquid—that is unfinished and in sketch form until I can show it to you. It is far sweeter and more cheerful than *Mona* but not without serious moments.
>
> If it pleases you I shall finish it. . . . So I hope I may ask you to keep a day or two free for me next summer. I can go anywhere you say and it will not take very long. . . . Please don't think I want you to assume any distasteful responsibility. I know you to be entirely honest and I have the highest confidence in your taste and judgment as well as in your skill.[3]

We know of several other operas by American composers from these years, some on American subjects, but lists of the operas actually submitted to either the Met's 1910 competition or this one remain unlocated. Henry Hadley's *Montezuma*, for example, was completed in 1914; we don't know whether it was submitted to this competition. Victor Herbert had already tried his hand at "serious" opera with *Natoma* (produced 1911) and returned to his more usual (and profitable) pursuit of operetta. John Philip Sousa likewise was able to get his stage works into production in New York and had no need (and probably no time) to take up this challenge. Scott Joplin's *Treemonisha* was completed by then; very likely he never heard about the competition, nor would they have let him enter. Other less-known possibilities ruled themselves out. Zitkala-Sa and William F. Hanson's *The Sun Dance Opera* had already been produced (in 1913) and was neither sufficiently competent to win nor suitable for a large-scale production.[4] Mary Carr Moore's *Narcissa, or, The Cost of Empire,* completed too late for the Met's competition, had already been produced in Seattle in 1912 and so was not eligible for this prize.[5] (Charles Wakefield Cadman's *Shanewis, or The Robin Woman* lay a few years in the future; he never completed *Daoma,* which was begun around this time.) All of these works had characteristics that made them sufficiently irregular that the judges may not have considered them truly "opera"; moreover, their composers might have been disqualified on the basis of race (Joplin and Will Marion Cook, composer of *Clorindy* and *In Dahomey*), sex (Moore), or (in William F. Hanson's case) religion. (Of course, all of their topics were straightforwardly "American," leading one to speculate long after the fact that "American" opera was not going to follow the rules imputed to "European" opera.) The National Federation of Music Clubs had announced that it did not want any immoral, unladylike figures like Carmen or Violetta Valery *(La Traviata)* in its prize opera, possibly discouraging some potential composers we are unaware of.

Given the already-established connection between Hertz and Parker, it is appropriate to ask whether the Los Angeles competition involved collusion or whether it was actually fixed. Parker's letter does not necessarily indicate that, despite the appearance. Alfred Hertz, one of the judges for the Met's competition, had not been favorably impressed by the submissions to the Met's competition, even by the eventual winner: "Eeny, meeny, miney, Mona" he wrote to another judge, and *Mona*'s reception in New York had been less than enthusiastic. Very likely some of the same opera scores came to the second set of judges (which again included Hertz), with the same weaknesses as before. The universe of American opera composers and experienced conductors of opera was not large, and exchanges among them should not be surprising. Hertz would have been genuinely interested in encouraging the best possible work in any case, especially if he might eventually have to conduct it; Parker would likewise have been interested in learning from his earlier mistakes and composing a better work.

That Parker had doubts about whether a competent production was possible in Los Angeles is clear from his correspondence with Blanchard after the prize was awarded. Starting in the fall of 1914, he insisted that artistic decisions be left to Hertz rather than any of the locals and that Temple Auditorium be used rather than the smaller Mason Opera House. The production did indeed challenge the city's resources, but Blanchard and Jamison took advantage of the widespread enthusiasm for the project to marshal the necessary forces. Newspaper publicity was continuous; even after the winning work was announced, it remained the "10,000 Dollar Opera" in the headlines.

Opening night was a great success, with extended ovations the order of the occasion. Even so, hints in the first round of reviews suggest that *Fairyland's* early success was to be fleeting. The music was dense, the singers couldn't be understood (or, often enough, even heard over the orchestra), the setting was puzzling, the plot impenetrable. Quickly made adjustments could not save subsequent performances. The opera itself raises the question of what was American about it. That both libretto (by Brian Hooker) and music were produced by Americans is clear. The topic, which at least one critic insisted was indeed American, is another matter. The location of the action is vaguely European, involving royalty and peasants. The hero, Auburn, is described as "the King—afterwards Prince of Fairyland." The chorus is characterized as "Chorus of Nuns, Men-at-arms and Common Folk (the People of the Hills, who are also Fairies)," and "The action takes place Once Upon a Time, and within the interval of a Year and a Day."

In other words, the topic draws more from the mid-nineteenth-century English literary and artistic interest in magic and fairies than from any specifically American folklore. (By the time it was produced, the term *fairy* may have begun to be applied to homosexual men in a derogatory sense, making the topic—and the title—even less viable.) Summarizing the story line is very difficult without getting lost in its twists and turns, which are a stretch even for opera lovers. (But then, so is the plot of Verdi's much-loved *Il Trovatore*.) King Auburn, who is bored with his royal position, gets hit on the head and mysteriously transported to Fairyland, creating the opportunity for a couple of dramatic—and confusing—transformation scenes. Eventually, despite the evil machinations of Corvain and the Abbess Myriel, the fair Rosamund renounces her nun's vows and joins King Auburn permanently. Neither the audience nor the critics could follow the story as it unfolded on stage.

In an impressive collaboration among normally competing musical interests, *Fairyland* was produced on schedule. Had it been more viable musically, its success might have lasted longer despite its setting or its impenetrable plot. Instead of an enduring triumph, however, it became one more of musical progressivism's two-steps-forward, one-step-back, equivocal successes, simultaneously a political triumph and an artistic failure. Needless to say, the original commitment, to bring the convention of the National Federation of Music Clubs to Los Angeles every four years and to stage a new American opera each time, was quickly forgotten.

Figure 17.   Cover, *Fairyland* program, 1915. Courtesy of Cambria Master
Recordings and Archives.

Figure 18. California Federation of Music Clubs, First Annual Convention, Oakland, California, May 1–4, 1919. Bottom row, left to right: Charles Wakefield Cadman; Carrie Jacobs Bond; Abbie Norton Jamison, first vice president, National Federation of Music Clubs; Sigmund Beel; Bessie Bartlett Frankel, president of the new state federation; and Gertrude Ross. Top row, left to right: George McManus; Grace Widney Mabee; Charles C. Draa, state publicity chairman; Sofia Newland Neustadt, state festival chairman; Mrs. M. J. Sweeney; Llewellyn B. Cain; and Anna Ruzena Sprotte. (Most of these are from Los Angeles.) *Musical America*, May 24, 1919, 9. Courtesy of Musical America Archives.

. . .

Now is a good moment to introduce the question of what was meant by "American" opera, anyway, though not to answer it. Americans had long been fond of theatrical entertainments in many forms, almost all of which included music, some of it composed by Americans. Virtually every town of any size had a theater or auditorium labeled "opera house," often of limited size and suitable only for modest, stripped-down productions. Opera on a grand scale, though, was still fundamentally a European genre, limited in the United States to a handful of large cities and considered the property of the elite. Everyday American ingredients such as minstrel tunes, ragtime, and the cakewalk were not considered appropriate to it. (Decades later, some critics refused to consider George Gershwin's masterful *Porgy and Bess* a "real" opera because it incorporated jazz elements; its all-black cast of characters may also have contributed to this judgment.)

When the National Opera Company visited in 1887, it was considered

American because some members of the company were Americans. Singing in English, the practice of some small touring companies, also served to Americanize the European repertoire. Also, some earlier operas had been composed by Americans, none of them successful for long (and none in the NOC's repertoire). *Fairyland* was composed by an American to a libretto by an American, still something of a novelty almost thirty years after the NOC's career. By 1915, though, the absence of specifically American references in either libretto or music was beginning to be a problem.[6] Possibly the presence of orchestral effects reminiscent of the German romantic tradition, with particular reference to the operas of Richard Strauss, had become problematic as well, given that World War I was already raging in Europe, and the wave of anti-German feeling that accompanied it was already evident by the time of the production.

After 1900, Arthur Farwell emerged as the most persistent, articulate, and peripatetic advocate for the acceptance of American music. In November 1904, his travels led him to Los Angeles, where he lectured to the Friday Morning Club. The *Times* quoted a member of Farwell's audience: "We are trying to develop a definite American musical art, which shall be indicative of the character of us in the same way that German music is of Germany, and Russian music is of Russia, and Bohemian music is of Bohemia."[7] Farwell's presentation included music derived from Indian and African American, as well as Yankee, sources. Later he collaborated with Charles Lummis in making field recordings of song sung by older, Spanish-speaking residents and transcribing them.[8] It was not uncommon in the discourse of the Progressive era to conflate religious purpose with the nation's Manifest Destiny as well as music. Farwell's audience borrowed from the language of patriotism as they absorbed his message. His evangelizing seemed to yield little in the way of immediate results, although many musicians in Los Angeles, as elsewhere, were quietly composing songs, church anthems, piano music, and other music for their own use. Yet, along with a follow-up visit five years later and the organization of a short-lived American Music Center by Gamut Club members, Farwell's persistence helped lay the groundwork for the "$10,000 Prize Opera," as well as for the People's Orchestra. *Fairyland* was intended to be an American opera in terms of its own time. The idea of inventing a tradition—in this case, elite "American" opera—is dramatically demonstrated in the run-up to *Fairyland*. Yet, like the other operas by Americans that were its contemporaries, even those with specifically American subjects, it failed as an aesthetic statement and did not find a place either in the popular imagination or the repertoire of grand opera.

10 Founding the Hollywood Bowl

On the evening of July 11, 1922, the first of the Symphonies under the Stars concerts took place at the Hollywood Bowl, a site still known to the audience as either Bolton Canyon or Daisy Dell, in the hills close behind the rapidly rising new Hollywood business center. The concert marked the inauguration of a summer series, which by now has become one of the longest-running in the United States. The Bowl's success represents the culmination of several attempts in the Los Angeles community, spread over the two preceding decades, to develop its own regional version of American high culture: symphony, opera, and oratorio as well as noncommercial theater and the fine arts, all transplanted to, created for, and participated in by a broad-based, essentially middle-class local arts community. The organizational conflicts that resulted in the establishment of the Bowl reveal much about the interests that had developed around the making of concert music in Los Angeles. The uneasy agreements that resulted from these struggles became the compromises that have constituted a source of the Bowl's long-term vitality.

For most of its history, the Bowl has been thought of as the summer home of the Los Angeles Philharmonic Orchestra. Yet, despite their common birth year (1919) and their long-time mutual dependence, the two institutions began in radically contrasting ways, forming a kind of yin-yang relationship. The Philharmonic was the creation of one individual, William Andrews Clark, Jr., who subsidized it for fifteen years, until his death in 1934. In stark contrast, the Bowl concerts, now so well known, would never have existed without extensive popular support, volunteer labor, and widespread but relatively limited private philanthropy. In addition to the absence of reliable funding, its organizers began their campaign without benefit of the extensive local newspaper support and coverage always enjoyed by the

Philharmonic. One could even say that, of all the arts enterprises inaugurated in Los Angeles immediately after World War I, the Bowl and its Symphonies under the Stars probably had the least propitious beginning. Yet the site soon became an icon among the city's spectacular natural surroundings and, not much later, an icon of its built environment.[1] Especially after its concerts came to be broadcast on network radio in the 1930s, it became a national monument to the ideal of low-priced symphony concerts, accessible to all (within limits, of course, for racial minorities were unwelcome in Hollywood after dark).

Two other ventures in the arts from this period—a time of growth and prosperity for Los Angeles in general and for high culture and commercial mass culture as well—were closely connected to the Bowl's beginnings. Community sings, started during World War I, drew large numbers of participants in Los Angeles as elsewhere. In the new town of Hollywood, the Community Sing grew to nine hundred members in its first year and, among other things, offered Artie Mason Carter an opportunity to discover her gift for charismatic leadership.[2] The other was the annual staging of the *Pilgrimage Play,* a dramatization of the life of Christ written and sponsored by Christine Wetherill Stevenson with support from the Theosophist colony at nearby Krotona, inaugurated in 1920. Several individuals involved in these two ventures played major parts in the Bowl's early history.

All accounts of the Bowl's beginnings tell us that everything about it was vigorously, continuously contested. The contestants, both male and female but mainly middle- to upper-class, included proponents of theater and champions of music; real estate developers and promoters of public parks; theosophists and agnostics, all in a kaleidoscope of unexpected, and unexpectedly shifting, alliances. Old issues from the waning Progressive era persisted. Questions of high and low culture, gender and class, patriotism, ethnicity, religion, and race lay beneath the surface issues, the economic conflicts, and the personal quirks of the combatants as the balance among educational, commercial, and "community uplift" factors was repeatedly negotiated. These conflicts, stated and unstated, both plagued and stimulated the process of inventing and developing the Bowl.

The Bowl's early history is summarized in a nine-page narrative, *A Brief History of Hollywood Bowl* (hereafter *Brief History*).[3] There are gaps, contradictions, and possibly even some misdirection in this terse, apparently objective, "official" pamphlet, which was issued in an effort to distance that year's board from the Bowl's early contentious history. As the first overview of the Bowl's origin and the closest one in time, it provides a convenient,

Figure 19.   Artie Mason Carter. Courtesy of the Hollywood
Bowl Museum.

though slanted, framework for this new narrative on the founding of the
Bowl.[4]

.   .   .

The early days of the Hollywood Bowl can best be understood by dividing
the activists into three groups, described here in the order in which they became involved in the Bowl's origin: first, Christine Wetherill Stevenson and
the colony of the Theosophical Society at Krotona in Hollywood; second,
the downtown business and professional men of Hollywood and Los Angeles; and third, Artie Mason Carter and the Hollywood Community Sing. Although these various groups overlapped considerably, especially at first, significant differences soon emerged. All started from the realization that a
permanent site for noncommercial outdoor arts events should be secured

before all possible locations were lost to private development.[5] Two theatrical productions, staged at other outdoor sites in the Hollywood Hills, inspired that realization. The first of these, mentioned in the *Brief History* and elsewhere, was an outdoor performance of Shakespeare's *Julius Caesar* on May 19, 1916, the tercentenary of the Bard's death. It attracted a crowd of nearly forty thousand people to another hilly location, nearby Beachwood Canyon. The site, called Beachwood Park Natural Amphitheatre in the publicity, was at or near Krotona, where a colony of the Theosophical Society had been organized a few years earlier.[6] Formally, *Julius Caesar* had little or nothing to do with the Theosophical Society beyond, maybe, the use of its property and the strong likelihood that individual theosophists were among the participants. Sponsorship came through the Hollywood Business Men's Club, the Hollywood Board of Trade, and the Women's Club of Hollywood, with substantial cooperation from the motion picture industry.[7] This production drew broad community attention to the spectacular possibilities of outdoor drama. Its role in the 1926 *Brief History*, which omits many early events actually held at the Bowl, was to show that the Bowl had precedents that included leadership from many segments of society, including the business community.[8]

The second event in the *Brief History* took place two years later. *The Light of Asia*, a retelling of the life of Buddha, ran for thirty-five performances, this time in the much smaller Krotona Stadium (capacity eight hundred) in the upper gardens of the Krotona Institute of the Theosophical Society, also in Beachwood Canyon. Camille Zekwer and Charles Wakefield Cadman, then living at Krotona, composed the music; Ruth St. Denis and dancers from Denishawn danced; and Louis Horst was musical director. Conceived on a more modest scale, this production lacked the support of the movie colony or the business community; it was, rather, the product of one individual's effort. Christine Wetherill Stevenson, a theosophist from Philadelphia, whose name does not appear on the program, commissioned the dramatization and sponsored the production.[9]

The *Brief History* tells us that, after *The Light of Asia* closed, Theodore Perceval Gerson and H. Gale Atwater, respectively a physician and a dentist, "called together a group of men and women . . . to devise ways and means for perpetuating these and other outdoor cultural events, and to promote artistic development in general." Another account has Stevenson approaching the Severance Club, a long-standing Los Angeles group with wide interests, to help her found at Krotona a home "for the seven arts of the theater: acting, music, dancing, painting, literature, sculpture, and architecture."[10] The Severance Club, whose purpose was "to promote political and industrial democracy in the cities, states and nations of the world," was skeptical, however, about the Theosophical Society as an appropriate sponsor for what Mrs. Stevenson presented as a broad-based community arts movement.[11]

Whoever initiated the dialogue, the Theatre Arts Alliance (TAA) was organized, with Stevenson as president and Gerson as first vice president, on May 26, 1919, some nine months after discussions had begun. Prominent members of the music community were recruited to become founding members and pledge one thousand dollars each.[12] Officers and board members included both theosophists and nontheosophists, members of the music community, and business people. The TAA's stated purpose, according to the *Brief History* and most other published accounts, was more general than Stevenson's: "to acquire . . . land for a community park and art center and kindred projects of a civic nature . . . to afford opportunities for the study, presentation and exhibition of all the arts, and opportunities for all classes of people to find congenial channels for the expression of their higher and best qualities."

True to its word, the TAA began to look for a site for an arts center in which music would play a subordinate, if essential, role.[13] One was soon located. Because proposed park sites were regularly preempted by fast-moving developers in the rapidly growing community, quick action to tie up the property was essential.[14] Stevenson and Marie Rankin Clarke (a veteran of the old Symphony's management) quickly came up with most of the money necessary to buy the property, which had been owned by three individuals, and took title to it themselves.[15]

The next major event reported in the *Brief History* was the formation of the Community Park and Art Association (CPAA) on October 25, 1920. The *Brief History* says only that the Theatre Arts Alliance presently "decided to abandon the project" and that, seventeen months later, "a small group of members . . . decided to reincorporate on a broader and more democratic basis."[16] What happened in those seventeen months between the May 1919 incorporation of the Theatre Arts Alliance and the formation of its successor organization is thus passed over in an uninformative sentence or two. It will be described here, however, for the conflicts that the Bowl's board wanted desperately to forget in 1926 are those that led to the compromises now hidden from view—the very ones that explain the vitality and success of the Bowl as a long-term venture.

. . .

Christine Wetherill Stevenson, theosophist-patron-dramatist and producer of *The Light of Asia* at Krotona in 1918, was the first moving spirit of the

Bowl. She represented a particular utopian conception of the TAA's purpose, which is reflected in its prospectus and quoted in the *Hollywood Weekly Citizen* of July 4, 1919, only a week after the new group was first mentioned. The prospectus, which does not appear in other published materials on the Bowl, differs significantly from the charter language, which is usually quoted, both because of its greater detail and because of its primary focus on theater:

> There is no movement which includes all the arts as does the modern theatre movement. It is . . . the synthesis of literature, music, acting, dancing, architecture, sculpture, painting, designing, lighting, costumes, crafts of all kinds. Therefore it seemed to provide the best nucleus for a great art impulse, and it was in recognition of its universality that the Theatre Arts Alliance was formed. . . . It will erect a playhouse convertible into an open-air theatre, also an outdoor Greek theatre, and other structures, in all of which the noblest and most distinguished in drama, music, and the allied arts may be given adequate expression. . . . Its possibilities for training in the arts are almost unlimited. . . . It may well grow into something unique in the world—a University of the Arts.[17]

The enthusiasm of theosophists for outdoor pageantlike presentations of Greek tragedy and Shakespeare was a part of a widespread pageantry movement in the United States, which was at its peak in the years immediately before World War I.[18] One often-quoted contemporary writer spoke of outdoor productions of Sophocles and Shakespeare as "gigantic co-operative efforts," constituting "a new art form, a sort of decorative drama that is more dependent upon the visual beauty of costumes, natural setting, grouping and dancing, and upon incidental poetry, than upon sustained emotional appeal."[19] Theosophy also heartily embraced the nineteenth-century romantic view of the uplifting power of music. Sound, wrote Mme Helena Blavatsky, the founder of Theosophy, is "the most potent and effectual magic agent, and the first of the keys which opens the door of communication between Mortals and Immortals."[20]

The differences of emphasis between Stevenson's prospectus and the nontheosophists' view did not seem unbridgeable at first. As it developed, she had a very specific agenda, a cycle of seven plays based on the lives of the prophets of the major religions, to be produced in a series, outdoors. Her own *Pilgrimage Play*, compiled from biblical accounts of the life of Christ, was the second in the series. *The Light of Asia*, based on the life of Buddha, had been the first, and a life of Confucius was to be the third. In keeping with this priority, she pushed for the immediate construction of one indoor theater and the development of the large Bowl as the site for the *Pilgrimage*

Play. By January 1920, when she was reelected president of the TAA, she had hired actors and commissioned music (from Dane Rudhyar) for a summer production. She proposed that the production be preceded by three weeks of extravagant theatrical and musical events, but the *Pilgrimage Play* was to be the centerpiece.[21]

Many members of the Theatre Arts Alliance Board resisted Stevenson, preferring the provision of their charter, "to present, produce and exhibit dramatic operatic and musical attractions, cantatas, pageants, community singing, oratory, sculpture, lectures, debates, discussions and intellectual and recreative performances of every kind and nature," to Stevenson's proposal. On February 16, 1920, she wrote to Gerson, apparently in response to criticism, that the TAA had organized to achieve "the annual production of such plays" as hers. She complained that she had paid for the architect to design a dramatic arts center, but he had insisted on designing a large "educational and general entertainment" institution instead. There was apparently some willingness to allow her play to go forward, but in a smaller theater, not in the large outdoor bowl. However, TAA members strongly resisted her next move, an offer to sell the Bowl property to private developers at a substantial profit, then purchase another canyon for the TAA's arts project.[22]

By April Stevenson found the opposition to her immediate plans insurmountable. She turned her attention instead to another hillside location only a few hundred yards from the Bowl, where she immediately began construction of her own thousand-seat outdoor theater.[23] The *Pilgrimage Play* opened on June 28 in the new Pilgrimage Bowl and ran for six weeks.[24] A few weeks after its opening, she resigned from the presidency of the Theatre Arts Alliance:

> The work that I had hoped to do through this organization I was forced to do individually and on my own property. . . .
> I am no longer free to aid further in a large community movement, which some of the members of the Board feel to be of more importance than the purely dramatic side of the Arts Alliance development, but any such movement that may develop under adequate auspices would have my hearty sympathy and such cooperation as I am still able to give, especially in the interest of community singing, drama, and pageantry.[25]

By the time her interest in the Bowl property was sold late in 1920, she was already in Palestine for a winter of research designed to improve the next year's production. Stevenson died unexpectedly in late 1922, after the *Pilgrimage Play*'s third season; her cycle of religious dramas remained a dream.[26] Her role in the initial acquisition of the Bowl property is recognized in the *Brief History*, but the importance of the religious and utopian interests she embodied to the Bowl's ultimate success is passed over.[27]

. . .

The second group involved in these early events, the business and professional men, is loosely tied together here by its oversight and management function. Its members' disparate interests ranged from physician Gerson's socialistic idealism to the more immediate capitalistic aspirations of Hollywood real estate developer Charles E. Toberman. (The *Brief History* says merely that Toberman was "involved with civic enterprises.") The group may safely be characterized as committed to the orderly, fiscally prudent development of an arts center. The men who led it viewed themselves as rational, while Stevenson and later Artie Mason Carter, both of whom were also heavily involved in management and finance, were seen as the irrational dreamers.

At first these men were among the community people who functioned to widen the appeal of the Theatre Arts Alliance and dilute its sectarian origin. Physician Gerson was its initial leader. It was Gerson, more than likely, who brought the architect Louis Christian Mullgardt into the picture. Mullgardt, whose fame had been established in the far West through his contributions to the design of the 1915 Panama-Pacific International Exposition in San Francisco, was invited in July 1919 to make recommendations for developing the Bowl site before the purchase of the property was completed.[28] His appointment, which soon followed, turned out to be a mistake, for his proposal was viewed as too pretentious for the highly valued rustic character of the Bowl property. Mullgardt threw himself into the TAA's politics, thereby creating another, quite superfluous, diversion. At the failure of his design proposal, he vented his spleen on Stevenson: "Mrs. Stevenson is considered a type of genius by some of her followers. It would be for the good of Society, to cage that type with the other Zoo-Exhibits at the expense of the Commonwealth, so as to escape the destructive claws which their thin virtuous Cloaks conceal. . . . Surely, the original purposes of the Theatre Arts Alliance were totally different in their sublime purposes, from those which Mrs. Stevenson's perversions have led to."[29] Even after Stevenson's death, Mullgardt placed the blame for the failure of his own plans for the property on "Mrs. Stevenson and her immediate sycophants" and on her "personal ambitions" and "caprices."[30]

Although Mullgardt's opinion of Stevenson has been quietly allowed to prevail in the various published histories, it should be remembered that the goals of using the Bowl for pageantry and drama as well as music and of having a school of the arts as an essential supporting element were major features of the original schemes for the Bowl's development. In 1920, the innovative dancer Ruth St. Denis, who had been involved from the start (and whose interest in Asian culture resonated with the teachings of Theosophy), wrote out her ideas for developing the Bowl as a school of the arts. She presented Gerson with a six-point plan to implement her ideas. She proposed that the TAA should divide its activities into a school section and a performance section and set up a two- to five-year program to achieve its economic goals. Heads of dance, theater, and music departments should be appointed first and their specific timetables and projects be developed; the architectural scheme should accommodate the recommendations of the department heads; no financial return should be expected for five years. She concluded that Stevenson's play be tentatively accepted for the first year, and "a large pageant of some kind" for the second year.[31] This plan, too, proved to be too grandiose.

Gerson remained closely associated with the Bowl, but others took turns at the leadership of the business and professional group and made invaluable contributions while the TAA dissolved itself and the Community Park and Art Association emerged. An attorney for the *Los Angeles Times*, E. N. Martin, probably first came in because of the *Times'* paranoia about anything utopian, especially if it involved Theosophy. Martin is credited with devising a way to avoid paying property taxes by giving the Bowl site to the county but still keeping control in the board's hands. Developer Toberman, who claimed to have proposed "an American Oberammergau" at the Bowl in 1914, made his construction equipment available for early grading and landscaping and served for many years as president of the Hollywood Bowl Association. His altruism, though genuine enough, had a strong element of self-interest, for it was his own development on Mulholland Drive that threatened the integrity of the Bowl's upper boundary in 1924. He is reported to have rectified the problem "at great expense to himself."[32] Ellis Reed, on-the-ground facilitator, actor, and day-to-day mediator between the Bowl and the *Pilgrimage Play* people, wanted to organize a school of the arts on the property after Ruth St. Denis's model; all are mentioned in the published histories.[33] Frederick W. Blanchard, Los Angeles' forgotten early entrepreneur of music, held his entrepreneurial success in common with the other business people; his long dedication to bringing art music to the people ("at popular prices") made him strongly sympathetic toward Artie Mason Carter and the community music movement that she led.

. . .

The third group in the Bowl's early history was led by Artie Mason Carter. Carter emerged as the preeminent leader of the Community Sing and community music movement in Hollywood just as the Theater Arts Alliance was at the impasse brought about by Mrs. Stevenson's defection. The Hollywood Community Sing had been organized in June 1917, two years before the organization of the TAA; it continued to grow in popularity even after the Armistice.[34] Carter was active in the Sing from its inception in 1917, becoming music chair in 1918, secretary in 1919, and president the following year. In the spring of 1920, she invited William Andrews Clark, Jr., to bring his new Philharmonic Orchestra to Hollywood for an Easter sunrise service. Clark sent the orchestra, although to a nearby site—now Barnsdall Park, then owned by Aline Barnsdall, one of Carter's allies—rather than to the Bowl.[35] That event established an association between the Philharmonic and the Sing.

The essence of Carter's style, learned through her Sing activity, was her reliance on the audience: "Big musical projects are not impossible to put through, provided you get the people themselves to work and divide the financial burden. We raised the first thousands by popular subscription. Then see how interested they all were in the Bowl, because it was their own! In no other way than by sharing the responsibility can we make music the veritable possession of the people."[36] The effectiveness of this approach is reflected in the number of people who revealed their personal investment in the Bowl by claiming to have been the first to discover the site of the Bowl, or given the first performance there, or made some other indispensable contribution. More to the point, it gave Carter a popular base that assured her a modicum of independence from the business interests.

The *Brief History* introduces Carter into the Bowl picture only in late October 1920, when she became secretary of the newly organized Community Park and Art Association, since "it was deemed expedient to seek the co-operation on a larger scale of the people of Hollywood," and "Mrs. Carter . . . brought to the Bowl the same dynamic enthusiasm and tireless energy that she exhibited in making the Community Sing a factor in musical circles of Los Angeles, and through her forceful leadership large numbers of the Chorus and others were induced to become active workers."[37] The availability of the newly accessible property and her leadership had in fact brought the members of the Sing and many other people into the Bowl months earlier than October. Arthur Farwell, then in Santa Barbara, had already led the Sing at a program in the Bowl on July 4, 1920, inaugurating a series of three Sunday-afternoon Sing-sponsored concerts. The Sing sponsored an Easter sunrise service there in 1921, a year before the one privileged by being listed as first in the *Brief History*. In addition to ignoring the high school production of *Twelfth Night* listed in the *Brief History*, the approved list ignores a series of band concerts and a variety of other concerts, pageants, fiestas, barbecues, conventions, and so forth, going back to July 1919. (Below are listed all known performances before the inauguration of the Symphonies under the Stars on July 11.)[38]

EVENTS IN THE HOLLYWOOD BOWL BEFORE JULY 11, 1922

(Complete information is not available for all events listed. HCS = Hollywood Community Sing.)

1919

July 20: Charles Dwight Edwards, singer, "tests acoustics"; public invited

August: Picnic of Finlanders entertained by a small Finnish orchestra. Occasional Sunday-evening musicales, including this program on August 10:

> Christine Wetherill Stevenson, talk
>
> Charles Farwell Edson, reading
>
> Mrs. Walker, vocal numbers
>
> The Misses Alberta and Lorena Davis, French horn and cornet
>
> Students of Miss Lillian Hayes of Normal Hill Center, classic dances
>
> Mr. and Mrs. Spencer-Kelley; announced but did not appear
>
> Leo Godowsky, Jr., violin; and Arthur Hickman, piano; attended but did not perform because there was no piano

Uncertain dates:

> Ernestine Schumann-Heink, Artie Mason Carter, Cosmo Morhan III, and others, acoustical experiments including pie pan and tenpenny nail
>
> Anna Ruzena Sprotte, contralto; Gertrude Ross, piano
>
> Gathering of African American choruses (Christmas)

1920

April 15: Hollywood May Festival Association. HCS, Hugo Kirchhofer, director; Carrie Jacobs Bond, singer-composer

May 15: HCS Chorus. Hugo Kirchhofer, director; Arthur Farwell, guest

Christine Wetherill Stevenson, speaker, described the *Pilgrimage Play*

July 4: HCS. Miss Florence Middaugh, mezzo-soprano; Miss Westphal, piano: "Blossom Song" by Needham

H. Ellis Reed, speaker

Leon Rice, dramatic tenor: "I Will Lift Up Mine Eyes" and "The Lord Is My Shepherd"

Eldridge Ladies Band (twelve pieces): "The Americans Come," "Tim Rooney's at the Fightin'," Jacobs Bond, "A Perfect Day" (cornet solo)

July 11: HCS. Margaret Messer (later Morris), soprano; Charles Wakefield Cadman, pianist-composer

July 18: HCS. Marion Woodley, soprano; Lillian Burkhardt Goldsmith, reader

November 27: HCS. Thanksgiving Sing with pageant by Hollywood High School students: "The Landing of the Pilgrims" (also called "The Arrival of the Pilgrim Fathers"), written by Hedwiga Reicher and teacher Elizabeth Waggoner; directed by Lionel Barrymore. ("First Production in the Hollywood Bowl")[39]

December 21: HCS. Christmas Community Sing

1921

March 27: HCS. Easter Sunrise Service, Los Angeles Philharmonic; Elizabeth Rothwell, soprano, soloist

May 14: Hollywood Business Men's Club Barbecue with American Legion Band and Community Sing. Kathleen Lockhart Manning, soprano; Frances Bullard, violin; Mrs. Bernard Brown, piano (rescheduled from May 7, a rare case of inclement weather; first event with electric lighting, placed there temporarily)

May 27: Shakespeare, *Twelfth Night*. Hollywood High School production; contest-winning Hollywood High School band

June 23: Shakespeare, *The Tempest*. Gwendolen Logan Hubbard, director; H. Ellis Reed, art and technical director; Pilgrimage Play chorus and orchestra, Arthur Farwell, director; Marion Morgan dancers

June 4: Hollywood Day:

American Legion Band

Hollywood Community Orchestra, Jay Plowe, conductor

Hollywood Woman's Club Chorus and Apollo Club, both under Hugo Kirchhofer

Wood-wind Society (band)

Quintet, Cornelia Rider Possart, piano; Sylvan Noack, violin; Josef Rosenfeld, viola; Alfred Wallenstein, cello; Albert Jaeger, bass: "Die Forelle" by Schubert

Community singing under Kirchhofer

Carrie Jacobs Bond, voice and piano: "A Perfect Day"

June 5: Mendelssohn, *Elijah*. Los Angeles Oratorio Society, John Smallman, conductor

July 17–September 11 (except August 14): Greater Los Angeles Municipal Band (sixty-three pieces), weekly concerts; Antonio P. Sarli, conductor

August 14–19: (Palestine) Pageant. Allen Moore, director

September 1: Hollywood Society Circus

September 12–14: Shakespeare, *A Midsummer Night's Dream*, with Mendelssohn's music. H. Ellis Reed, director; Denishawn company and Marion Morgan, dancers

September 15–17: Shakespeare, *The Taming of the Shrew*. H. Ellis Reed, director

September 23: Community Party. Picnic, bonfire, dancing in the pavilion to a jazz orchestra

October 15–19: Knights of Pythias Carnival; dancing nightly until 11:30; theatrical entertainment, barbecue on closing night

November 11: Armistice Day Mother's Peace Service. Ernestine Schumann-Heink, contralto; Gertrude Ross, piano

December 24: HCS. Christmas songs, tree planting

1922

March 19: Christian Endeavor convention

April 16: Easter Sunrise Service. Los Angeles Philharmonic, Hollywood Community Chorus

May 29: National Association of Real Estate Dealers

June 3: Al Malaikha Temple, Shrine carnival

Figure 20. Greater Los Angeles Municipal Band, Sunday afternoon concert at the Hollywood Bowl, 1921, showing the benches that followed the contours of the hill before it was bulldozed in 1926. There is no shell yet. Courtesy of the Hollywood Bowl Museum.

June 10: Rotary International Convention

July 7: Evangelical Synod of Missouri, Ohio, etc. (Lutheran). Music by Otto Backhaus (Long Beach); piano, church choir, and soloists

July 8: Bizet, *Carmen.* Opera produced by Hall, Bevani, and Schostedt

On Saturday afternoon, May 15, 1920, for example, two thousand people came to the Bowl for an open-air sing. At Carter's behest, Stevenson described to the crowd her plans to produce her "Christ" play at the stadium (the Pilgrimage Bowl), then nearing completion a few hundred yards away. Composer-singer Carrie Jacobs Bond, newly moved to Hollywood but very well known to the audience for "A Perfect Day" and other songs, offered a "spontaneous remark" that led to the taking of a collection for the projected *Pilgrimage Play.* Two months later, the Sing made a point of offering its first series of events at the Bowl on Sundays, the one day of the week when the *Pilgrimage Play* was not performed. Clearly, Stevenson's production was seen by this audience and by Carter not as a rival to a successful Bowl but as an admirable and complementary operation, just as the Bowl was viewed supportively by Stevenson in her otherwise acrimonious letter of resignation from the Theatre Arts Alliance, quoted earlier.[40] Later, Stevenson and Gerson both were said to have favored Carter to succeed Stevenson as president of the new Community Park and Art Association.[41] Thus, Carter and Stevenson saw themselves as allies, not rivals, in their respective commitments to the arts.

.　.　.

While Stevenson was building her own outdoor theater and staging her play in the summer of 1920, the Bowl property languished, its fate uncertain. A few benches and a barbecue pit, with little or no lighting, were the sum total of its "improvements"; its growing popularity as a gathering place and the aspirations of the remaining TAA members were all that prevented its commercial development. One source has Stevenson giving a thirty-day option to the TAA in the late summer of 1920.[42] At this point, a major step was taken that is omitted from the *Brief History* and from the other readily available published accounts as well. With the help of other Hollywood business people and Sing activists, Carter formed a new group, the Community Arts Alliance, in early September. The CAA attempted to succeed the TAA as operators of the Bowl property.[43] Her new proposed included a national center for art and music, with a much smaller stadium than in earlier proposals. Drama is conspicuously absent from this plan. A new board is proposed, overlapping the previous TAA Board but omitting most of the previously active business and professional men.[44] On September 24, a ten-day extension on the Carter organization's option to purchase the Bowl property was granted, on the grounds that the new fundraising attempt had already come within ten thousand dollars of the purchase price, earlier reported as one hundred thousand dollars. The San Francisco–based *Pacific Coast Musical Review*, whose Los Angeles correspondent was well acquainted with the Krotona colony, reported that sixty thousand dollars had already been raised in this September campaign.[45]

Within a week, the picture had changed dramatically, for the businessmen reentered the picture. A new and much more ambitions organization was being formed, the Sing audience was now told, to raise $350,000 in the entire Los Angeles area for the Bowl and for the extensive developments, probably intended to implement Mullgardt's proposal. A brochure circulated by the newly formed Community Park and Art Association (CPAA) proposes extensive development adding up to a million dollars of "living memorials," to include:

a major open-air theater	$200,000
small open-air theaters	$150,000
a community house	$150,000

an administration building	$100,000
purchase of a community park and beautification of its grounds	$100,000
a waterfall open air theater	$50,000
an art display building	$50,000
an enclosed theater	$50,000
an ornamental gateway entrance	$50,000
a lagoon and waterfall	$50,000
a hanging bridge	$50,000[46]

"Some of the big men of down-town institutions" were now interested, it was reported. (Their main interest was probably to prevent the construction of an arts center that would challenge the hegemony of downtown Los Angeles.) For the first time, professional fundraisers were introduced.[47] Three weeks later, the new board of the Community Park and Art Association, the group that is generally credited with succeeding the TAA and starting the Bowl concerts, was announced, with Frederick W. Blanchard as president and Carter as secretary.[48] A new (or extended) thirty-day option was announced. The fundraising brochure refers to "Men and Women of Broad Vision" and was addressed to "all classes of citizens." It stressed the Bowl as a business-endorsed enterprise: "Successful business men are men of analytical, astute minds. Whatever the issue at hand, they require that the need shall be established and that when supplied, the results shall justify every dollar and cent expended. THAT'S BUSINESS."

By early December, the new CPAA had managed to close the deal on the property, if not on the proposed construction. The terms were seriously deflated from those described two months earlier, either by Carter's ephemeral organization or by the CPAA's brochure. The purchase price had dropped to $67,000. The CPAA did not come close to raising even that reduced amount, let alone the $350,000 it had originally sought. The hired fundraisers had achieved nothing. In fact, only $18,000 was collected, the lion's share from board members themselves; the rest was covered by a mortgage and an open note signed by four members of the new CPAA.

What had happened to Carter's earlier campaign and her pledges, said to total $60,000? Here, there is no direct evidence. The difference between her claimed $60,000 and the $18,000 actually raised is exactly the amount initially invested by Stevenson and Marie Rankin Clarke in the Bowl property, $42,000. Did Carter have a commitment from Stevenson and Clarke to donate the property to her group, or did she have some reason to believe they would? If their presumed donation was not available to the business group that formed the new CPAA, it is understandable that they would have wanted to suppress this part of the story. As signers of the open note, however, they were in a position to give the Bowl a chance to succeed—and to acquire some real estate of rapidly escalating value if it failed.

·   ·   ·

However it was achieved, the sale of Stevenson's interest in the Bowl property finalized the divorce of the Bowl from the Theosophical Society and initiated a new and shaky alliance between the charismatic Carter and the business interests. In theory, at least, the new CPAA reincorporated theater into the Bowl's grand design. Therefore, the statement that "Mrs. Carter and F. W. Blanchard deserve praise above all others for the successes of the Summer Symphony Concerts" represents a qualified endorsement in the *Brief History*.[49] It certainly does not say that Carter, with help from Blanchard and others, virtually willed the summer symphony concerts into existence in the face of skepticism and outright opposition from the business-dominated board of directors, not once but at least three times.[50]

When she herself was uncertain whether the concerts should be attempted, Carter asked the question of the thousand members of the Sing gathered at the 1922 Easter sunrise service. The favorable answer did not dispel the outspoken skepticism of other CPAA members, the Hollywood Chamber of Commerce (which never did endorse the season), and such experts as L. E. Behymer.[51] The season went forward, but failure loomed when, in the fifth week of the projected ten-week season, there was not enough money to cover immediate expenses. After a consultation, Hollywood businessmen offered to resolve the problem by taking over the Bowl's operation themselves, ending the symphony programs and offering cheaper band concerts in their place. Carter again took the problem and the proposed solution to the audience; she came away with a resounding vote of confidence for her program in the form of enough money to finish the symphony season.[52] The CPAA's board regarded this success as a fluke and refused to back a second symphony season at all. A separate music committee, including Carter, Gerson, Blanchard, and two newcomers, had to run the 1923 season on their own.[53]

Carter continued as president, first of the Community Park and Art Association, and then of its successor, the Hollywood Bowl Association, until the spring of 1926. She became a member of the newly organized Hollywood Chamber of Commerce; her support there was substantial enough to elect her to its first board of directors in 1921. She served on the Hollywood

Planning Commission, helped found the Hollywood Art Association, and held office in the Woman's Club of Hollywood. Her mainstream support does not appear to have suffered from her public jabs at the local banks, who had not contributed to the Bowl campaigns, and at the "build and sell, build and sell" mentality of local business interests. In fact, her public came to the rescue when, in April 1923, the CPAA Board elected another secretary in her absence, without bothering to consult with her. (He "graciously" stepped aside when she "reappeared.")[54]

Clearly the business interests had had more than enough of the outspoken, independent Mrs. Carter when they forced her out of the Bowl management before the 1926 season. She left with a public blast at the board that contrasted her ideals with their "policy of money grubbing," complained of the "ever-present antagonism" of the other board members, and enjoined her followers to "keep the Hollywood Bowl democratic."

> It is no longer possible for me and the present board of directors to work together in harmony . . . [her] ideals . . . a policy of money grubbing. . . .
> The utter lack of sympathetic understanding and the ever-present antagonism has killed my spirit. I am a living dead soul. Had the men of the board killed me it would have been better for me. . . .
> Wherever I go, I go gladly, for the joy of giving. Mine is a community spirit. All the combined wealth of the board could not pay me for my humble service. My priceless compensation is the thought that people came and loved the music. I had faith in them and they kept faith with me. . . .
> Keep the Hollywood Bowl democratic.
> Keep the Hollywood Bowl ideals and standards planted there![55]

Her departure was page-one news for several days, in sharp contrast to the early events in this narrative. The public response of an unnamed former board member reveals that the hostility was mutual: "Mrs. Carter ruled easily enough when she had to do only with the bowl in its early stages, when it was experimental and doubtful. But later, when heavy business interests entered the project, and big men became financially interested in the development of the bowl, Mrs. Carter found stiff opposition which she could not overcome."[56] The chronicler whose book was underwritten by Toberman wrote of her later this way: "Like all dreamers, and crusaders for a cause, Mrs. Carter was emotional and sometimes lacked the restraint of realism in her business dealings." "Carter was NOT a businesswoman but a crusader with the zeal of a fanatic," "up to her pretty ears" in her cause.[57]

The issue was not really control over the choice of artists, as was later said, for the first announcement by Raymond Brite, the newly hired business manager, after her departure was to confirm that the conductors she had chosen for the 1926 season would in fact be hired.[58] It is more likely that the four hundred new boxes planned as part of one hundred thousand dollars for seating "improvements" were a final, devastating affront to her sense of democracy, leading her to comment that her community's democratic experiment in beauty had "degenerated into a money-making machine."[59]

Carter's flowery style, her charisma (both all too evident in her letters to Alfred Hertz), and her utopian politics no doubt irritated the businessmen, who were probably apprehensive anyway about her influence over the Bowl's audience. The newspaper quotation that "she is not well" simply reflects the Victorian language still used, by both Carter and her adversaries on the Bowl board, to ease the departure, either enforced or voluntary, of a female individual.[60] The constant use of stereotypically gendered language suggests that the businessmen were representing their takeover as the inevitable result of a conflict between responsible businessmen and irresponsible, emotion-driven arts women. When Toberman later acknowledged that the capital improvements of 1926, to which Carter objected, had permanently damaged the acoustics of the Bowl, he did not recognize this as an indirect admission that Carter might have been at least partly right in the dispute that ended her formal association with the Bowl.[61]

•   •   •

The "authorized and approved" *Brief History* appeared in print less than three months after Carter's departure. It reflects the moment of triumph of the second of the three groups who struggled to develop the Bowl, crediting Carter and Blanchard "for the successes of the Summer Symphony Concerts" but not for the success of the Bowl itself. Although the long career of the Bowl as well as the Symphonies under the Stars that emerged from these early events is a remarkable success story from the point of view of symphonic music in America, it has realized only a fragment of the organizers' original goal of affording "opportunities for the study, presentation and exhibition of all the arts." So strong was the hold of this dream, spelled out in Ruth St. Denis's typescript from 1920, that, as late as 1935, Gerson was still attempting to expand the range of the Bowl's activities. He wrote to Allan C. Balch, a major Los Angeles philanthropist: "The original Bowl concept as 'dreamed,' and as expressed through its Articles of Incorporation, is far more alluring and comprehensive than most people realize and not unless this is made articulate by comprehensive planning, can the real ultimate Bowl destiny be grasped."[62] Ever the practical businessman, Toberman took a very dim view of Gerson's initiative: "If the tone of my voice seemed to indicate irritation it was only due to the fact that I was extremely anxious to impress upon you my belief in the futility of a program at this time involving the acquisition of the land you propose to add to the Bowl grounds."[63]

Even the alliance between the Bowl and the Philharmonic, now taken for granted, was at first anything but secure. The 1919 discussions had included representatives of the old Symphony, then still very much alive, who were eager for their orchestra to participate. (While the Philharmonic was playing an Easter sunrise service in 1920 at Barnsdall Park in Hollywood, the Symphony was giving its own outdoor Easter sunrise concert in Pasadena.) Just before the first of the Symphonies under the Stars concerts, Walter Henry Rothwell, conductor of the Philharmonic, saw the Bowl concerts as an unsuitable activity for the orchestra and tried to dissuade his friend Alfred Hertz from conducting them.[64] A year later, the CPAA Board expressed doubts about the fifty-thousand-dollar offer of William Andrews Clark, Jr., to underwrite the Bowl's second season. Clark withdrew the offer, to Carter's disgust. The two organizations were fully integrated only in 1966, decades after supporters of the old Symphony, many of them early Bowl activists, were gone, and their old diffidence toward the Philharmonic's founder forgotten.[65]

In terms of the broad range of its founders' aspirations, the Bowl's success was incomplete. The cycle of dramas about the world's major religions was forgotten in favor of the annual Easter sunrise service, a more narrowly focused religious use of the site than the one conceived by the Theosophists of Krotona and one that continued in the minds of many long-time Bowl supporters to be the most significant event in the Bowl's annual calendar. The center for drama never emerged, nor did the complex of theaters, museums, and galleries conceived at the start. A school of the arts was not organized on the site, nor was the necessary additional property for such a project acquired. (Most of the spaces they would have occupied are now tastefully landscaped parking areas.) Although audiences have often been large, the Bowl has mainly attracted the largely white middle- and upper-class population characteristic of Hollywood and Los Angeles circa 1920; it has rarely found a way to attract the wider audience for which some of its founders once hoped.[66] The Bowl's role as a potential regional or even a national arts center was quietly forgotten after Gerson's last effort in 1935, after construction of the Hollywood Freeway further damaged the acoustics in the 1950s, driving a concrete chasm between it and the Pilgrimage Bowl site, and especially after the opening of the downtown Music Center in 1964.

Nevertheless, the achievement of the Bowl was remarkable. The first season of Symphonies under the Stars consisted of forty concerts in ten weeks, compared with the regular winter season of the fledgling Philharmonic of a mere twelve pairs of concerts. In an interview soon after the close of that season, Hertz, who had, over his career up to that point, already conducted more than fourteen hundred opera performances in Europe and America, commented, "I believe that I have done more to spread the gospel of good music during the last ten weeks than in all my life before." He wrote later of the great success of Carter's "most original plan to democratize music in the southern part of California" and compared the widespread public support and participation in the Bowl favorably with "the relatively small group of wealthy people who were controlling the destiny" of his own orchestra in San Francisco.[67]

The *Brief History* itself uses concise language and apparent reasonableness to promote the image of a rational, efficient managerial group, motivated by altruism, moving steadily toward an agreed-on goal. One need not look far beyond this façade to recognize it for what it is. The extent to which images of emotional women and rational men influenced the all-male business group's language is striking, especially considering that many of Stevenson's and Carter's supporters were themselves men. One could even argue that the businessmen came forward only when they saw that Carter and the Sing members, who were the biggest risk takers in the Bowl's early history, were on the brink of success. The businessmen's understanding of the need to accommodate both of the other groups was demonstrated later by their appointment of Mrs. Irish and their later dependence on her for fundraising and management. (That appointment can also be seen as a failure of the male-only, "professional" managers they had appointed in Carter's place.)[68] That understanding is also revealed, perhaps inadvertently, in the idealistic language of the final paragraph of their *Brief History*: "Thus is evolving in the hills of Hollywood a great force, making for the new civilization, a civilization built upon beauty: physical beauty, intellectual beauty, and spiritual beauty."

The multiple roles of (nonsectarian) religious commitment, community participation, rational management, and business interest—in which women and men both took leading roles—all contributed to create the Bowl as a vital institution. Stevenson left the TAA, Carter was driven out of the CPAA, and both were trivialized by the triumphant businessmen in their

Brief History. Yet, partly because of this hidden, controversial history and the widespread public commitment the institution represented, the Bowl became an enduring monument to the early twentieth-century American dream of art music for the people. It remains a symbol for a longed-for, never-achieved era of public participation in the culture of symphonic music, one of the goals to which the leaders of all three groups were, ultimately, committed. Whether it can remain a symbol for high aspirations in the arts as those aspirations are regularly reconstructed for a new century remains a question.

PART III

From Progressive to Ultramodern

11   Old Competitors, New Opera Companies in 1925

The short-lived National Opera Company had arrived in town in 1887 with its own orchestra, ballet, and chorus, along with a trainload of stage sets. Five planned performances expanded to seven, literally by popular demand. Its visit was so successful, in fact, that more than half the town turned out to see and hear it, makeshift opera house and all. To accommodate a similar turnout in the 1920s, when the city had grown many times larger, would have required several such companies, each of them running for weeks on end.

Of course that never happened. Among other things, opera had been bypassed by recordings, vaudeville, and especially the movies (still silent, but routinely accompanied by live musicians), all of which now competed for the audiences that had once patronized visiting opera companies. In fact, promoters of grand opera had given up on the "popular" audience by the 1920s. Julian Johnson's 1906 pronouncement that "the problem of dollar opera" had been solved by the Bevani Company in the newly opened Temple Auditorium was long forgotten. Grand opera had become obsolete as popular entertainment and was now considered elite, with a repertoire fixed in the era just past. In Los Angeles, the proof of that pudding emerged unequivocally in October 1925, when two opera companies undertook back-to-back week-long runs. Even two weeks of grand opera turned out to be too much, despite the hugely increased potential audience of LA residents over the intervening decades. That was the conclusion reached by old rival impresarios L. E. Behymer and James T. Fitzgerald, after they had exhausted themselves and their financial backers with their back-to-back, rival week-long "seasons."

Gaetano Merola and his fledgling San Francisco Opera precipitated the competition. Merola moved to bring a version of his one-year-old company to Southern California in 1924. The Los Angeles Grand Opera Company (LAGOC) was formed under his leadership.[1] As was discussed in chapter 4, Merle Armitage, then working for one of the New York concert management agencies, had distinguished himself a few years earlier by rescuing a touring Russian opera company stranded in Seattle and shepherding it successfully through a nationwide tour. He had been recruited as a rival concert manager to Behymer by J. T. Fitzgerald, the music store operator who had once been F. W. Blanchard's partner and had quietly kept his hand in the concert business even after Behymer had risen to prominence. Armitage was joined by George Leslie Smith, a former contractor who had already replaced Behymer as manager of the Philharmonic. In this undertaking Behymer was bypassed entirely.

Merola's Grand Opera season was successfully promoted as an elite social event that would (yet again) enhance the city's prestige and the people's taste. The old Friday Morning Club and the Gamut Club, as well as the newer Los Angeles Opera and Fine Arts Club and many other groups, supported the project and helped fill Philharmonic Auditorium for the weeklong season in October. Operas from the French and Italian repertoires were performed: *Andrea Chenier* (Giordano, 1896), *Manon, Romeo and Juliet* (Gounod, 1867), *La Traviata*, and the double bill of *Gianni Schicchi* (Puccini, 1918) and *L'Amico Fritz* (Mascagni, 1892).

On the heels of this success, a second season was announced for the following fall. A funny thing happened within days of that announcement, however; Merola abruptly canceled his connection with the Los Angeles Grand Opera Company. Public expressions of wonder and disappointment at this development followed with no clear explanation. Presently Merola announced that, instead, he would bring his San Francisco company for a week, but another Los Angeles company, the new California Grand Opera Association (CGOA), would serve as presenter. With one successful season under their belts, the organizers of the first company (LAGOC) decided to go forward anyway, hiring the distinguished Richard Hageman as their conductor, finding enough star-quality singers, and shutting the upstart rival company out of Philharmonic Auditorium. The result, in October 1925, was two back-to-back week-long seasons of grand opera instead of one. The first was offered by the LA Grand Opera Association at Philharmonic Auditorium and the second by the CGOA at the spanking new Olympic Auditorium, a structure that had so far—like the long-ago Hazard's Pavilion—been used for boxing and wrestling matches and was now being promoted as an all-purpose venue.[2]

What was the reason for this sudden, unexpected, and extravagant competition, with its off-putting array of similarly named "grand opera" companies? The trail leads straight to our old friend L. E. Behymer. Deliberately cut out of the first company's 1924 season by the Fitzgerald-Armitage partnership, long-time impresario Behymer was now flexing his entrepreneurial muscle. It turned out that Behymer's web of contractual arrangements included control over the Southern California appearances of many of Merola's star singers. Although the point seems never to have been made in the press and is only indirectly confirmed even in Howard Swan's book, it is clear that Behymer's threat to enforce those contracts for the season just past left Merola with little choice but to do things Behymer's way and work with CGOA rather than LAGOC if he wanted to keep the singers he was planning to use, even in San Francisco.[3]

Having gotten his way with Merola, Behymer pulled out all the stops to make a success of his own week-long season, which was piggybacked on the rival one already announced. He took his cue from his early rivalry with F. W. Blanchard, reversing his pattern of many years and setting lower ticket prices than those charged by the other company. (He was able to obtain Olympic Auditorium rent-free, suggesting that he had quietly maintained his ties to the world of prizefights.) Then, he promoted the new theater as a suitable venue with some preparatory events that used stars from the now well-established world of commercial mass entertainment. (Sally Rand, Fred Waring's Pennsylvanians, Dolores Del Rio and the dog Rin-Tin-Tin were among them.) Needless to say, he also worked his long-time subscriber lists, developed over decades for his Philharmonic Concert Courses.

As with the rivalry five years earlier between the Symphony and the Philharmonic, this competition could not continue. After that one near-ruinous double season, peace was discreetly declared.[4] Now the competing companies were folded together. Armitage remained as general manager (and later as manager of Philharmonic Auditorium). But Behymer had made his point, once again taking a place in these elite events and reaping his agent's fees, even though he was no longer active in the management. The association with Merola and the San Francisco Opera continued for several years. It lapsed after the 1931 season in the face of the Great Depression, but in 1937 the San Francisco company began a long series of regular visits to Southern California, ending only in 1969.

•   •   •

Things had changed radically since the days of the small touring English-language opera companies that had played the old Grand Opera House and Los Angeles Theater for several weeks at a time thirty years earlier. A major issue in Los Angeles' musical life in the Progressive era and later, and, indeed, in American musical life, had to do with settling the social role that opera would play, in reference both to the commercialized mass culture that took shape at the turn of the century and afterward and to the formation of a model for an elite, specifically "American" culture. By 1925, opera was definitively established as an elite event, dependent for its backing on its social standing as a plaything of the wealthy and on gaining support as an opportunity for the elaborately dressed, glamorous audiences to be part of the show—a little like the Oscars of today.

Or was it? The depth of opera's presence across social classes worked against its use as a tool for social stratification for a long time. In his seminal *Highbrow/Lowbrow: The Emergence of Cultural Hierarchy in America,* Lawrence Levine argues that the currently understood distinctions between popular and elite culture in the cases of music and theater developed in the course of the nineteenth century in the service of carefully cultivated class distinctions. Symphony concerts are not a major focus of Levine's thesis, and they do not fit easily into his scheme. (For Los Angeles, we have seen that symphony concerts began as elite entertainments, with efforts to broaden the audience rather than further restrict it continuing long after 1900, efforts such as the short-lived People's Orchestra and the still-thriving Hollywood Bowl.) Opera, however, is more central to Levine's argument.[5] Well after 1900, opera in Los Angeles resisted the restrictions that would have made it exclusively an elite genre. The process of turning a popular entertainment, such as nineteenth-century opera, into an elite one was both longer and bumpier than Levine would have it. In fact, the great Grand Opera compromise that followed the duel of 1925 is not the end of the story.

It would seem that the process posited by Levine was completed (insofar as it ever was completed) because of pressure from the emergence of commercial mass culture as much as from efforts to make opera emblematic of elite culture. It is likely no coincidence that the transformation became complete only when opera became a technologically backward-looking genre on the margin of a newly developed and fabulously profitable commercial movie industry. The long contest between opera as popular culture and opera as an exclusive event subsidized by a social elite ended at the same time that the movies became the dominant element of commercial mass culture. This is demonstrated in Los Angeles, where in 1915 Temple Auditorium became Clune's, featuring full-length silent films (with orchestral accompaniment) for several years. It is worth a thought that the Baptist board of directors controlling the auditorium considered that movies would be an appropriate weeknight use for their hall, which continued to host the Symphony concerts and, of course, Sunday services. This practice came to an end only when William Andrews Clark, Jr., was able to buy out Clune's lease in 1920, capturing and even renaming the hall for his elite new Philharmonic.

In fact, opera and film have had a curious relationship, worth a short digression here, especially given the seemingly paradoxical absence of any other discussion of the film industry from a book on music in Los Angeles. These two entertainment categories have not always seemed as distant from each other as they did by the late twentieth century, when they were set in concrete as different genres with different conventions and different (if overlapping) audiences. Both represent self-conscious fusions of the arts, though in the case of opera the composer often dominated, while movies are much more of a collective enterprise in which the composer dominates very seldom indeed. The presence of commercial mass culture and the new technology that went with it requires us to reconsider the basic conception of opera, a multigenre mix that has been radically rethought and reinvented periodically ever since it emerged in late sixteenth-century Italy. Through all that time, it has bounced back and forth between being a popular and an aristocratic entertainment, influencing, influenced by, and occasionally overlapping with other forms of theater that included music. The nature, application, and relative importance of its various components (singing, instrumental music, drama, spoken versus sung language, subject matter, dance, stage settings, etc.) have been stoutly contested on a fairly regular basis. Since many kinds of musical theater involve essentially these same components, arguments in the twentieth century raged over whether a given entertainment added up to "opera." (As previously mentioned, Gershwin's *Porgy and Bess* was declared not a "real" opera for some years, for example.) Does the addition of film or of recorded sound to the mix mean that a particular event is no longer an "opera"? Can the term apply only to something taking place in an opera house? to something witnessed by an audience dominated by a particular class?

The analogy with film is stronger if "opera" is given a relatively inclusive meaning, as suggested, for example, by the innumerable optimistically named, small-town opera houses that dotted the American West in the nineteenth century. The difference between opera and musical theater (and, by analogy, film) has sometimes been a matter of different aspirations or different audiences, expressed through the use of different performance venues, different musical styles, and the presence or absence of spoken dialogue. By the time of the competing grand opera companies in 1925, the Hollywood film colony had made its transition from one- and two-reel shorts played in storefront film parlors to full-length feature films played in elaborate movie palaces. The transition had been dramatically initiated in 1915 by D. W. Griffith's *Birth of a Nation,* considered by film critics to be the first masterpiece of filmmaking. The film debuted in Los Angeles as *The Clansman,* where it played in Clune's (formerly Temple) Auditorium. At Clune's, the orchestra played a score by Carli Elinor, director of the house orchestra, compiled from orchestral music by other composers, the most common practice during the silent film era. When the film opened in New York City a few weeks later, however, an original score composed by Joseph Carl Breil (1870–1926) in collaboration with Griffith was used.[6] Despite the success of this score, through-composed scores intended for specific movies, analogous to those composed for operas, remain rare.

Douglas Fairbanks, Sr., he of the 1916 outdoor production of Shakespeare's *Julius Caesar* in the Hollywood Hills, which was a forerunner of the Hollywood Bowl, is a major figure in a mid-1920s experiment aimed at making movies more operatic, raising them to the level of high art. Fairbanks left behind a highly successful career as a comic when he formed United Artists in 1919 (with D. W. Griffith, Mary Pickford, and Charlie Chaplin) in search of a new standard of artistic excellence and began to make the adventure epics for which he is now known.[7] As part of that effort he commissioned original, newly composed scores for three feature films from then-prominent composer Mortimer Wilson. Wilson, a gifted Iowa native who had composed symphonies and chamber music and was well established as a teacher in New York City, traveled to California to compose new scores for *The Thief of Baghdad* (1924), *Don Q—Son of Zorro* (1925), and *The Black Pirate* (1926).[8]

This one moment in the saga of silent film when it seemed possible to create a film-based genre analogous to opera, fusing the new medium with the older staged arts of music, drama, dance, and scenery, went by, overwhelmed first by the visual and dramatic (and financial) success of these films and then by the experiments with sound film that followed within a few years. (Wilson died in 1931, just after the initial triumph of sound film, and so could not follow up on his success with these scores.) Instead, his three film scores have remained almost unknown, even to film music buffs, their claim as an incipient high-art genre overwhelmed by the popular success of Hollywood on one hand and the emergence of the "ultramodern" on the other.[9]

.   .   .

Despite the failure of music to assume the dominant position in film that it held in opera and the divergent paths taken by these genres, opera did not

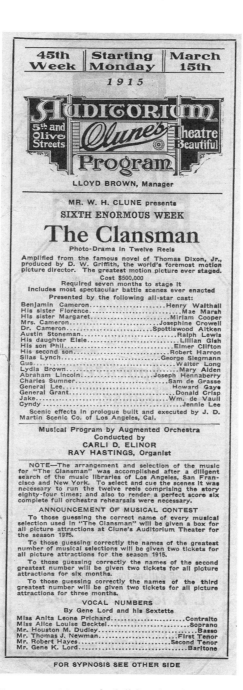

Figure 21. Movie playbill for *The Clansman* (soon renamed *Birth of a Nation*), the 1915 version of Thomas F. Dixon's popular 1905 novel that became a landmark of American popular culture. Courtesy of Cambria Master Recordings and Archives.

remain comfortably in the elite pigeonhole to which the development of commercial mass culture had consigned it. Low-budget opera managed to reemerge, though in different formats and for different audiences than in the days of those ubiquitous traveling companies. In 1924, the Euterpe Opera Theater was organized as a largely volunteer-run local organization designed to give concert or partly staged, cut-down versions of standard operas, using local singers, many of them promising students. The idea found a substantial following. The organization grew to several thousand members within a few years; soon seasons of five or six operas were using this format. Another organization, the Los Angeles Opera and Fine Arts Club, operated on a somewhat similar pattern, with comparable success. The performances were often in the daytime, sometimes even in the morning. Audience members bought memberships in these clubs; mainly they were middle-class white women. Thus, the audiences, large and enthusiastic as they were, were quite different from the mixed-class, mixed-sex audiences who had regularly attended the touring opera companies offered at the Los Angeles Theater several decades earlier.

As the larger, elite opera companies came to dominate the scene, their repertoire tended to remain grounded in the nineteenth-century repertoire. New operas, if they were produced at all, tended to be treated as ad hoc productions, often using the extensive club structure that was so important to local performers and composers. Horatio Parker's *Fairyland* (1915), the first and by far the most ambitious of these (in terms of budget), was, as we have seen, produced by an alliance of civic and musical backers and the California and National Federations of Women's Clubs. Homer Grunn's *The Isle of Cuckoo* (1931) was produced at the Ellis Club, on Wilshire Boulevard. Mary Carr Moore succeeded in getting ad hoc productions of several operas in Los Angeles after World War I: *Los Rubios* in 1931 (outdoors in the Greek Theater in Griffith Park); *David Rizzio* in 1932 (at the Shrine Auditorium, revived by Euterpe several years later), and, after many years' efforts, her American landmark *Narcissa, or, The Cost of Empire,* in 1945.[10] The Federal Music Project in Los Angeles briefly attempted an opera company, with mixed results. Apart from occasional productions of operas composed by faculty members (Charles E. Pemberton, *The Painter of Dreams,* 1934; Pauline Alderman, *Bombastes furioso,* 1938), regularly scheduled opera workshops in an academic or conservatory setting did not begin until after World War II; the earliest was established at the University of Southern California in 1951, when the opera reading clubs began to shrink and resources available to academic institutions grew.[11] The question of what

"American" opera might be remained on the margins of this by-now marginalized genre.

From the specifics, especially the frequent uncertainties of the Los Angeles picture, one draws the uncertain conclusion that the outcome of the sacralization process for opera was in doubt for much longer than one might have otherwise guessed. Opera was, and still is, just too challenging and too satisfying to perish from the weight of class distinctions.

12 The New Negro Movement in Los Angeles

> Race relations are historically contingent and regionally
> specific, varying in meaning over time as within different
> regions of the country. . . . The primary and secondary
> historical materials collected here cannot be made to
> conform to some analytical edifices drawn from the
> black/white experience in other regions of the country.
>
> TOMÁS ALMAGUER, *Racial Fault Lines: The Historical Origins
> of White Supremacy in California* (Berkeley and Los Angeles:
> University of California Press, 1994), 205–6

A few generations after the founding of the Spanish mission that became
Los Angeles, Mexicans, Chinese, and African Americans were among the
gold seekers, railroad builders, and other fortune hunters who supplanted
the area's once-numerous indigenous peoples. Given Los Angeles' origin as
a part of Mexico, it is to be expected that the city had a larger Latino population than most other American cities, but the presence of the largest
African American community on the West Coast may come as a surprise.
(In contrast, San Francisco had few Mexicans or blacks; Chinese were by far
its most numerous racial minority.) Although it is difficult to quantify the
Latino presence, neither Latinos nor African Americans were very numerous. There were somewhat more persons of Asian descent (mostly Chinese,
with increasing numbers of Japanese after 1900) than African Americans in
1910, though the balance shifted when Asian immigration shrank. According to the U.S. Census, which counted each group on a different scale, persons of Mexican descent and African Americans appeared to be nearly equal
around 1910, but after 1920 the Mexican-identified population clearly grew
faster. The generally xenophobic *Times* experimented with a daily news
summary in Spanish in the early 1920s, suggesting a more influential and
considerably larger Spanish-speaking presence than the census figures
imply.[1] The black population grew in proportion to the city's growth, but
never exceeded 2 percent of the city's total population until the boom of the
1940s. Taken together, persons counted as racial minorities (i.e., African
Americans and Asians) plus ethnic Mexicans (counted as a national minority only if they chose to identify as such) numbered about 13 percent of the

city's population in 1940. Even though the period covered by this book was one of extreme Anglo dominance in Los Angeles culture and politics, the presence and influence of these and other minorities were always a factor, whether recognized directly or not by the dominant group, as will become clear.

In his "History," for example, Bagley describes La Banda Union, a band organized in the late 1870s by Manuel Valasco, which was active "for many years." He lists some twenty-five musicians, only about half with obviously Hispanic names, as among its members over the years; a few of these also performed with Anglo bands in the same time. La Banda was apparently the first nonmilitary band to dress distinctively, for it "had very showy costumes consisting of a cutaway coat, blue, trimmed with white, trousers of the same color, gold lace, epaulets, and the whole surmounted with a helmet and plume."[2] The apparent non-Hispanic participation in La Banda suggests the interactions that were a continuing factor in the city's cultural life and that are not adequately represented by census figures.

By the 1890s, Bagley reports musical activities that reflect the changing ethnic variety to be found in the stream of professional music making in the city. On a December evening in 1891, for example, A. J. Stamm presented his students in a "grand concert" at Turnverein Hall; M. S. Arévalo's Guitar Club performed at the YMCA, and W. F. Arend's orchestra played for a ball at the Grand Opera House Hall in Pasadena, illustrating the everyday presence of German-, Hispanic-, and Anglo-American music makers; each of the three was prominent among the city's ethnic groups of the time.[3] A few years later, Y. Escobar directed the Mexican Philharmonic Band, whose frequent performances included weekly concerts at Terminal Island (near San Pedro) and whose membership of twenty-nine made it one of the largest of the local bands.[4] Somewhat later, C. S. De Lano's Guitar, Banjo, and Mandolin Club offered a regular series of concerts with as many as ten events per season.

Ironically, Bagley, who later did his best to maintain segregated locals in the musicians' union (helping to organize both Local 47 and Local 767 and resisting their later merger), is also the source of one of the earliest reports of public music making by African Americans in Los Angeles: "They were few in number and accurate information regarding them is lacking, but the first colored brass ensemble . . . the Concord band of 12 pieces, organized in 1897 or 1898, under the leadership of Samuel Lenard. I think Mr. H. L. Toney also had this band for a time, as he appears a number of times as leader. . . . My information is that Mr. Toney also organized the first colored orchestra of seven pieces about 1895. . . . the Concord Band frequently ap-

Figure 22.   African American band, circa 1895. SHADES OF L.A. ARCHIVES/Los Angeles Public Library.

peared in the parades of the period."[5] He also provides more information than the U.S. Census, which lists four "colored" musicians and teachers of music, possibly Chinese, in 1890. Ten years later, the U.S. Census reports twelve "colored" musicians and teachers of music, including eight "Negroes." Not only did the census understate information about minorities; it made a distinction between "race" and "nationality" that reduces its value as a source here, since it collected information that is not directly comparable for each category. Most important, it reports occupations for racial minorities but not for ethnic groups, meaning that it reports the occupations of Asians but not of the Latino population in the Progressive era.[6] Adding to the confusion, very few of the minority musicians mentioned by Bagley would have listed music as their principal occupation; of necessity, they held separate "day jobs" well into the 1920s.[7]

The changing configurations of these racial and ethnic groups, different for Southern California and the north, shaped the cultures of the city's music making in the Progressive era and beyond. Differences in the experiences of each (as well as among the white majority, itself a jumble of ethnicities and languages) have much to do with geography ("regionally specific" in the quotation from Tomás Almaguer at the head of this chapter) and with the presence and relative influence of other minorities ("historically contingent"). Mexican and Asian minorities played larger roles regionally, interacting with the city's African Americans in the neighborhoods they shared, than in other parts of the United States.[8] The presence of various minorities and their roles in the white imagination, visible in the devising and chronicling of public events such as La Fiesta, in the city's political and theatrical history, and later in the movies, were always important in Los Angeles, as in other parts of the United States. Almaguer's statement was designed for a general history of white supremacy in Los Angeles, and it also applies to music making within that history, including the music making of the New Negroes, which is the focus of this chapter.[9] Because the cultures of these ethnic and racial groups were uniquely intertwined in Los Angeles, I offer an anecdote that illustrates the state of the white imagination and the role of music in it, then a few details about these groups of "others."

A formal celebration intended to honor the fiftieth anniversary of the Emancipation Proclamation was scheduled on the eve of Lincoln's birthday in 1913. The *Los Angeles Evening Express* carried a story headlined "Dr. Locke to Repeat Lecture for Negroes." The title of his address alone tells us what a different world it was: "Was Abraham Lincoln Justified in Issuing the Emancipation Proclamation; or Is the Negro Making Good?" Music was promised: "A chorus of the combined choirs of the negro *[sic]* churches of the city, under the direction of Rev. T. J. Hill, pastor of the Mount Zion Baptist church, will sing old plantation melodies." The announcement incorporates an unusual detail, clearly turning the customary local practice on its ear: "The floor of the main auditorium will be reserved for negroes until 7:50 P.M. All the rest of the large auditorium will be open to white people." It concludes, "Cordial invitations are extended to all people to be present. It probably will be the most notable gathering of the kind ever held in Los Angeles."[10] Blacks saw Los Angeles as a relatively open city, but second-class citizenship, including restrictions on where they might sit in white churches, remained a fact of life for its people of color.

By 1890, much of the older Spanish-speaking population had assimilated into the general middle-class white population, at least to a degree.[11] The number of working-class Mexican residents increased when heavy labor was needed for construction projects in the 1890s and surged again during the period of civil war in Mexico after 1910. By 1920, one source estimated their number as about 50 percent higher than the 21,598 reported in the U.S. Census.[12] These new workers often considered themselves temporary residents, resisting the idea of taking U.S. citizenship.[13] Most of the recent arrivals were crowded into substandard housing courts in an area near the original Plaza, north of downtown. When Union Station was constructed in the 1930s on the site of the old Plaza, the Mexicans moved to Boyle Heights or to the increasingly ghettoized Central Avenue district.

After 1910, in keeping with the growing Mexican population, Spanish-language theatrical activity expanded.[14] (By the time the old Los Angeles Theater was torn down in the 1950s, for example, it had been a Spanish-language movie house for some years.) Hollywood studios accommodated Spanish-speaking audiences worldwide by making separate Spanish-language versions of many films, using the same sets and costumes and first translating the written text in the subtitles of silent films, later dubbing in the spoken dialogue.[15] Among Hispanics to work early in the film colony was the actress Beatriz Michelena Myrtle Gonzales; Dolores Del Rio achieved fame somewhat later. Angela Gomez, born in San Bernardino, was an extra in some three hundred movies. Guatemala-born José Rodríguez worked in radio in the 1920s and wrote trenchant music and film criticism for the liberal *Rob Wagner's Script* starting in 1930. Mexican-born baritone Rodolfo Hoyos did radio programs, recorded, appeared in films, sang in an occasional local opera production, and organized a zarzuela troupe.

Cantonese-speaking Chinese were present in Los Angeles from the 1850s. Mostly male, they found employment as laundry men, market gardeners, agricultural workers, ranch hands, and road builders. More severely ghetto-bound than either Mexicans or African Americans and more often subjected to violent repression at the hands of the white population, the Chinese were also displaced from the Union Station area in the 1930s; they were moved to the present Chinatown area, north of downtown. Occasional entertainers traveled from the much larger San Francisco Chinatown, and in 1890 a Chinese theater featuring an orchestra of six (later eleven) musicians who produced, to Bagley's ears, "far eastern cacophony," opened at least briefly.[16] A few years later, a six-piece Chinese band performed at a fair at its opening, drawing imitations from a white band on subsequent evenings.[17] Given the repeated early bans on Chinese immigration and the periodic anti-Chinese violence, their survival is impressive.

In the 1890s, farmworkers were brought from Japan to work in the produce industry. In the 1920s, their success led to restrictions on their right to own property or to attain citizenship.[18] The considerable interest among middle-class whites in Japanese culture (shown, for example, in the "oriental" borrowings of dancer Ruth St. Denis and the success of a few touring Japanese dancers such as Michio Ito) was offset by politically fostered hostility toward working-class Japanese residents. The level of white paranoia about various minorities is exemplified in this report from the weekly *Los Angeles Graphic* of a new play on a Japanese theme that was about to open in October 1912: "That the white race's dominance of the world is doomed to be overthrown by a wave of Japanese conquest and that the awakened Orientals will rule supreme is the hypothesis upon which is founded 'The Typhoon,' which will be given its first Pacific coast presentation by McKee Rankin, Margaret Drew and company at the Mason Opera House."[19]

The presence of minorities other than blacks in substantial numbers had another effect. White hostility toward nonwhite "others" often focused on Asians and Mexicans, inadvertently creating a buffer that made African Americans targets for white violence less often, one reason why blacks considered Southern California a relatively desirable place to live. This chapter focuses on aspects of the black music-making experience.

. . .

Los Angeles' geographic distance from the more heavily populated and longer-established areas of the United States meant that relatively few African Americans had the means to settle there. Within the physically expansive city, they were relatively spread out in the early years, divided among communities around Holmes Avenue, Temple Street, the West Side, and Central Avenue. (The latter district became the dominant one.) Only in the 1920s were sharply segregated neighborhoods formed and restrictive covenants adopted by the city, later than for the larger eastern U.S. cities. Racially mixed schools were the rule. Brought to Los Angeles as an infant in 1905, Arna Bontemps, later a prominent Harlem Renaissance poet, reported being the only black child in the Ascot Street elementary school on East Forty-fifth Street, two blocks east of South Central Avenue, and of his parents' evident wish to "forget the past" and assimilate.[20] Strong music programs in community, church, and the public school system gave a number of well-known musicians their start and influenced the character of their music making; this was true for whites as well as blacks. Given the limitations on other opportunities, however, these school music programs were particularly important to the careers of blacks, especially black men. They contributed to another characteristic that the LA black population shared with the white majority, namely, a high level of musical literacy.

According to Henry Sampson's *The Ghost Walks*, the first large black minstrel companies to tour in the Far West were Callender's Georgia Minstrels, featuring Billy Kersands and the Hyers Sisters, both in 1883.[21] Lew Johnson's Baby Boy Colored Minstrels came west in 1887 and 1888. None of these apparently came to Los Angeles, though the smaller McKanlass Colored Comedy Company got as far south as Santa Barbara in 1887. Richards and Pringle's Famous Georgia Minstrels, featuring Billy Kersands and others, played the Los Angeles Theater in 1889. In December 1889, their performance at the Grand Opera House was described in the pages of the *Los Angeles Times:* "As fine a brass band as ever traveled through California or any other state. Every member is an artist and the show is first class. One of the best features of the show was the performance of W. G. Huff on a small harmonica, and the singing by the quartette was exceedingly fine."[22]

The following year, Lew Johnson's Minstrels came. In the fall, McCabe and Young's Operatic Minstrels appeared at the cavernous Hazard's Pavilion with thirty-five performers, opening their performances with an "Operatic Flower-garden" and concluding with "Our Diplomatic Olio." Thereafter minstrel companies, both white and black (and occasionally one mixing white and black performers), appeared regularly. In 1898, W. C. Handy was a part of Mahara's Big City Minstrel and Pickaninny Show at the Los Angeles Theater. James P. Johnson also appeared with his A Trip to Coontown company, and Will Marion Cook managed an appearance in this period as well.

The black artists who performed what we now think of as the European classical or operatic repertoire early on included the Hyers Sisters (originally from Sacramento), Sissieretta Jones (the "Black Patti"), and Flora Batson, all singers.[23] When they made return visits, as all of the singers did, they often came as part of larger companies that performed in a wide variety of styles, comfortably mixing what now would be considered the "popular" with the "classical." The Hyers Sisters returned with a company playing "Out of Bondage, or, Before and After the War." When Jones came back the first time, she appeared in the smaller Music Hall with the Nashville Jubilee Singers.[24] A few years later, she lent her nickname to a larger company, Black Patti's Troubadours. The company's 1901–2 tour included nearly a month in California, more than half of it in Southern California.[25] Its performances began with sketches employing the expected stereotypes; the cakewalk (newly popularized by the wildly successful team of Williams and Walker, originally formed in California) ended the first half. After the intermission, an operatic "kaleidoscope" offered scenes from the most popular operas, such as *Faust, Lucia di Lammermoor,* and *Il Trovatore,* including arias sung by Jones.[26] Black entertainers remained popular in Los Angeles; at least one all-California vocal group, the Imperial Quartette, is reported in 1904, organized by L. E. Behymer, who, charlatan that he was, had an eye for promising performers.[27] In an East Coast turnabout of sorts, the local community of Watts became the setting for a stereotype-laden Broadway musical a few years later.[28]

. . .

By the turn of the twentieth century, signs of change were appearing, and public entertainments reflected, however imperfectly, changing realities off-stage. A variety of new local organizations devoted to the general welfare was emerging in LA's black community. The Los Angeles Forum (organized in 1903) was a men's discussion group that encouraged a diversity of opinion on current issues, enabling its participants to develop their ideas but not functioning as an action group. Very likely the Sojourner Truth Industrial Club (from 1904) for women was responsible for starting a YWCA for women of color. Both of these met at the First AME Church. A day nursery opened at the Wesley Chapel AME in 1907. Branches of national organizations with differing approaches to black progress were established. W. E. B. Du Bois visited Los Angeles in 1913 to kick off a chapter of the National Association for the Advancement of Colored People (NAACP). A chapter of Marcus Garvey's United Negro Improvement Association (UNIA) attracted much attention (and a much larger membership) in 1919, and two years after that a chapter of the Urban League, an offshoot of Booker T. Washington's Tuskegee movement, was organized.[29]

Other local changes were appearing on the horizon as well. The weekly *California Eagle,* long the dominant black paper, had begun publication in 1879. Few (if any) issues survive before 1913, leaving the impression—not necessarily correct—that the city's African Americans rarely spoke for themselves in print in those early years.[30] Charlotta Bass, who edited the *Eagle* for several decades, later published a collection of her editorials that shows her paper's longtime role in the community's activism.[31] (In terms of music making, the *Eagle*'s relative social conservatism prevented it from covering commercial music making in the news columns, despite its importance to the black community. It can be tracked, however, through ads that appeared there.) The pioneering librarian-writer Delilah M. Beasley (1871–1934) provided a column, "Activities among Negroes," for the (white) *Oakland Tribune* (in Northern California), partly intended to counter the negative stereotypes that were routine in the white press. Beasley traveled to Southern California repeatedly over a period of eight years, gathering information for her landmark *Negro Trail Blazers of California* (1919). In it, she lists a number of church organists and music teachers in Los Angeles.[32]

Characteristics of the black community reported in the U.S. Census (however imperfectly) are significant to music making. Blacks in Los Angeles were far better educated than their generally low-paid, menial occupations suggested.[33] The census shows a literacy rate for blacks that was much higher than for urban areas nationally (93.5 percent in 1910 versus 82.4 percent in all urban areas and a horrendous 64 percent in rural areas), especially for persons under age forty-five.[34] Music performance, always a precarious occupation, offered one of the few open professions. In the 1910 Census, only ministers were more numerous than musicians among blacks for the professional occupations listed; very few other professions included any blacks at all. As with musicians in the white population, the women were often teachers and the men, performers. Segregation extended to union membership, formally closing certain jobs to black musicians and keeping their wages low. Even so, more blacks entered the professions in the decade of the 1910s, including music, which remained very prominent. By 1920, there were forty-nine clergymen, twenty-one actors, and ten lawyers who were black men, along with a handful of other professional people to go with the forty-eight musicians and music teachers. Among black women, there were twenty-five schoolteachers, nineteen trained nurses, and sixteen actors, along with twenty-five musicians and music teachers. The groundwork was laid for the emergence of a more substantial, educated black middle class in the next decade.

Concert music had a prominent place in the black community and in the training of its musicians, more than later writers have wanted to recognize because of its growing, and increasingly painful, class associations. John S. Gray and William T. Wilkins operated music schools that trained generations of African Americans to read and perform so-called serious music.[35] Black churches had vigorous music programs. Modern authors Jacqueline DjeDje and Bette Yarbrough Cox, who collected oral histories of some musicians active before 1920, describe early black church music (especially a unique regional form of gospel) and concert music, respectively.[36] Large choirs existed in the churches and in the community; Jester Hairston, Hall Johnson, Eva Jessye, Freita Shaw Johnson, and Mrs. A. C. Bilbrew were among their directors. Bilbrew was also a prominent church organist, along with Elmer Bartlett. (Bartlett, part of the NAACP's old guard, was a stalwart in bringing off Du Bois's *The Star of Ethiopia* in the face of the boycott described below.) An independent gospel style developed at the Azusa Street Church, replaced only after World War II by Thomas A. Dorsey's Chicago gospel style. Concerts and musicales were abundant in the black churches. Very early in his career, in 1918, famous tenor Roland Hayes performed before an integrated audience in Los Angeles, said to be a first for the city.

Figure 23.   Alma Hightower (at piano, back to camera) with students, 1939.
Photo by Fred William Carter. SECURITY PACIFIC COLLECTION/Los Angeles Public
Library.

Among other exceptional performers were pianist Lorenza Jordan-Cole, violinist Bessie Dones, and singer Ivan Harold Browning. All of these taught,
to the enormous benefit of the community. Several teachers were prominent and notably successful in preparing jazz musicians. Alma Hightower,
drummer and bandleader, led a WPA "training" band that included Melba
Liston, Clora Bryant, Doris Jarrett, Minnie Hightower, and Dexter Gordon;
she also taught Vi Redd, saxophonist. All of these had careers as jazz musicians.[37] In 1936, Samuel Browne began the legendary teaching career at Jefferson Middle School that produced many of the black studio musicians and
jazz artists who emerged after World War II.

  In sum, it is clear that the black population was relatively small, unusually literate, and relatively stable, prosperous, and conservative. Bontemps
paints a loving picture of this Los Angeles in the novel *God Sends Sunday*
(1931) and again in his combined history-reminiscence *They Seek a City*.
He gave the generic label "Mudtown" to Watts and the semirural Furlong
Tract.[38] The town he describes grew up around an old farmhouse in an area
surrounded by railroad tracks, first subdivided, then overtaken by an influx

of laborers, first Mexican, then African American. Streets were unpaved, cows and goats wandered the area, and housing ranged from hovels to substantial cottages, yet[39]

> there are those who remember this community fondly. Some talk about the picnics held in a lantern-hung summerhouse and under the pepper trees that surrounded it. They recall ribbons and bright silks in the Fourth of July sunshine, and bands playing under the trees at night. They mention unforgettable services in one or the other of the two little Mudtown churches, particularly the Sunday night when the quartet of boys from Tuskegee gave a program which started folks to humming spirituals they thought had been left down home. . . .
> And in this Mudtown, as in all the others, there was a sprinkling of the sheltered homes of educated Negroes trying earnestly to inspire and maintain ideals and aspirations in their children. . . . Among the offspring of this group were some girls who would soon become public school teachers in the Los Angeles system; some boys who were headed for better-than-average pulpits; a prospective dentist was among them, a lawyer, and a couple of doctors—all in a community without a sidewalk, a community served by a single street lamp.[40]

These became the schoolteachers, musicians, and ministers counted in the 1920 Census. Bontemps claimed as his home this modest working-class community of southern migrants, Mexicans, and others, now conflated with Watts and renamed "South Central" in the twenty-first century, and remarks that it also produced several high achievers (in addition to himself) in the arts and the entertainment world, among them the actor James Lowe, the UCLA football and track star Woody Strowe, the prizefighter Babe Slaughter, the Hollywood architect Paul Revere Williams, and the trumpeter Arthur Whetsol.[41]

.　.　.

By 1920, after several decades of steady growth in both numbers and level of education, the stage was set for a further flowering of black cultural activity, a far western version of the New Negro movement with its own style. In it we can see the fruits of unusually strong educational opportunity, increasing prosperity, and geographic mobility, all gained in the face of increasing white racism. Among the more numerous black voices that appeared after World War I, I have already quoted Arna Bontemps, who became a well-known Harlem Renaissance figure. Wallace Thurman, later a playwright and editor, produced *The Blacker the Berry* (1932), set in Los Angeles, where he lived before going to New York. Thurman's novel satirizes the hierarchy of color within the black community as well as outside it, especially at the University of Southern California, where his heroine is a student who is shunned by her lighter-skinned fellows solely because of her unusually dark skin.

Fragmentary runs of at least fifteen black newspapers published at some point in the 1920s or 1930s in Los Angeles (and five more in Oakland) survive and speak to the community's modest prosperity as well as the diverse range of opinion it contained. In the 1920s, in addition to the *California Eagle,* there were the *New Age Dispatch,* the *Negro World,* the *Pacific Defender,* the *Pacific Enterprise,* the *Western Clarion,* the *Western Dispatch,* and the *Western Herald.* More followed, even in the lean years of the Great Depression.[42] Most were weeklies. Some were church-oriented. Marcus Garvey's United Negro Improvement Association had a journal that served its large following. The middle-class nature of even this group, whose hallmark nationally was its attraction for the urban poor, is obvious from its pattern of oftentimes holding meetings and fundraisers in middle-class homes after the pervasive model of women's clubs.

Membership in the local chapter of the NAACP, never very large, dwindled in the face of emerging competition from the UNIA in the early '20s. The Junior Division, organized in 1924 and led most prominently by James McGregor, Naida Portia McCullough (pianist), and Fay M. Jackson, attempted to revive the moribund chapter. McGregor and McCullough were students at the University of Southern California; Jackson, a recent graduate, was already writing columns for the *Eagle.* The iconoclastic Harold Bruce Forsythe (of whom more below) was still in high school but was closely associated with all three. Members of the Junior Division self-consciously styled themselves "New Negroes" and sought to use their university training to advocate for black freedom and progress. At one point some of them produced a letterhead that styled them as "The Iconoclasts / Down with Tradition."[43] They took their inspiration from W. E. B. Du Bois, Langston Hughes, their own Arna Bontemps, and other emerging black artists and intellectuals. Seeking a way to express their aspirations, they hit on the ambitious idea of staging Du Bois's pageant, *The Star of Ethiopia,* which had been produced a decade earlier in New York and Washington, DC. Their venue was to be the Hollywood Bowl, a bold commitment given the level of discrimination in that neighborhood.

A generational confrontation soon arose. When Du Bois himself traveled west to supervise the production, he backed the older, more established membership, taking the casting and direction of the pageant away from the Junior Division. Suddenly shut out of the pageant's management, the would-be insurgent young people promptly quit the project and declared a boycott. The production took place anyway but was poorly attended. Recriminations about the resulting deficit of over seven hundred dollars went on for several years.

Presently the same group of young people focused on a weekly literary journal, *Flash*. The magazine survived for a little more than a year, in 1929. Fay M. Jackson, its editor, later served as the Hollywood reporter for the Associated Negro News Service; James McGregor was associate editor. In hindsight but unrecognized at the time, Harold Bruce Forsythe is the most important writer to emerge in *Flash*. Like Bontemps, Forsythe was brought to Los Angeles as a small child. He was trained there as a musician and was a gifted pianist as well as a composer and writer, studying with Wilkins, McCullough, and Charles E. Pemberton, the last a long-time (white) faculty member at USC. Some of Forsythe's writing suggests a familiarity with theosophy, perhaps gleaned in part from the teachings of Dane Rudhyar. A few years after *Flash* folded, Forsythe edited probably no more than two issues of another, even more ephemeral journal, the *Hamitic Review*.[44] Later, having come to appreciate the monumental challenge of expressing the African American experience in terms of the European-based cultural tradition with which it was so troublesomely entangled, Forsythe wrote passionately about the music of William Grant Still, who he believed had uniquely mastered that challenge. Ill health prevented him from realizing his own multifaceted promise.[45]

.   .   .

William Grant Still came to Los Angeles in 1934 and composed four of his five symphonies and all eight of his operas there. Other works from his Los Angeles years include film music, arrangements for radio and TV, ballets, and chamber music. (Will Vodery, who had given Still a hand earlier, was the first African American to work as an arranger in the movie studios.) Still came west initially to prepare the orchestrations for Paul Whiteman's weekly radio broadcasts of the *Old Gold Hour* in 1929–30. Finding the atmosphere more comfortable than that of New York City, where he had worked since 1919, he returned to Los Angeles permanently after winning a Guggenheim fellowship in 1934. Later he worked with Langston Hughes on his second opera, *Troubled Island* (produced in New York in 1949 but composed in the 1930s), and with Katherine Garrison Chapin on *And They Lynched Him on a Tree*, a protest piece that premiered in New York City in 1940. In 1939, he married Los Angeles pianist Verna Arvey, the daughter of eastern European Jewish immigrants; she provided the rest of his librettos.[46]

He worked in the film colony occasionally and continued to make popular arrangements (an important source of income in addition to his several fellowships) but mainly composed concert music and opera in his Los Angeles years. In the 1930s and '40s, his music was very widely performed by symphony orchestras in the United States.[47]

Black engagement with concert music in the New Negro period was vital but was already being ignored by most black intellectuals. Alain Locke is an important exception, for he had written of Still's controversial *From the Land of Dreams* after its 1925 New York premier: "Up to the present, the resources of Negro music have been tentatively exploited in only one direction at a time,—melodically here, rhythmically there, harmonically in a third direction. . . . The modernistic, *From the Land of Dreams*, by Grant Still . . . [is an] experimental tapping in still other directions into the rich veins of this new musical ore."[48] Locke recognized the work's novelty and, with a seemingly unique perception, assumed that Still had tapped "the resources of Negro music" to achieve his new effects. (White critics expected to hear jazz from a black composer and were sometimes querulous when they failed to find it.)[49] A dozen years later he remarked, after the premiere of Still's second symphony, "It is so strange that nowhere among Negro musicians do you find any really intellectual interest in new works and experimenting," but Locke himself contributed little beyond generalities about this generality.[50]

For that reason, Forsythe's work as a writer (unpublished and unknown to Locke) is the more important. The draft novel, variously titled "Masks" and "Frailest Leaves," satirizes middle-class black music making and what Forsythe perceived as its superficiality.[51] Yet he was enormously interested in William Grant Still's work, finding in it more than hints of West African culture and other characteristics that he read as subversions of white racism. A few quotations from his monograph on Still, "A Study in Contradictions," give an idea of his views on the local black concert culture:

It is increasingly difficult to write of a Negro of talent. The Negro press itself is impossible. Each day there appears in its columns lengthy accounts of tea-party musicales. . . . The Negro is not the prodigiously talented individual his sheets assure him that he is, as he is not so downtrodden and forlorn as these same rags contend. Quite to the contrary he seems to be a race of harmless and polite mediocrities. . . . Some men, [Countee] Cullen, [Langston] Hughes, [Wallace] Thurman, [Claude] McKay, [Eric] Walrond, [Frederick] Douglass; have done excellent work. Perhaps in Jean Toomer he has a genius, as in Walrond. In [Roland] Hayes and [Paul] Robeson he has men of very exceptional talent; but in the art with which we have to deal, he has very little to offer on the creative side. . . .

The intelligent white press is of course suspicious of Aframerican composers. . . . the Negro has little inclination or aptitude for music. A facile and fundamental sense of rhythm and harmony, and a group of excellent folk songs have given rise to the absurd nonsense about the Aframerican's "inherent musical genius."

The intransigence of Forsythe's early activity with the Junior Division of the NAACP did not fade; indeed, he was not an easy figure to work with. Yet, alone among black critics, he understood Still's contribution: "But for the inevitable exception . . . This man, William Grant Still, is without doubt the most talented Negro ever to compose music in America, and the only man of his race to abandon the past on one hand, to cling to it successfully on the other, and to make a successful and original artistic cohesion of the two."[52]

Another column, which may or may not have been published in some form, spoke of Still's and Hall Johnson's appearances at the Hollywood Bowl in 1936:

Still's music, for many years has been hailed by ofay critics, in America and abroad.

. . . we are concerned with the Amerafric of Angelean denomination, and it is with his rheumatic intellectual gasps that we take issue.

. . . If we think that a few isolated and brilliant examples of the Amerafric can materially aid the degraded condition of the rest of us, we're sadly mistaken. Group action alone can do that. . . .

Hall Johnson, who has handled the Negro folk-music with greater artistry than anyone else, who has stripped it of the gaudy harmonic trappings other musicians have given it, who has restored the fervor the ofay arrangers have taken from it, and who has restored it to its final character, the fervent gaunt splendor and passionate religious implication that marked its inception. William Grant Still, who has looked behind the Spiritual into the seething ancestral stuffs within him and about him. Still, who has pushed a vision of the blues and the jazz impulse far beyond any other composer's ability. Still, who with a curious inner alchemy has wrought an eloquent, exquisitely textured music. Hall Johnson has summed up the Spiritual and the worksong and made them artistic mechanisms. Still is both a fulfillment and a promise of what a composer of genuine talent can do.[53]

Forsythe agreed to supply an introduction for the score of Still's ballet *Sahdji*, completed in 1931.[54] At 110-plus pages, it turned out to be unsuitably long; very likely Still considered its extravagant literary style inappropriate as well. An excerpt is illustrative of both Forsythe's enthusiasm for newly available materials on African culture and his fantasy-laden imagination:

> The Chanter is phylogenetically paramount. He is the deep, heavy stream of ethnic history. He is more than a chorus, more than a type. . . . Sahdji is a floating, flaming bubble on the surface of the Chanter. . . .
>
> She assumes the form of the Fire-god's child. Konombju has no persona or no appearance. . . . He is a link cementing Sahdji to the Chanter. . . . Mrabo is even more vague. He is a mere beauty-illusion of Sahdji, the dream for which all aesthetic emotionalism is a longing.[55]

Forsythe's work, hyper quality and all, suggests a promising critical approach to concert music by black composers, including Still's, that has yet to be thoroughly pursued. It is regrettable that he never had the opportunity to write about Still's *Africa*, an orchestral suite, or the much better-known *Afro-American Symphony*.

. . .

In Los Angeles' smallish African American community, the music making most fully endorsed by the middle class (and covered by the *California Eagle*) took place in church, sometimes in the form of concerts and of course as part of the services. These "genteel" concerts, in churches, clubs, and other public places, are often now dismissed as merely emulative of performances by white artists, yet they played an important role, rather different from such concerts given by white musicians.[56] Their later reputation has suffered partly because they did not achieve the universal success of black "popular" music—ragtime, jazz, blues, gospel, and other popular music with roots in African American culture—across most boundaries of race, ethnicity, class, and gender. The class connotation of these concerts came to be more obvious and less supportable for black audiences much sooner and much more definitively than concert music ever did for white audiences. Many saw racial overtones in the sharp distinction drawn between the classical and the popular by white critics, reinforcing their suspicion of these "genteel" concerts. The differences greatly frustrated another generation of black critics, impatient in the 1960s for long-delayed political and social change.[57] The association of jazz with masculinity and dismissal of concert music as effeminate among many white males may also have influenced this outcome. More practically, blacks who were expert concert musicians could not make a living performing in all-black venues and generally could not cross the color line to play in symphonies, sing in opera companies, or teach on white faculties. At least partly as a matter of necessity, they became church musicians or chose to perform various kinds of commercial music whose audience was white as well as black. Superb bassist Charles Mingus (1922–78), who grew up in Watts and started on the cello, is the most famous of these.[58]

It may be time to reconsider the total omission of black concert music from critical appraisal, if only to complete the historical record. But there is an even better reason than that. In these concerts, blacks were concertizing for one another, adapting the European tradition for themselves rather than for white audiences. The emulation of middle-class white concert music was never literal; black concert music always had its own inflections. (By contrast, more popular black music is almost always heard in forms commodified for mainly white audiences or adjusted by its black performers for white middle-class paying audiences. The difference is a matter of degree, not of principle.) Ignoring this aspect of black music making is suggestive of the sexism visible in white male critics' low opinion of the white music club culture of the same period. Indeed, black composers of both sexes have suffered (along with white women) because the revolutionary nature of their speech in these white-male-dominated genres has not been sufficiently recognized. Beyond that, the musical distinctions among these genres was never so absolute as white writers have maintained. The role of concert music in the training of jazz musicians and in the materials they used demands further exploration.

Many popular entertainers later found their way to the film colony in Hollywood, where they struggled to maintain their personal integrity even as they were expected to play stereotyped, menial roles by white filmmakers. In 1916, early in the film industry, Noble M. Johnson founded the Los Angeles–based Lincoln Motion Picture Company, one of the earliest and most successful of the black film companies, abandoning it in 1921 in favor of an economically viable career as a bit player in stereotyped black and Native American roles.[59] Arranger Will Vodery, actors Clarence Muse, Bill "Bojangles" Robinson, and the Nicholas brothers are among the many entertainers who remained in California and continued to work in Hollywood, often biting their tongues while working the stereotypes to their advantage when they could.

· · ·

As one of the focuses for the migrations that were fundamental to the New Negro movement, Los Angeles made little-known but important contributions to the early development of jazz. Black musicians from New Orleans and elsewhere had early found their way to San Francisco, still a much larger city. A few blocks of rough black-operated dives had appeared there along Pacific Street, collectively labeled the Barbary Coast by the late 1890s. One of the centers where a protojazz elaboration of ragtime was performed, the Barbary Coast burst into the consciousness of the white middle-class public with a series of new dances having a New Orleans flavor, starting soon after 1900 with the shimmy, or the shim-me-sha-wobble. After 1908 came the turkey trot, bunny hug, chicken glide, Texas Tommy, pony prance, grizzly bear, and other imaginatively named close and acrobatic dances.[60] Sid Le Protti's So Different Orchestra was the most active performing group, gradually incorporating features of the new style.

San Francisco's Barbary Coast, which was commercially viable only through its ancillary nonmusical and often extralegal activities, was shut down in the course of World War I. Some of the musicians remained in the Bay Area, holding day jobs and performing on weekends. Others migrated south, where there was a much larger African American population. Along with new migrants from New Orleans, they brought the new style to the budding Central Avenue district in LA, where, after the centuries-old fashion of itinerant entertainers and migrating musicians, they adapted it to local practices, generating new hybrid styles in the process.[61]

In Los Angeles' relatively conservative atmosphere, local musicians and much of the audience (white and black) had some formal music training and were quite familiar with aspects of the European concert and operatic tradition. Musicians were expected to read music readily and perform in many styles. They played, among other places, in the street, on the back of trucks, and at prizefights.[62] Leaders of several local bands that played jazz required their musicians to play from written arrangements. Of the New Orleans musicians who came to Los Angeles, those who were formally trained (many of them Creole, reflecting class distinctions significant in New Orleans) were more successful than those who relied entirely on memory and did not read the notes. Bill Johnson and Ernest Coycault had played in Los Angeles as early as 1908; Coycault remained and Johnson returned in 1912, possibly with Jelly Roll Morton. Freddie Keppard had arrived by 1914, the year he formed the Original Creole Band, made up of six New Orleans musicians who had also emigrated westward. This last ensemble was "discovered" while entertaining at a boxing match in Los Angeles and hired to perform as part of an act on the Pantages vaudeville circuit in that year. (One wonders whether our old friend Behymer was part of the picture; in any case, the crossover between professional athletic events and other kinds of public entertainment, along with the ubiquity of music, is visible here.) For the next four years, the Original Creole Band toured the United States, playing in vaudeville houses and making their version of the New Orleans style, still often termed "ragtime," known to a wide audience. In 1917, Jelly Roll Morton began what turned into a stay of five years, pursuing a variety of business interests along with music.[63] Trombonist Kid Ory, who arrived in 1919 and also stayed for five years before joining Louis Armstrong in Chicago, organized a series of recordings on the Sunshine label in 1921. These are usually considered the first recordings of instrumental jazz by an African American band; their style is clearly Dixieland.

Several bands and musicians stayed in the Los Angeles area, anchoring the Central Avenue music scene and launching the careers of many well-known musicians. From 1919, the Spikes Brothers ran a music business on Central Avenue that served as a booking agency for black musicians and became the forerunner of the black union, Local 767.[64] One of Reb Spikes's bands was the Legion Club 45s. Other important bandleaders and bands included Mutt Carey, Harry Southard's Black and Tan Jazz Orchestra, Sonny Clay's Stompin' Six, Charlie Lawrence's Sunnyland Jazz Band, Paul Howard's Quality Serenaders, Les Hite, and Curtis Mosby's Dixieland Blue Blowers. Lionel Hampton, who achieved international fame for his vibraphone playing in the late 1930s, got his start as a drummer with Hite, Howard, and Mosby.

In his novel *God Sends Sunday*, Arna Bontemps describes a celebration in the Furlong Tract–Watts neighborhood that strongly resonates with later descriptions of early jazz performances outside the city limits, where a city-imposed midnight closing hour could not be enforced. The weekly festivities began in the afternoon, when whole families, dressed in their Sunday best, arrived at a park with a bandstand and a slightly decrepit merry-go-round. Some of them set up booths with things to sell, mostly foodstuffs; gaming concessions and gypsies appeared. "As the park darkened, a portion of the folks dispersed. The ironic flying horses of the merry-go-round stopped, their heads still unbended, and the exhausted young riders toppled from their backs. It became quite dark; beneath a remote tree where there had been a fire some coals glowed softly, uttering a faint smoke like breath. Soon afterward the pavilion was lighted and the dance music commenced. . . . 'Let's strut.'"[65]

Trombone, clarinet, piano, and cymbals are the instruments mentioned in Bontemps's narrative.

> Directly in front of the musicians there was a bit of space where the floor was brighter than elsewhere because of the extra lights for the orchestra. . . . A flashy pair were showing a new dance that they had picked up in the city, on Central Avenue, in some of the less respectable

places, and were attracting considerable attention. It was a dance in which the shoulders and hips twitched rhythmically, but in which the feet made no steps. . . . In those days it [the shimmy] was regarded as a low, unseemly dance, and the young country girls felt a little outraged at seeing it done there so boldly.[66]

Bontemps's description is consistent with Jelly Roll Morton's account of an enterprise he ran. The city had ordered the dance halls on Central Avenue (including Morton's) to close at midnight. "To get around the restriction he [Morton] 'went partners with Pops Woodward, the trombone player, and we opened up the Wayside Park at Leek's [also Leakes'] Lake out in Watts County [actually an incorporated city at the time]. There we could stay open all night.'" Around 1922, Morton was playing there on Thursdays and Saturdays, drawing large crowds ranging from families to young adults.[67]

．　　．　　．

Black musicians worked for much lower wages than white musicians, whether they played for all-white, all-black, or racially mixed audiences. Local 47 did not recruit the African American musicians who began to arrive in Los Angeles following World War I. As the Central Avenue clubs developed and expanded in the 1920s, black musicians formed a separate local, with help from "Lee" Bagley, the longtime union functionary who by then served as legal adviser to Local 47. Bagley's collection, now at USC, includes copies of the black local's bylaws (which he apparently wrote) and several of its directories. His role in organizing Local 767 and in maintaining the segregated locals is implicit in Marl Young's account of the integration of the two locals, which took place only in 1953. Young, a bandleader and an attorney who represented Local 767 in the complex post–World War II negotiations that led to the merger, reports that a difficult-to-achieve two-thirds vote of the black local was necessary in order to dissolve it so that the amalgamation could take place. Despite pressure from the American Federation of Musicians to merge the locals, with their very different assets, wage scales, and work rules, the board of Local 47 opposed the merger, yielding only after the proposal carried in a vote of the membership.[68]

African Americans and other minorities suffered greatly in the Depression of the 1930s. Of the WPA agencies that attempted to create jobs for the huge numbers of unemployed, the Federal Theatre Project proved a more reliable employer of minority musicians than did the more rigid Federal Music Project. With the start of World War II, the black population of Los Angeles soared, bringing further change and a new set of issues. Whether there was a distinct, laid-back "West Coast style" associated with jazz in the years of the New Negro movement is still not entirely clear. What is clear is that a lively jazz scene emerged out of the community's now-forgotten, rich music-making tradition that fostered the early careers of many later-famous musicians. Although much of the black community's varied music making is now unknown (true for other racial and ethnic minorities as well), the groundwork had been laid for the emergence in Los Angeles of post–World War II rhythm and blues as well as cool jazz.

13   Welcoming the Ultramodern

> A new music is being born facing the classical music of
> old and its belated imitations. . . . it is growing with a
> momentum that no old-fashioned argument may stay,
> that no personal preference may challenge.
>
> Program, New Music Society of California, first concert,
> October 22, 1925

"Southern California . . . probably has the smallest audience for new music
to be found anywhere," wrote Jerome Moross in the journal *Modern Music*
in 1941.[1] Henry Cowell's selection of Los Angeles as the site for the first
New Music Society concert in October 1925 has seemed a quixotic choice,
for Moross's judgment has been widely shared.[2] Indeed, by the time
Evenings on the Roof, the first long-running concert series in Los Angeles
devoted to high modernism, got started in 1939 (drawing minuscule audiences in its first seasons), several such series had come and gone in New
York, *Modern Music* was well into its second decade, Arnold Schoenberg
was ensconced at UCLA, and the Depression-era Federal Music Project had
just been reorganized. Yet it is a mistake to date high modernism in Los Angeles from the start of the Evenings on the Roof series. Actually, the city had
had a phase of receptiveness to the "ultramodern" in the early 1920s.

Los Angeles had a huge base of community music making in the 1920s.
From it came the enormous community sings of the late 1910s and the large
audiences for the Hollywood Bowl concerts and for many other kinds of
music. Contrary to more recent views, Cowell had every reason to expect
that from this base he could develop a receptive audience for his New Music
Society. In hopes of understanding why that did not happen, I start from a
description of music making in the city. One caveat—I shall use the terms
new, modernism, and *ultramodern* as they appeared at the time, without
venturing into the quicksand of precise definition.[3] As has been the case all
along, my choices of what to discuss are highly selective, probably even
more so here than earlier in this book.

Postcards from Los Angeles in the 1920s tend to show modest frame
farmhouses set amid groves of orange trees that extend for miles toward
snow-capped mountains, a reminder of the great physical beauty as well as

the semirural quality of the city even as its population approached and passed the million mark.[4] Music making, an important element of everyday life all along, was at a high point and growing, much of it seemingly unchanged in nature, although now it coexisted less comfortably with commercial mass culture, which was growing even faster.

A small but lively interest in the "new" is visible in the extensive press coverage of music-making events. The *Pacific Coast Musician,* at first a monthly, then a biweekly, was well established as the main reporter of the concert-giving activities of the local white musicians. It was aimed at the large population of music teachers and their students. *Los Angeles Saturday Night,* the latest in a series of weeklies and biweeklies that began in the 1890s with the *Los Angeles Capital* and continued with the *Western Graphic,* reported on the larger concert music events as part of its extensive coverage of the arts.[5] Most of the daily papers also maintained music critics, at least as stringers. At the *Times,* Isabel Morse Jones, once a member of the Los Angeles Women's Orchestra (and often assisted by Edwin Schallert at the paper), and the German-trained Bruno David Ussher, who arrived in 1919 at *Saturday Night* and later the *Hollywood Citizen-News,* were the most prominent, but the *LA Evening Express* and the *LA Examiner* also published music criticism regularly, thereby acknowledging the role concert music played in the lives of their readers.[6] For the most part, commercial music making at the local level could be followed through advertisements but was not covered by the paid reporting staff.

A promotional pamphlet published in 1927 outlines the city's massive and diffuse art music establishment in more detail but ignores much commercial music, including the vigorous activity on Central Avenue that we now celebrate, as well as that of the city's Asian and Mexican populations. Its writers saw their city as partaking of a spirit of freedom and cultural enterprise unique to the West, particularly Los Angeles:

> There is a spirit abroad throughout the entire western slope of the United States which is peculiarly favorable to a strong native art development. People, who come west from eastern cities and farms, undergo a subtle spiritual change of which they are scarcely conscious until they return to their old place of residence. Then they discover a lack of freedom, a sense of being cramped, a feeling that there are things impossible of attainment, and find themselves in a state of mind from which the Pacific slope with its vast distances, cheerful living conditions, natural, rather than traditional, mode of life, had entirely released them.[7]

The pamphlet enumerates the city's achievements in painting, sculpture, and architecture before getting around to music, where it focuses on large concerts and on school and club activities. Its list of musical institutions begins, as might be expected, with the Philharmonic and the Hollywood Bowl but continues with the Tandler Little Symphony (a struggling remnant of the old, now-defunct Symphony, retaining a certain social cachet), the Women's Orchestra (by now the oldest of its kind in the United States, illustrating the local staying power of the individuals and especially the ideas behind it); and community orchestras in Hollywood, Long Beach, and Glendale (newer, often semiprofessional). (More of these were organized later on.) These groups were supplemented by various school, church, theater, and even industrial orchestras.[8] The touring San Carlo Opera Company, a remnant of the premovie culture of traveling low-budget opera troupes, visited for three weeks every year, and the much more prestigious (i.e., high-budget) San Francisco Opera came for one.[9] Local chamber music ensembles, such as the Zoellner Quartet, toured widely.[10] Blanche Rogers Lott was the anchor of several respected series of piano-violin-cello trios and other ensembles from the late 1890s for three decades and more and founder of the Los Angeles Chamber Music Society. Paloma Schramm (later Baruch), once LA's favorite piano prodigy, was often heard in chamber concerts in the early 1920s. The Coleman Chamber Music Association in Pasadena, initiated by the local musician and patron Alice Coleman Batchelder, originated in 1926 and continues to this day. After sponsoring a chamber music festival in Ojai in 1926, Elizabeth Sprague Coolidge (of Coolidge Auditorium, Library of Congress, fame) backed other chamber concerts in Los Angeles; these are the proverbial tip of the iceberg.[11] Network radio was in its infancy, but local radio stations were already offering live music performances. By 1933, stations broadcasting concert music included KFI-KECA, KHJ, and KNX.[12]

The musical hierarchy implied by that 1927 pamphlet was now quite rigid. The Philharmonic, with its foreign-born conductors, all-male membership, and mostly European visiting soloists, had stood at the lonely peak from the moment of its founding in 1919, though it soon lent its prestige (and its repertoire) to the more democratic Hollywood Bowl with its much larger audiences. Adulatory star status and high fees were conferred on such traveling virtuosi as Heifetz, Piatigorsky, and Rubinstein, whose visits were still controlled by Behymer, though he now had competition from Merle Armitage's Auditorium Artist series. Plenty of newspaper space, though with fewer pictures and smaller headlines, was reserved for the far less well-rewarded activities of local performers, organizations, music patrons, and teachers, as well as the "resident" composers. The music clubs, whose multitudinous members were mostly women, provided the basic audience for all these activities, as did students from the classes of the numerous music teachers.

The popularity of music study is clear from the sheer number of music conservatories in Los Angeles. The Methodist-founded University of Southern California (USC) already had a large music school, which offered bachelor's and master's degrees and, surprising from our vantage point, actually turned a profit for the rest of the university. The University of California at Los Angeles (UCLA) was still known as the Southern Branch of the University of California and had its campus on Vermont Avenue, near downtown Los Angeles, though the present Westwood campus was already under construction.[13] In music, the Southern Branch offered only a normal (i.e., teacher-training) program; its students supplemented their work with classes at nearby California Christian College (later Chapman College, now in Orange County). The Hollywood Conservatory, Olga Steeb Piano School, Zoellner Conservatory, Institute of Musical Art, Los Angeles Music School Settlement, Los Angeles Conservatory, South West College, and fourteen more private schools offered various kinds of music programs to students of all ages, as did any number of individual teachers working from their own studios. There were nine schools of drama and dancing as well, among them the Denishawn School of Dancing and Related Arts, a spawning ground for modernism in dance, operated by Ruth St. Denis and Ted Shawn.[14]

Music clubs included oratorio and choral groups, opera study clubs, church choirs, industrial choruses, and school choruses. (The oldest of these, the all-male Ellis Club, a descendant of the old German singing societies, had been active since 1888; the Apollo and Lyric clubs were almost as old.) Some of these sponsored their own series of public concerts. The Wa-Wan (formerly Schubert) Club claimed to be the largest of the music clubs and was also one of the older ones, at nineteen, in 1926. The Women's Lyric Club acknowledged 130 members in a 1927 program. The Euterpe Opera Reading Club, which concentrated on low-budget, daytime concert performances of operas using local singers and piano accompaniment rather than orchestra, was able to expand its membership from 23 at its inception in 1925 to 956 after only five years of activity. No fewer than 178 women's clubs are included in the list of cultural resources mentioned in the 1927 pamphlet.

A sizable group of composers, including many women, was active in Los Angeles by 1926. Many composed (or had composed, since they included musicians retired from other cities) for local churches, schools, and clubs; some were established as teachers, patrons, critics, or performers. A few had wider reputations. A 1919 photo of the founders of the California Federation of Music Clubs includes many delegates from Los Angeles: composer–club performer–lecturer Charles Wakefield Cadman; composer-singer-publisher Carrie Jacobs Bond; patron-clubwomen-composers Abbie Norton Jamison, Bessie Bartlett Frankel, Gertrude Ross, and Grace W. Mabee; professor-composer George Stewart McManus; and singer-pianist-clubwoman Anna Ruzena Sprotte, all of them among the Southern California delegation to the state federation's first convention (see figure 18).[15] Fourteen years later, the *Who's Who in Music and Dance in Southern California*, designed to celebrate the area's achievements and opportunities, lists many composers, a third of them women, among its 520 names. By far the most prominent among them was still Cadman, permanently enriched by the success of one early song and assured a place in history as one of those rare Americans who had an opera produced and later revived at the Metropolitan Opera in New York.[16] Gertrude Ross, Homer Grunn, and Fannie Dillon were also frequently recognized.[17] Mary Carr Moore joined them in 1926, moving from San Francisco to teach at the Steeb school and presently at California Christian College/Chapman. The rather younger Elinor Remick Warren, with her winning combination of talent, continuing study, and strong financial backing, would eventually gain national recognition.[18] Most maintained teaching studios; some accompanied touring singers in their West Coast appearances. Dillon taught music at Los Angeles High School, where she almost certainly taught the young John Cage.

All in all, the city's resident composers were producing a surprising amount of music for a large audience, although little of their music was memorable.[19] This pre-émigré culture was dominated by women in terms of sheer numbers, but it always included a number of foreign-born male musicians and was always at least somewhat cognizant of its resident composers, providing them with enough support for survival. Although it has faded from view along with the culture that fostered it, this beehive of indigenous musical activity, centered in the very large white middle-class population, is sufficiently substantial that I have dubbed it the "first Los Angeles school" elsewhere.[20] The resident composers mostly labored in isolation from the rest of the country, working in the shadow of the domination of American art music by Europeans. They rarely received top billing, even in their own region. They were more conservative in their musical tastes and their politics than were most of the now better-known (and often younger) American "ultramodernists" of the same period. But opportunities were greater, especially for the women among them, in this rapidly growing young city than in more established centers, such as San Francisco or New York. Relatively few new composers emerged in the 1920s, and even fewer after that, however, yielding one small hint of the changes to come.

In a more democratic direction, music making cropped up in publicly supported programs. Partly as a result of a nationwide movement for subsidized urban recreation, the Los Angeles Department of Playground and Recreation under Glenn M. Tindall started a music program in 1927, institutionalizing the widespread, persistent belief in the power of music to improve the lives and characters of the city's residents as well as to hasten the "Americanization" of the immigrants among them. The playground programs included choruses and glee clubs as well as harmonica bands, ukulele orchestras, and "toy symphonies" for children "too young to understand or participate in a more advanced type of musical activity." The enormous population of do-it-yourself music makers among Los Angelenos is reflected in statistics from this program, however exaggerated they may be: in February 1927, 762 participants; twenty-eight months later, 613,463 participants—an eight hundred–fold increase.[21]

Most of this massive quantity of music making reflected the interests of the white middle class, who saw it as both a source of satisfaction and pride for themselves and a means to impart moral as well as musical values to workers and new arrivals, thereby helping to integrate them into the mainstream culture. Yet all the music making described so far in this chapter does not include the substantial numbers of (mostly male) working-class musicians employed in restaurants, hotels, and bars, let alone those working in the splendid new silent movie palaces. In the early 1920s, large orchestras were employed in seven of the largest movie theaters in Los Angeles. The orchestras sometimes gave free or low-priced Sunday morning concerts, playing complete numbers, giving their members opportunities to play solos, and providing satisfaction for themselves and their audiences as well.[22] The larger movie orchestras became less common as the decade progressed and producers found that fewer musicians were sufficient to support the drama (or the comedy).

• • •

One of the numerous fine pianists and teachers in the city, Olga Steeb, deserves attention here as a successful artist and teacher who remained open to the "new" in music. Steeb's school was the largest and most consistently successful of the many private conservatories that operated in Los Angeles during the 1920s and 1930s. By 1934 the school had its own building, complete with studios, an auditorium, and even living quarters for some of the teachers, on Wilshire Boulevard.[23] Such was Steeb's reputation that her school had several branches in the metropolitan area.

Born in Los Angeles in 1892 to musical German-born parents, Steeb

Figure 24. Olga Steeb. Her "Historic Recitals" in 1925–26 broke new ground in LA. Gift of Lillian Steeb French. Author's collection.

studied with Thilo Becker, whose students made a major contribution to the high level of piano playing prevalent there, as previously discussed. She passed the years 1909–15 in Berlin. The English-language *Continental Times* wrote: "Besides being the possessor of an enormous repertoire Miss Steeb is the possessor of a perfect technic, is not surpassed by any pianist in variety of tone color, has the rarely heard 'grand tone' and is wonderfully poetic in her readings, has absolutely no mannerisms and in gradation of power in crescendos and diminuendos no living artist surpasses if anyone equals her."[24] Two years after this initial story, she played nine concertos in the space of two weeks with the Berlin Philharmonic, one of several tours de force in the course of her career.[25] World War I broke out as she launched her career, forcing her to return home, her prospects further limited by the wave of anti-German feeling associated with the war.

In addition to her teaching, Steeb demonstrated her extraordinary memory and technical command in the series "Historic Recitals," surveying the piano repertoire with unprecedented breadth for Los Angeles, also in frequent chamber recitals. She made more than a dozen appearances with the Philharmonic, each time with a different concerto. On one occasion, she substituted for touring Russian virtuoso Mischa Levitski (1898–1941) on two hours' notice, playing a concerto by Saint-Saëns as if she had rehearsed it thoroughly. For this feat, both the orchestra musicians and the audience gave her a standing ovation. Steeb cherished a strong interest in the "new." She brought composer Mary Carr Moore to Los Angeles to teach music theory in her conservatory and pledged financial support for a revival of Moore's major American opera, *Narcissa,* though the Depression forced a long postponement of that project. Her support for the new extended to the current ultramoderns. She attended the first classes given by Arnold Schoenberg in Los Angeles in 1935, contributing by performing the music examples for his lectures. Late in December 1941, a few weeks after the United States entered World War II, Steeb died of cancer. Within a year, her school had disappeared.[26] We have little direct evidence of her work as a performer. All that survives of her art as a concert pianist are two short Duo-Art piano rolls, two Edison disks, and a few acetate records.

·   ·   ·

Several patrons put their individual stamps on the concert music scene. Most prominent was William Andrews Clark, Jr., founder of the Philharmonic. Bessie Bartlett Frankel was a prominent supporter of the Philharmonic and chamber music in Los Angeles. Daughter of a longtime music store owner, A. G. Bartlett, and trained as a musician, as were many other patrons, Frankel became a powerful opponent of the new.[27] Florence Irish was another supporter of the Philharmonic, taking over many administrative responsibilities for the Bowl in the 1930s and '40s.

Among the friends and supporters of Artie Mason Carter, founder of the Hollywood Bowl concerts and their manager until 1926, was Aline Barnsdall, who briefly but significantly supported Henry Cowell's New Music, an unlikely adventure in musical modernism in Los Angeles. Less firmly attached to Los Angeles than the other patrons described here and not musically trained as the others were, Barnsdall was only peripherally interested in music, although she made some key financial contributions to the Bowl in its early years.[28] She had sponsored innovative theatrical productions in

Chicago as early as 1914. Her 1916 backing of the abortive *Thunderbird,* a play by Norman Bel Geddes based on a Blackfoot myth, was the first of her modernist projects in Los Angeles. Charles Wakefield Cadman, who introduced Geddes to Barnsdall, composed an orchestral suite for it, later published in its piano version. Barnsdall commissioned and purchased a number of costumes from native makers in anticipation of the production. They canceled the project when, after conducting extensive auditions, they could not find actors who could portray the Blackfoot people convincingly.[29] In the late 1920s Barnsdall sponsored several other theatrical productions in Los Angeles in a theater rented for the purpose.

In addition to her interest in the arts, Barnsdall was a pacifist and an anarchist who was not reluctant to use her wealth in support of her political views. Her outspoken defense (and financial support) of Tom Mooney, a labor organizer in San Francisco falsely convicted of a deadly bombing in 1916, and her strong financial support of Emma Goldman three years later, when Goldman was being deported, brought the unwelcome attention of the FBI in the form of hints of subversiveness and a possible communist affiliation, enough to deny her a passport at one point.[30] (Mooney's cause remained in the limelight for some years; his death sentence was commuted, but he was not freed until 1939. The "Free Mooney!" billboards Barnsdall placed on her Olive Hill property remained a thorn in the side of the conservative LA establishment.) Barnsdall's radical politics eventually estranged her even from the liberal Mrs. Carter and may have helped estrange her other causes, including modernism, from the conservative *Times.*

More spectacular and lasting of her projects was Barnsdall's star-crossed commissioning of architect Frank Lloyd Wright to build a home and theater complex at Olive Hill, a sizable property in Hollywood now known as Barnsdall Park. The project dragged on for ten years and was never entirely completed, though Hollyhock House remains a Los Angeles landmark.[31] Barnsdall resigned from the Bowl's board in 1926 in protest against the forced departure of her friend Mrs. Carter from its management. Her support of Henry Cowell's first New Music Society Concert, to be described below, was probably something of an afterthought.[32]

· · ·

For almost two decades, accounts of outrageous ultramodern performances in Europe or, very occasionally, in New York appeared in national music periodicals such as *Musical America* and the *Etude.* These had taken on something of a local flavor only when Marcella Craft, who had grown up in nearby Riverside, became Richard Strauss's choice for the role of Salome in the Munich revival of that opera in 1912.[33] Regional composers, however, generally satisfied themselves with Debussy-inspired whole-tone experiments; an example is Mary Carr Moore's 1919 song, "Immortal Birth," set to her own spiritualist-influenced text.

The strong Progressive-era motivation to spread the Americanist "New Gospel of Music" (a phrase Arthur Farwell was still using in early 1923) that had achieved so much in its heyday had acquired, by the 1920s, a certain institutionalized, conservative character, demonstrated, among other ways, in the changing face of the *Pacific Coast Musician*, whose early vitality was long gone.[34] Nevertheless, the practice of performing newly composed music was alive and well. The Philharmonic season of 1922–23 included unheard works by Europeans such as Mahler, d'Indy, and Rachmaninoff (the last two still active), also works by composers born or resident in America such as Paolo Gallico, Lazare Saminsky, Howard Hanson (still a Californian at the time), Ernest Bloch, and John Alden Carpenter. Many others were being heard in concerts by the new Los Angeles Chamber Music Society and elsewhere.

Two composers dominate the trickle of avant-garde music that was heard in 1920s Los Angeles; they will serve here as bellwethers for the shift in attitudes toward the new. Dane Rudhyar came to Los Angeles at the invitation of Christine Wetherill Stevenson, specifically to compose the music for her *Pilgrimage Play*, first produced in the summer of 1920. His score was not used the following year, but in 1922 Rudhyar was asked to supply more music, which critic Bruno David Ussher favorably compared with his earlier effort. Rudhyar served on the music committee of the Hollywood Bowl and later took a hand in the organization of the local Pro Musica chapter, but his biggest success was winning a prize of two thousand dollars in a 1922 composition competition sponsored by the LA Philharmonic for his tone poem *Surge of Fire*. Prize or not, the Philharmonic refused to perform it, even though its conductor (Walter Henry Rothwell) had been one of the judges who awarded the prize. At one time a prominent modernist, Rudhyar has become a footnote in the history of high modernism, his unexpected (and, for him, anomalous) role in the aesthetic shift long forgotten.[35]

The much more famous Henry Cowell, a San Francisco product, had begun concertizing in 1914, demonstrating his tone clusters and under-the-lid piano techniques there and (starting even earlier) in Carmel, an artist colony and favorite vacation spot south of San Francisco.[36] The youthful Cowell's work must have been known to some of the Los Angelenos who visited Carmel, but he probably did not perform in the southland until the

Figure 25.   Dane Rudhyar. Courtesy of Department of Special
Collections, California State University, Long Beach.

fall of 1922. In October of that year, a series of "modern interpretive
recitals" by Cowell, "himself a composer of exceedingly modern characteristics," was announced in the *Times*.[37] The announcement fails to give the
dates and locations of these events, an unusual and puzzling omission. Not
until early December can we read about them. At that point Bruno David
Ussher broke the critical silence with a lengthy discussion in the pages of
the weekly *Saturday Night*. "Los Angeles made the acquaintance of 'tone
clusters,' when Henry Cowell, young American composer, incidentally a
Californian, presented a program of his piano compositions," he began. His
evaluation of Cowell was generally positive: "Cowell is not only sincere and
thoughtful . . . but in him burns the poetic flame," he wrote; also "Cowell's
music is fascinatingly novel in its use of means." After describing various

pieces in which Cowell combined his novel pianistic techniques with "thematic episodes in the more usual form of pianistic style," he elaborated on the novel techniques:

> Cowell's almost orchestral use of the piano, based on the overtone-theory of all-embracing blending, undoubtedly sensed by him through an uncanny sixth sense, which one might name "multiplicity of tone-consciousness" or "multiple tone-thinking," is, needless to say, startling, at least, and to the listener not prepared for extremes, also jarring physically and esthetically. . . .
>
> To this method he adds a virtuosity of pedalling. One can hardly speak of thematic in the two pieces mentioned, at least, not in the traditional sense. His themes are sequences, tremendous double of chords [sic], based on the frankest use of atonality. While he shows virtuosity in playing "tone-clusters" (the term chosen by the composer as explained in the prefaces to his published works), yet one cannot accept his performance as piano-playing, and, perhaps, not as music for the piano. At least, not for the piano of yesterday and today.

Ussher's conclusion confirms that he had heard Cowell perform on at least two occasions, though it is a little less positive: "Observation is to the extent that Cowell's music, per se, does not gain upon second hearing, though his use of means becomes clearer. His is, as he has himself hinted, music in the transition stage. It would be unwise to deny it, for it possesses great germinal qualities."[38]

Why were Cowell's performances not reported in the daily press, where they had been announced, sans place and time? The most likely reason is that they took place at Krotona, the Theosophist colony in the Hollywood Hills. Cowell had had a long association with theosophists in Menlo Park and Pismo Beach. His colleague and friend Rudhyar's ties may have been even closer, since he first came to Los Angeles at the behest of Mrs. Stevenson. Various forms of spiritualism (including Theosophy) remained popular in the area. However, the *Times* had waged a private war against the sect, having paid at least one libel judgment as a result. By 1920, it had banished all references to Theosophy from its pages. (The consequence for music historians who rely on the *Times* for their information is that these events have to all intents been erased from the record.) In any case, Cowell's warm reception at these concerts, together with the extensive music making that was part of the Los Angeles scene, provided a good reason for him to return later on.

Even so, Cowell's next known public appearance in Los Angeles was not until three years later, as part of the inaugural performance of his New

Music Society. This time he was able to secure a more central concert hall (the Biltmore Theater), plus a sponsoring committee and the patronage of Aline Barnsdall, which allowed him to use several local musicians, including Adolf Tandler, conductor of the old Symphony, and pianists Wesley Kuhnle and Winifred Hooke.[39] The program included music by Darius Milhaud, Carl Ruggles, Feodor Kolin, Leo Ornstein, Arnold Schoenberg, and Rudhyar's prizewinning but previously unperformed *Surge of Fire*, though in a cut-down arrangement.

The concert was reasonably well attended and reasonably well reviewed, even though it announced itself as "revolutionary" and featured composers who "face the powerfully organized majority of the day." Though Ussher was seriously offended by Edgard Varèse's *Octandre*, he described Ruggles's work as having "a sort of agonized mysticism" and Rudhyar's as "undoubtedly a work of great talent and strength and struggle."[40] Other critics were even more positive, welcoming the fresh voices. A few months later, Winifred Hooke played a new work of Cowell's for "string piano" (i.e., piano played directly on the strings instead of from the keyboard) and small orchestra with the Tandler Little Symphony.[41] Already, Ussher, who had shown signs of becoming an advocate for the new, instead had grown tired of Cowell's pianistic effects:

> I think Mr. Cowell, whom I believe to be of a highly gifted and profoundly poetic nature, has entered a musical "cul de sac." . . . The piano should be "swept" only by way of exterior treatment. Perhaps, it would be more polite to call this an experiment, as it is a safe thing to do when one is confronted with extravagantly modern music. But the music heard in that manner was really not modern. It is as old as the spinet or harpsichord. The public was not enthusiastic. A composer of sweet songs spoke of the Cowellian innovation as a charming novelty, whatever that may imply. As charming, indeed, as it was brave on Mr. Tandler's part to include the musical charm in his program. I believe Mr. Cowell is too sane, not to realize that he has made a plaything out of an instrument.[42]

Tandler, who was clearly more interested, continued to program music by Cowell.[43]

Cowell planned a second New Music Society concert for the fall of 1926. This time the performers were the Persinger Quartet from San Francisco, with Dene Denny, a Carmel-based pianist, and Cowell himself; the program consisted of string quartets by Milhaud, Alfredo Casella, Ruggles, and Cowell, along with piano music by Schoenberg, Rudhyar, and Cowell. Barnsdall did not back this concert, and thereafter the New Music Society gave its concerts in San Francisco.[44] The inference has been that she disliked the music, but other reasons are at least as likely, for she continued to correspond with Cowell and even met him on at least one occasion. She had some serious distractions. Her long-running struggle with architect Frank Lloyd Wright over the construction of Hollyhock House absorbed her energy and financial resources. In addition she faced the dual threats of unfriendly nearby development and condemnation of her property by the city, which had long dragged its feet over Wright's structural innovation and considered her radicalism a public nuisance.[45] Her falling out with Artie Mason Carter may also have played a role, since Carter may have been among those who suggested she support the first concert. It is even possible that her subsidization of the first concert was intended primarily for the support of conductor Adolf Tandler, who still had a following after the demise of the old Symphony.

In any case, the second concert was received more than politely. Patterson Greene wrote in the *Los Angeles Examiner*:

> The large audience that listened thoughtfully and appreciatively to the New Music Society testified that contemporary developments in composition will receive due consideration in Los Angeles. These programs would be welcome at more frequent intervals. They are sometimes disconcerting but always stimulating.
>
> Henry Cowell's "tone clusters"—meaning groups of notes played on the piano with the flat of the hand or even with the forearm—sounded far less startling in actuality than in theory. They are really an outgrowth of piano pedaling, and can be so managed as to produce gorgeous sonorities. . . .
>
> The five piano pieces by Schoenberg were a demonstration of remarkable musical memory on the part of Dene Denny, who played them. To the average ear they were a chaos of unreasoned acoustic accidents, but Miss Denny seemed to find sufficient continuity in them to retain them in her mind. Piano numbers by D. Rudhyar were interesting studies in dissonant overtones.[46]

Ussher admired Milhaud's quartet but was less impressed by the rest. He was puzzled by the Schoenberg pieces and described Ruggles's *Lilacs* as "perverted into something much more aptly called poison gas, or 'In the Wake of the Garbage Cart.'" Of Rudhyar's *Moments,* he remarked that they were "very personal, often intensive, to me . . . non-conveying, unoriginal manifestations of 'subjective experiences, fragments of the inner life of the soul.'" He deferred judgment about Cowell's quartet, expressing doubts about the application of clusters to stringed instruments. Of the piano pieces, including the now-famous *Banshee,* he said, "As concert music it is a clever but limited mode of expression."[47] Ussher, the only local critic to follow the new with any sympathy at all, would grow steadily more impatient with Cowell's pianistic discoveries, though his coverage remained courteous.

Contrary to many later assumptions, Los Angeles music culture was clearly perceived as very strong and open in the early 1920s. That perception would soon change, dramatically.

14 Second Thoughts

No sooner had the New Music Society folded its tent in Los Angeles than a local chapter of Pro Musica, a national organization whose purpose was to present European modernists to American audiences, was organized.[1] The charismatic Artie Mason Carter, newly fired from the Bowl, emerged as chapter president, a move that carried with it the promise of an interested, friendly following. A single concert by the visiting Pro Arte string quartet in spring 1927 constituted the first season of the local Pro Musica chapter. The Pro Arte generated a positive response with an uncontroversial, not-so-modern concert of music by Debussy, Beethoven, and Glazounov (the last, at least, still among living modernists). The following fall, a four-concert season was announced, with programs to be presented by touring com-posers Imre Weisshaus (a Hungarian who also used the name Paul Arma), Alexandre Tansman (Russian), Béla Bartók (another, older Hungarian), and Maurice Ravel (French).[2]

Weisshaus led off the series. Winifred Hooke, the English-born pianist who performed and taught Cowell's music regularly from her Hollywood studio, reported on it in a distinctly ironic tone:

> Here are a few items regarding the great Imre's arrival in L.A. and his concert.
>
> At first (at breakfast) we saw he wished to play his own sonata and, hearing a few measures encouraged him to do so (displacing Vivaldi which we can hear at any time). Ladies of the board—"a great pity" (before they heard sonata)—At concert—indignation meetings held in doorways and passages of concert hall—one prominent composer <u>Gertrude</u> [Ross?]—announces herself ashamed to have anything more to do with Pro Musica—laughter, giggles. . . . Ladies of board retire <u>in-furiated.</u> Times critic [Isabel Morse Jones] <u>stunned</u>—unable to report

concert—asks Rudhyar to do it in her place (for which thank you God). . . . Ussher's indignation you have read. I've got a real crush on Mrs. J. J. [Artie Mason] Carter who flirted outrageously with him but unfortunately didn't understand a word he said.[3]

Ussher was indeed indignant, concluding his lengthy diatribe:

> Americans, even more gifted than he, would be ridiculed and scorned abroad, were they to perpetrate such contortions, such impudently pretentious balderdash as his "Sonata No. 1." It was a sign of good nature and faith that the audience received the Hungarian visitor in a lenient, quietly quizzical mood. I am glad, at least, one person had the courage of conviction and hissed. Suffice it to add that Weisshaus was sponsored by the local Pro-Musica chapter at the instigation of Henry Cowell. It is hard to understand this from an artist, so sensitive, genuinely creative and poetic as the latter.[4]

Times critic Isabel Morse Jones preferred to write up a recital offered by a visiting Metropolitan Opera soprano the same evening. Responding to her invitation, Rudhyar wrote a lengthy review of the Weisshaus concert, far different from anything Jones might have written and quite likely different also from what Jones might have expected him to write, given the reputation he had established from his music for the *Pilgrimage Play*, his lectures to local groups, and his writings in the New York–based journals *Eolian Review* and *Musical Quarterly* (the latter probably more widely circulated in Los Angeles).[5] Rudhyar is known among scholars of 1920s modernism as a devotee of Theosophy and astrology with a substantial knowledge of "oriental" musics, and as someone who made a point of associating dissonance with the spiritual rather than the formal. Eschewing the musically specific in his essays, he expressed a preference for abstract ideas of "tone" and "mode" as opposed to the more specific "note" and the fatally transposable "scale." Music, he argued, is both mystical and magical; it "has not to do primarily with forms but with the soul that expresses itself through these forms, the collective life that manifests itself as a culture." He also wrote that composers "all represent the various aspects of a unique impulse; *the desire to express the innermost and occult essence of life.*"[6]

Rudhyar's review of Weisshaus's concert is worth paying some attention to, for it suggests an aesthetic shift, or at least a different emphasis. Downplaying the spiritual associations for which he has been known, he framed his arguments in this case quite differently. This time, he expressed the racial essentialism and idealized masculinism that, along with an implicit misogyny, were widespread in the culture and becoming more and more characteristic of ultramodernist aesthetic statements.[7] After recognizing that much of the audience was puzzled by the concert, which included sonatas by other living Hungarian composers (Béla Bartók, 1881–1945; Zoltán Kodály, 1882–1967; and Pál Kadosa, 1903–88) as well as Weisshaus's (1905–87) own work, Rudhyar continued: "To me it was a wonderful revelation, a great cry of hope and life in the desert of European music which has become stale and corpse-like in its neo-classic futile efforts of the last seven years. Here was the expression of essential vitality, the virility of a race which in spite of defeat and humiliation [i.e., the dissolution of the Austro-Hungarian Empire after World War I] is finding the power to sing in bare, austere and rigid outlines its deepmost soul."[8]

As he described Weisshaus's program in this *Times* review, Rudhyar wrote of Bartók's music as the "point of departure" for the rest. "It is clear, open, rhythmic; it smells the soil—but thus is very physical and perhaps lacks human depth." Kodály he described as "a Hungarian Debussy." Kadosa, he says, "has overcome such a sensibility."[9] "We are going farther away from European sentimentality, from femininity. His music is essentially masculine, strong, rugged, bare. It is almost solely melodic, but melodic in an entirely non-European sense. Dissonant, cutting, passionate melodies which at times lash. Now we feel the Mogol [sic] heroic soul riding the steppes, a conqueror's soul devouring space, exalted by infinite horizons to be mastered. His "Sonata" . . . is to my mind a chef-d'oeuvre which will live forever. . . . nothing is superfluous in it; it is all necessary, unavoidable, relentless."

Finally reaching Weisshaus's own work, Rudhyar made an attempt to reconcile the violent, masculinist racism he has just heard in the music with his own theosophically tinged spiritualism.

> With Weisshaus' "Sonata" . . . we go farther toward racial beginnings. Here we have music which is based on magical performances, the music of the "primitive," but which is so only in so far as it goes to beginnings of things, to the very roots of human life, to the magical sense of tones, of incantations. Magical is the technic of reiteration of tone masses or tone-formulas, a technic used by Stravinsky in his "Sacre du Printemps," but with much less purity and spontaneity. Magical also, in that it is a music of will-power, not trying to give sensorial pleasure (a preoccupation foreign to any real artist), but to exalt, to stir, to regenerate.[10]

The *Times* inserted an editorial disclaimer at the beginning: "The following appreciation of Imre Weisshaus, the young Hungarian pianist-composer who startled local musical circles by his strange recital for Pro-Musica on Thursday evening, was written by D. Rudhyar, well-known musical internationalist." The adjective *internationalist* was anything but a compliment in the *Times'* isolationist editorial lexicon, as will become clear.

Under Mrs. Carter, Pro Musica lasted several more seasons, but no one else, even Bartók later that season or Paul Hindemith the next, managed to offend so thoroughly as had Weisshaus. From that point on, Cowell could no longer find a platform or a sponsor for performances in Los Angeles.[11]

. . .

The mid-1920s run at exposing Los Angeles concert audiences to ultra-modernism ended abruptly after one further event having a rather different aspect—Aaron Copland's appearance at the Hollywood Bowl on July 20, 1928, as soloist in his own piano concerto. This performance, as Ussher reported in the *Express,* "amused, puzzled and offended listeners," provoking an unusually lively audience reaction and a correspondingly vehement press response.[12] The copious scrapbooks kept by the Los Angeles Philharmonic include more reviews of that concert than for any of the others around it. The *Los Angeles Record,* the *Illustrated Daily News,* and the *Santa Monica Outlook* were among the smaller papers that weighed in. Surprisingly, these reviews are more mixed than Copland's most recent biographer now suggests.[13] Most of the writers emphasized the tumultuous audience response, with only limited references to the music that had precipitated the storm of cheers, catcalls, hisses, and whistles that brought the soloist out three times to acknowledge them. The *Times'* headline told the story: "Bowl Stirred Up to Frenzy / Fans Greet Sophisticated Jazz with Derision / Catcalls, Hisses, Laughs and Applause Follow Pianist." Under the provocative headline, critic Isabel Morse Jones remarked,

> Played last night in the Hollywood Bowl, with Copland at the piano, it outdid in noise and impudence anything ever heard there in seven summers of symphony concerts which have prided themselves in bringing to the Pacific Coast quantities of new music. . . .
>
> Applause and whistles, both jeering and encouraging, greeted the piece. Some claimed it to be "typically American"; others said it was "like a bad dream you can't forget." But everyone talked about it. And when [conductor Albert] Coates ostentatiously closed the piano and literally "washed his hands" of it, at its close, he won still louder laughter and applause.[14]

Ussher was relatively circumspect about expressing his reaction:

> It is a sincere utterance. There can be no doubt. What it does utter is a question answerable in more than one manner, or not at all. It is not a concerto, not even in the newer, symphonic sense of the word. The

piano plays an important part, a sort of essential obligato, which at times, determines mood and pace. Too much has been made of the jazz elements in the second half of the score. Instrumentally they offer nothing new. . . . It is the rhythmic, in fact, unusual, inner-rhythmic vitality and complexities of this score which constitutes its chief asset.

Copland . . . is an extremist in the formulation of themes and harmony. . . . On the whole, it is small, if vehement material, treated smallish and vehemently. There throbs and agitates a certain demonic feverishness in the music. Mr. Copland writes evidently as he must and as an American. . . . Copland works in tart, strident, sometimes compelling sonorities and he plays the piano in that manner. . . .

Mr. Copland . . . creates music natural to him, expressive of him and his environment, as he has done in the past without part of the audience chuckling. But the concerto is provoking in more than one way. If some of the applause was not ironic, then it was due largely to the efforts of Conductor Coates and the orchestra.[15]

Gregory Goss hinted at a more positive response in the *Examiner:*

Conversational echoes followed musical reverberations last night at Hollywood Bowl. Aaron Copland's concerto for piano and orchestra, with the composer at the keyboard, was responsible. At the conclusion of this much anticipated number the large audience showed a disposition to dissolve in impromptu debating groups to determine whether fame or notoriety should be accorded the young musician.

Seldom has interest been so stimulated. Musical modernism was rampant and the reception at the Bowl indicated enthusiasm for the courage of the composer in shaking off conventional shackles and pleasure at the opportunity of hearing a brilliant rendition of the opus over which controversy has raged.[16]

Another, otherwise unknown critic liked the work and suggested a generational factor in the audience's mixed response:

YOUNGER FANS CHEER PIANIST

Did young Mr. Aaron Copland, composer-pianist, desecrate Hollywood Bowl last night when with the help of the local symphony orchestra, he played his wicked "Concerto for Piano and Orchestra"?

"That, sir," said a refined elderly gentleman sitting next to a critic, "violates all prevailing conceptions of music." . . .

The older generations were mystified, when not outraged. But all up and down the vast auditorium the young folk listened tensely. . . . The truth seems to be that an entirely new sense of what constitutes rhythm and harmony and form is pervading the oncoming populace.

And so last night when the exciting notes of Copland's concerto were stilled a chorus of whistles resounded from up and down the big auditorium. There was loud hand-clapping, but the whistles were the significant response—whistles of approval are seldom heard at the Bowl.

We make no attempt at reporting the concerto, save to say that it was "new" and in spots meandered about under no compulsion of "form" while exhibiting the sauciest and most impertinent orchestral elaborations. The "jazz" spots were just viciously syncopated—it ain't fair to put over "rhythms" that are lost to a fellow in the forties.

Copland was recalled three times. The "classicists" had better begin sounding a call to arms![17]

The "classicists" did indeed sound a call to arms. The following fall, Cowell wrote to the Bowl management asking, as he had earlier asked Pro Musica, to appear as piano soloist in his own work the next season (1929). Raymond Brite, then the manager, replied as diplomatically as he could: "The reaction of the Bowl public to Mr. Copland's *Concerto* this season was so unfavorable, on the whole, that our Committee is rather hesitant to make further excursions into ultra modern music."[18]

There were no further experiments in ultramodernism at the Bowl for several years, until Nicolas Slonimsky was hired to conduct five concerts in the first two weeks of the 1933 season. Slonimsky's programming was imaginative, to say the least. He conducted Cowell's *Reel,* finally giving Cowell the Bowl premiere he had sought several years earlier. He located (or commissioned) a series of "fanfares" by living composers, including José Ardévol, Arnold Bax, Arthur Bliss, Alejándro García Caturla, Manuel de Falla, Hamilton Harty, Gian Francisco Malipiero, Milhaud, Serge Prokofiev, and Igor Stravinsky, all of which probably had the virtue of being relatively short. His programming of Varèse's *Ionisation* (for thirteen percussionists) provoked another storm, foreclosing the possibility that Slonimsky might have other conducting opportunities in Los Angeles.[19] Fifteen months after this last hurrah, Arnold Schoenberg arrived in Los Angeles and, unbeknown to concert audiences, performing musicians, and the general public for some years, the so-called Golden Age of music in Los Angeles began.[20] Perhaps, from another point of view, that is the moment when a Golden Age of sorts came to an end.

. . .

If the Pandora's box of ultramodernism had in fact cracked open in Los Angeles as early as 1922, how is it that after 1926, "ultramodernism" met such

Figure 26. Program, Symphonies under the Stars at the Hollywood Bowl, Nicolas Slonimsky conducting, July 16, 1933. Slonimsky claimed that this performance of Varèse's *Ionisation* cost him the opportunity to become the regular conductor of the Philharmonic. Courtesy of Hollywood Bowl Museum.

strong resistance, did not find a continuing audience, and generally failed to thrive? Many of the essential ingredients were there at the start. There were composers such as Cowell and Rudhyar to bring new ideas and styles from elsewhere, patrons and promoters such as Barnsdall and Carter to see that concerts were scheduled and publicized, critics such as Bruno David Ussher and (presently) José Rodríguez to write or speak effectively and often sympathetically about the music, and musicians such as Adolf Tandler, Winifred

Hooke, and Wesley Kuhnle to navigate their difficulties with both skill and goodwill. Most surprising of all are the relatively large audiences for these earlier adventures in the ultramodern, much larger than those who turned out starting in 1939, when Evenings on the Roof, the concert series regularly touted as the beginning of high modernism in Los Angeles, began.[21] It is true that the level of patronage and audience support may have been below some necessary critical mass. It is also possible that, had the Bowl management cultivated the part of the audience that had cheered Copland's 1928 appearance, a consistent audience for high modernism might have developed more easily. One can speculate further that obvious differences in style and aesthetic between Cowell's work and Copland's, or that of other ultramodernists, had something to do with this outcome.

Here, however, I propose to draw on the threads pursued up to this point, along with some other contemporary events, to argue that the negative reaction to the ultramodern documented here is symptomatic of a wider cultural shift. The changes in music making involve the (now redefined) popular, the technological, the entrepreneurial, and the gender related. They took place against a changing political background that is worth a passing reference here. The 1917 Communist revolution in Russia and the civil war that followed provided a motive for political reaction and xenophobia in the United States. The *Times,* by then rapidly taking its place as the dominant paper in Los Angeles, advocated these attitudes almost as stridently as did the Hearst-owned *Herald.* (The *Times* building had been bombed in 1910, supposedly by labor agitators.) Among the national issues were the Red scare of 1919–20, which gave J. Edgar Hoover his start at the FBI, the Immigration Act of 1924, which closed U.S. borders to unlimited European immigration, and the disputed execution of anarchists Sacco and Vanzetti in 1927. Asians in California were explicitly denied citizenship; the state authorized segregated schools for all racial minorities in the 1920s as well. The severe limitation placed on immigration was also tied to anti-Semitism, more evident in Los Angeles as the film colony grew. The nationwide surge in membership in the Ku Klux Klan is an obvious indication of increasing racism, one of the motivations underlying the growing perception of cultural distance between the classical and the popular. (Not everyone was pleased that the Central Avenue music community was growing rapidly, attracting a racially mixed audience to the new Dunbar Hotel, the Lincoln Theater, the Club Alabam, and other night spots; recall that Jelly Roll Morton had moved his music making outside the city limits to escape police harassment.) In addition, the 1920s are often seen as a period of reaction following ratification in 1920 of the constitutional amendment giving women the vote.

A striking analog to the shifting attitudes toward the "new" in music, appropriate to this Southern California–oriented discussion, may be found in the political career of Hiram W. Johnson, governor of California from 1910 to 1916. Elected at first with the support of the state's Progressive Party, Governor Johnson provided the leadership for numerous statewide reforms. As a (Republican) U.S. senator (from 1916 until his death in 1945), he became a reactionary, voting against U.S. entry into both the League of Nations in 1919 and, a quarter century later, the United Nations. The association of the new in elite concert music with internationalism did not help the former in Los Angeles. The radical new music that came from Europe was seen by some as part of the dangerously non-Anglo anarchism emanating from that decadent source. (The brochure quoted in chapter 13 about the "subtle spiritual change" and new possibilities available in the far west takes on a richer and more questionable meaning in this context, as does the racial language in Rudhyar's critique.)[22] One could also read in Ussher's generous reviews of Cowell's 1922 performances a certain sympathy based on his perception of Cowell's sexual orientation and a reluctant reversal of that sympathy in his later review of Copland's concerto.[23] That these generally "conservative" attitudes occasionally conflicted (for example, antiwoman views on one hand versus anti-internationalism on the other) did not, apparently, weaken their influence on the society in general or on music making in particular.

How much the expansion of public religiosity in this cultural climate had to do with the closing of the Los Angeles audience to new music is unclear, but one notes the increasing visibility of Theosophy and Christian Science just as the ultramodern composers were turning away from the spirituality laid out by Rudhyar. The *Pilgrimage Play, Mission Play,* the annual Easter sunrise services at several outdoor sites (including Barnsdall Park and the Hollywood Bowl), and the flamboyant ministry of Aimee Semple McPherson all illustrate this growing phenomenon. More likely, the attachment of an increasing religiosity to music making had a damping effect on the new as the decade wore on. Cowell's modernism, with its spiritual associations, was acceptable to much of LA's concert audience; Imre Weisshaus's, with its "foreignness," and Copland's, with its use of jazz, were much less so.

More directly related, one notes that popular music making (in the older sense of music for the people) had greatly expanded with the establishment of the Hollywood Bowl concerts. But, it had not expanded anywhere near as fast as the commercial popular music that was so large and important a part of the new mass culture, creating a new audience as it grew. Although the two audiences often overlapped, the emergence of a whole class of wage earners with leisure time and discretionary money to spend dwarfed the development of the Bowl's concert audience. Technological advances in the recording industry, early radio, and continuing experiments with sound films were obviously changing the way that large numbers of people whose music making had been relatively passive now participated. All this is evident from the boom in the construction of elaborate movie palaces, the new customers (often male) drawn to phonograph records and recording technology, and the steady decline in the sale of pianos, all trends that had begun by the mid-1910s and continued in the '20s.

Two shifts in the politics of local concert management coincided with the decline of interest in the musical ultramodern. In 1925, long-established impresario L. E. Behymer was able to reaffirm and even consolidate his stranglehold on the top of the concert-giving pyramid, in spite of challenges from Merle Armitage's Auditorium Artist series (backed by an old rival, music store owner James T. Fitzgerald) and from the short-lived Los Angeles Grand Opera Company. Subsequent perception of Behymer's domination of the concert business as hopelessly reactionary was so strong that, even twenty years later, Peter Yates could write, in connection with his Evenings on the Roof concert series, that a major purpose of the new enterprise was to "break up the Behymer monopoly."[24] The following year, the Hollywood Bowl's founder-manager, Artie Mason Carter, whose initiative and charisma had made the Bowl into a viable enterprise, was replaced by a salaried manager. Her departure was engineered by the businessmen who had been (sometimes only peripherally) involved from the start. Thus Behymer, purveyor of the tried-and-true, triumphed, while Carter, the musical innovator, went under, finding a new (if more limited) role as a champion of the ultramodern Pro Musica series.

Carter's departure from the Bowl smacked of misogyny and was a local cause célèbre.[25] Certainly a power differential was involved in these different outcomes for Behymer and Carter; Behymer had the backing of the now-powerful *Times* as well as financial support and a host of contractual commitments with prominent performers that assured him of some level of control. Yet the juxtaposition of these contrasting outcomes raises questions about the role of gender in the change in audience taste that was marked by Weisshaus's and Copland's performances in 1927 and '28. One notes that in 1925 Ethel Leginska drew a very large audience (some thirty thousand) when she conducted at the Bowl, but she met serious passive resistance from the orchestra. Isabel Morse Jones wrote of "the attitude of hostility expressed by the orchestra men in words and in their playing"; she concluded that Leginska "may be a master of music but she has not yet learned that soft words make masters of men." Bruno Ussher, her male counterpart as a critic, also noted the "unfriendly or openly derisive attitude" of the players but concluded quite the opposite, that she needed to be more forceful, not less. The players' resistance triumphed, and the experiment of hiring a woman conductor was not repeated.

The gender issue becomes more pressing because of an accompanying population trend: while the number of male performers increased sharply in the 1920s, the proportion of women among teachers of music was falling off, meaning that the overall presence of women among visible, professional music makers was declining. Yet the role of women as audience members was more important than ever. Music clubs, with their overwhelmingly female membership, were reaching a peak in membership (as were religious organizations such as the Theosophists and the Christian Scientists, both clearly perceived as woman-friendly). Women made up the majority of the concert audience in Los Angeles, as they did in many other American cities. The new in Los Angeles was introduced through the operation of (mainly female) clubs and private societies, as shown by Cowell's early performances at Krotona. (For this we have one piece of concrete evidence involving Cowell, though not for Los Angeles; Cowell's San Francisco audiences were overwhelmingly made up of women.)[26]

Music had long been seen in the United States as a feminine/feminizing/effeminate occupation, leading the younger male American composers to adopt a vocabulary of masculinist, misogynist language in their writings about music. Such language is readily found; it came from both straight and gay male composers.[27] Cowell, and for that matter Rudhyar, had earlier managed to avoid the strong antiwoman language that is so abundant among the male modernists.[28] In Rudhyar's 1927 review of Weisshaus's concert, his insistence on the "virility" of the music he admired—just one of any number of misogynist remarks by male composers in the 1920s that I have chronicled elsewhere—had a chilling effect, helping to alienate the overwhelmingly female concert audience.[29] His insistence on the non-Caucasian, violent racial essence of Weisshaus's music may also have alienated parts of the audience, as Copland's use of jazz-derived syncopation, with its suggestion of African American and Jewish influences, obviously did.[30] In seeking to distance themselves from the older "effeminate" model of concert music in America, the younger composers came to antagonize and eventually lose what had been the most reliable audience for concert music, middle-class white women. This is not to ignore or contest that the younger composers employed different styles from, say, Cadman, but to insist that their well-advertised antiwoman attitudes left audiences less willing to open themselves to the new sounds they were offered than they might otherwise have been. The result of all these things was the marginalization of the club-dominated concert music scene in the larger picture of music making via the new media, across a wider array of class and ethnicity, and through its ever-stronger characterization as "feminine." (It is particularly ironic that the antiwoman rhetoric was also implicitly homophobic and that Theosophy had been more tolerant of gender difference than what followed.)

The later suppression of the role of women in public music making can be seen in the long-time misrepresentation of his Los Angeles years by John Cage, long hailed as the most important avant-garde composer of the mid- and late twentieth century. (Cage was a student at Los Angeles High School, still contemplating a career in the ministry, when Weisshaus gave his infamous concert.) Cage drew heavily on the "feminized" musical culture of Los Angeles, though he later downplayed these influences consistently, choosing instead to stress a more tenuous short-term contact with Arnold Schoenberg in the mid-1930s. In particular, he suppressed the formative influence of his maternal aunt, Phoebe James, a progressive music teacher who was a major mentor as he struggled to find a compositional style.[31]

• • •

The Progressive-era culture of music making, which had been so vital and receptive in the years immediately before and after World War I, changed significantly after 1926. By that point it had lost its resilience and begun a long period of shrinkage that led to its virtual disappearance by the 1950s. Along with this turning of the tide came increasing conservatism, expressed in many ways, including resistance to many forms of the new in music, seen increasingly as disruptive and even adversarial. The widespread reaction against the culmination of the first wave of feminism—the ratification of the Nineteenth Amendment in 1920, giving the vote to women— had found its way unerringly to the world of music making in Los Angeles, and elsewhere as well. Thus, Rudhyar's critique of Weisshaus's concert, quoted at length above, strongly reinforced cultural as well as technological and political trends already visible elsewhere in California and the United States.

If this investigation of music making in Los Angeles shows us anything, it is that viewing the first decades of the twentieth century as musically uninteresting in that city is the result of, not the absence of music and music making, but the blinkers we ourselves have worn for the past half century as we have focused on a too narrowly defined "new" in American music. The blinkers come from comments such as the one by Moross in the pages of *Modern Music*—that in 1941 "Southern California . . . probably has the smallest audience for new music to be found anywhere," already quoted from New York's little magazine of musical high modernism at the start of chapter 13. The change was contemporary with other changes in the music-making establishment and in the wider culture. The modernist turn away from mysticism (as, for example, in Theosophy) toward a rationalist, quasi-scientific approach to composition was so strong that this earlier, more spiritual and woman-friendly aspect of the movement was forgotten and generally suppressed. Early 1920s modernism, nurtured by the Progressive-era culture of music making, has been so deeply buried that, as late as 1980, a writer as thorough and insightful as Rita Mead could accept the usage of the day without examination and speak of "contemporary music" in the 1920s as referring only to modernist music, as if the overwhelming preponderance of music making did not exist.[32] Even in 2003, one could read in *Opera News* that "in some quarters of America, the notion of a sophisticated cultural life thriving in Los Angeles is still something of an oxymoron."[33] The music club culture, which provided the basic audience for concert music, had once been recognized, for all its faults, as "the one and only force to which music may look for nurture and development."[34]

The city was indeed exposed to musical ultramodernism in the 1920s. Audiences were receptive to it at the start. After 1926, this changed along with a change in the modernist aesthetic. Self-conscious, high ultramodernism had a long, hard struggle in Los Angeles after 1926, a struggle that lasted well beyond Moross's remark.

15 Calling the Tune

The Los Angeles Federal Music Project

Opportunities for working musicians expanded in the 1920s, in Los Angeles as elsewhere, bringing what would turn out to be their highest level of paid employment in the twentieth century. After 1930, though, everything changed. Sound films definitively replaced the silents, resulting in the demise of the theater orchestras that had routinely supported the movies in the larger theaters and the firing of the organists and pianists who had worked in the smaller ones. The American Federation of Musicians estimated that eighteen thousand of what had been twenty-two thousand movie theater jobs disappeared soon after 1929.[1] As the Great Depression deepened, clubs and restaurants struggled to survive; they had little choice but to let their entertainers go. Furthermore, the spread of jukeboxes made these losses, too, permanent. Legitimate theaters, which had virtually always employed house musicians, cut back or went dark for longer and longer periods. Substantial job losses were also sustained among other entertainers in the theater industry, in parallel with those in music. The close connection between music and theater is seen in these losses. The campaign to salvage or at least cushion the devastation in both professions makes it important to discuss both here.[2]

By the time Franklin D. Roosevelt took office in March 1933, the situation of musicians and others in the arts, like that of many other kinds of workers, was desperate. Three years later, a few months after the Federal Music Project got underway, Modest Altschuler described their situation in his first report as conductor of Federal Symphony no. 1 of Los Angeles: "The first problem encountered was the inability of the players to perform acceptably. . . . First, many of them were physically not able to stand the required hours of rehearsal, due basically to mal-nutrition and hardship suffered prior to the advent of the [Federal Music] project. Psychologically their morale was poor; they were in many instances incapable of sufficient concentration to enable them to correctly count the measures of rest and hence frequently came in before or after they should have."[3]

Those who were eventually hired by the Federal Music Project (and the few who fell under Altschuler's observation) were the lucky ones. Local 47's monthly magazine, much reduced in size, carried long lists of musicians who were dropped for nonpayment of dues. FMP files are sprinkled with pathetic letters from longtime musicians, recounting their sufferings and begging for a chance to work again.

·   ·   ·

Relief programs for the poor had always been the province of cities and counties, but such local agencies were, to put it mildly, unequipped for such extensive and persistent unemployment. The new national administration undertook to turn things around. Within two months of Roosevelt's inauguration, a program of federal grants to the states (FERA, the Federal Emergency Relief Administration) was under way.[4] By December, the Reconstruction Finance Corporation (RFC) was in place, and the Civil Works Administration (CWA) put workers, including musicians, on the federal payroll. Struck down by a Supreme Court decision within a few months, these new agencies were replaced with a series of smaller federal grants to the states, this time through the State Emergency Relief Administration (SERA), while the government struggled to devise another program that would put people to work on a large scale and still pass constitutional muster.[5]

In California and other states, the pre-WPA programs had included musicians and actors. They were administered variously through existing education, recreation, and women's programs. They fell far short of the need, but they represented considerable improvement over such drop-in-the-bucket, one-shot gestures as that of the Los Angeles Musicians' Union (Local 47), which had organized four Sunday-afternoon symphony concerts in the summer of 1931, in which the seventy-five otherwise unemployed musicians shared the gate after expenses were paid.[6] In Los Angeles, the federally subsidized programs were administered through the county (the Los Angeles County Relief Administration, LACRA). The *Pacific Coast Musician* reported the following in early 1934: "The two local RFC-sponsored 45-piece orchestras, fostered by the government in its program of aiding through employment, unemployed musicians, artists, sculptors, et cetera, has been taken over by the Civil Work Service Project 8297, which also has added to its musical care another orchestra of like size, a concert band, three chamber music groups, a male choir and other ensembles. These units are available for programs open to the public and no charge is made."[7] A few months later, as the local SERA program went through one of its periodic reorganizations, Adolf Tandler, formerly director of the Los Angeles Symphony Orchestra, by then defunct for fifteen years, was appointed to direct an orchestra of forty-five unemployed musicians with symphonic experience to play some radio broadcasts.[8] These efforts, too, came nowhere near meeting the need.

The pre-FMP music programs in Los Angeles, strongly influenced by the musicians' union, had not supported singers, who by and large were not included in its membership. Because the union was racially segregated and most of the funds went to Local 47 rather than Local 767, black instrumentalists were also rarely supported. The early Drama and Choral Division of SERA, under J. Howard Miller and George Gerwing, took up some of the slack, maintaining a choral program that employed black musicians, very likely including some who were primarily instrumentalists. A scrapbook in the Library of Congress shows that this division assembled a vaudeville show that included black singers and a típica orchestra, staffed and led by men with Spanish surnames. This took place on July 21, 1934; a month later (on August 29), the Negro Dramatic Unit presented a one-act play at Los Angeles High School. A panoramic photo shows the full chorus, with fifty-two whites in the center and a total of twenty-seven slightly out-of-focus African Americans grouped on each side.[9]

The cluster of federally supported work programs—FERA, CWA, SERA—starting soon after Roosevelt took office in March 1933, served as pilot projects for the much larger WPA programs that followed. These early programs were funded as supplements to the old idea of relief, that is, as a dole intended for the bare survival of the unemployed. Achieving a quality artistic product was not an explicit priority; by no coincidence, the music performances in these early programs were reportedly dismal and, to judge from the spotty Los Angeles record, singularly unambitious. (Among other things, rehearsals were unpaid, and there was no budget to acquire music.) As finally adopted, the arts projects of the new WPA (the Work Projects Administration after the 1939 reorganization the Works Progress Administration), grouped together at first as Federal One, incorporated a significant new approach. Rather than serve as a dole, the arts projects aspired to restore the skills and self-respect of the unemployed through the production of quality work, bringing the arts to new audiences around the country in the process. These several goals—putting people to work, creating a high-quality artistic product, and reaching new audiences—coexisted only with difficulty in the Music Project.

.   .   .

By their nature, the arts projects were always a highly visible, if nevertheless a numerically small part of the WPA as legislated by Congress in August 1935. At the start, Federal One included the Federal Music Project (FMP), the Federal Art Project, the Federal Writers' Project, the Federal Theatre Project (FTP), and the Historical Records Project. Although it was revamped several times and the FTP was dropped in 1939, the other programs ended definitively only after the entry of the United States into World War II, when the wartime economy created almost instant full employment. The Federal Music Project was the largest of the Federal One arts projects. Nationwide, starting in late 1935, the FMP began by providing work for about sixteen thousand of the unemployed musicians who could qualify for relief.

A look at the national leadership of the Federal Music and Theatre projects sheds light on their local implementation and on the issues the projects raised. Differences in the philosophies of the directors of these two agencies affected their achievements, and they help to illuminate some of the issues that plagued the Music Project locally and brought unwelcome attention, both national and local, to the administration of the Federal One agencies. Under its controversial national director, Hallie Flanagan, the Theatre Project approached its mission quite differently from the Music Project, under Nikolai Sokoloff. In notably broader consultations with directors of commercial, nonprofit, and university theater companies around the country, Flanagan came up with an eclectic range of theatrical enterprises, all conceived to avoid competition with existing commercial theater while achieving her project's goals, which, according to the enabling legislation, were similar to those of the Music Project. The FTP's units produced new plays, classical drama, revivals of Broadway productions, modern and foreign drama, children's and marionette theater, revues, musicals, vaudeville, dance, early Americana, and pageants. Some units functioned as stock companies; others assembled new companies for each production. The FTP contributed to a project on American scene design in cooperation with the Federal Art Project. It formed photographic and radio divisions. (The radio division produced three thousand broadcasts in 1937 alone; its Los Angeles unit was very active in this program.) Some of its productions tackled current events and social issues, one reason why the Theatre Project eventually became a lightning rod for congressional criticism.[10] Through the life of the project, Negro, Yiddish, Italian, Spanish, German, and French units could be found where there were urban populations to support them. (Its diversity may also have made it a favorite congressional target.) In January 1939, 1,395 people were working in the Federal Theatre Project in California, most of them in Los Angeles. They were distributed among drama, dance, marionette, children's, Negro, and vaudeville units; at other times there were Yiddish and French units.[11]

All this contrasts with the way the Music Project under the direction of Nikolai Sokoloff went about its business. In the course of his fifteen-year tenure as the first conductor of the Cleveland Orchestra (ending in 1933), Sokoloff had been enterprising in reaching out to the public through regional touring, educational concerts, commercial recordings, and radio broadcasts, seemingly a good preparation for the federal job.[12] Yet the range of his vision was clearly narrower than Flanagan's. His conception for the FMP is summed up in his approach to the project's stated goals. Presidential Letter number 5020, dated in early November 1935, states the project's purposes: "to rehabilitate musicians, to retrain them for new forms of work in music and allied fields, to establish high standards of musicianship and to educate the public in an appreciation of musical opportunities." But the statement on the first page of the *Federal Music Project Manual: Preliminary Statement of Information* (1935) reorders these goals, making "to establish high standards of musicianship" the first stated purpose of the project rather than the next to last.[13]

In practice, Sokoloff made high standards his top priority. That meant, in practice, symphonic music (and opera, in the case of Los Angeles) would be strongly privileged over other genres. The ranks of his national advisory board reflected his conviction and buttressed it; the board's membership included five prominent symphony conductors, the director of the Metropolitan Opera, directors of three major conservatories and a sprinkling of other music educators, two representatives of the music club movement, two publishers, and several composers of concert music. Seemingly as afterthoughts, the president of the American Federation of Musicians and two representatives of the field of popular music are also listed. All, needless to say, were white.[14] Fourteen of the twenty-five were based in New York City. Even though some projects managed to maintain greater diversity than did those in California, it seems fair to say that the board's membership was more supportive of Sokoloff's intent to use the project to "elevate" the public's taste in music (i.e., increase its exposure to symphony and opera) than it was in creating jobs for unemployed commercial musicians, let alone preparing them for emerging technologies such as television.

With this orientation, the Music Project was not likely to disturb the class-based artistic hierarchy, which by then had firmly placed symphony and opera at the top and endowed them optimistically with the power to up-lift the lives of the masses. (The Roosevelt administration's general support of labor unions never translated into an assault on the class structure that had grown up around symphony and opera.) The Federal Music Project thus did not fashion itself as an agent for change, as the Federal Theatre Project did. (Almost inadvertently, it facilitated some changes anyway, while the more imaginative FTP paid dearly in the end for its enterprise.) I strongly disagree, however, with Kenneth J. Bindas's judgment that the FMP was a failure because of Sokoloff's symphonic bias.[15] That particular bias on the part of its leadership was pretty much inevitable, given the artistic climate of the time.

The comparison with Hallie Flanagan, Sokoloff's FTP counterpart, is re-vealing. Quite apart from his overall approach, moreover, Sokoloff's lead-ership skills did not transfer well to his new role. He did not inspire unit leaders to develop new models for music making, although some did any-way. He was not, apparently, sensitive to regional differences or to the old questions about "American" music—how much and what kinds to play, whether to commission music from working composers, how much oppor-tunity to provide for younger, often U.S.-born musicians. Ashley Pettis's Composers Forum Laboratory, designed to showcase individual composers, is perhaps an exception, although it was developed by the New York City project and did not translate easily to Los Angeles, despite many directives from Washington. In addition, Sokoloff was unwilling to make the task of collecting and recording indigenous folk music from around the country a part of the FMP, even though this activity was analogous to other Federal One projects, such as collecting narratives from surviving ex-slaves and photographing migrant workers.[16] This difference meant that the policies of the FTP and its predecessors were generally more inclusive than those of the FMP. The Federal Theatre Project started with a very wide variety of the-atrical units, as did the FMP, but the FTP kept them through the life of the project. Even so, the Los Angeles Music Project was, like the FTP, quite di-verse at the start, though racial and ethnic segregation was the rule.

·   ·   ·

California had the largest FMP organization of any state, with thirty-two hundred employees. Half of these were in Los Angeles, making it the sec-ond largest unit in the country; the rest were divided among smaller South-ern California cities and the San Francisco Bay Area. The FTP was between half and three-quarters as large.[17] Within a few months, a wide range of music performances was offered. There were symphonies, concert orchestras (smaller in size), and bands, but also string quartets, stage bands (code for jazz groups), típica orchestras, and choruses of various kinds. The FMP maintained separate Negro units, including a string quartet, chorus, and several stage bands. (Elmer Keeton and later Carlyle Scott directed the Negro chorus.) Latinos were assigned to a típica orchestra. The list below shows twenty-four highly diversified concerts, all of them free to the public, in one seven-day period, distributed among twenty-one different Los Angeles locations.

FEDERAL MUSIC PROJECTS:
LOS ANGELES DISTRICT NO. 11: SCHEDULE OF FREE MUSICAL
EVENTS, WEEK OF MARCH 2–8, 1936, INCLUSIVE

Opera: *Tales of Hoffman,* 2 performances

Hawaiian Orchestra (José García), 2 performances

Mexican Típica Orchestra (José García), 3 performances

Colored Military Band (Ed Perkins), 1 performance

Bessie Chapin String Trio, 2 performances

Hungarian Symphonette (Josef Feckete), 1 performance

Concert Band (Don Philippini), 2 performances

Concert Orchestra (Harry Clifford), 1 performance

Bob Dunham Dance Orchestra, 3 performances

Archie Morris Dance Orchestra, 2 performances

Long Beach Dance Orchestra #1 (Dick Dixon), 1 performance

Long Beach Dance Orchestra #2 (Dick Dixon), 2 performances

Dance Orchestra (George Eckhardt), 1 performance

Dance Orchestra (Ed Perkins), 1 performance[18]

Unfortunately, the non-Anglo units became the first victims when Congress began to cut the number of musicians it would support, though they were also periodically restored, generally with fewer musicians.[19]

The local press, firmly Republican, led a chorus of objection to the invasion of the federal government into what had been a local or state responsibility, and it tended to give the activities of Federal One agencies minimal coverage. This was not at all unique to Los Angeles, but the way this policy played out for the FMP there is closely tied to local practices. By the 1930s, the habit of giving priority to press releases from our old friend L. E. Behymer for his regular stable of "attractions" was long ingrained; reports of FMP performances could not hope to supplant his customary space, and the papers were not disposed to expand their music coverage to accommodate the goals of the new agencies. It is well worth noting that Behymer, long allied with the *Times,* demonstrated a certain ambivalence about the FMP. He was well aware of the need, for he took advantage of the program to protect his personal interests; yet he criticized its wastefulness regularly in his correspondence and dragged his feet from his position as a member of its local advisory board.[20] More legitimately, he was concerned that competition from the proposed federally subsidized orchestras might threaten the existence of the Philharmonic, already reeling from the unexpected death in 1934 of its creator and long-term guarantor, William Andrews Clark, Jr., whose will contained no further provision for the orchestra.

The choices made in organizing and administering the FMP and its successor, the WPA Music Project, vividly reflect certain unresolved issues in the world of music making and, more generally, societal divisions, cutting among them in contradictory ways, locally as well as nationally. The contrasts already drawn with the Federal Theatre Project illustrate some of them, as do the two specific FMP incidents I describe below. In addition, there was something of an administrative gap between the sister agencies on the local as well as the national levels. The Federal Theatre Project, operating in the same strongly Republican, anti–New Deal atmosphere fanned by the local press in Los Angeles, kept in place the successful administrators from the previous SERA program in Los Angeles (J. Howard Miller and George Gerwing in particular); these had already created a viable way to meet their diverse goals. The FMP did not have the luxury of retaining strong administrators who carried over from SERA, which was not Sokoloff's fault, since he was not involved with FMP's predecessors and seems not to have consulted with them when he took over. Sokoloff's actions in the opera-related incident described below were bound to counter any hope of developing such leadership. Of the two incidents to be described, the first, which concerns a production of *La Traviata* in the fall of 1936, exposes the arrogance of those at the top of the musical hierarchy, especially Sokoloff, whose sovereign contempt for his project's organization and intended purpose in this case created the brouhaha. (Violation of the "10 percent" rule—that 90 percent of any project's personnel must be financially eligible for relief—was a glaring example.) It also earned the project this sobriquet, "the stormy petrel of the government unemployment relief organizations here," from the anti-WPA *Times*.[21] The second incident deals with the efforts of local composers to get their music performed by FMP units and raises perennial issues around the fundamental nature of American music and culture.

THE FEDERAL MUSIC PROJECT'S 1936 PRODUCTION OF *LA TRAVIATA*

As soon as the Federal Music Project was funded, late in 1935, an opera department was organized in Los Angeles, reflecting the long-time popularity of the genre and the lack of a resident company. Its initial musical director was long-time Los Angeles resident Dr. Alois Reiser, a Czech-born cellist, composer, and conductor.[22] By March 1936, with cooperation from the Theatre Project, Reiser was able to present Jacques Offenbach's *Les Contes de Hoffman*, locally translated as *Love Tales of Hoffman*, in Long Beach, San Bernardino, and Pasadena, to large and enthusiastic audiences. Emanuel Wolf-Ferrari's *Secret of Suzanne* and Otto Nicolai's *Merry Wives of Windsor* were in rehearsal.[23] Later that year, on October 27, 1936, under entirely different circumstances, a production of Verdi's *La Traviata* opened for a short run at Philharmonic Auditorium. The production tells a cautionary tale about Sokoloff's leadership.

Some weeks after *Love Tales of Hoffman*, Max Rabinoff, who had earlier achieved success with opera productions in Boston, arrived in Los Angeles with the intention of forming an opera company using FMP resources. Perversely, his role was not clarified for the local staff, even those who were already producing operas. This is evident from a July 9 letter written by Bruno David Ussher (the knowledgeable music critic previously met, whose paper had folded and who was at this point based in Salt Lake City as the FMP western regional director) to Sokoloff in Washington: "The fact that Mr. Rabinoff deliberately or unwittingly gives the impression that he has been sent here from Washington, that he has various commitments from you to take over the opera unit, is perhaps a minor point, but it gives him a nimbus . . . which makes it difficult . . . in case the whole affair should prove not the success of which Mr. Rabinoff is so sure."

Ussher went on to point out that Rabinoff had been unsuccessful in his attempts to form a committee of guarantors, that he was unrealistic in his estimate of the cost of bringing in major artists and in his financial projections (which would have had a troupe of 270 persons self-supporting in six months), and that he had committed the "treachery" of complaining about

Figure 27. Cover, *The Baton,* April 1937. Published monthly, July 1936–July 1937, by the Federal Music Project of California. Courtesy of National Archives and Records Administration, RG 69, FMP Correspondence 1936–40, 1936–37, California Miscellaneous.

the recalcitrance of Ussher, Behymer, and others to the Democratic Central Committee. At the same time, according to Ussher, Rabinoff repeatedly denied that he had any personal interest in taking over the opera project. Ussher then offered his own more modest plans for setting up a company.[24] From his Washington office, Sokoloff not only overruled Ussher's more cautious counterproposal; he also emphatically decreed full cooperation with Rabinoff by all project employees at the peril of their jobs.

The new grand opera unit had begun with organizational meetings involving Rabinoff, the local volunteer advisory board, and an assortment of local project administrators. At one of these meetings it was collectively decided to produce grand opera in English, thus reviving the fondly remembered, older concept of opera as popular entertainment. Discussion of choice of opera revolved chiefly around two comic operas, *Martha* and *The Merry Wives of Windsor*. Rabinoff overruled this consensus:

> The majority of the committee were, in fact with one exception—(Mr. Rabinoff)—in favor of "Merry Wives," as it was thought that this opera was a novelty, that the production costs would not be too great, and that the roles could be handled without much difficulty, chiefly by singers already on the project. . . . The sentiment of the committee also was strongly against using an opera which depended chiefly upon the soprano or tenor roles, and which had already been exploited by famous artists. It was felt that opera in America should endeavor to divorce itself as far as possible from the Star system of opera at present in vogue. On the other hand, that the Federal Project should endeavor to produce successful opera from the standpoint of ensemble, rather than a Star cast. However, in spite of this committee sentiment, Mr. Rabinoff selected *La Traviata* which calls for a soprano and a tenor of a very high calibre.[25]

Since the necessary paperwork was not completed in a timely fashion, some of the artists Rabinoff hired from outside the local project went unpaid. When the conductor he had hired resigned, Rabinoff found another one outside the project, then bypassed the project staff entirely in hiring outside publicity people to promote himself and his production.[26]

Rabinoff's "free hand," decreed by Sokoloff from Washington, created problems that went beyond these issues, drawing unfavorable public attention to the project. Rumors of maladministration and abuse of the project's primary relief function, enthusiastically fanned by the local papers, were particularly unwelcome in the last weeks of President Roosevelt's fall 1936 campaign for reelection. A letter signed by the members of the Glendale, California, FMP concert band complained to Harry Hopkins, Roosevelt's close associate and an architect of the WPA, that the symphony and opera were getting too much of the project's attention. They added, "Why are non-relief persons being surreptitiously infiltrated in the orchestras and other units, and men and women being dismissed by a system of auditions that are too obvious in their vicious intentions?"[27] The fiercely anti-Roosevelt *Times* gleefully reported a split among project workers over the opera.

Despite the public rumors and behind-the-scenes confusion, the opera opened as planned, drawing the usual reviews from local music critics. There was a second kind of coverage as well. The *Times*, like other papers in the area, ran two stories after its opening. The first was a review by its regular music critic, Isabel Morse Jones: "*La Traviata* as staged and directed by the eminent impresario, Max Rabinoff, attracted a record crowd to the Philharmonic Auditorium last night. . . . The local project loaned the opera its principal orchestra and a large chorus, both of which were successful in the effort to make this a major musical event." Jones's review was cut from later editions.[28]

The second *Times* story, unsigned and not cut from later editions, ran in the news section and carried the headline "Opera Venture Draws Fire." It reported the politically explosive fact that many more of the opera's personnel were not certified as on relief than the 10 percent permitted by the FMP's enabling legislation.

> Around the Max Rabinoff grand opera venture in the Federal Music Project . . . is revolving a cyclonic discussion that is stirring local musical circles.
>
> Financed with public funds appropriated to give jobs to unemployed musicians in Los Angeles county, Rabinoff's undertaking in grand opera production starts with three principals, none of whom is on relief and includes eight in minor roles, only one of whom is on relief.
>
> The entire ballet of twenty-four includes none on relief. Likewise, only a proportion of those in the large chorus, in the musicians' pit, backstage and otherwise supporting the production are on relief.
>
> In all, 32 percent of the entire aggregation has been selected from non-relief circles, according to official figures, while unofficial figures from persons connected with the project place the non-relief proportion at about 50 percent.[29]

Two days later, the *Times* published a follow-up story, using the opera production as its example.

RELIEF AND NON-RELIEF

> The farther the administration's program of made-work relief goes, the heavier becomes its load upon the public and the farther it gets from the purpose for which it was created. . . .
>
> Even the percentage of 25 to 75 does not hold for Federal Music Projects, however, if the Max Rabinoff grand opera at the Philharmonic is typical. This runs up to 32 per cent, . . . but even that does not tell the story. Of a cast of twelve only one . . . was drawn from the relief list, and none of the ballet of twenty-four was so drawn. . . . The best-paid performers were never on relief. In the entire Federal Music Project here 17 per cent are non-relief workers and draw 19 per cent of the pay.
>
> At least they will until after [next week's presidential] election.[30]

Immediately following the opening, Harlé Jervis (California state director, based in Los Angeles) wired Sokoloff jubilantly: "Opening of *Traviata* in Los Angeles last night attracted capacity house tremendous enthusiasm shown by audience many curtain calls and spontaneous applause stop federal opera attracted great many people who never saw opera before and they liked it" (October 28). That very day, scrupulously observing the project's organizational chain of command, Jervis endorsed a staff recommendation that opera productions cease and Rabinoff be dismissed following the close of the production. She relayed the recommendation to Ussher, who added his approval and garnered that of Clayton E. Triggs, a WPA administrator not subordinate to Sokoloff, before sending it on to Sokoloff. Ussher added "leading members of the advisory board" to his list of supporters, probably indicating that Behymer (chair of the unpaid local advisory board, with long experience at sidestepping public disasters) acceded to the dismissal.[31]

At first Sokoloff responded to Jervis: "In view your enthusiastic telegram relative huge success opera performance cannot understand your subsequent recommendation to cancel opera project and dismiss Rabinoff. . . . Under no circumstances dismiss Rabinoff until you hear from me nor do anything about closing opera." However, Triggs had already reported to his own and Sokoloff's superiors. In a memo, "Personal and Confidential to Ellen S. Woodward, Asst. Administrator, WPA, DC," he noted that "Mr. Rabinoff's 'Traviata' has caused much criticism from the public and the press." Citing the figure that nonrelief personnel were sometimes up to 50 percent of the opera project's staff, he mentioned Sokoloff's "direct orders . . . to give Max Rabinoff 'anything he wanted'" as a leading source of the trouble. He wrote that it was "impossible to defend this. . . . The pleasant way for this to be handled would, of course, be for Dr. Sokoloff to inform Dr. Ussher 'that he agrees' with the recommendation to discontinue Grand Opera in Los Angeles "until it can be put on a relief basis."

Thus overruled from above, Sokoloff had to abandon Rabinoff, sealing the fate of the Los Angeles grand opera project even before the run of *La Traviata* was over. A final scene concerning its even shorter-term fate is contained in a report filed a few days later, entitled "Failure of Opera Performance Friday Night, November 6th." Rabinoff, advised that he would be dismissed following the final performance, retaliated by advising the principals he had brought in that the last performance had been canceled. Local administrator Loren Greene struggled to bring about the performance while the audience waited, but he had to abandon the effort, apologize to the waiting audience for the hour-long delay consumed by acrimonious backstage discussions, and refund their admissions.

At approximately 11:00 o'clock Friday morning, Mr. Rabinoff called me informing me that the ballet group was not going to appear and that Rodolfo Hoyos, the baritone, was seriously ill. . . . In the meantime, Michio Ito and his assistant of the ballet group came in and informed me that Mr. Rabinoff, at 11:00 A.M. Friday, had announced to them that they were through Thursday night, November 5th, and would not be paid for their Friday night's performance. I proved to Mr. Ito that Mr. Rabinoff had misinformed him and at about 4:00 o'clock in the afternoon he agreed to have the ballet ready for performance Friday night if it were humanly possible. . . . At about 3:30 P.M. Friday, Rabinoff again called me and told me that it was impossible for Hoyos to sing, so I told him that I would make every effort to get a baritone for him. . . . Finally at about 4:30 P.M. [I] lined up Claudio Frigerio, who according to the reports to me, knew the part very well having sung it with the Metropolitan Opera Company. . . .

Upon my arrival back stage in the Pasadena Civic Auditorium about 7:15, Mr. Rabinoff met me and I told him that I had secured the services of Frigerio to sing the part. . . . He then said that the show would not be put on without his being allowed to go in front of the curtain and announce to the crowd what a "dirty deal" he had gotten from the Federal Music Project. Of course, I informed him that would be impossible but that if he wished I would send a man out to make the announcement that Mr. Rabinoff was not to be credited with the production. Mr. Rabinoff then said "alright, if we are going to put on the show get Frigerio down here so that we can run over the parts with Miss de Philippe and Felix Knight." . . . Mr. Rabinoff immediately took us in to Miss de Philippe's dressing room where . . . [she] flared up and stated she would not go on as it would ruin her reputation. . . . Mr. Frigerio asked her point-blank if she and Mr. Knight felt that it would be detrimental to their reputation to sing with him, to which they both replied very vehemently in the negative. Miss de Philippe then took it upon herself to give approximately a 10 minute lecture to me about what a "dirty deal" various people connected with the Federal Music Project had played on Mr. Rabinoff and her. . . . Miss de Philippe made statements to the effect that representatives of the Federal Music Project, not under my jurisdiction, had bought off the newspapers to be sure that publicity given her and Mr. Rabinoff was detrimental. . . . In the meantime, I had gone out on the stage with Felix Knight pleading with him to see the necessity of putting on the performance, with most of the company listening to our discussion. Mr. Knight then weakened somewhat, and the company standing around pleaded with him to get ready and put on the show with them as they wanted to go on. . . . At about 9:05 after having made an announcement to the crowd that we were slightly delayed, [I was told that] . . . Miss de Philippe might go on and to get Felix Knight ready. When I turned to get Mr. Knight, I was informed that he had gotten in his car and gone home. Realizing the impossibility of putting on any kind of a professional performance, I felt that it was necessary to abandon the idea and refund the money.[32]

As an immediate outcome of this fiasco, the opera program in Southern California was canceled. Ussher was fired from the project a month later; the position of western regional director, which he had occupied, was never again filled. Sokoloff left the project at the time of its 1939 reorganization to conduct the Seattle Symphony. Jervis, who had been the only female state director in the entire FMP, left in 1938; she went to study in Paris with Nadia Boulanger before joining the Department of State.[33] The opera project was restored, with new personnel and carefully limited conditions, eight months after the close of *La Traviata*.[34] A year later, reductions in project personnel forced it to shut down permanently. (The light opera unit was not directly affected by the *La Traviata* brouhaha. It gradually commanded more and more of the Los Angeles project's attention, expanding to two companies and generating its own set of problems, until further quota reductions caused it, too, to close down. It was eventually able to continue on its own.) In late 1939, the reorganized Southern California project was still the nation's largest, with thirteen hundred persons; in January 1940 it was reduced to five hundred. Earl V. Moore, who succeeded Sokoloff as national director, found it appropriate to state early and often that "the Federal Music Project was, and its successor, the WPA Music Program, *is*, an agency for the emergency relief of musicians."[35]

THE "SOCIETY OF NATIVE AMERICAN COMPOSERS" AND THE FEDERAL SYMPHONY

All of the arts projects were extensively reorganized by Congress in 1939. One of the most publicized results of the new legislation was the elimination of the Federal Theatre Project.[36] The reorganization also shifted control of the program away from its federal agency, turning it over to the states and stressing local participation and responsibility. Thus the Los Angeles Music Project's final year of symphony concerts began to reflect local interests more fully. If much of what it did was new, it was also distinctly conservative.

Florence Lawrence, the *Examiner*'s critic, had authored a supplemental story about the *La Traviata* production that raised the underlying issues around "American" music with a xenophobic twist. Under the heading "U.S. Cash Spent on Alien Art," she wrote:

American dollars are being expended this year to develop musical art and intelligence in this country. American composers are working and waiting patiently for a hearing of their own compositions. And last week Government financed a grand opera production, at what was obviously considerable cost, and presented an old Verdi opera, on an even older French theme, sung in Italian.

The performance supplied, to be sure, a temporary entertainment for some two or three thousand persons. But did it do anything for native creative art? Did it provide anything novel for either listeners or singers. It did not. . . .

The opera already has been sung here many times and will be given again and again by opera companies for years to come. . . .

If these United States are to sponsor music of grand opera caliber, it would be interesting to build it along lines which will make for a stronger and more comprehensive national taste in music. . . .

"Pretty good for dollar opera," a comment heard frequently during the performance of last week, is not sufficient basis for approval.

The dollars which clinked into the box office did not begin to pay for such a lavish—and not always dextrous [sic]—production. If funds are to be supplied by the national treasury for the purpose of providing grand opera, how much more significant if the operas were selected from American works, and so cast and staged that they may become a compelling feature of local cultural life. . . .

If the Music Project contemplates a continuance of such operatic ventures, how doubly interesting the productions would be by exploiting native language, composers and traditions.[37]

By 1940–41, the final full season in which the reorganized Los Angeles Music Project operated, the xenophobic tone of Lawrence's diatribe had become much more prominent, indeed, had definitively taken over the long-standing American music movement. Nationally, the project's administrators had found they could garner the necessary annual congressional appropriation more easily by emphasizing the "American" aspects of the project. Local units were asked to report on what American music they had performed, and lists were appended to the project's regular reports to Congress.[38]

Locally, the question of American music had been raised even before Florence Lawrence's 1936 critique, though to relatively little effect. Over the decades before the Depression, several clubs dedicated to the performance of music by American composers had existed, dating from Arthur Farwell's pre–World War I travels and his organization of American Music Centers in many U.S. cities, including Los Angeles. (He had visited Los Angeles as early as 1904; around 1920 he served as composer in residence and director of the Community Sing in Pasadena.) In the 1920s, the National Federation of Women's Clubs had published a bibliography of American music suited to performance at music clubs; the California Federation of Music Clubs had published its own list of compositions by residents of the state in 1919, as one of its first actions.[39] In Southern California, the Cadman Creative Club (later the Creative Arts Club) and the local Society for the Advancement of American Music, along with many other clubs, had explicitly supported performances of the music of local composers at their meetings. The production of Parker's *Fairyland* in 1915 was also a result of this movement. While this practice had kept the work of some Americans before one part of the public—mostly middle-class white women—it did not replace the rather larger audiences that performances of new works by the old Los Angeles Symphony had reached in its twenty-odd years or the People's Orchestra had in its less than two. The division that removed most "American" and most other "new" music from the repertoire of symphony orchestras and opera companies and consigned it largely to the music clubs in the 1920s—the pre-Depression decade of prosperity—was one indication of the hardening of the lines among various categories of music that was a characteristic of the decade following World War I. Since symphony, opera, and the performances of a selected few traveling virtuosi had far larger budgets and were considered more public, music club performances were increasingly assumed to be tainted by an aura of amateurism, presumably connected to the domination of their membership by women.[40] Thus, American concert music was minimally supported, slipping ever further into the background and lower in the musical hierarchy.

Los Angeles' numerous resident composers, most of them politically and musically conservative, watched as the FMP was organized, and when its local orchestras focused on the usual European repertoire, not much changed from two decades earlier. In mid-1936, Charles Wakefield Cadman, Homer Grunn, and Mary Carr Moore, three of the most prominent of the local composers whose music was regularly performed in club venues, agreed on their common need to organize in order to seek performances of their music by the new project's performing groups. These ensembles had been started under the direction of various old-line European-born conductors, a group that had always relied heavily on the European concert repertoire in their programming. Fittingly, these local composers conducted their initial discussion at the annual dinner of the local Music Teachers' Association, the group that had once organized the People's Orchestra. Mostly they wanted a chance to be heard, as Moore wrote: "It is hoped that the combined efforts of this group will eventually succeed in gaining the attention of Symphony and Opera conductors, most of whom are foreigners and cannot know of the material available, unless it is brought to their attention."[41]

Local critic-composer Richard Drake Saunders, who was also present, added the tone of xenophobia that soon came back to haunt the group:

> The real fact is that European trained artists have long held a virtual monopoly, which they are desperately afraid of losing. If the American public takes to American works, it will obviously soon progress to taking up American performers, and the third-rate Europeans who have long flooded this country will find their jobs non-existent.
>
> But in the last year a new factor has been injected into the equation, the WPA music projects. There are now symphonic orchestras available, and moreover symphony orchestras which have no prejudice against American music, but which are willing to lend a helpful hand.[42]

The newly organized California Society of Composers produced two substantial festivals of American music in 1937 and 1938, each of which included one concert by an FMP orchestra along with concerts of chamber music. These festivals were among the city's first devoted to American music. In all, music by some twenty-seven composers, nearly all of them Los Angeles residents, was performed.[43] Other festivals or concerts that programmed new music (not all by Americans) and were organized at the same time or soon after included Arthur Leslie Jacobs's Festival of Modern Music; the New Music Forum, the public readings held by the American Society of Music Arrangers, and, in 1939, the long-lasting, more avant-garde-oriented Evenings on the Roof.[44]

The California Society of Composers' orientation was toward the work of older composers in what had come to be considered relatively conservative styles. Though the issues that broke it up now seem to have turned on these stylistic differences, the society came apart over the ugly issue of whether the foreign-born, even longtime residents and naturalized citizens, could be considered "American" composers and therefore hold office in their group. The controversy was very public, and it could scarcely have been more destructive. Hoping to broaden the society's scope, several younger members, most of them employed in the movie studios, organized a write-in campaign, resulting in the election of English-born arranger Vernon Leftwich as president. Two new organizations emerged from the ruins. The Hollywood composers organized the American Society of Music Arrangers and

Figure 28. California Society of Composers, circa 1937. Standing, from left: Frank Colby (editor of the *Pacific Coast Musician*), Zhar Bickford, Baruch Klein, Hugo Davise, Homer Grunn, and Ernest Douglas. Seated, from left: Scott Bradley, Mabel Woodworth (USC faculty), Vernon Leftwich, Mary Carr Moore, Frances Marion Ralston, and Arthur Carr. On floor: Ethel Dofflemeyer. Courtesy of Cambria Master Recordings and Archives.

Composers, a group that remains active today. The older composers reorganized as the Society of Native American Composers, with an explicit place-of-birth requirement. They attempted to increase their membership by removing the older requirement that members must have composed in "the larger forms," thus opening its ranks to more women, many of them composers of songs and short piano pieces. In addition, they sought to become a national organization, garnering support briefly from such national figures as Amy Beach, Howard Hanson, Carl Ruggles, and Charles Ives. (The generous Ives sent a donation of fifty dollars before he began to have second thoughts.)[45]

Others saw the Society of Native American Composers (SNAC) as a logical extension of the need to help American composers. Richard Drake Saunders argued, for example, that the organization, "definitely nationalistic in its formation and intention," was a necessary step.[46] On the other hand,

Ussher, whose coverage of new music and the work of local composers in general had been the most thorough and interested among the city's critics since his arrival from Germany in 1919 (and who by now had returned from his FMP sinecure to writing criticism), took another view, writing somewhat later with more than a suggestion of bitterness,

> I take it that emphasis is laid by the sponsoring society on the fact that composers are native to these shores. I am wondering whether the spirit of true Americanism as distilled in the ink of official signatures necessarily differs when used in the bureau of vital statistics from that of the immigration office.
>
> Sometimes I wonder, too, whether the real nationality of music does not come with the emotional perception and expressional objective of the composer, rather than with the mere facts of locality of birth.
>
> Had the music performed particular flavor which one could easily recognize as American? . . . I have not been able to discover the "American" quality.[47]

In fact, had the members of SNAC been able to characterize a style as specifically "American" that applied to the work of every working American composer, they might have avoided couching their discussion in such starkly and unattractively nativist terms. It must be said, though, that no such term or phrase has yet been coined, nor has an unoffending code word been devised for such a style. Even among the relatively small group of composers directly involved in any of these three societies, the diversity of interests involved would almost certainly have overwhelmed even the best intentions.[48]

Before it was overcome by World War II and the aging of its leading members, SNAC presented a number of small concerts and workshops, but never with the publicity and public support garnered by the California Society of Composer's earlier festivals. Its most important public success was one in which its influence was diluted in the very manner that had led its organizers to leave the CSC in the first place. SNAC became the formal sponsor of the Federal Symphony's entire 1940–41 season. Each of the orchestra's sixteen concerts at the Embassy Auditorium (the FMP was generally shut out of the acoustically superior Philharmonic Auditorium; the aborted opera project seems to have been the exception) bore the rubric, "The Society of Native American Composers presents the Southern California Symphony." Three members of the selection committee (never a majority), which conductor James Sample had organized to screen compositions submitted for performance, were members of SNAC. In that season, works by forty-six Americans, including several Latin Americans and many émigrés, were performed. Only nine of the forty-six were members of SNAC; the rest ran the gamut from actor Lionel Barrymore through composers Samuel Barber, Erich Korngold, Vernon Leftwich, and Eugene Zador.[49] The New York–based journal *Modern Music* took negative notice: "The WPA Symphony runs a series in connection with an organization called 'The Society of Native American Composers.' Until now the output has been very depressing, the usual program featuring items like the *Symphony* by Charles Wakefield Cadman about which the less said the better."[50]

Others saw a need for SNAC and supported it, regardless of the nativism that had been one aspect of the old Progressive movement and now, as the émigrés from Hitler gathered in Los Angeles, seemed uglier than ever. After all, American composers, especially those not based in New York City, did need help in getting their works heard. European composers and musicians dominated the art music establishment to the virtual exclusion of others; there was no argument about that. How, and even whether, to absorb music by Americans into the canon of symphonic music remained a problem. Like others Americans, composers in the United States, including Los Angeles, encompassed a diversity of backgrounds, prejudices, political positions, and musical styles. SNAC was led by a group of older composers of both sexes who hoped to sustain a regional culture of music making already under siege from a wide range of cultural forces. To say the least, they chose an unnecessarily problematic response to the old conundrum about American concert music, a response that proved self-limiting and even destructive to their cause.

·   ·   ·

In the end, the Federal Music Project, even in conservative Los Angeles, overcame the foibles of its administrators to achieve its goals of putting musicians to work, playing a lot of music, and reaching large new audiences. In doing so, it served some musicians, genres, and audiences better than it did others. Among the positives, it gave some U.S.-born musicians the professional experience that prepared them to take principal chairs in major symphonies after World War II. (Until then, these chairs were almost entirely filled by European-born musicians.) Although relatively few women were served by the FMP, there were some breakthroughs. Modest Altschuler, the Russian-born conductor who is quoted near the start of this chapter, was promptly and firmly overruled when he refused even to audition women applicants for the FMP orchestras at the start of the project. By the end, about 15 percent of the Southern California Symphony musicians were

Figure 29. WPA Orchestra and dance troupe. SHADES OF L.A. ARCHIVES/Los Angeles Public Library.

women, including its concertmaster, Eunice Wennermark. (Like other major American orchestras, the Los Angeles Philharmonic did not accept women as members at that time.) Elsewhere in the country, in Buffalo and Oklahoma City, for example, orchestras organized under the FMP continued long after World War II brought a resounding conclusion to the Great Depression. In New York, the practice of public sponsorship of the arts led to the organization of the City Center for Music and Drama, which was unable to sustain a symphony orchestra but fostered a major, long-lasting opera company, the New York City Opera. Regrettably, there was no such aftereffect in Los Angeles.

Sokoloff's apparent lack of interest in the organization and administration of the Federal Music Project is notable. His would-be imperial gesture in trying to bestow the Los Angeles project's resources on Max Rabinoff to develop a grand opera company would seem to have been a result of that indifference. That scheme backfired resoundingly, partly from its own weight and partly because of local political machinations. Given such political imbroglios, it is not surprising that strong local leadership did not materialize.

And, given the public influence of the California Society of Composers and its successor, it is unlikely that radical new music in any genre would have found a strong welcome, though it might have gained a bigger toehold. One may speculate that, had local composers' symphonic or band music been welcomed at the start, more of it might have emerged by the end of the Federal Music Project, and the regrettable, deceptively labeled Society of Native American Composers might never have emerged at all.

The Federal One arts projects and their shorter-term predecessors were the first U.S. experiments with federal aid to the arts. Among other things, the Music Project demonstrated how such a program, conceived as a radical departure from earlier practice, was actually implemented in a way that now seems surprisingly conservative as well as, sometimes, downright clumsy. Nationally, the emphasis on symphonic music harked back to Progressive-era ideas of "improving" the public taste, morals, and general quality of life, with all the unresolved issues about ethnic and religious background, immigration status, race, gender, and class that were implicit when the doctrine of musical meliorism was put into practice. It also reflects the central position held by symphonic music in the Progressive era. Although the Music Project became more responsive to local needs as time went on, steady reductions in its budget and then the advent of World War II meant that, at least for Los Angeles, the project never found a way to rise definitively above the limitations imposed by this background. Given its peculiar combination of the new and the old, it serves here as a coda—and provides an indecisive farewell with suitably mixed implications—to this account of music making in Progressive-era Los Angeles.

Los Angeles Population Growth, with Racial and Ethnic Distribution

Data in the tables that follow are taken from decennial reports of the United States Census.

TABLE 1. Los Angeles Population Growth

Year	City of Los Angeles	Los Angeles County
1850	1,610	3,530
1860	4,392	11,333
1870	5,728	15,309
1880	11,183	33,381
1890	50,395	101,454
1900	102,479	170,298
1910	319,198	504,131
1920	576,673	936,455
1930	1,238,048	2,208,492
1940	1,504,277	2,785,643

NOTE: The population of Los Angeles (city and county) grew very rapidly through this period. Table 2 shows that it was always very white. Counting methods do not reflect the Mexican/Hispanic presence or, starting in 1870, the Native American presence.

TABLE 2. Population Characteristics of Los Angeles
and San Francisco, 1930

	Los Angeles	San Francisco
Total population	1,238,048	634,394
Native white, native parentage	49.9%	37.1%
Native white, foreign or mixed parentage	22.1%	32.5%
Foreign-born white	14.7%	24.2%
Negro or other race (includes Indians, Chinese, Japanese, and other nonwhites)	13.3%	6.2%

NOTES: Neither city had large racial minorities. Los Angeles had a much smaller proportion of foreign-born persons and native-born persons with one foreign-born parent than San Francisco, an older city that was a gateway for immigration. The proportion of foreign-born persons in both cities was higher in earlier decades but was never as high in Los Angeles as in San Francisco. In 1870, for example, 49 percent of the population of San Francisco was foreign-born, but only 35 percent was in Los Angeles.

ETHNIC DISTRIBUTION: The white population given here includes both native- and foreign-born whites. Generally, U.S.-born whites account for 65 to 75 percent or more of the white population in LA County during this time period. In 1910, for example, there were 60,584 foreign-born whites, fewer than 20 percent of the city's population. By 1920, after a decade in which the overall population of Los Angeles doubled, reaching a million, Mexicans were significantly more numerous than blacks in the city (21,598 to 15,579, as counted by the U.S. Census). (At least one estimate of the Mexican population was almost 50 percent higher than that of the U.S. Census.) Asians, no longer separated in the U.S. Census by country of origin, numbered 14,230.

TABLE 3. Principal Ethnic Origins of the 60,584
Foreign-Born Whites in Los Angeles County, 1910

Germany or Austria	20.1%
England, Scotland, or Wales	15.8
Canada	13.6
Mexico	9.3
Sweden, Norway, or Denmark	9.1
Russia	7.9
Ireland	6.3

NOTE: The ethnic mix was different in San Francisco, which had
more Italians and Chinese and fewer Mexicans and African Americans.

TABLE 4. Racial Distribution as Counted by the United States Census: Los Angeles County

Year	Total	White	Indian (Native American)	Chinese	Japanese	Free Colored/African Descent
1850	3,530	3,518	—	—	—	12
1860	11,333	9,221	2,014	11	—	87
1870	15,309	14,720	219	236	—	134
1880	33,381	31,717	316	1,160	—	188
1890	101,454	95,033	144	4,424	36	1,817
1900	170,198	163,875	69	3,209	204	2,841
1910	504,131	483,547	97	2,602	8,461	9,424

NOTES: A dash indicates that the category was not counted at all in that year. The Mexican population was not counted separately in determining racial distribution. While the Native American population declined sharply after 1860, the Chinese population increased steadily, declining only after 1890. Japanese, mostly farmworkers, increased sharply after 1900.

TABLE 5. Gender Distribution in Los Angeles
and San Francisco: Ratio of Males per 100 Females

	Total Population		African American Population	
	1910	1920	1910	1920
Los Angeles	103.9	97.8	94.0	90.2
San Francisco	131.6	116.6	166.1	129.5

NOTE: Males normally outnumber females in the population. However, the imbalance was much less pronounced in Los Angeles than in, for example, San Francisco, and even was reversed at times. The gold discoveries of 1849 brought a disproportionate number of males to San Francisco, and the proportion remained high sixty years later. Los Angeles had no comparable population-changing event. In 1880, before the railroad made immigration easier, there were 112.1 males per 100 females in Los Angeles. The coming of direct rail transportation in 1886 made immigration from the eastern United States easier, attracting more women.

Musicians and Teachers of Music in the United States and Los Angeles

TABLE 6. Musicians and Teachers of Music (Separately) in the United States, by Gender, in 1870 and 1910

	Musicians			Teachers of Music		
Year	Total Number	% Male	% Female	Total Number	% Male	% Female
1870	6,519	97	3	9,491	59	41
1910	54,832	71	29	83,851	19	81

NOTES: The professions of musician and teacher of music were counted separately through the 1910 Census; afterward they were grouped together. Both professions grew much faster than the overall population between 1870 and 1910. The proportion of women in both professions grew even faster in those years, though that trend was reversed after 1910. Even though the proportion of women musicians grew tenfold in that period, they remained a minority. Not so for teachers of music, a profession that came to be dominated by women, reaching what turned out to be a high point in 1910.

Table 7 shows that, when the two professions are grouped together, the gender differences remain but are not so pronounced. It also shows that the proportion of women in the twin professions declined after 1910; even the absolute number of women declined, while the total number of people engaged in these professions continued to grow.

Table 8 shows how these trends worked after 1910, nationally, in both Los Angeles and New York City. Both cities diverged progressively from the national average and from each other.

SOURCE: These data are taken from decennial reports of the United States Census.

TABLE 7. Musicians and Teachers of Music (in Total) in the United States, by Gender, 1870–1930

Year	Total Number of Musicians and Teachers of Music	% Male	% Female	Total U.S. Population
1870	16,010	64	36	38,558,371
1890	62,155	44	56	62,622,250
1910	138,683	39	61	91,972,266
1930	165,128	52	48	122,775,046

SOURCE: These data are taken from decennial reports of the United States Census.

TABLE 8. Musicians and Teachers of Music, by Gender
(Percentages Only)

Year	Nationwide		Los Angeles		New York City	
	% Male	% Female	% Male	% Female	% Male	% Female
1910	39	61	40	60	62	38
1920	44	56	47	53	66	34
1930	52	48	59	41	72	28
1940	54	46	67	33	74	26

SOURCE: These data are taken from decennial reports of the United States Census.

TABLE 9. Racial Minorities: Musicians and Teachers of Music in Los Angeles

	1910	*1920*
Black	9 men, 13 women	48 men, 25 women
Asian	None	5 (gender not recorded)

SOURCE: These data are taken from decennial reports of the United States Census.

TABLE 10. Musicians and Teachers of Music per
10,000 Population in 1910, by City

City	Musicians and Teachers of Music
Los Angeles	45.8
Denver	42.1
Boston	38.9
San Francisco	38.2
Seattle	37.9
Oakland (CA)	36.6
Kansas City (MO)	35.6
Portland (OR)	35.5
Spokane	33.4
Minneapolis	32.7
Albany (NY)	32.3
New York City	31.8

NOTE: Seven of the first eight cities listed here are in the western
United States.

SOURCE: These figures are discussed in Henry J. Harris, "The Occupation of Musician in the United States," *Musical Quarterly* 1,
no. 2 (April 1915): 299–311. Harris drew his statistics from the
1910 Census.

A Music Chronology for Los Angeles, 1781–1941

1781   First European settlement

1850   California becomes a part of the United States

1869   First transcontinental railroad completed (to San Francisco)

1876   Southern Pacific Railroad from San Francisco to Los Angeles opens

1879   Unitarian Thursdays

1880   Los Angeles population exceeds 11,000

1884   O. W. Child's Grand Opera House opens

1886   Atchison, Topeka, and Santa Fe Railroad, direct to LA from Kansas City, opens

1887   Visit of National Opera Company; Hazard's Pavilion opens

1888   Los Angeles Theater opens; first efforts to organize a philharmonic society; Ellis Club (men's chorus) organized

1889   Treble Clef Club (women's chorus) organized

1893   LA Women's Orchestra organized; Tally Brothers open a phonograph parlor

1893   A. J. Stamm's Philharmonic (first concert)

1896   Vitascope movies shown at Orpheum Theater, on vaudeville bill, at Tally's Edison Phonograph and Kinetoscope Parlor on South Spring Street

1897   LA Symphony organized (first concert in 1898); U.S. premiere of Puccini's opera *La Bohème*

1899   Chutes Park opens at Washington Gardens

1900   LA's population reaches 100,000

1902   Tally's Electric Theatre (claimed by some to be the first theater in the United States devoted exclusively to motion pictures)

1904   Gamut Club organized

1906   Temple/Clune's/Philharmonic Auditorium opens on site of Hazard's

1912   People's Orchestra organized

1915   Opera *Fairyland* produced for National Federation of Music Clubs; *Birth of a Nation* (movie) opens at Clune's

1917   Community Sings organized

1918   LA Philharmonic organized (first concerts 1919)

1919   Final concert of LA Symphony; first Hollywood Bowl organization; Grauman's Million Dollar Theater, a movie palace on South Broadway, opens

1920   *Pilgrimage Play* first performed (outdoors, near Bowl)

1921   Nordskog/Sunshine Records issued, with Kid Ory

1922   Symphonies under the Stars inaugurated at Hollywood Bowl; Henry Cowell's first performances in LA

1923   Biltmore Hotel opens; early 1920s, Spikes Brothers active; Apex Club (later Club Alabam) opens on Central Avenue

1924   Euterpe Opera Reading Club organized

1925   First concert of Henry Cowell's New Music Society presented; competing week-long seasons by Los Angeles Grand Opera Company and California Grand Opera Association

1927   *The Jazz Singer,* first successful sound film

1928   Copland's Concerto for Piano performed at the Hollywood Bowl

1929   Dunbar Hotel opens on Central Avenue

1930   City of LA population goes over 1 million

1934   William Grant Still and Arnold Schoenberg arrive

1935   Federal Music Project begins

1939 Co-Art Turntable recordings; WPA reorganized; Federal Theatre Project closes; first Evenings on the Roof concert

1941 United States enters World War II, contributing to major changes in Los Angeles culture, including its music making

Notes

PREFACE AND ACKNOWLEDGMENTS

1. Catherine Parsons Smith and Cynthia S. Richardson, *Mary Carr Moore, American Composer* (Ann Arbor: University of Michigan Press, 1987). Moore (1873–1954) enjoyed a strong local reputation from the time she arrived (1926) until the advent of World War II and even for a few years beyond. Several of her operas received local semiprofessional productions. For a list of sometime composers, see Smith, "Primary Documentation of California Composers," in Steven Fry, ed., *California's Musical Wealth* (Los Angeles: Southern California Music Library Association, 1988), 1–8.

1. MUSIC MAKING AS POPULAR PRACTICE

1. Dorothy Lamb Crawford, *Evenings On and Off the Roof: Pioneering Concerts in Los Angeles, 1939–1971* (Berkeley and Los Angeles: University of California Press, 1995), describes the advent of high modernism in Los Angeles from 1939, posits "hostile cultural surroundings" for it (1), refers to "the anti-intellectual, culturally unfocused Los Angeles" (13), and so forth. See also Jerome Moross, "Hollywood Music without Movies," *Modern Music* 18 (1941): 261. It is precisely Crawford's "culturally unfocused" Los Angeles that is my topic. Some of the ideas in this book were initially considered in my "Inventing Tradition: Symphony and Opera in Progressive-Era Los Angeles," in Michael Saffle, ed., *Music and Culture in America, 1861–1918* (New York: Garland Publishing, 1998), 299–322.

2. The 1910 Census shows 45.8 per 10,000 population, in comparison to 32.7 for Minneapolis and 31.8 for New York City. That means about 1,400 musicians and music teachers for the city of around 300,000 total population. See appendix B, table 10, for more detail. For contemporary discussions of these figures, see Henry J. Harris, "The Occupation of Musician in the United States," *Musical Quarterly* 1, no. 2 (April 1915): 299–311; also Joseph A. Hill, *Women in*

Gainful Occupations: 1870 to 1920, Census Monographs 9 (Washington, DC: U.S. Department of Commerce, 1929).

3. T. J. Jackson Lears, *No Place of Grace: Antimodernism and the Transformation of American Culture, 1880–1920* (New York: Pantheon, 1981), has regrettably little to say about music.

4. Lawrence Levine, *Highbrow/Lowbrow: The Emergence of Cultural Hierarchy in America* (Cambridge, MA: Harvard University Press, 1988), has been especially provocative for historians of American music.

5. The "music-making" approach used here is similar to the concept of "musicking" in Christopher Small, *Musicking: The Meanings of Performing and Listening* (Hanover, NH: University Press of New England, 1998). Here it is applied to concert music, opera, and church and domestic music in contrast to Small's usage.

6. See the essays in John C. Tibbetts, ed., *Dvořák in America, 1892–95* (Portland, OR: Amadeus Press, 1993). Genres that drew heavily on the African American experience, such as ragtime, blues, and early jazz, are absent from those turn-of-the-century discussions about "American" music.

7. For example, Howard Swan, *Music in the Southwest* (San Marino, CA: Huntington Library, 1952), focuses on the career of impresario L. E. Behymer; Crawford, *Evenings On and Off the Roof*, focuses on one high modernist concert series.

8. Michael Broyles, "Art Music from 1860 to 1920," in David Nicholls, ed., *The Cambridge History of American Music* (Cambridge: Cambridge University Press, 1998), 216.

9. For Los Angeles, some examples are Caroline Estes Smith, *The Philharmonic Orchestra of Los Angeles: The First Decade, 1919–1929* (Los Angeles: Press of United Printing Company, 1930); Robert Morell Stevenson, ed., numerous articles in *Inter-American Music Review*, 1978–present, passim; John Koegel, "Mexican American Music in Nineteenth-Century Southern California: The Lummis Wax Cylinder Collection at the Southwest Museum, Los Angeles," PhD dissertation, Claremont Graduate University, 1994; Sharyn Wiley Yeoman, "Messages from the Promised Land: Bohemian Los Angeles, 1880–1920," PhD dissertation, University of Colorado at Boulder, 2003; Julian Kyle, "Sounding the City: Jazz, African American Nightlife, and the Articulation of Race in 1940s Los Angeles," PhD dissertation, University of California, Irvine, 2000; Brian Scott Walls, "Chamber Music in Los Angeles, 1922–1954: A History of Concert Series, Ensembles, and Repertoire," MA thesis, California State University, Long Beach, 1980; Burton Lewis Karson, "Music Criticism in Los Angeles, 1895–1910," doctor of musical arts (hereafter DMA) dissertation, University of Southern California, 1964; Francis Hill Baxter, "A History of Music Education in the Los Angeles City Schools," DMA dissertation, University of Southern California, 1960; Janice Ann Foy, "Croatian Sacred Musical Tradition in Los Angeles: History, Style, and Meaning," PhD dissertation, University of California, Los Angeles, 1990.

For a more politically oriented study of Progressive-era music making in another city, see Derek Vaillant, *Sounds of Reform: Progressivism and Music in Chicago, 1873–1935* (Chapel Hill: University of North Carolina Press, 2003). Chicago's longer history, its larger size, its very large immigrant population, and its greater accessibility to the East Coast all figure in creating a significantly different history.

10. Henry W. Splitter, "Music in Los Angeles," *Historical Society of Southern California Quarterly* (December 1956): 307–44. In addition, see Jeannie G. Pool, "Music in Los Angeles, 1860–1900," MA thesis, California State University, Northridge, 1987; and, more recently, Kenneth Marcus, *Musical Metropolis: Los Angeles and the Creation of a Music Culture, 1880–1940* (London: Palgrave Macmillan, 2004), which does not duplicate the contents of this book. Marcus devotes a chapter to music education in Los Angeles; most of the rest deals with the development of radio, recordings, and the film colony, topics I have generally avoided because they already have long bibliographies. Robert Murrell Stevenson, "Los Angeles," in H. Wiley Hitchcock and Stanley Sadie, eds., *The New Grove Dictionary of American Music*, vol. 3 (London: Macmillan Press, 1986), 107–15, available in a shortened version in *New Grove Online*, is the best and far the most accurate summary of the city's early music history.

11. The most important of these numerous histories, given in the order of their first editions, are as follow: Louis C. Elson, *The History of American Music* (New York: Macmillan, 1904; rev. ed., 1915); John Tasker Howard, *Our American Music: Three Hundred Years of It* (New York: Thomas Y. Crowell Co., 1931, rev. 1939, 1946, and 1954); Gilbert Chase, *America's Music, from the Pilgrims to the Present*, 3rd ed. (New York: McGraw-Hill, 1955; rev. eds., New York: McGraw-Hill, 1966, and Champaign: University of Illinois Press, 1987); H. Wiley Hitchcock, *Music in the United States: A Historical Introduction* (Englewood Cliffs, NJ: Prentice-Hall, 1969, rev. 1974, 1988, and 2000); Charles Hamm, *Music in the New World* (New York: Norton, 1983); David Nicholls, ed., *The Cambridge History of American Music* (Cambridge: Cambridge University Press, 1998); and Richard Crawford, *America's Musical Life: A History* (New York: Norton, 2001).

12. Surveys of Southern California history, useful for background but containing little about music, include Carey McWilliams, *Southern California Country: An Island on the Land* (New York: Duell, Sloan and Pearce, 1946); Kevin Starr, *Material Dreams: Southern California through the 1920s* (New York: Oxford University Press, 1990); Kevin Starr, *Inventing the Dream: California through the Progressive Era* (New York: Oxford University Press, 1985); Kevin Starr, *Endangered Dreams: The Great Depression in California* (New York: Oxford University Press, 1996); Kevin Starr, *The Dream Endures: California Enters the 1940s* (New York: Oxford University Press, 1997).

13. See especially Judith Fetterley, *Writing out of Place: Regionalism, Women, and American Literary Culture* (Urbana: University of Illinois Press, 2003). Fetterley argues that writers other than white males tend to be assigned to the category of "regional" authors as a way to minimize the value of their work.

14. According to the U.S. Census, females made up 39 percent of San Francisco's population in 1890, while they constituted 47 percent of Los Angeles'. In 1900, 50 percent of the population over fifteen years of age in Los Angeles was female, as compared with 43 percent for San Francisco.

15. My "'A Distinguishing Virility': On Feminism and Modernism in American Art Music," in S. Cook and J. Tsou, eds., *Cecilia Reclaimed: Perspectives on Gender and Music* (Urbana: University of Illinois Press, 1994), 90–106, quotes many statements reflecting this attitude.

16. See, for example, Robert M. Lewis, ed., *From Traveling Show to Vaudeville: Theatrical Spectacle in America, 1830–1910* (Baltimore: Johns Hopkins University Press, 2003).

17. Mary Louise Pratt, *Imperial Eyes: Travel Writing and Transculturation* (London: Routledge, 1992), uses *transculturation* in describing "how subordinated or marginal groups select and invent from material transmitted to them by a dominant or metropolitan culture" (6), relevant to this study because of its distance and historical subordination from eastern urban centers in the United States. Los Angeles, which was not among the top fifty U.S. cities in 1880, had become the tenth largest in 1920, the first time its population outnumbered that of San Francisco.

18. Julian Johnson, "Music and Musicians," *Los Angeles Times*, June 6, 1909, sec. III, 2.

19. For more on commercial mass culture, see Lary L. May, *Screening Out the Past: The Birth of Mass Culture and the Motion Picture Industry* (New York: Oxford University Press, 1980); Lary L. May, *The Big Tomorrow: Hollywood and the Politics of the American Way* (Chicago: University of Chicago Press, 2000); Kathy Lee Peiss, *Cheap Amusements: Working Women and Leisure in Turn-of-the-Century New York* (Philadelphia: Temple University Press, 1986); and Roy Rosenzweig, *Eight Hours for What We Will: Workers and Leisure in an Industrial City, 1870–1920* (Cambridge: Cambridge University Press, 1983).

20. Los Angeles was not a union town, partly because the *Los Angeles Times* mounted an unrelenting, decades-long anti-union campaign. Because the *Times* is the only Los Angeles daily that continues to publish and because its microfilm archive is easier to read and more readily searchable than those of its defunct rivals, its idiosyncratic early views have tended to prevail. For recent descriptions of how the *Los Angeles Times* became the city's dominant newspaper in this period and the influence of its long-time owner, Col. Harrison Gray Otis, see Dennis McDougal, *Privileged Son: Otis Chandler and the Rise and Fall of the L.A. Times Dynasty* (Cambridge, MA: Perseus Publishing, 2001).

21. Attitudes toward the influence of the European concert tradition on American music have changed in the late twentieth and early twenty-first centuries. For example, "Europe versus America" is a chapter title in the 1955 edition of Chase's *America's Music from the Pilgrims to the Present*. The chapter claimed that "the products, the techniques, and the carriers of European musical culture had no organic—that is, no true cultural—relationship to the struc-

ture of American society . . . [they] proved sterile . . . they failed to provide the American composer with 'a usable past'" (323). The chapter title is retained in the third edition (1987), but the quotation is deleted.

German music is singled out for its powerful influence in Hitchcock, *Music in the United States: A Historical Introduction*, 3rd edition (1988). See 89–93 and especially 140–45. The introduction to his section "The Cultivated Tradition" refers to the "highwater mark" reached in the period 1865–1920 by "Germanophilia" in music (140).

Adrienne Fried Block, "New York's Orchestras and the 'American' Composer: A Nineteenth-Century View," in John Graziano, ed., *Importing Culture: European Music and Musicians in New York, 1840–1890* (Rochester, NY: University of Rochester Press, 2006), 114–34, takes the position that the many German-speakers who immigrated in the nineteenth century brought their cultural traditions along, and these evolved slowly as the immigrants assimilated.

All these discussions helped create what Eric Hobsbawm has called "invented traditions" in his introduction to Hobsbawm and Terence Ranger, eds., *The Invention of Tradition* (Cambridge: Cambridge University Press, 1983), 1. See also Hobsbawm's essay in the same collection, "Mass-Producing Traditions: Europe, 1870–1914," 263–307. An "invented tradition" is defined as "a set of symbolic ritual practices that function to inculcate values and behavior patterns signifying continuity with the past" (introduction, 1).

22. Emanuel Rubin, "Jeannette Meyer Thurber (1850–1946): Music for a Democracy," in Ralph P. Locke and Cyrilla Barr, eds., *Cultivating Music in America: Women Patrons and Activists since 1860* (Berkeley and Los Angeles: University of California Press, 1997), 134–63, is a recent detailed account of the National Opera Company that fails to mention its Los Angeles visit.

23. William Deverell, *Whitewashed Adobe: The Rise of Los Angeles and the Remaking of Its Mexican Past* (Berkeley and Los Angeles: University of California Press, 2004); Michael E. Engh, *Frontier Faiths: Church, Temple, and Synagogue in Los Angeles, 1846–1888* (Albuquerque: University of New Mexico Press, 1992); Steven Joseph Loza, *Barrio Rhythm: Mexican American Music in Los Angeles* (Urbana: University of Illinois Press, 1993); Douglas Monroy, "Rebirth: Mexican Los Angeles from the Great Migration to the Great Depression* (Berkeley and Los Angeles: University of California Press, 1999); Douglas Monroy, *Thrown among Strangers: The Making of Mexican Culture in Frontier California* (Berkeley and Los Angeles: University of California Press, 1990); Douglas Monroy, "Making Mexico in Los Angeles." In Thomas Sitton and William Deverell, eds., *Metropolis in the Making: Los Angeles in the 1920s* (Berkeley and Los Angeles: University of California Press, 2001), 161–78; G. Bromley Oxnam, director, Los Angeles City Survey, *The Mexican in Los Angeles: Los Angeles City Survey* (Los Angeles: Interchurch World Movement of North America, June 1920); Roberto R. Trevino, *Becoming Mexican American: The Spanish-Language Press and the Biculturation of California Elites, 1852–1870* (Stanford, CA: Stanford Center for Chicano Research, Working Paper Series, no. 27, 1989).

Concerning Latin music in the United States more generally, see John Storm Roberts, *The Latin Tinge: The Impact of Latin American Music on the United States,* 2nd ed. (New York: Oxford University Press, 1999); Louise K. Stein, "Before the Latin Tinge: Spanish Music and the 'Spanish Idiom' in the United States, 1778–1940," in Richard L. Kagan, ed., *Spain in America: The Origins of Hispanism in the United States* (Urbana: University of Illinois Press, 1990), 193–246; Robert Stevenson, "The Latin Tinge, 1800–1900," *Inter-American Music Review* 2, no. 2 (Spring–Summer 1980): 73–101.

2. "THE LARGEST AND MOST ENTHUSIASTIC AUDIENCE THAT EVER HAS ASSEMBLED IN THE CITY"

1. Pio Pico, per *Don Pio Pico's Historical Narrative* (July 1848), translated by Arthur P. Botello, edited by Martin Cole and Henry Welcome (Glendale, CA: A. H. Clark, 1973).

2. The image was launched with Helen Hunt Jackson's immensely popular *Ramona* (1884) and was continued in Charles F. Lummis, *The Spanish Pioneers* (Chicago: A. C. McClurg, 1893); Charles F. Lummis, *The Land of Poco Tiempo* (New York: C. Scribner's Sons, 1921); and other titles in the years between. For recent discussions of Lummis's contributions, see John Koegel, "Preserving the Sounds of the 'Old' Southwest: Charles Lummis and His Cylinder Collection of Mexican American and Indian Music," *Association for Recorded Sound Collections Journal* 29 (1998): 1–29; and Yeoman, "Messages from the Promised Land."

3. U.S. Bureau of the Census, *Tenth Census of the United States, 1880* (Washington, DC: Government Printing Office, 1883), vol. 19, 781. Toberman also reported that twenty miles of the city's two hundred miles of streets were paved, and there were horse-drawn railroads (mileage unspecified).

By 1930, there were, among other things designed to support the growth, several monumental water projects extending for hundreds of miles, which had required federal complicity and support. Land speculation was even more prevalent than music making throughout the period.

4. No schedule of German-language events is available. For Spanish-language events, see John Koegel, "*Canciones del país:* Mexican Musical Life in California after the Gold Rush," *California History* 78, no. 3 (1999): 160–87, 215–19, see especially 182. See also Koegel, "Calendar of Southern California Amusements 1852–1897; Designed for the Spanish-Speaking Public," *Inter-American Music Review* 13, no. 2 (1993): 115–43; and Koegel, "Mexican and Mexican-American Musical Life in Southern California, 1850–1900," *Inter-American Music Review* 13, no. 2 (1993): 111–14. Examples from the "Calendar" (139) are these references to music for 1887: January 29, an ad by Arévalo for a benefit performance at Armory Hall to help build a Catholic church in Wilmington; September 5 to 14, Zerega's Royal Spanish Troubadours at the Grand Opera House (three nights), San Bernardino Opera House (one night), San Diego (two nights), and Pomona (one night). For 1888 (149): April 29, the

Great Zarzuela Spanish Opera Bouffe Company, Grand Opera House (*Boccaccio*, von Suppé; *Les Noces d'Olivette*, Edmond Audran); and May 12 to 18, the Hispano-Mexicano Opera Company (*El Reloj de Lucerna*, Barbieri; *El Sargento Federico*, Gaztambide).

5. Sue Wolfer Earnest, "An Historical Study of the Growth of the Theatre in Southern California," PhD dissertation, University of Southern California, 1947, contains an invaluable Day Book listing theatrical events in vol. 3, part 2: 1–178, the source of information in the following paragraph.

6. Marra returned to Los Angeles in 1882; Fabbri, in 1876, 1881, and later.

7. Ticket prices for the National Opera Company ranged from one to four dollars per performance, with special prices for season tickets. This was more expensive than the usual theatrical scale in Los Angeles but well below the prices charged in San Francisco, for example. The box office for the first three nights was said to be seventeen thousand dollars.

8. A few operas on American subjects, and some by American composers, existed but had not entered the repertoire. Verdi's *Un Ballo in maschera*, transplanted to Boston for political reasons unrelated to U.S. history and culture, is the exception.

9. For more on the remarkable and significant career of Theodore Thomas in the United States, see Rose Fay Thomas, ed., *Memoirs of Theodore Thomas* (1911; reprint, Freeport, NY: Books for Libraries Press, 1971). Lawrence Levine, *Highbrow/Lowbrow*, devotes a chapter to Thomas's efforts to "raise" musical standards in the United States. Named the American Opera Company in its first season (1886), it was reorganized in its second year, when it traveled to the West Coast, as the National Opera Company. It folded permanently a few weeks after leaving behind its Los Angeles success, stranding its members in Buffalo.

10. *Los Angeles Tribune*, May 1887, ads, passim. Baird's Minstrels played the first week of May; Mr. and Mrs. Knight played May 10–14; and Professor Carpenter opened on Sunday, May 16.

11. *Los Angeles Tribune*, May 12, 1887. The names attached were N. A. Covarrubias, president, and E. A. DeCamp, secretary.

12. *Los Angeles Tribune*, May 12, 1887. See chapter 6 for more on Washington Gardens around 1900.

13. For more on Los Angeles newspapers before 1900, see Henry Winfred Splitter, "Newspapers of Los Angeles: The First Fifty Years, 1851–1900," *Journal of the West* 2 (1963): 435–58.

14. *Los Angeles Evening Express*, May 19, 1887, 5.

15. *Los Angeles Tribune*, May 19, 1887, 5, col. 1.

16. *Los Angeles Times*, May 17, 1887, 4, "The World's Musical Advance," unsigned; possibly by W. F. Kubel.

17. *Los Angeles Evening Express*, May 19, 1887, 5.

18. Between 1880 (population 11,000) and 1890 (population 50,000), the average growth rate was between 16 and 17 percent per year. By this estimate, in 1887 there were about 32,000 persons in Los Angeles, of whom 65 percent, or 20,800, were age fifteen and over.

19. *Los Angeles Times,* May 19, 1887, 4. The *Times* would later change its position on ticket prices.

20. *Los Angeles Herald,* May 20, 1887, 4.

21. Theodore Thomas, handwritten note in scrapbook, vol. 25, Theodore Thomas Collection, Music Division, Library of Congress, 148. I am grateful to Wayne Shirley for calling this to my attention. No published sketches or interviews with Thomas have been located in the Los Angeles papers.

22. Ezra Schabas, "Thomas, Theodore," in H. Wiley Hitchcock and S. Sadie, eds., *Grove Dictionary of American Music,* vol. 3, 381 (London: Macmillan, 1896).

3. "A PRECARIOUS MEANS OF LIVING"

1. Charles Leland Bagley (1873–1965), "History of the Band and Orchestra Business in Los Angeles," *Overture* 4, no. 12 (October 1, 1924): 5. The final installment appeared in vol. 16, no. 12 (April 1937): 7. The *Overture* published semimonthly and, later on, monthly. Bagley announced a second project, a history of Local 47 and of the American Federation of Musicians, along with its predecessors, dating back to the 1870s. Although he never got to it, the materials he collected are in the Bagley Collection in the Archival Research Center at the University of Southern California.

2. Bagley, "History," *Overture* 4, no. 15 (November 15, 1924): 5.

3. Bagley arrived in Southern California on November 16, 1887. An early activist in the musicians' union by 1894, he served Local 47 as secretary (1902–10), president (1911–13), vice president (1918–22), and legal counsel (1922–61). He was a vice president of the American Federation of Musicians from 1931 to 1959. He was admitted to the California bar in 1909 and received law degrees from USC in 1910 and 1911.

4. Clarinet was his primary instrument. Cornet was a common double for musicians at that time; even violinist and later conductor Harley Hamilton played cornet occasionally in the early years.

5. Bagley's list of musicians and their day jobs includes Harley Hamilton, violinist and printer. Others who left the music profession to become prominent elsewhere include physicians H. H. Smith (flute) and F. J. Nutting (trombone), banker W. C. McQuillen (flute), dentist J. N. Larraia (violin), vice president of Southern California Edison Russell H. Ballard (cello), sheriff John C. Cline (cornet), deputy sheriff D. D. Parten (drums), capitalist G. Allan Hancock (cello and cornet), and several who were successful in the real estate business. Bagley, "History," *Overture* 8, no. 2 (June 1928): 6.

6. Bagley, "History," *Overture* 6, no. 1 (April 15, 1926): 5.

7. List and pay scale in box 4, Bagley Collection, Archival Research Center, University of Southern California.

8. The material on La Fiesta is from album 62, Behymer Ephemera Collection, Huntington Library (hereafter HL). Hobsbawm's concept of "invented" traditions (see chapter 1, n. 21), intended to cultivate a particular view of his-

tory, is particularly apt to La Fiesta. For the health-seeker image (long an embarrassment to the city's boosters), see John E. Baur, *The Health Seekers of Southern California, 1870–1900* (San Marino, CA: Huntington Library, 1959); Robert V. Hine, *California's Utopian Colonies* (San Marino, CA: Huntington Library, 1953); also Ralph E. Shaffer, *"Crazy Shaw": Frederick M. Shaw, Southern California's Forgotten Dreamer* (Pomona, CA: author, 2007).

9. Mamie Perry (Mrs. Charles Modini-Wood) had made a successful debut at La Scala in Milan some years earlier but had not been permitted by her wealthy father, William H. Perry, to pursue a career as a singer or to sing in public except for charitable occasions. Modini-Wood was a tenor who comanaged the Los Angeles Theater for a time.

10. I am grateful to Paul Charosh for this information.

11. The 1894 Fiesta took place from April 10 to 13. There were parades, a Carnival Night, a Children's Day, and a Floral Military Day. The first year's program book was published by R. W. Pridham and the Merchants and Manufacturers Association of Los Angeles. Among the numerous committees were one for music, including J. O. Koepfli, M. H. Newmark, H. T. Kubel, and L. Loeb, and one for entertainment, including H. C. Wyatt, C. N. Pike, J. H. Surk, C. Modini-Wood, and Lawrence Hanley.

12. *La Fiesta de Los Angeles, Official Program, 1897* (Los Angeles: R. W. Pridham, 1897).

13. "The Concert," *La Fiesta, 1897, Report of Committee of 30 to Commercial Bodies,* dated May 22, album 154, p. 13, Behymer Ephemera Collection, HL.

14. "Patriotic concert," Scrapbook, vol. 1, Press Clippings, Nov. 23, 1897—July 22, 1898, pp. 215–16, Behymer Ephemera Collection, HL. The Los Angeles Theater ad for this concert: "Monday night, May 9, 8 o'clock/Grand Concert/Addresses by Rev Burt Estes Howard, W. A. Harris Esq. Soloists: Mary Linck, prima donna contralto, J. Bond Francisco, violinist, Dr. Ludwig Semler, baritone, T. E. Rowan, Jr., tenor. Fiesta chorus, 200 voices, Seventh Regiment Band, 45 pieces, 500 seats at 50c. Frederick Stevenson, choral director; George Cann, band director. Frederick W. Blanchard was the impresario." (For more on Blanchard as an impresario, see chapter 4.)

15. Program courtesy of Cambria Master Recordings and Archives, Lomita, California.

16. *Los Angeles Times,* June 13, 1897, 26, the source of the "wheezy band." Among the comments of this review: "Faust himself might just about as well as not have stayed comfortably at home." Bagley, "History," *Overture* 7, no. 9 (January 1928): 4, reports a total of four performances. Arnold Kirofly was in charge of the production.

17. The band played three concerts in two days, then and on later visits, to packed houses. Bagley reported that the gate from the 1892 visit was five thousand dollars, more than the gate from the band's concerts in then-larger San Francisco. Bagley, "History," *Overture* 5, no. 20 (February 1, 1926): 5.

18. Swan (*Music in the Southwest,* 177) lists several amateur orchestras, be-

ginning around 1887; he considers Willhartitz's Philharmonic of 1888–89 the first symphony orchestra in Los Angeles. Smith, *The Philharmonic Orchestra of Los Angeles*, gives a clear and accurate account of Willhartitz's Philharmonic and A. J. Stamm's later orchestra, along with some information about the founding of the Los Angeles Women's Orchestra, in chapter 1, "Los Angeles' Early Symphonic Awakening," 15–24.

Bagley omits the Los Angeles Orchestral Society, under Harley Hamilton, a group that included business people and music students that gave at least one concert in 1890 (see chapter 5).

19. Letter, Edna Foy to her sister Cora Foy, February 18, 1892, Foy Family Papers, file cabinet C3, folder 25, HL. The letter continues, "Also a fine pianist. The program lasted until about 9 o'clock. They had the orchestra out in one of the halls, and dancing began at about 10 o'clock. All the floors were waxed and with that superb music it was enough to drive a person in a fit." Romandy died a few years later at age thirty-five.

20. Bagley, "History," *Overture* 5, no. 18 (January 1, 1926): 11.

21. Helena Modjeska (1844–1909) immigrated with a group of Polish people at the height of her success as an actress in Europe to a cooperative farm in Anaheim, California, in 1876. The venture was unsuccessful. She then learned English and became even more successful as an actress in her new language, in the United States and England.

22. Bagley, "History," *Overture* 5, no. 24 (April 1, 1926): 6; and 6, no. 1 (April 15, 1926): 6.

23. For more on Clark (1877–1934), an important Los Angeles patron, see Robert Murrell Stevenson and William E. Conway, *William Andrews Clark, Jr., His Cultural Legacy; Papers Read at a Clark Library Seminar, 7 November 1981* (Los Angeles: William Andrews Clark Memorial Library, 1985). For a muckraking account of Clark, see William D. Mangram, *The Clarks: An American Phenomenon* (New York: Silver Bow Press, 1941). Clark was the son of a U.S. senator (from Montana, not California) and an heir to a copper fortune. An amateur violinist and bibliophile, he lived for part of each year in Montana, Los Angeles, and Paris. His support of the Philharmonic is said to have been frowned on within his own family. His will contained no bequest for the orchestra. His library and home in Los Angeles became the William Andrews Clark Memorial Library, a part of the University of California, Los Angeles. William Severns reported that Clark decided to found his own orchestra, at least partly because his offer of assistance to the Los Angeles Symphony Orchestra had been snubbed.

24. Bagley, "History," *Overture* 6, no. 1 (April 15, 1926): 6. For a general account of pitch in Europe and the United States, see Bruce Haynes, "Pitch," I.2.vii, in Stanley Sadie, ed., *Revised New Grove Dictionary of Music and Musicians*, vol. 19 (London: Macmillan, 2000), 800. Through most of the nineteenth and twentieth centuries European orchestras have played at a'' = c.446 vibrations per second or higher. In 1858, European countries adopted the *diapason normal* of a'' = 435; the current standard of a'' = 440 was adopted in 1939. Vic-

torian English "sharp pitch" approximated a'' = 452. Bands in the western Unites States played at that high pitch or higher.

25. Bagley, "History," *Overture* 7, no. 5 (September 1927): 4, 5.

26. Adolf Tandler, violinist, had come to Los Angeles from Vienna in 1907 as part of a quartet. He conducted the old Los Angeles Symphony from 1913 until its demise in 1920. Later he organized the Tandler Little Symphony, directed theater orchestras, and played occasionally in the new Philharmonic.

27. Mrs. Dean Mason, "The Los Angeles Symphony Orchestra," chapter 2 in Smith, *The Philharmonic Orchestra of Los Angeles,* 27–38, is a clear contemporary exposition of the Symphony's history by one of its board members. Bagley's conclusion about "intrigue" is confirmed by the decision of Marie Rankin (Mrs. Chauncey D.) Clarke, a long-time board member who had acquired considerable wealth from oil discoveries in the city, not to endow the Symphony; instead, she became a major supporter of Claremont College. See George R. Martin, *The Clarke Story: Chauncey Dwight Clarke, Marie Rankin Clarke and the Claremont Colleges,* 3rd ed. (Claremont, CA: Claremont Graduate School and University Center, 1964).

28. Mrs. Mason's account differs from Bagley's and supplies additional detail. Mason reports that Mrs. Emily Earl guaranteed the orchestra three thousand dollars per year, starting in the second season ("The Los Angeles Symphony Orchestra," 33–34). The performance venue was supplied by W. H. Perry, owner of the Los Angeles Theater, and H. C. Wyatt and Charles Modini-Wood, its operators; at first they performed in a small upstairs theater next door, the Music Hall; after a year or two they moved to the larger theater.

29. Bagley, "History," *Overture* 15, no. 7 (November 1935): 6.

30. *Pacific Coast Musician* 8, no. 4 (April 1919): 4. Frank Colby, the magazine's editor, is the probable author of the editorial.

31. Bagley, "History," *Overture* 6, no. 14 (June 14, 1900): 8.

32. See chapter 12.

33. Bagley, "History," *Overture* 5, no. 20 (March 1926): 6–7.

34. Bagley, "History," *Overture* 15, no. 10 (February 1936): 8.

35. Victor O. Geoffrion, "The Outlook in the South," *Musical and Theatrical News* 1, no. 1 (January 15, 1920): 1, 10.

36. For an account of the nationwide difficulties created by the advent of sound films, see James P. Kraft, *Stage to Studio: Musicians and the Sound Revolutions, 1890–1950* (Baltimore: Johns Hopkins University Press, 1996), especially chapter 2, "Boom and Bust in Early Movie Theaters," 33–58.

37. Letter, Bagley to Nikolai Sokoloff, national head of the Federal Music Project, July 14, 1936, Behymer Papers, Manuscript Collection, folder "Federal Music Project."

38. Swan, *Music in the Southwest,* 166–67. In 1878, Day put together a large chorus and sang the Hallelujah Chorus with "the city's first concert band." Some years later, another large choral concert was reviewed in the *Times,* March 18, 1886, 2, "The Chorus Concert." A letter, signed "Tonic," reported an audience of three thousand, a chorus of four hundred, plus solos "a wonderful per-

formance" music by Handel, Beethoven, Rossini, Gounod, Bellini, Verdi. "A great treat, it was, and, it is confessed, a rather unexpected one, to hear in Los Angeles such grand music, and to hear so good directing as was done by Prof. Day." I am grateful to R. E. Shaffer for calling my attention to this reference.

39. See William Beck, "The Ellis-Orpheus Men's Chorus: The Story of Its First Century," *Hazard's Pavilion* 5 (1988): 1–33. Vaillant, *Sounds of Reform,* 28, credits the large number of *Mannerchor* in 1870s Chicago as a source for the audience for European concert music in that period.

4. "POPULAR PRICES WILL PREVAIL"

1. "Treasurer's Statements, New Los Angeles Theater," Behymer Manuscript Collection, HL. Daily box office receipts and attendance are recorded circa 1892–1902. Statements showing expenditures for each attraction exist for the season 1900–1901.

2. For more on Will Marion Cook (1869–1944), see Thomas L. Morgan, "Will Marion Cook," www.jass.com/wcook.html (accessed December 13, 2005); Maurice Peress, *Dvořák to Duke Ellington* (Oxford: Oxford University Press, 2004), especially chapter 13; and Marva Griffin Carter, "The Life and Music of Will Marion Cook," PhD dissertation, University of Illinois, 1988. Many of his sheet music publications are reproduced on the voluminous Library of Congress "American Memory" Web site: http://memory.loc.gov (accessed December 13, 2005).

3. Rogers married Clifford Lott, a baritone with whom she often appeared in concert. Later on, a son, Sinclair Lott, became the principal French horn in the Los Angeles Philharmonic. Arnold Krauss, violin, with whom she often performed in the Lott-Krauss concerts, was concertmaster of the Symphony under Harley Hamilton.

4. For information on Barnhart, see Claude Bragdon, *More Lives Than One* (New York: Alfred A. Knopf, 1938), especially 69–75 and 110–15; also *Western Graphic* 6, April 8, 1899, 13–14. Barnhart's appearance at the Friday Morning Club in Los Angeles in 1904 is chronicled in the scrapbooks of the Friday Morning Club at the Huntington Library. Barnhart was already associated with Arthur Farwell's American Music movement. Later he was very successful as an organizer of community choruses in New York City, Rochester, and elsewhere; he was also prominently associated with the pageantry movement. DeLano's ads frequently appear in newspapers of the time.

5. Bagley, "History," *Overture* 8, no. 2 (June 1928): 5.

6. "Treasurer's Statement, New Los Angeles Theater, 1900–1901," Behymer Manuscript Collection, HL.

7. For more on Mamie Perry, see chapter 3, n. 9.

8. The *Los Angeles Herald* (May 25, 1900) reported that the Los Angeles Theater was now controlled by Meyerfeldt, director of the Orpheum vaudeville circuit; three days later, the *Express* reported that the same theater was under the control of the Al Hayman theater syndicate. In August, the *Herald* reported that Wyatt

had leased the theater from Meyerfeldt, with the proviso that he not engage in price competition with the Orpheum. Clippings in Behymer Ephemera Collection, Press Clippings Scrapbook no. 6, HL. Charles W. Stern, *American Vaudeville* (New York: Da Capo Press, 1984), 4, reports that Keith and E. F. Albee organized the Vaudeville Managers' Association, a central vaudeville booking office, in 1900, establishing a vaudeville trust comparable to the existing theater trust.

9. See M. B. Leavitt, *Fifty Years in Theatrical Management* (New York: Broadway Publishing Company, 1912), 254–55; also Bagley, "History," *Overture* 5, no. 2 (May 1, 1925): 4. Bagley is the more reliable source for Los Angeles events. Shortly before his death in 1910, Wyatt is described as a local representative of "the syndicate." "H. C. Wyatt Seriously Ill," *Los Angeles Times,* July 21, 1910, I14.

10. *Los Angeles Times,* Los Angeles Theatre ads, October 9–30, 1. The first U.S. performance of *Bohème* took place on October 14, 1897.

11. "Box Office Receipts, Los Angeles Theater," Behymer Manuscript Collection, vol. "Feb–Dec, 1897," HL. Italian Grand Opera Co. (Del Conte); the gate was divided between the company and the house on a 75–25 percent basis. The first number is the attendance; the second, the gate. (Partial list only.)

Tues., 10/12/97, *La Gioconda,* 679, $541

Wed., 10/13, *Un Ballo in Maschera,* 396, $304.25

Thurs., 10/14, *La Bohème,* 523, $436.25 (company share, $327.20; house, $109.05)

Fri., 10/15, *Ernani,* 779, $603.

Sat., 10/16, matinee, *La Bohème,* 625, $412.50

Sat., 10/16, evening, *Il Trovatore,* 1,252, $995.25

Mon., 10/18, *Otello,* 601, $417.75

Tues., 10/19, *Rigoletto,* 430, $318.00

Wed., 10/20, matinee, *Il Trovatore,* 684, $459.50

Wed., 10/20, *Cavalleria rusticana* and *I Pagliacci,* 1,168, $959.75

12. *Los Angeles Capital* 6, no. 15, October 9, 1897, 6.

13. *Los Angeles Herald,* October 24, 1897, as quoted in Swan, *Music in the Southwest,* 188.

14. *Western Graphic* 6, no. 21 (May 27, 1899): 6.

15. Much of the material on Blanchard comes from an obituary notice in the *Los Angeles Evening Express,* September 22, 1928. See also "Blanchard, Fred W.," in *Who's Who in the Pacific Southwest: A Compilation of Authentic Biographical Sketches of Citizens of Southern California and Arizona* (Los Angeles: Times-Mirror Printing and Binding House, 1913), 47. His papers remain with his family and were not accessible when this was written; see Beverly Blanchard Nelson and Pamela T. Lundquist, *F. W. Blanchard: First President of the Hollywood Bowl* (Victoria, BC: Trafford Publishing Co., 2006).

16. Bagley, "History," *Overture* 7, no. 9 (January 1928): 4, reports that Harris Newmark, a prosperous merchant who had owned the property, built the Music and Art Building and that Blanchard ran it as Newmark's lessee.

17. W. Francis Gates (WFG), generally a reliable reporter, wrote for *Musical America* (June 7, 1919): 14, that Fred W. Blanchard, not Behymer, had been the Symphony's manager for the three seasons ending in spring 1919, "during which the debt of the orchestra of $30,000 has been paid and the audiences attending the concerts have been much increased in size."

18. The flyers are bound into Scrapbook no. 3, Behymer Ephemera Collection, HL. Some other artists sponsored by Fitzgerald in this time period were, according to the *Western Graphic* and the *Los Angeles Saturday Post*, January–June 1899, Gerome Helmont, boy violinist, at Simpson's; Mae Martinez, "In a Persian Garden," at Blanchard Hall; and Lisetta Regina Mariani, soprano. Fitzgerald, who had published some of his own music, came to Los Angeles in 1891. He continued in business into the late 1940s.

19. The performers were the Euterpean Male Quartet, assisted by a soprano and a pianist. The group was local.

20. Records of the Redpath Lyceum Bureau, a large supplier of traveling lecturers and musicians, are at the University of Iowa, but there is apparently nothing concerning Los Angeles.

21. *Los Angeles Saturday Post: A Family Story Paper* 4, no. 10, September 7, 1901, 7; 4, no. 21, November 23, 1901, 7.

22. Behymer's concert series were always called courses, reflecting their origin in the early educational lecture and concert series organized by his rivals. He initially offered his series as the "Star Concert Course," copying the title used by Blanchard the year before. Pressured, he quickly changed the name to the "Philharmonic Course," a name he retained for the next forty-five years.

23. One of Blanchard's publicity promotions read, "The marked demand for seats at 'popular-priced' entertainments this season has been greater than ever, and the Star, Imperial and People's courses, blocked out months in advance, have been readily taken to by the local public." *Los Angeles Saturday Post* 10, no. 15, October 8, 1904, 10. Blanchard's claim, "ninety-five out of every hundred contracts for [lyceum] events . . . on the Coast are issued from [Blanchard & Venter's] Los Angeles office. Courses of from five to ten events have already been closed by most of the leading cities of the Pacific Coast, including about a dozen in southern California," appeared two months earlier. *Los Angeles Saturday Post* 10, no. 7, August 13, 1904, 11.

24. Frederick Stevenson, column, *Los Angeles Graphic* 22, no. 10, April 8, 1905, 10.

25. *Los Angeles Saturday Post* 9, no. 18, April 30, 1904, 10–11. Sembrich performed on May 2; the Oratorio Society gave Bruch's *Arminius* on May 21 (both at Hazard's Pavilion); Watkins Mills, basso, and others appeared at "a Grand Lyric concert" at Simpson's Auditorium, on May 24. The railroad snafu prevented most of the delegates from arriving in time for Sembrich's perfor-

mance, but it gave an opportunity to repeat the Blanchard and Barnhart concert of May 3 some days later.

The *Los Angeles Times,* May 1, 1904, sec. vi, 2, gives the soloists and the program for the Blanchard-Barnhart concert: Maud Reese-Davies, soprano; Harriet Longstreet, contralto; Spencer Robinson, tenor; Lalla Fage, violinist; Blanche Williams, pianist; Alfred Butler, organist; William Mead, flutist. This was the program:

Weber, *Der Freischütz,* overture (orchestra)

Gounod, *By Babylon's Wave* (chorus & orchestra)

Delibes, "Bell Song," *Lakmé* (Davies & Mead)

Reinecke, "Evening Hymn" (chorus and tenor)

Wagner, *Lohengrin,* selections (orchestra)

Mendelssohn, "Thirteenth Psalm" (chorus and contralto)

Bohm, "Thine Only" (Robinson)

Rossini, "Inflammatus" (orchestra and Davies)

Gillett, "Loin du bal"

Mascagni, "Intermezzo," *Cavalleria rusticana*

Mendelssohn, "Wedding March"

Handel, "Hallelujah" (chorus and orchestra)

26. *Los Angeles Times,* Thursday, May 26, 1904, 6.

27. *Los Angeles Saturday Post* 10, no. 24, December 10, 1904, 10, carries the competing claims.

28. *Los Angeles Saturday Post* 10, no. 1, July 2, 1904, 15. Compare with Behymer's 1913 "too many concerts" in chapter 8, "Something of Good for the Future."

29. *Los Angeles Graphic* 22, no. 5, March 4, 1905, 23.

30. Stevenson made his opinion of Behymer and Jahn's production clear: "'Elijah' was, I regret to say, not one whit better than 'The Messiah.' . . . wherein then lay the failure? Briefly, and frankly, in the soloists and in the conductor. . . . I would have little respect for myself and less for my readers if these columns permitted that this 'Elijah' was either the 'Elijah' of Mendelssohn or in the slightest degree representative of Los Angeles." *Los Angeles Graphic* 22, no. 9, April 1, 1905, 23–24.

The Los Angeles Oratorio Society was successfully revived in 1918, under John Smallman; it continued to perform for several decades.

31. Johnson, "Music and Musicians." Johnson had actually written about theater more than music. His byline disappears very soon after this.

32. In 1900, a year after the contest got started in earnest, the city's population had reached one hundred thousand. Since the city's population tripled between 1900 and 1910, one might guess that the potential concert audience in-

creased by at least 50 percent in the four years immediately before the twin *Messiahs.*

33. *Los Angeles Saturday Post* 10, no. 15, October 8, 1904, 10.

34. Bagley reports that in January 1914 there were thirty-two movie theaters in Los Angeles that were advertising in the local papers. "History," *Overture* 11, no. 8 (December 1931): 8.

35. Clipping, probably from the *Los Angeles Times,* in album "Programs, 1903–1922," Friday Morning Club Collection, HL. On November 4, 1904, Arthur Farwell, assisted by local artists, delivered a lecture there, "Toward American Music: A Study in National Progress, with Special Reference to the Music of the American Indians." For more on Farwell, see Evelyn Davis Culbertson, *He Heard America Singing: Arthur Farwell, Composer and Crusading Music Educator* (Metuchen, NJ: Scarecrow Press, 1992); also Arthur Farwell, *"Wanderjahre of a Revolutionist" and Other Essays on American Music,* edited by Thomas Stoner (Rochester, NY: University of Rochester Press, 1995).

36. Charles F. Lummis, collector and translator; Arthur Farwell, piano accompaniments, *Spanish Songs of Old California,* reprint, ed. Michael Heisley (1st ed., 1923; Los Angeles: Historical Society of Southern California, 1987). The earliest discussion so far located on folk influences in European and American music in Los Angeles is by Edward F. Kubel in *Western Graphic* 9, no. 4 (July 28, 1900): 9–10. Kubel mentions Edward Everett Hale, Dvořák, and Krehbiel, but not Farwell.

5. AMATEURS, PROFESSIONALS, AND SYMPHONIES

1. Some wealthy males who had acquired performance skills also became patrons. William Andrews Clark, Jr., violinist and heir to a copper fortune, was one; G. Allan Hancock, cellist, yachtsman, and heir to an oil fortune, was another.

2. Women had worked in lower-paid, lower-status ensembles in restaurants and cafés all along; Bagley reports a Hungarian Ladies Orchestra as a regular feature of one of the city's cafés, as well as other such groups. For instance, Bagley ("History," *Overture* 9, no. 1 [May 1927]: 8, 9, 11) mentions the Venetian Ladies' Orchestra and the Klaus Ladies' Orchestra, both shorter-lived groups. Late in the life of the LA Symphony, Elsa Bierlich von Grofé, a cellist, became the orchestra's first female member. (She is better known now as the mother of composer Ferde Grofé.) Later, in the 1920s, some women worked in pit orchestras in the movie palaces.

3. Hamilton was the first violinist; the other members were Robert Paulson, violin; J. Bond Francisco, viola (later a successful artist); Herman Wangerman or Will Schilling, cello; and Max Leneberg, flute. In 1892 Hamilton organized another chamber ensemble, the Lorelei Quartette, with Mrs. M. A. Larrabee (piano), W. C. McQuillen (flute), and one of the musical Bierlich family (instrument not given).

4. *Pacific Coast Musical Review* (hereafter *PCMR*) 22, no. 5 (May 4, 1912):

4, reports the Women's Orchestra gave Hamilton a benefit after his illness in 1907, resulting in a gift of one thousand dollars for a trip abroad. See also Julian Johnson's column, *PCMR* 2, no. 1 (April 8, 1911): 6.

5. Noted in the *PCMR* 17, no. 12 (December 18, 1909): 19.

6. Hamilton also continued to conduct the (amateur) LA Orchestral Society after the Women's Orchestra was organized and at least for a time after the Symphony was under way. A story in the *Western Graphic* 6, no. 14 (April 8, 1899): 17, lists the members and reports Hamilton as the conductor of the "First Congregational Orchestra." The orchestra apparently continued, at least intermittently in some form, though it was not often reported in the press. The Los Angeles Symphony Club, conducted by Ilya Bronson, who was said to have organized it in 1912, is reported in the *Pacific Coast Musician* (hereafter *PCM*) 23, no. 19 (May 12, 1934): 3. At that point it had moved out of both church and theater; it gave annual concerts at the Ebell Club, on Wilshire Boulevard, starting in 1926.

7. *Los Angeles Graphic* 40, no. 12, February 14, 1914, 7.

8. Bagley reports that, when this became public knowledge at the close of the Symphony's second season, the musicians held a benefit concert for him. "History," *Overture* 7, no. 9 (January 1928): 4.

9. "Complex marriage" meant that community members were discouraged from "special" relationships (even when they joined the colony as married couples) and were encouraged to engage in consensual sex with others in the community, a practice that aroused objections among outsiders. Men were responsible for birth control; reproduction was encouraged after 1869.

10. Robert S. Fogarty, ed., *Desire and Duty at Oneida: Tirzah Miller's Intimate Memoir* (Bloomington: Indiana University Press, 2000). Fogarty's introduction, 3–44, describes the community in some detail. See also Fogarty, *All Things New: American Communes and Utopian Movements, 1860–1914* (Chicago: University of Chicago Press, 1990); and Louis J. Kern, *An Ordered Love: Sex Roles and Sexuality in Victorian Utopias: The Shakers, the Mormons, and the Oneida Community* (Chapel Hill: University of North Carolina Press, 1981). The community's buildings survived as of May 2004, although in some disrepair. The area has been preserved as a nonprofit foundation, separate from the long-prosperous manufacturing business that closed in 2005.

11. "Agreement concerning Harley Hamilton," H. H. Noyes Collection/Hamilton, Arents Research Library, Syracuse University. Harley later chose "Burnham" as his middle name.

12. "Musicians of Los Angeles: Embracing 150 Singers, Instrumentalists and Teachers, and including the Choirs of 21 Churches as constituted at the time of writing. Plates used by courtesy of the *Los Angeles Evening Express.* 1904–05." Found in album 156, "Memories," Behymer Ephemera Collection. These appear to be the newspaper clippings rather than a separate publication. The musicians are grouped on pages, by specialties. The emphasis is on church choirs, with sketches of choir directors, organists, and paid vocal soloists. The directors include Fred A. Bacon, Harley Hamilton, Julius A. Jahn, William H. Lott, William H. Mead, and Henry Schoenefeld.

Hamilton's daughter, Viola Hamilton Taylor, was interviewed in 1978–79 by Marian G. Cannon, author of "His Music Left an Echo: A Biography of Harley Hamilton, 1861–1933," *The Californians* (May/June 1983): 31–34. Taylor confirms his study in New York and further study abroad. Hamilton also went abroad in the summers, especially to Munich, while he was conducting. Taylor adds that on his 1912 trip he consulted specialists concerning his hearing. She reports that his students included Mabel Otis, daughter of the publisher of the Los Angeles *Times*, as well as the Foy sisters.

13. John B. Teeple, *The Oneida Family: Genealogy of a 19th Century Perfectionist Commune* (Cazenovia, NY: Gleaner Press, 1985), 14–17, 222.

14. Inslee left the Oneida Community several years before it broke up. One aspect of his disagreements with the community's founder, John H. Noyes, is described from Tirzah Miller's position in Fogarty, ed., *Desire and Duty at Oneida*, passim. Inslee named one of his community children "Haydn," an indication of the importance of music in his life.

15. *Dwight's Journal of Music* (Boston, 1852–81; reprinted in multivolume set, New York: Johnson Reprint Corporation, 1968). See also Judith Tick, "Passed Away Is the Piano Girl," in Jane Bowers and Judith Tick, eds., *Women Making Music: The Western Art Tradition, 1150–1950* (Urbana: University of Illinois Press, 1986), 325–48.

16. Alfred Metzger, *PCMR* 18, no. 6 (May 7, 1910): 10.

17. W. Francis Gates, *Los Angeles Graphic* 38, no. 24 (May 10, 1913): 8.

18. At one point in 1907, she was invited to perform with a women's orchestra being organized to play in a hotel for the summer. Apparently she did not take the position.

19. Foy Family Papers (hereafter FFP), white shirt box 2, folder 1, HL. Along with his brother, John Calvert Foy (born in Washington, DC, 1830), he also ran a cattle business for several years, some of the time in San Bernardino. The father of Samuel and John had immigrated from Northern Ireland.

20. The children were Samuel Calvert Foy (1860–60), Mary Emily Foy (1862–1962), James Calvert Foy (1865–1922), Oscar Foy (1867–67), Cora Calvert Foy (1870–1920), Samuel Calvert Foy (1873–74), Edna Calvert Foy (1875–1971), Irma Calvert Foy (1878–96), Alma Calvert Foy (1880–?), and Florence Calvert Foy (1883–?).

21. A temporary, summertime-only tent city continued for several more decades farther south, on the beach at Coronado.

22. Letter, Edna, at Santa Monica with the family, to Cora, at Mt. Shasta, July 30, 1891; and letter, Alma to Cora, from Santa Monica, July 14, 1891; FFP, Foy file cabinet C3 (2), folder 17, HL.

23. Letter, Cora to Edna, from San Diego, September 28, 1892, FFP, file cabinet B3C1, loose at back of 1892 folder (20), HL. Cora attended with her father. A program from a similar event in 1894 also survives in file cabinet B3D3, folder 33a: *Vest Pocket Guide to Cabrillo Celebration, San Diego, September 27, 28, 29, 1894.* Events include "Boulevard Race for Wheelmen"; aquatic sports, horse races, arrival and landing of Cabrillo; fireworks, Indian Village, Military Camp,

military drill, and, on the third morning, the farewell and departure of Cabrillo. Bands include the Golden Gate Park Band of San Francisco, Alfred Roncovieri, director, also the Los Angeles Military Band and City Guard Band.

24. Letter, Edna to Mama, "Sat." [1895], FFP, carton III, folder 3, "Foy letters—miscellaneous 2)," HL. Mary, Cora, and "Auntie" were also there at Camp Indolence.

25. Letter, Edna to Cora, December 18, 1891[92?], FFP, Foy file cabinet C3, folder 23, HL.

26. Maud Powell (1867–1920) did, in fact, earn this recognition; her early and continuing success made the violin an acceptable instrument for women to study. I have found no evidence that Powell concertized in Los Angeles.

27. Letters, Edna to Cora, December 29, 1891, and December 31, 1891, FFP, file cabinet C3, folder 24, HL.

28. Letter, Edna to Cora, February 7, 1892, FFP, file cabinet C3, folder 25, HL.

29. Letter, Edna to Cora, March 24, 1892, FFP, file cabinet C3, folder 25, HL.

30. "A Musical Debutante," *Los Angeles Capital* 2, no. 24, December 14, 1895, 8. An excerpt: "As she stepped upon the platform at Blanchard-Fitzgerald Hall, to which Mr. Harley Hamilton had invited a large number of discriminating music-lovers," she played Beethoven opus 30, no. 2; Henri Vieuxtemps, *Reverie*, opus 22; and Louis Spohr, *Duo*, opus 3, no. 2. A singer completed the program.

31. Hancock Banning was a developer of Catalina Island. Charles E. Pemberton, a violinist, played the oboe in the first seasons of the Los Angeles Symphony Orchestra before returning to the violin section. He taught for decades at the University of Southern California School of Music. William H. Mead, the organizer of this orchestra and an amateur flutist, helped organize the first musicians' union and later became a bank president. He was a member of the Water Board that undertook the Owens River Project. Banning and Mead were on the orchestra's board of directors, which was chaired by Dr. W. O. Green, also the concertmaster.

32. "Amateur Actors Give an Entertainment at [St. Paul's Church] Guild Hall," unidentified clipping enclosed in letter, Edna to Cora, September 16, 1893, FFP, white shirt box 2, folder 1, HL. "Led," in this context, means that Edna was concertmaster, not conductor. Very likely Julius Stamm, Harry Wood, Arthur Wood, and Julius Bierlich, listed as orchestra members, were the children of prominent musicians bearing the same surnames.

33. Letter, Edna to Cora, April 1, 1892, FFP, file cabinet C3, folder 26, HL.

34. Letter, Mama to Cora, November 20, 1891, FFP, file cabinet C3, folder 23, HL.

35. Having studied elocution and acting with G. A. Dobinson, Marion ("Mamie") Short taught elocution in Los Angeles in the 1880s (very likely to Cora, among others), giving recitations and acting in local Owl Club productions in 1888 and '89 before going to New York. A series of photos are in FFP, file cabinet A1 (4), folder "Marion Short," HL. George C. D. Odell, *Annals of the New York Stage*, vol. 15, *1891–94* (New York: Columbia University Press,

1927–49), 552, lists Marion Short as a "popular reciter" during the 1892–93 season. Her last noted appearance was on June 1, 1893, at Griffith Hall, Port Richmond. Short wrote to Cora that she turned down at least one dramatic role offered her by Major Pond. Eventually she returned to Los Angeles, where she coauthored a play, *Sweet Clover*, produced at the Mason Opera House, in October 1904 (*Los Angeles Herald*, Sunday supplement, October 9, 1904, 5).

36. Letter, Mama to Cora, February 22, 1892, FFP, file cabinet C3, folder 25, HL.

37. Letter, front page and date missing, FFP, white shirt box 2, folder 7, HL. This is almost certainly an earlier performance than the one in 1905 referred to in chapter 4, " 'Popular Prices Will Prevail.' "

38. Some of the musicians may have objected to Foy's exclusion from the Symphony. A. Willhartitz, who organized the Philharmonic concert of 1888, published "Woman in Music," *Musical Courier* 37, no. 9 (August 31, 1898): 29, intended as a reply to an earlier article in the same journal published June 22, 1892. Willhartitz lists 153 works by women composers. His focus is on women as composers, not as performers, however.

39. Letter, front page and date missing, FFP, white shirt box 2, folder 7, HL.

40. E. F. Kubel published a weekly music newspaper, the *Los Angeles World*, of which only a handful of issues survives.

41. Letter, Edna to Cora, February 18, 1898, FFP, white shirt box 2, folder 7, HL.

42. Letter, Mama to "My dear daughter" [i.e., Mary], March 2, 1898, FFP, white shirt box 2, folder 7, HL.

43. E. F. Kubel, concert review, *Los Angeles Times*, March 2, 1898, 10.

44. Émile Sauret (1852–1920) performed in Los Angeles in 1875, touring with pianist Teresa Carreño (1853–1917), to whom he was married. See Robert Stevenson, "Carreño's 1875 California Appearances," *Inter-American Music Review* 5, no. 2 (1983): 9–15. They performed in Turnverein Hall (opened 1872) June 25–28 and July 3. Frederik Christian Frederiksen (1869–1929), Norwegian violinist and conductor, studied at the Leipzig Conservatory and with Sauret in Berlin, taught in London at the Royal Academy of Music and later at Chicago Musical College.

45. It is doubtful that she completed it.

46. The letters from London are in FFP, boxes I/5 and IV/5, HL. A typed transcription is part of the collection.

47. Edna and Mary both wrote voluminous letters, carefully preserved and transcribed by the family.

48. Program, Ebell Society Musicale, FFP, carton VII, folder 4, HL. The quartet (Foy, Beatrice Kohler, Vella Knox, and Sarah Simons) played Schubert's *March Militaire*, an unidentified "Andante" by Mozart, Handel's famous "Largo," Boccherini's "Minuet" from op. 13, no. 5, Schumann's *Traumerei*, and a gavotte by Catlin. Edna played two solos, *Souvenir de Bade*, by Leonard, and *Reverie* by Vieuxtemps. Mrs. J. S. Rice sang two numbers; the pianist was Wenona Huntley.

49. Estelle Lawton Lindsey, "Woman's Symphony Now One of the Foremost Orchestras in the World," *Los Angeles Record*, 1907, n.d., FFP, carton I (boxes 1–4), 2, 3–4, HL. A program dated April 22, 1910, in the Behymer Ephemera Collection (album 154, HL), lists Hamilton as conductor and Mrs. Edna Foy Neher as concertmaster. The group's club-style organization is revealed by its list of officers: Cora Foy, president; Beatrice Atkins, vice president; Mrs. L. M. Loeb, secretary; Florence Longly, treasurer. Other members of the board of directors were Daisy Walters, Winifred Haig, Mrs. Hubert Parker, and Harley Hamilton. Behymer was manager. The list of personnel includes twenty-three violins, seven violas, six cellos, six basses, three flutes, two oboes (Gertrude Barrett is listed as "on leave of absence"), two clarinets, two bassoons, four horns, three trumpets, two trombones, and two tympani (Cora Foy is also "on leave of absence").

50. Jane Apostal, "Mary Emily Foy: 'Miss Los Angeles Herself,'" *Southern California Quarterly* 78, no. 2 (Summer 1996): 112, reports that Edna eloped with architect Otto Neher, whose firm designed the old Federal Bank Building in Lincoln Heights.

51. Letter, Edna to Cora, FFP, box 3, folder B3 (4), HL.

52. For general histories of women's clubs, see Karen Blair, *The Clubwoman as Feminist: True Womanhood Redefined, 1868–1914* (New York: Holmes and Meir Publishers, 1980); and Theodora Penny Martin, *The Sound of Our Own Voices: Women's Study Clubs, 1860–1910* (Boston: Beacon Press, 1987). For women's clubs in Los Angeles, see Mrs. Burton M. Williamson, ed., *Ladies Clubs and Societies in Los Angeles in 1892* (Los Angeles: Elmer King, 1925); Thelma Lee Hubbell and Gloria Ricci Lothrop, "The Friday Morning Club: A Los Angeles Legacy," *Southern California Quarterly* 50, no. 1 (Spring 1968): 59–90; Gloria Ricci Lothrop, "Strength Made Stronger: The Role of Women in Southern California Philanthropy," *Southern California Quarterly* 71, no. 2 (Summer 1989): 143–94; Joan Jensen, "After Slavery: Caroline Severance in Los Angeles," *Quarterly of the Historical Society of Southern California* 48, no. 2 (June 1966): 175–86. For an example of the importance of women's clubs to an area composer, see Smith and Richardson, *Mary Carr Moore, American Composer*, chapters 12–20, passim, especially 14, "Promoting and Surviving," 126–35.

53. Gertrude Barrett's letters to Cora (FFP, file cabinet B3 [A], HL) over several years describe her career as a professional oboist playing in all-girl summer park orchestras, first in San Bernardino, then in Santa Cruz and neighboring towns. Later she joined the Boston Fadettes, studied the oboe with a member of the Boston Symphony, and toured with the Fadettes before returning to Los Angeles and the LA Women's Orchestra by circa 1915.

For more on the Fadettes, which was active from circa 1888 to 1920, see Blanche Naylor, *The Anthology of the Fadettes* (n.p., n.d.) and an article in *Women in Music* (February 1936). For more on women's orchestras in general (but not the LA Women's Orchestra), see Christine Ammer, *Unsung: A History of Women in American Music*, 2nd ed. (Portland, OR: Amadeus, 2001), chapter

5, "Apartheid—The All-Women's Orchestras," 119–38. One recording of a brass ensemble from the Fadettes exists: "Morning Serenade," on Berliner 366 (1897).

54. Mary Foy, obituary notice, *Los Angeles Times*, February 19, 1962, A1, A8, clipping in Lummis Collection, MS 614, Southwest Museum. The fullest account is Apostal, "Mary Emily Foy." Mary Foy's position as librarian began the year after she graduated from LA High School. After teaching in the elementary schools and attending the State Normal School (predecessor of UCLA), she returned to teach English at the high school in 1893. She worked on the campaign for women's suffrage, which passed in California in 1911, and was active in Democratic politics, serving several times as Democratic National Committeeman. In 1952, she authored a series of articles ("as told to Don Ryan") for the column "Schoolteacher" in the *Los Angeles Herald & Express* (March 17–21, 1952). Clippings from Lummis Collection, MS 614, Southwest Museum. See also Ella F. O'Gorman, "Foy and Allied Families," *Americana Illustrated* 25 (April 1931).

55. Letters, Edna to Mama, FFP, carton VII, folder 4: "9/28/1921ff.," HL, letters, from Idylwild (San Bernardino Mountains), Yosemite, Grand Canyon, etc.

56. "Women Line Up to Fight / Organize to Oppose Militant Suffragettes / Believe Politics a Baneful Influence in Homes / Declare Principles and Open Headquarters," unidentified clipping, October 28, 1910 (FFP, carton VII, folder 2, HL), lists Mrs. Otto H. Neher as a member of the executive committee of the Southern California Association Opposed to Woman Suffrage. In 1910, the family was riven by a lawsuit filed by Alma Foy, demanding that the assets listed in the estate of Samuel C. Foy be distributed to the heirs. It seems likely that Edna's position on suffrage had something to do with the family feud; Mary Foy had been an advocate of women's suffrage for some years.

57. For an example of these letters, see Edna to Cora, February 19, 1920, FFP, file cabinet B3, folder 2, HL.

> We were asked to the Dreyfus concert by the Beckers last Monday. . . . Estelle looked nicer than she ever did and the whole stage picture was the best the Trinity ever looked. . . .
>
> With our party were Mr. & Mrs. Tollerton? (she is Mrs. B's niece), Carla Schramm, and Isabel Morse [later Jones]. We went to the B's after for a little cozy supper and after Thilo [Becker] read from the "Young Visitors." They have asked us to have dinner with them tomorrow at Mrs. Schramm's, where they take their dinners as a rule.

58. FFP, carton VII, folder 2, HL.

59. Isabel Morse Jones, "Words and Music" column, *Los Angeles Times*, November 3, 1935, A8.

6. "OUR AWE STRUCK VISION"

1. See, for example, Starr, *Material Dreams*, 165. Calling Behymer "the impresarial rootstock of the region," he reports inaccurately that "for nearly thirty

years, L. E. Behymer had functioned as the first demiurge and impresario of the performing arts in the Southland. Driven from the Dakota Territory to Los Angeles in 1886 when a cyclone destroyed his general store, Behymer . . ."

Even the online catalog of the Huntington Library contains erroneous biographical information about him in the entry for his collection: "He came to Los Angeles in 1886 and soon afterwards brought the first important operatic organization to Los Angeles. In 1898 Behymer founded, and then managed, the Los Angeles Symphony, and in 1918 he formed the Los Angeles Philharmonic Symphony for William Andrews Clark, Jr." Beyond the date of his arrival in Los Angeles, none of those statements is accurate. Catalog entry at the Huntington Library for the Papers of Lynden Ellsworth Behymer, 1881–1948: http://catalog .huntington.org (accessed January 19, 2007). See Behymer's obituary, *Los Angeles Times*, December 17, 1947, A1, for more claims, some of them accurate.

2. Stevenson, "Los Angeles." See also his "Los Angeles," in Stanley Sadie, ed., *The New Grove Dictionary of Opera*, vol. 3 (London: Macmillan Press Limited; and New York: Grove's Dictionaries of Music, Inc., 1992), 51–52. Both articles appear, somewhat condensed, in *The Revised New Grove Dictionary of Music and Musicians*, online version (www.grovemusic.com), 2000 and later (accessed December 14, 2006). In "Music in Southern California: A Tale of Two Cities," *Inter American Music Review* 10, no. 1 (1988): 51–111, Stevenson ad dresses some of Behymer's activities.

3. Swan, *Music in the Southwest*. See especially chapters 11 through 14.

4. Crawford, *Evenings On and Off the Roof*, 19, 141.

5. The Behymer Ephemera Collection at the Huntington Library include an 1885 graduation program from the State Normal School, Fredonia, New York; Nettie A. Sparkes is listed as a graduate in the "Classical" program. "Minette" sometimes appears as "Minetta" or "Nettie."

6. *Hyde County Bulletin*, February 13, 1886, 1, "local news."

7. "Behymer, Lynden Ellsworth, Theatrical Manager," *Who's Who in the Pacific Southwest*. There is no entry for Behymer in *Hyde Heritage, 1880s to 1977* (Highmore, SD: Hyde County Historical and Genealogical Society, 1977), nor is he mentioned in the account of the organization and early history of Hyde County on pp. 3–4. I am grateful to the Reference Department, South Dakota State Library, Pierre, for this information.

8. *Hyde County Bulletin*, April 24, 1886, 4. The dateline is St. Cloud, MN, April 14. A four-column story details some fifty thousand dollars in property damage and lists the names of the dead and injured. Probably at least two separate tornadoes occurred, since there were deaths and damage in a second town as well.

9. After she was widowed, Minette Behymer produced a lengthy typescript memoir describing her career. My thanks to Lynn Hoffman for making this memoir available.

10. Los Angeles city directories, 1886–1910.

11. Swan, *Music in the Southwest*, 199–200. A letter of complaint to the *Los Angeles Times*, February 24, 1888, 6, signed "Drama Lover," found in Ralph E.

Shaffer, "Culture," *Letters from the People: The Los Angeles Times Letters Column, 1881–1889,* www.intranet.csupomona.edu/~reshaffer/cultrx.htm (1999), complains of scalping and may refer to Behymer. A handwritten agreement in the manuscript section of the Behymer papers dated August 18, 1893, and good for one year gives Behymer an arrangement similar to the ones he had at the Los Angeles Theater and the Grand Opera House for the new Burbank Theater. Behymer was to publish the official program and sell candy, popcorn, shelled peanuts, photos, fans, and song books in lobby, foyer, auditorium, balcony, and gallery; also to rent opera glasses, manage the checkroom, and furnish as many ushers as might be needed to seat the audience.

12. In her (undated) typescript memoir, Minette Behymer (p. 29) quotes a letter from Behymer dated November 2, 1893.

13. "La Fiesta Programs with Special Folders, 1893–1903," album 62, Behymer Ephemera Collection, HL. Behymer is not named in the programs for 1893 or '94. He became "official programmer" only in 1897 and was never on the Music Committee.

14. *Los Angeles Capital* 9, no. 15, April 8, 1899, 10. The writer claimed to have followed the city's theatrical activities for almost a decade when he wrote.

The ad on page 11 of the same journal indicates that McLaren was booked at the Los Angeles Theater for three evenings and a matinee beginning April 13, 1899. "Ian McLaren" was a pseudonym of the Reverend John Watson (1850–1907), a Scottish Presbyterian minister. Major James B. Pond, in *Eccentricities of Genius: Memories of Famous Men and Women of the Platform and Stage* (New York: G. W. Dillingham Company, 1900): 405–51, describes McLaren's first American tour, which got no farther west than Iowa, in 1896.

15. "Morosco Has Rivals: Four Prospective Managers Contest for the Burbank . . . Len Behymer and Harry Mears Would Each Like to Secure the Theater," *Los Angeles Record,* July 2, 1899. Oliver Morosco (c. 1876–1945) made a success of Morosco's Burbank Theater and soon moved on to Broadway, where he produced forty-two plays between 1912 and 1926.

16. Letter, "Dear Wife, Babies and Dad," Lawrence, KS, October 7, 1899, quoted in Minette Behymer, typescript memoir.

17. "Colored Entertainers," *Musical Critic* 2, no. 4 (October 1904): 7, edited by Raymond F. Wolfsohn, probably used by Behymer as a house organ, found in Behymer Ephemera Collection, HL. The promo was strong on hyperbole: "Richard B. Harrison, reader, who probably has no equal as a delineator of negro dialect verse, and is considered by Paul Laurence Dunbar as the most perfect in his rendition of Dunbar's poems. This quartette should prove the strongest body of colored entertainers who have ever concerted throughout Southern California."

18. The *Los Angeles Evening Express,* founded in 1877, was owned by Edwin T. Earl, a millionaire Progressive activist, from 1900 until his death in 1919. It was operated by Earl's estate until 1928; publication ceased at the end of 1931.

19. Behymer, quoted in newspaper clipping, *Los Angeles Herald,* August 27, 1900, in album 146, "Personal," Behymer Ephemera Collection, HL.

20. E. F. Kubel, more often a music critic, writing in an unidentified "At the Theaters" column printed on glossy paper, in album 49, Behymer Ephemera Collection, HL. Kubel devoted most of this column to a withering critique of an "unwholesome 'Parisian Romance'" by Sardou, playing at the Burbank Theater, with which he contrasts the vaudeville house's fare. Although several of Sardou's plays were performed by traveling theatrical companies, this probably refers to *A Scrap of Paper*, which played in December 1898.

21. For more on Chutes Park, see Jan Berman and Sesar Carreno, "The Short Life of a Downtown Amusement Park," http://downtownnews.com/articles/2006/09/04/news/news03.txt (accessed December 14, 2006).

22. Folder "Addendum: Business Papers; Contracts," Behymer Manuscript Collection, HL.

23. Register of Licenses, 1904, City of Los Angeles Archives. A clipping from *The Musical Leader and Concert Goer*, Chicago, 1904, reports that Behymer was sponsoring Ellery's Royal Italian Band at Chutes Park, three concerts a week, admission ten cents.

24. Frank T. Searight, "Schumann-Heink—Isn't She on at the Orpheum?" *Los Angeles Record*, March 29, 1905, praises Behymer for his entrepreneurial nerve.

25. The Behymer Manuscript Collection, HL, includes a receipt showing that "L. Behymer" paid nine dollars to the city and in return was "hereby granted License to transact the business of Amusement at Hazards Pavilion for March 16–17–22, 1903." A boxing match between two African American heavyweight fighters was the last event at Hazard's before it was leased by the new Temple Baptist Church, in October 1903.

26. Album 52, Behymer Ephemera Collection, HL.

27. Unidentified clipping dated December 12, 1933, album 86, Behymer Ephemera Collection, HL. Other references to fights are in album 152.

28. Behymer Manuscript Collection, box 1, HL.

29. William Severns, who worked as an assistant to Behymer as a college student before he became part of the management of the Los Angeles Philharmonic, confirmed that late in life Behymer had not lost the taste for fights and wrestling matches, as documented in a 1979 interview on *Los Angeles: Wasteland or Cultural Wellspring*, narrated by Carl Princi, KFAC Radio (master tape at Cambria Master Recordings and Archives). See also my telephone interview with Severns, May 7, 1990; my interview with Lance Bowling, February 7, 1995; and Severn's interview with Lance Bowling and Carol Merrill-Mirsky, November 1, 1994; tapes at Cambria.

30. *Los Angeles Evening Express*, November 22, 1902.

31. A six-page, unsigned, typed memo in Harriet Williams (Russell) Strong Collection, folder HS851, "Los Angeles Symphony," HL, concerning the campaign by supporters of the old Symphony to effect a merger with the new Philharmonic concludes: "There is in our midst a mischievous little B, with, I fear, the proverbial sting. This little B has considerably buzzed about, 'That we will let Symphony die quietly.' SHALL WE?"

W. Francis Gates (WFG), generally a reliable reporter, wrote for *Musical America* (June 7, 1919): 14, that Frederick W. Blanchard, not Behymer, had been the Symphony's manager for the three seasons ending in the spring of 1919, "during which the debt of the orchestra of $30,000 has been paid and the audiences attending the concerts have been much increased in size."

32. Alfred Hertz, typed memoir, 114–15, box 45, item 274, Alfred Hertz Collection, Music Library, University of California, Berkeley.

33. Robert Grau, *The Business Man in the Amusement World: A Volume of Progress in the Field of the Theatre* (New York: Broadway Publishing Company, 1910), 218, quotes Behymer thus: "There is much agitation at the present time over the possibility of arranging for a public library, art gallery and music hall combined, so that the big musical affairs may have a permanent home, and the symphony concerts be given at a minimum admission. Manager Behymer has taken these matters in hand and assures the musical world that within the next two years Los Angeles will stand at the head of musical endeavor in the great West."

34. At one point later on, there was an attempt to make the Gamut Club follow the model of San Francisco's Bohemian Club, with its annual Grove Plays at its Russian River site in Mendocino County. The Gamut Club's Sylvan Gambol of 1912 offered an all-male production of *California*, a "scenic allegory" contrived by G. Carl Bronson (at other times a cellist and sometime critic), held at Providencia Rancho.

35. *PCMR* 15, no. 20 (February 13, 1909): 14, quoted from an article by W. Francis Gates in "a recent issue" of the weekly *Music News of Chicago*.

36. For biographical information on Edson and his better-known spouse, Katherine Philips Edson, see chapter 8, notes 3 and 4.

37. *Los Angeles Saturday Post*, October 7, 1905.

38. *PCMR* 9, no. 6 (October 1906): 85.

39. Grau, *The Business Man in the Amusement World*, 213–22, is quoted extensively in *PCMR* 19, no. 14 (December 31, 1910): 13–14, "L. E. Behymer's Tremendous Influence in Southern California: A Tribute to a Musical Force That Has Transformed a Rather Barren Musical Territory into One of the Most Remarkable Musical Centers of the World." See also Leavitt, *Fifty Years in Theatrical Management*; and *Los Angeles Evening Express*, Behymer interview series, December 20, 1912.

40. Metzger's lengthy quotation from Grau in a later *PCMR* issue (24, no. 14 [July 5, 1913]: 6) exaggerates Grau's claims.

41. Program, Gamut Club dinner, November 4, 1924, Cambria Master Recordings and Archives. Behymer's dates were checked against contemporary newspaper ads in the *Proquest Historical Newspapers Los Angeles Times*, consulted in December 2006 and February 2007. In addition to the lecture by African explorer Henry M. Stanley, two of these events were theatrical rather than musical. Edwin Booth (1833–93) and Lawrence Barrett (1838–91) were Shakespearean actors; Sarah Bernhardt (1844–1923) was a famous actress.

After he was established as an impresario, Behymer sponsored return visits by both Patti and, very successfully, Paderewski.

42. Behymer probably chose to lead his list with the National Opera Company because it was the best-remembered of these events among his 1924 audience.

43. I am indebted to Lance Bowling, at Cambria, for discovering this hoax.

44. See, for example, a letter dated August 16, 1926, from Behymer to conductor Alfred Hertz, in box 43, folder 228, Alfred Hertz Collection, Music Library, University of California, Berkeley.

45. John Sanders, "Los Angeles Grand Opera Association: The Formative Years, 1924–26," *Southern California Quarterly* 55, no. 3 (Fall 1973): 261–302, describes the competition and the social milieu of these seasons. Cardell Bishop, *The Los Angeles Grand Opera Association—1924–1934: A Short Career in a Big City* (Santa Monica: Bishop, 1979), lists the operas produced and the singers, with added information about the singers' careers.

46. Reported in Minette Behymer, typescript memoir. His partners were Ellis Reed of the Hollywood Bowl and Simeon Gest; they used the Figueroa Theater. Minette says she mortgaged an apartment house to pay his share of the loss.

47. Merle Armitage (1893–1975) began his career in concert management in New York, working for the firm of Charles L. Wagner and providing the artists for a concert course in Los Angeles sponsored by Fitzgerald Concert Direction. In 1921 he took over the visiting Russian Grand Opera Company, which was stranded in Seattle, and worked it out of debt; it completed its tour in New York five months later. A brochure prepared by Armitage in 1930, when he left the Los Angeles Grand Opera Association, describes a varied career as a concert manager, teacher of mechanical engineering, poet, novelist, book designer, and art historian. In 1946 he was mentioned as a candidate for director of the new LA County Museum of Art. His papers are at the Harry Ransom Humanities Research Center, University of Texas; also the University of Iowa, where the online finding aid to his papers contains a biographical sketch; and the University of Arizona.

48. Behymer used his position as chair of the local FMP advisory board to discourage the FMP from competing directly with his own series or the established music organizations, especially the Philharmonic. He encouraged a federally sponsored opera project in Riverside, in direct competition with Marcella Craft's community opera program, which did not book his artists. Most egregiously, he pressured Bruno David Ussher, western regional director, to keep certain unqualified individuals on the FMP's payroll. See folder "Federal Music Project," no box number, Behymer Manuscript Collection, HL, especially the letter, Behymer to Ussher, May 13, 1936: "I am afraid it would worry me a bit if some of those I had recommended were dismissed, or reduced in pay. . . . and still I do know that in all such enterprises there are some undeserving persons creeping under the cloak of the deserving."

7. THE "TRUE TEMPLE OF ART"

1. Maria L. Sanford, "The Influence of Good Art and Literature on Character," *California Outlook* 14, no. 14 (March 29, 1913): 15.

2. *California Outlook* 13, no. 12 (September 14, 1912): 14. Other women carried signs advocating specific issues. The following week's *Outlook* (11) reported that only about seven hundred women, including "a score" of blacks, were able to get into the building because of the large crowd. In general, the Progressive movement partook of the racism of its time.

3. Quoted in Hitchcock, *Music in the United States,* chapter 6, "The Cultivated Tradition, 1865–1920," 142. See also Crawford, *America's Musical Life,* 300–304. Dwight was a divinity school graduate who had a strong influence as a music critic. *Dwight's Journal of Music,* which championed European concert music (especially that of the German-speaking countries) and its moral value, appeared continuously from 1852 to 1881.

4. Thilo Becker, "Thoughts relating Principally to Music," typescript, n.d., n.p. In Mrs. Albert Atwood Collection, Special Collections, Music Library, University of California, Los Angeles (hereafter UCLA).

5. Walter Henry Rothwell to William Andrews Clark, Jr., Christmas 1919, Behymer Ephemera Collection, album 123, HL.

6. For another account of the founding of Temple Auditorium (eventually renamed Philharmonic Auditorium) and something of its later history, written at the time it was torn down, see Henry A. Sutherland, "Requiem for the Los Angeles Philharmonic Auditorium," *Southern California Quarterly* (September 1965): 303–31.

7. For more on Burdette (1855–1954), see Dorothy Grace Miller, "Within the Bounds of Propriety: Clara Burdette and the Women's Movement," PhD dissertation, University of California, Riverside, 1984.

8. *Los Angeles Evening Express,* October 1, 1902. The fact that she owned stock in that paper's archrival, the *Times,* may have made her a more attractive target for the editor of the *Express.*

9. "Mrs. Burdette's Reply to Her Maligners," *Los Angeles Times,* October 3, 1902, A1.

10. Clara B. Burdette, *The Rainbow and the Pot of Gold* (Pasadena: Clara Vista Press, 1907), 60.

11. The Methodist church, also known as Simpson's Auditorium, had been a frequent site for concerts for at least a decade, despite its poor acoustics. The building was sold to the University of Southern California, which continued to use it for concerts until 1913, when it was once again sold.

12. Burdette, *The Rainbow and the Pot of Gold,* 2.

13. "New Church Is 'Temple': Rev. Robert J. Burdette Is Flock's Leader," *Los Angeles Times,* July 18, 1903.

14. *Los Angeles Times,* October 7, 1904, A1.

15. Ibid.

16. Opened as the Tremont Theatre in 1827 and rebuilt several times, the Baptist Tremont Temple that Burdette visited was built in the 1870s.

17. The building committee included J. O. Koepfli, president of the Chamber of Commerce; W. H. Mead, once organizer of an amateur orchestra in which Edna Foy had played alongside several prominent businessmen; and Ella C. Crowell, a wealthy landowner.

18. *Los Angeles Examiner,* October 7, 1904, A1.

19. Letters dated "Wed. night" [April 26] and April 28, 1905, box 34, Clara Bradley Burdette Collection, HL.

20. Jane Apostal, "They Said It with Flowers: The Los Angeles Flower Festival Society," *Southern California Quarterly* 64, no. 1 (Spring 1980): 67–76.

21. By the time Temple Auditorium was completed, however, most chamber concerts and recitals had moved to the new Blanchard Hall, part of a building designed to accommodate the studios of artists and musicians.

8. "SOMETHING OF GOOD FOR THE FUTURE"

1. Some examples: In New York City, the People's Orchestra existed as early as 1906, and Claire Reis organized People's Concerts starting in 1910. The Chicago Civic Music Association was formed in 1913. In San Francisco, the People's Orchestra gave its first concert a few days after the debut of the LA orchestra discussed in this chapter.

2. *Los Angeles Evening Express,* November 1, 1912, 4, 8. In the same paper are found a sample ballot and an article giving some specifics of the California Progressive Party's platform: minimum wage for women, occupational safety, workmen's compensation, protection of small investors, opposition to legalized racetrack gambling.

Although they were not covered by the conservative *Los Angeles Times,* the paper to which historians most often turn, the new orchestra's activities were reported and reviewed by the progressive *Express* (Frank Colby), the weekly *Municipal News* (Alfred A. Butler), the *Graphic* (W. Francis Gates), the *California Outlook,* and the monthly *Pacific Coast Musician* (Colby and Gates).

3. Katherine Philips Edson (1870–1932) was a prominent reformer in Los Angeles from circa 1900 and director of the successful 1911 campaign for women's suffrage in California. Later, she was appointed to the California State Industrial Welfare Commission, in which she served under four governors. In 1910, she served on the Los Angeles Charter Revision Committee, probably one reason why her husband cherished the notion of municipal subsidies for music. See Charles Farwell Edson, Jr., and Katharane Edson Mershon, *Katherine Philips Edson Remembered,* Jacqueline R. Braitman, interviewer (Oral History Program, University of California, Los Angeles, copyright 1987); and Jacqueline R. Braitman, "A California Stateswoman: The Public Career of Katherine Philips Edson," *California History: The Magazine of the California Historical Society* 65 (1986): 82–95, 151–52. Katherine Edson's activism, encouraged by

her spouse, began through the Friday Morning Club. The couple divorced in 1925; she died in 1932 at the age of sixty-two.

4. Charles Farwell Edson (1864–1936) was born in Lake Forest, Illinois. His mother, Maria Louise Farwell, was luxuriously supported by an annuity from her brother, a wealthy Chicago developer. Thus, Charles grew up in an atmosphere of wealth, although he was never wealthy himself. After their marriage in 1890, the Edsons came to Southern California to farm a tract in the Antelope Valley (near Los Angeles, in the Mojave Desert), given to them as a wedding present. In 1899, having failed to develop enough water to farm, they moved to Los Angeles. The family lived on his mother's annuity until her death. Edson operated his "American Studio," where he taught voice, but was a poor breadwinner. The Edsons increasingly lived apart for about nine years before their divorce in 1925.

The oral histories taken from their two surviving children by Braitman give contrasting images of both parents, especially the father. The son represented him as disorganized, unrealistic, and lazy; the daughter saw him as a creative visionary. Both agreed that the mother was highly organized and successful, but the daughter blamed Katherine for not sending her to college, although her two brothers went. For a general statement of Edson's progressive ideas, see his collection of poems, *The Stranger* (Los Angeles: Braxton Press, 1930), which contains "transcriptions" of messages he reported were delivered by a Christ figure. The first three poems, "Christ to the People," "Christ to Women," and "Christ to Youth," are dated October 11 and 23, 1912, when the People's Orchestra was being formed.

5. *Los Angeles Evening Express,* November 11, 1912, 3.

6. The well-regarded Lebegott was the son of a German-born father who directed a provincial Italian opera house. He first visited Los Angeles with the Lambardi company in 1906 and was briefly director of the National Conservatory in Guatemala after that. Later he conducted at the Majestic Theater in Los Angeles. After the People's Orchestra collapsed, the *Pacific Coast Musician* suggested that the orchestra had actually been started because of Lebegott's presence and his interest in the project.

7. The Symphony's scale was six dollars for five rehearsals and one concert. (*California Outlook,* January 21, 1912, 8–9.)

8. Only two programs have been located, in the Katherine Philips Edson Papers, box 13/4, collection 235, Special Collections, Charles E. Young Research Library, UCLA. They were regularly reported in the *Express* and the *Graphic* but are most fully chronicled in Bagley, "History," *Overture* 11, no. 4 (August 1931) through 11, no. 12 (April 1932.)

9. *Los Angeles Evening Express,* 11 November 1912, 3.

10. Southern California [Los Angeles] Music Teachers Association (hereafter SCMTA), minutes. A. D. Hunter, secretary-treasurer, typed this version some years after the fact, from the notes he took at the time. I am grateful to Helen Nash and Lance Bowling for making these minutes available.

11. For example, Mrs. Tiffany, the soloist at the first concert, saw the policy

of presenting local soloists as the orchestra's main purpose: "The aim of the People's orchestra is to give Los Angeles soloists an opportunity of playing and singing with orchestral accompaniment" (*Los Angeles Evening Express*, November 9, 1912, 3).

12. *Los Angeles Evening Express*, November 10, 1912–January 4, 1914.

13. *PCMR* (November 7, 1908): 11. Johnson's models included Herman Klein's popular Sunday concerts in New York and similar concerts in the various boroughs of London.

14. *Los Angeles Times*, January 24, 1909, quoted in the *PCMR* (January 30, 1909): 3–4. *PCMR* editor Alfred Metzger added, "California composers should receive attention, California artists should be soloists."

15. City of Los Angeles Archives, box B-2420, folder "Municipal Music, June 22, 1909–April 25, 1910." The municipal band may not have been renewed for legal reasons. Chapter 420, *The Statutes of California and Amendments to the Codes Passed at the Extra Session of the Thirty-ninth Legislature, 1911* (Sacramento: Superintendent State Printing, 1911), authorizes cities to levy and collect a tax for park, music, and advertising purposes but requires that such a tax be confirmed by the voters. The act was approved on April 10, 1911.

16. "Music in the City's Life," speech by L. E. Behymer to the City Club, August 14, 1909, as reported in the *California Outlook* (August 21, 1909): 7. Behymer listed Denver, Seattle, and St. Paul as cities that gave public support to their orchestras. He prefaced his remarks by saying, "Man represents the commercial, woman the artistic and it is time there was a wedding of the two in this city."

17. Julius Johnson, "Music in Los Angeles," *PCMR* 9, no. 16 (January 7, 1911): 5.

18. *Final Calendar of Legislative Business 1909, Thirty-eighth Session* (Sacramento: Superintendent State Printing, 1909). The bill was introduced on January 15 by A. B. Transue, Republican of Los Angeles. As A.B. 424, it passed the Assembly but died in the Senate Committee on Education when the legislature adjourned on March 24. The bill was opposed by Alfred Metzger, San Francisco–based editor of the *PCMR*, because it did not go far enough.

19. SCMTA minutes, December 17, 1910.

20. SCMTA minutes, June 6, 1913. Fred Ellis and Mrs. L. J. Selby were the envoys to the Symphony board meeting.

21. Letter, June 5, 1913, quoted in SCMTA minutes of June 6. Signers were the members of the SCMTA board: Fred Ellis, president; Grace Carroll Elliot, secretary; A. D. Hunter, treasurer; Mrs. L. J. Selby, G. Carl Bronson, and Eugene E. Davis, directors.

22. This list reproduces the information in a flyer found in the National Archives and Records Administration (hereafter NARA), RG 69, Central Files, General, 211.1, box 0378.

23. "The People's Orchestra and Its Program," *California Outlook* (September 20, 1913): 11. The article is a reprint of, or is reprinted from, the reverse of a flyer, *The People's Orchestra and Its Program*, NARA, Federal Music Project, RG 69, Central Files, General, 211.1, box 0378.

24. The Los Angeles Symphony ceased operation after the 1919–20 season. William Andrews Clark, Jr., founded the present Philharmonic in 1919 and funded it until his death in 1934.

25. SCMTA minutes, June 26, 1913. A. J. Stamm, with a second from Frank Colby (editor of the *Pacific Coast Musician*), moved that the board had no authority to "contract debts for the association without a guarantee or some other tangible asset; that the board, officers, and employees must agree to personally assume such debt." Ellis and Edson replied that the state MTA had no responsibility for the orchestra's deficit. When Edson "gave Mr. Ellis a personal letter, saying that he would hold himself personally responsible for anything due," the motion was withdrawn.

26. SCMTA minutes, October 28, 1913; November 4, 1913 ("a complete reversal of policy as to the programs, and with discretion, cater to the desires and wishes of the people"); November 7, 1913 ("it did not mean tawdry music, nor all popular music," "lighter numbers for encores," "suggested that members of the Association hand their suggestions for more popular numbers to Mr. Lebegott," "a large majority voted for this change").

27. SCMTA minutes, November 4, 1913. The board of the SCMTA agreed to accompany Edson and a committee of music club presidents on one last trip to the LA City Council to ask for an appropriation in support of the orchestra.

28. I do so with a little help from recent historians of American culture, among them David Glassberg, *American Historical Pageantry: The Uses of Tradition in the Early Twentieth Century* (Chapel Hill: University of North Carolina Press, 1990); Levine, *Highbrow/Lowbrow*; and Lary May, *Screening Out the Past*; also Peiss, *Cheap Amusements*; and Rosenzweig, *Eight Hours for What We Will*.

29. Michael Broyles, "Music and Class Structure in Antebellum Boston," *Journal of the American Musicological Society* 44 (1991): 451–93, documents the decision by upper-class Bostonians to adopt symphonic concerts as a form of elite entertainment in the 1840s. In the process, he shows that Levine's thesis (in *Highbrow/Lowbrow*) is too broadly drawn.

30. *Los Angeles Evening Express*, November 9, 1912, 3.

31. "SENDS WARNING TO EASTERN MANAGERS / L. E. Behymer Calls a Halt on Overcrowding Western Territory with Musical Artists," *Musical America* (July 12, 1913): 1. The article appears to be based on an interview with Behymer. It refers to the Symphony as "the backbone of local musical activity," and reports that its "usefulness . . . was greatly impaired by the institution of a popular orchestra playing popular music on Sundays, the seats selling for twenty-five and fifty cents. . . . the invasion of the popular music idea came as a severe blow to those who were laboring for what they believed to be a cause of far higher value to the musical development of the city."

The editorial response (July 19, 1913, 16) is unsigned; John C. Freund was the magazine's editor.

32. Information on the kinetoscope comes from ads in the *Los Angeles*

Times, passim. I am grateful to Clyde Allen and Lance Bowling for assembling this material.

33. *California Outlook* (September 14, 1912): 14.

34. *Report of the State Recreational Inquiry Committee,* September 28, 1914 (Sacramento: California State Printing Office, 1914), 11–13, 55.

35. Hobsbawm, "Introduction: Inventing Traditions," 1.

36. Levine, *Highbrow/Lowbrow,* 229.

37. In 1890, the U.S. Census counted 203 musicians and music teachers in Los Angeles, 47 percent of them male. In 1900, the total number was 607; the proportion of males had declined to 36 percent. See also appendix B; and U.S. Bureau of the Census, *Occupations of the Twelfth Census* (Washington, DC: Government Printing Office, 1904), 590–93.

9. PRODUCING *FAIRYLAND*, 1915

1. Mrs. William H. Jamison [Abbie Norton Jamison], "The Birth of Fairyland," program book, National Federation of Music Clubs, 1915, 27, in Behymer Ephemera Collection, album 75, HL. Jamison wrote in her capacity as secretary of the local American Opera Association and vice president for the Western District of the National Federation of Music Clubs. See also "Los Angeles Opera Committee Organizes: Agreement with Federation of Music Clubs Anent Production of Prize American Opera Is Ratified," *Musical America* 18, no. 6 (14 June 1913): 25. W. F. G., who signed the article, is W. Francis Gates, the regular Los Angeles correspondent of *Musical America,* a founder of the Gamut Club and writer on music. And see "Ten Thousand Dollars for American Opera," *PCMR* 24, no. 11 (June 14, 1913): 3.

2. Blanchard was president of the American Opera Association of Los Angeles, organized to handle the competition and the production. The executive board consisted of Blanchard, Jamison (secretary), Dr. Norman Bridge (a long-time benefactor of the arts and Progressive activist), Behymer, Mrs. Gertrude Parsons (a music teacher), and Joseph P. Dupuy (director of the Ellis Club, a long-established men's chorus.) The list of contributors to the ten-thousand-dollar prize is impressive: the Los Angeles County Public School Music Teachers Association, the Gamut Club, Blanchard, Jamison, N. D. Wade, Behymer, Edson, the Orpheus Club (another men's chorus), William H. Jamison, Los Angeles Title & Trust Company, the Friday Morning Club, the Lyric Club (a women's chorus), the Ellis Club, R. H. Norton, Mrs. L. J. Shelby, Charles A. Elder, Frank E. Haitian, J. B. Yountz, Volney S. Beardsley, Estate of A. Willhartitz, C. E. Gilhousen, the Gamut Club Triple Quartet, Charles H. Eager, the Southern California Music Teachers Association, the Ebell Club, Walter B. Cline, John H. Francis, R. W. Hefflefinger, James T. Fitzgerald, J. F. Salyer, G. Allan Hancock, F. Q. Story, Mrs. M. H. Whittier, Lyric Club members, Holmes Music Co., Pacific Electric Co., the Retail Dry Goods Merchants Association, the St. Cecilia Club, the City of Los Angeles, Southern California Music Co., the

County of Los Angeles, the Musicians Mutual Protective Association (Local 47 AFM), Los Angeles Gas & Electric Corp., Stoddard Jess, and Dr. Norman Bridge.

3. Letter, Horatio Parker to Alfred Hertz, Alfred Hertz Papers, San Francisco Public Library. Parker's letters to Hertz are in the San Francisco Public Library; Hertz's letters to Parker are at Yale University.

4. Catherine Parsons Smith, "An Operatic Skeleton on the Western Frontier: Zitkala Sa, William F. Hanson, and *The Sun Dance Opera.*" *Women & Music: A Journal of Gender and Culture* 5 (2001): 1–30.

5. Extensively described in Smith and Richardson, *Mary Carr Moore, American Composer.* See especially chapter 9, 69–83, and chapter 20, 187–93.

6. Edward F. Kubel, *Western Graphic* 9, no. 4 (July 28, 1900): 9–10, is the earliest discussion so far located on folk influences in European and American music in Los Angeles. Kubel mentions Edward Everett Hale, Dvořák, and Krehbiel, but not Farwell, who had yet to make an impression. None of the Americans he mentions was a composer of opera.

7. Clipping dated November 5, 1904, probably from the *Los Angeles Times,* in album "Programs, 1903–1922," Friday Morning Club Collection, HL. On November 4, 1904, Arthur Farwell, assisted by local artists, delivered a lecture titled "Toward American Music: A Study in National Progress, with Special Reference to the Music of the American Indians." He was assisted by Alice Coleman (later Batchelder), piano, and Harry Barnhart, baritone. They performed music by Henry F. Gilbert, John P. Beach, Carlos Troyer, and Farwell. Farwell's *Wanderjahre of a Revolutionist and Other Essays on American Music* collects his many writings on the topic of American music.

8. Lummis and Farwell, *Spanish Songs of Old California.*

10. FOUNDING THE HOLLYWOOD BOWL

1. Carol Reese, "The Hollywood Bowl 1919–1989: The Land, the People, and the Music," published serially in *Performing Arts* (Los Angeles), July 1989: 17–34; August 1989: 9–25; September 1989: 25–32. These articles concentrate on the architectural history of the Bowl and describe some of the theatrical productions that took advantage of its physical features. Reese's articles, which appeared in the Philharmonic's summer program book, stress the Philharmonic's association with the Bowl partly by ignoring the Bowl's pre-1922 concert history.

2. Artie Mason Carter was born in Salisbury, Missouri, in 1881 and died in Los Angeles in 1967. She graduated from the Christian College Conservatory of Music, Columbia, Missouri, in 1900, and then taught school. In 1902, she married Joseph J. Carter, a physician, and moved to Kansas City, where she studied piano with Moissaye Boguslawski and earned a second bachelor's degree in 1911 from the Kansas City Conservatory. She and her husband lived in Vienna, where she studied with Theodor Leschetizky from 1911 to 1914. They came to Los Angeles on their return. She apparently did not perform publicly. After Carter left the Bowl, she helped organize the Los Angeles chapter of Pro Musica and was involved in other music-making activities.

I have located no collection of Carter's papers beyond a group of letters to Alfred Hertz, first conductor of the Symphonies under the Stars, in the Alfred Hertz Collection, Music Department, San Francisco Public Library.

3. Board of Directors, Hollywood Bowl Association, *A Brief History of Hollywood Bowl: Authorized and Approved by the Board of Directors of the Hollywood Bowl Association,* June 11, 1926, unpaginated pamphlet, in T. Perceval Gerson Collection, Department of Special Collections, Charles E. Young Research Library, UCLA, box 5; reprinted in Bruno David Ussher, *Who's Who in Music and Dance in Southern California* (Hollywood: Bureau of Musical Research, 1933), 29–34.

4. The most useful extended accounts of the Bowl are Isabel Morse Jones, *Hollywood Bowl* (New York: G. Schirmer, 1936), marred by its lack of documentation or bibliography but written by a close observer and the *Times* music critic; and Grace G. Koopal, *Miracle of Music* (Los Angeles: Charles E. Toberman, 1972), privately published, which contains the most complete list of Bowl events from July 1922 on. Shorter accounts include Raymond Brite, "Hollywood Bowl and the 'Symphonies under the Stars,'" in Caroline Estes Smith, *The Philharmonic Orchestra of Los Angeles: The First Decade, 1919–1929* (Los Angeles: United Printing Company, 1930); Andrae Arne Nordskog, "The Earliest Musical History in the Hollywood Bowl: 1920 and 1921" (typescript, copyright 1957); John Orlando Northcutt, *Symphony: The Story of the Los Angeles Philharmonic Orchestra* (Los Angeles: Southern California Symphony Association, 1963); John Orlando Northcutt, *Magic Valley: The Story of Hollywood Bowl* (Los Angeles: Osherenko, 1967); John Orlando Northcutt, "The Philharmonic and the Bowl," in Jose Rodriguez, ed., *Music and Dance in California* (Hollywood: Bureau of Musical Research, 1940); Naima Prevots-Wallen, "The Hollywood Bowl and Los Angeles Dance, 1926–1941: Performance Theory and Practice," PhD dissertation, University of Southern California, 1983; and Glenn M. Tindall, "Symphonies under the Stars: Concerts in the Hills of Hollywood," in Bruno David Ussher, ed., *Who's Who in Music and Dance in Southern California* (Hollywood: Bureau of Musical Research, 1933), 27–28. More general accounts include George Brookwell, *Saturdays in the Hollywood Bowl* (Hollywood: Suttonhouse Publishers, 1940); Ann Wardell Saunders, "Hollywood-Los Angeles," in Richard Drake Saunders, ed., *Music and Dance in California and the West* (Hollywood: Bureau of Musical Research, 1948), 153, 282–83; Starr, *Material Dreams*; Southern California Writers Project, *Los Angeles: A Guide to the City and Its Environs* (New York: Hastings House, 1941, 1951); Michael Buckland and John Henken, eds., *The Hollywood Bowl: Tales of Summer Nights* (Los Angeles: Balcony Press, 1996); and Swan, *Music in the Southwest*. A complete run of program books is located in the Hollywood Bowl Museum, on the Bowl grounds.

I have relied heavily on contemporary running accounts in the local paper, the *Hollywood Weekly Citizen,* whose publisher appears to have attended the early events he reports (the *Citizen* became a daily on October 3, 1921); also on two collections of the papers of T. Perceval Gerson (1872–1960) at the Charles E. Young Research Library, UCLA, and at the Huntington Library.

5. A downtown municipal arts center had been proposed as early as 1907; the most recent (unsuccessful) proposal occurred in early 1919. See *Los Angeles Times*, editorial, February 5, 1919; also "Dead or Live Memorial? Which Does Los Angeles Want? Representatives of a Hundred Thousand Persons in and near Los Angeles Declare for Central Memorial Building: Uniting for Centrally Located Allied Arts and Convention Hall Memorial," *Pacific Coast Musician* 8, no. 3 (March 1919): 5.

6. Joseph E. Ross, letter to the author, March 12, 1990. Ross is the author of *Krotona of Old Hollywood* (Montecito, CA: El Montecito Oaks Press, 1989), the first of a projected four-volume history of the Krotona colony, which was located in Hollywood from 1912 to 1926.

7. Edwin O. Palmer, *History of Hollywood* (Hollywood: Arthur H. Cawston, 1937), 1:201. The outdoor production and a second, indoor, performance of *Julius Caesar* on June 5, 1916, this time underwritten by D. W. Griffith and Mack Sennett, at the Majestic Theater in Los Angeles, both were benefits for the Actor's Fund of America. (Program courtesy of Lynn Hoffman.)

8. According to the printed program, G. G. Greenwood was director of concessions, H. T. Wright was secretary for the production, and George L. Eastman was director of ushering. Greenwood became one of four treasurers of the Theatre Arts Alliance; Mrs. H. T. Palmer became an officer in the Hollywood Community Sing; Eastman was a member of the Community Park and Art Association. Several names on the list of patronesses were among those who, either on their own or through their spouses, were later active in the Theatre Arts Alliance or the Community Park and Art Association. The participation of the film colony in this community event was not repeated; the prominent actors who took roles in *Julius Caesar* are for the most part conspicuous by their absence from accounts of Bowl history.

9. Christine Wetherill (Mrs. W. York[e]) Stevenson, 1878–1922, the daughter of an industrialist associated with New Jersey Zinc and Westmoreland (later Pittsburgh) Paint, was a resident of Philadelphia who never lived permanently in Southern California. Before her Southern California activities, she was a founder of the Philadelphia Arts Alliance.

According to the prospectus but not the printed program, the play's subtitle was "A Miracle Play Dramatizing the True Story of the Buddha." Stevenson commissioned Georgina Jones Walton's dramatization of the text of the same name by Edwin Arnold. Walter Hampden played the leading role. The play was originally scheduled to run for nineteen performances. A copy of the prospectus, kindly provided by Joseph E. Ross, includes a map with directions for reaching the stadium by streetcar.

Krotona, which took its name from a colony of Pythagoreans in pre-Roman Italy, was the national headquarters of the American section of the Theosophical Society, Annie Besant, president; it operated independently of other theosophist colonies in Southern California.

10. Jones, *Hollywood Bowl*, 11–12. Jones was music critic for the *Los Angeles Times*. She had been a volunteer worker under Artie Mason Carter in 1922.

Jones's sources, which are not cited, appear to include Gerson, Artie Mason Carter, and others associated with the Bowl's founding. Gerson and Atwater were both active in the Severance Club, so this account may also be accurate.

Mrs. Stevenson wrote later that the meeting took place the day after the production closed. Letter, Stevenson to "Dear Members of the Theatre Arts Alliance," February 16, 1920, T. Perceval Gerson Collection (724), box 13, Charles E. Young Research Library, UCLA.

11. The Severance Club was organized in 1907 by Madame Caroline Severance, prominent suffragist, reformer, Unitarian, and founder of the Friday Morning Club. In addition to the goal of "social democracy," the club took its motto "Justice and Courage" from Mme Severance, "who explained that in her view 'Justice' includes, and demands, love to the neighbors, of all races and conditions. And that 'Courage' leads one to stand as stoutly for all the rights and opportunities of that neighbor, as oneself." Severance, "Address before Women's Parliament of Southern California," quoted in Ella Giles Ruddy, ed., *The Mother of Clubs: Caroline M. Severance, an Estimate and an Appreciation* (Los Angeles: Baumgardt Publishing Company, 1906), unpaginated. John R. Haynes, a prominent Los Angeles Progressive, was the club's first president. Dr. and Mrs. Gerson were among the charter members. The fact that it was open to both women and men made it unusual among Los Angeles clubs.

The mix of politics, social action, and music was not new for Mme Severance; she is credited with initiating "Unitarian Thursdays," important to the history of Los Angeles's concert life, in the late 1870s.

12. Jones, *Hollywood Bowl*, 13, lists these charter members (each of whom pledged a thousand dollars to the project): "Mrs. Stevenson, Dr. Gerson, Katherine Yarnell and H. Sheridan Brickers, newspaperman; Louis Horst, now a well known composer-pianist . . . Mr. and Mrs. Frank Keenan, actors; Thilo Becker, leader among pianists, and Elizabeth Carrick, then a loved vocal teacher, now long since returned to Scotland; Wayland Smith, man of society and the arts, and Abbie Norton Jamison, teacher and club leader; Dr. Gale Atwater, dentist; Desidir Vescei, pianist, and Dr. Sven Lokrantz, physician, now identified with the public schools . . . A. P. Warrington, of Krotona." It is likely that Aline Barnsdall was among the group, since in 1926 she asked that her name be removed as a founding member.

On the next page, Jones lists these officers: Stevenson, president; Gerson and Atwater, vice presidents; H. Ellis Reed, secretary; G. G. Greenwood, Mrs. Marie Rankin Clarke, Frank Keenan, Ted Shawn and A. P. Warrington, all treasurers. She then gives the more familiar list of charter members: L. E. Behymer, Carrie Jacobs Bond, Charles Wakefield Cadman, Charles Farwell Edson, William Farnum, Kate Crane Gartz, Leopold Godowsky, Robert Brunton, Lillian Burkhardt Goldsmith, D. W. Griffith, Ruth St. Denis, C. E. Toberman, Mrs. Georgina Jones Walton, and Allan C. Balch. E. N. Martin is apparently omitted from her list by mistake.

A Theatre Arts Alliance letterhead from February 1920 adds these charter members: Leopold Godowsky, Sarah W. Logan, and Ted Shawn, Ruth St. Denis's partner.

13. Jones, *Hollywood Bowl*, 13–14.

14. In 1919 and 1920, however, there were other parks created in the area. Griffith J. Griffith donated twenty-five hundred acres that became Griffith Park, several miles west of the newly developing downtown; although a five-thousand-seat Greek theater was eventually built on it, the land was probably considered too mountainous for development. In addition, Aline Barnsdall, whose name is associated with Henry Cowell's New Music concert in 1925 (more on this in chapter 12), contributed a corner site for a community theater, now Barnsdall Park. A community park association was also formed to create neighborhood parks and a local World War I memorial. Although it was unsuccessful in this endeavor, this association eventually played a part in the formation of the Bowl.

15. Fifty of the site's fifty-nine acres were acquired from Myra Hershey, owner of the Hollywood Hotel, for twenty thousand dollars. A second owner had purchased part of the canyon bottom in 1914, through developer Charles E. Toberman, in order to operate a carpet-cleaning plant in an out-of-the-way location. Marie Rankin Clarke (Mrs. Chauncey D. Clarke) was probably a member of the Theosophical Society (Joseph E. Ross, phone conversation with the author).

16. Board of Directors, Hollywood Bowl Association, *A Brief History,* "Early Plans for Music" and "Reorganization on Broader Basis."

17. *Hollywood Weekly Citizen,* July 4, 1919, 4.

18. Some early examples in Southern California were La Fiesta de Los Angeles (1894–97), *Califia* (1898), and *Mission Play* (1912).

19. Sheldon Cheney, *The Open-Air Theater* (New York, 1918), 36, quoted in Hine, *California's Utopian Colonies,* 50. For a recent account of the pageantry movement, see Glassberg, *American Historical Pageantry.*

20. Helena P. Blavatsky, *The Secret Doctrine* (I, 464), quoted in Daniel de Lange, "Thoughts on Music, Part IV," *Theosophical Path* 13 (July–December 1913): 117. See also Daniel de Lange, "Thoughts on Music," *Theosophical Path* 11 (July–December 1916): 553. For another view of the relationship between Theosophy and American composers of this period, see Judith Tick, "Ruth Crawford's 'Spiritual Concept': The Sound-Ideals of an Early American Modernist," *Journal of the American Musicological Society* 44, no. 2 (Summer 1991): 221–61. See chapter 13, "Welcoming the Ultramodern," for another aspect of the Krotona Colony's music connections.

21. Back East, Stevenson had already recruited Sheldon Cheney and unnamed others to work on the text; Walter Hampden to play the Christ; Dane Rudhyar, recommended by Leopold Stokowski, to work on the music; and Winold Reiss, who wanted to involve "the Duncan dancers"; and Ruth St. Denis, to design scenery and costumes. (Later on, Gertrude Ross and Arthur Farwell also composed music for it. None has been located, however.) Stevenson was discussing an alliance with the Theatre Guild, which would become a branch of the TAA, and the possibility of securing painting and sculpture through the Philadelphia Arts Alliance to exhibit during the intermissions. She further proposed that a drama festival open on June 1 with an imported Theatre Guild pro-

duction in the projected small indoor theater; that Shakespeare's *Midsummer Night's Dream,* in an existing production by Granville Barker, open in the large amphitheater on June 7; that Michio Ito's and Theodor Kosloff's dance companies, already performing in the East, perform in the Bowl between June 14 and 19; and that a week-long "Festival of Light," to include a staged version of Franck's *Beatitudes,* be preceded each evening by a choral vespers lead-up to the opening of "our passion play." "Excerpts from Letters of Mrs. Stevenson, Chairman of the Theatre Arts Alliance, in regard to the Passion Play and Other Entertainments," undated two-page typescript in the T. Perceval Gerson Collection, box 13/22, Charles E. Young Research Library, UCLA. On the basis of their content, we can tell the letters were sent to Gerson from Philadelphia or New York. A three-page typed "Prospectus of the Play," then titled "Light Eternal," which accompanies Stevenson's proposal, shows that most of her attention had been given to the play itself.

22. Jones, *Hollywood Bowl,* 23. Mrs. Stevenson had also bought the Pilgrimage Bowl site. According to Dane Rudhyar, she might have bought a third site, Bryn Mawr, the hill behind the Pilgrimage Bowl, which was vacant, but she offered it instead to A. P. Warrington, head of the Krotona colony, who turned it down (Rudhyar, Oral History, ed. Sheila Finch Rayner, Arts Archive, California State University, Long Beach, 1977, interview of May 19, 1975, 2). "Her idea was to have those hills where the *Pilgrimage Play* was to be made into a great spiritual center, with the Bowl giving all the big performances, choruses and so on, and where the *Pilgrimage Play* now was to be all for arts and crafts with bungalows and everything like that for the artists. What is now the Bryn Mawr section of the hills was to be developed with cottages and motels and things like that for the visitors. Well, that was a great vision, which in 1920 in California didn't find any echo!"

23. Jones reports that Stevenson bought El Camino Real Canyon (the site of the Pilgrimage Bowl) with the proceeds from the sale of her interest in the Bowl property to the Community Park and Art Association.

24. The play opened on June 28, 1920. Its publicity campaign was underwritten by a ten-thousand-dollar grant from the Los Angeles County Board of Supervisors. *Hollywood Weekly Citizen,* June 6–July 23, 1920.

25. Letter, Stevenson to "Dear Member of the Arts Alliance," July 24, 1920, T. Perceval Gerson Collection, box 13/3, Charles E. Young Research Library, UCLA.

26. The obituary notice in the *Philadelphia Public Ledger,* November 22, 1922, gave the cause of death as overwork. Her husband, W. Yorke Stevenson, and his parents had all died earlier in 1922.

27. Several members of the TAA Board, the later CPAA Board, and the Hollywood Bowl Association, including both Gerson and Carter, served on the board of the Pilgrimage Play Foundation after Stevenson's death. The Hollywood Bowl Association eventually produced the *Pilgrimage Play* in addition to its Bowl events. The former Pilgrimage Bowl is now owned by Los Angeles County and operated as the John Anson Ford Bowl.

28. Letter, Mullgardt to Gerson, October 6, 1919, acknowledges Gerson's invitation; a telegram authorizing Mullgardt to proceed is dated November 9, 1919; T. Perceval Gerson Collection, box 13/1, Charles E. Young Research Library, UCLA.

29. Letter, Mullgardt to Gerson, July 5, 1921, T. Perceval Gerson Collection, box 2/10, Charles E. Young Research Library, UCLA.

30. Letter, Mullgardt to Gerson, July 9, 1923, T. Perceval Gerson Collection, box 2, Charles E. Young Research Library, UCLA.

31. "By Ruth St. Denis," undated typescript, T. Perceval Gerson Collection, box 13, Charles E. Young Research Library, UCLA.

32. Koopal, *Miracle of Music*, 86.

33. Martin devised the scheme of public ownership of the property with a ninety-nine-year lease for the Hollywood Bowl Association, thus protecting it from other uses. From time to time the lease has been renegotiated, usually with added improvements by the county. Toberman, who had arranged for the sale of the property to the carpet cleaner in 1914, sent in his construction equipment to level the floor of the canyon. Koopal based her account of the Bowl's history on Toberman's papers. See especially the options reproduced at the front of *Miracle of Music*.

34. The Community Sing movement was begun by Arthur Farwell and Harry Barnhart in 1916; its growth was stimulated nationwide by the United States' 1917 entry into World War I. Palmer, *History of Hollywood*, 1:206–7, details the start of the Hollywood group: Mrs. Cecil (Bessie Bartlett) Frankel called a meeting on June 16, 1917, at the Hollywood Public Library, which resulted in the organization of the Hollywood Community Sing. Weekly meetings began on June 23. Frankel served as president the first year; Mrs. C. F. Wade became president in 1918, and William Palmer in 1919. Hugo Kirchhofer was director. Membership grew from thirty-five to nine hundred in the first fourteen months. For one other sing in the region, see "Santa Barbara Joins in Brilliant Concert by Mr. Farwell's Choristers," *Musical America* 31, no. 13 (January 24, 1920): 13, a report of a concert by the Santa Barbara Community Chorus of three thousand on December 28, 1919.

35. Norman M. and Dorothy K. Karasick, *The Oilman's Daughter: A Biography of Aline Barnsdall* (Encino, CA: Carleston Publishing, 1993).

36. Quoted in Jones, *Hollywood Bowl*, 37.

37. Board of Directors, Hollywood Bowl Association, *A Brief History*, "The Community Park and Art Association," and "Greater Participation Sought." "Hollywood Bowl," (T. Perceval Gerson Collection, box 1, HL), an undated manuscript in Gerson's hand, probably for a speech given in 1935, says:

Approximately one year following the incidents and developments mentioned [i.e., after May 26, 1919], it was deemed advisable to enlist the interest of more Hollywood people.

With that motive I secured an introductory letter to Mrs. Artie Mason Carter, President of the Hollywood Community Chorus, who

received me most graciously and promised unreservedly the cooperation of her splendid organization. To say that this has been given
effectively, is to put it mildly.

In fact, this meeting must have taken place before the Community Sing met in
the Bowl on May 15 (see below).

38. Principal sources are the *Hollywood Weekly Citizen;* Nordskog, "The
Earliest Musical History in the Hollywood Bowl"; Jones, *Hollywood Bowl;* and
Koopal, *Miracle of Music.* The only conflict among these sources is Jones's (and
Koopal's identical) report that Arthur Farwell led the Sing on July 4, 1919, when
he was in fact conducting his own music in the Greek Theater, Berkeley; they
must have referred to his appearance at the Bowl on May 15, 1920, or to his
guest conducting of the Sing there on July 4, 1920.

39. Hedwiga Reicher (undated résumé, two-page typescript, courtesy of
Lance Bowling) makes this claim and lists the second title as "First Production
in the Hollywood Bowl," date not given.

40. *Hollywood Weekly Citizen,* May 21, 1920, 1, 8. Bond suggested fifty
cents apiece for the collection; three hundred dollars was raised.

41. Jones, *Hollywood Bowl,* 33.

42. Jones, *Hollywood Bowl,* 23. Jones's chronology here is flawed, however.

43. "'Community Arts Alliance' Will Meet Tonight to Make Permanent
New Organization for Hollywood," *Hollywood Weekly Citizen,* September 3,
1920, 1, 8. Carter chaired the meeting; she appointed as temporary trustees Mrs.
H. T. Wright, president of the Women's Club of Hollywood; [town] Supervisor
Frank E. Woodley, E. G. Mansfield, board member of the Hollywood Community Chorus and business manager of the Hollywood Community Orchestra;
George L. Eastman, president of the Hollywood Chamber of Commerce; and
Chester T. Hoag. Marie Rankin Clarke, Christine W. Stevenson, Madame Ire-
nee Pavloska, composer Charles Wakefield Cadman, singer Mariska Aldrich, actors Frank Keenan and H. Ellis Reed, and J. W. McLellan all spoke in support of
"the movement to create a beautiful community center which shall become
even a national center of art and music." An open-air theater seating from five
thousand to eight thousand was mentioned; it was said that the sum of one hundred thousand dollars had to be raised; and a community Christmas pageant was
announced for the site, made available by co-owner Clarke.

44. Omitted were Ellis Reed, George L. Eastman, and Charles Wakefield
Cadman, in addition to Carter, Clarke, and Stevenson.

45. *PCMR* 39, no. 1 (October 1, 1920): 6. "The seventy-acre site of the Theatre and Arts Alliance will soon be taken over by the Community Arts Alliance
of Hollywood. Mrs. J. J. Carter, the indefatigable prophet of the Hollywood
Community Chorus, has been mainly the moving factor in a campaign during
which close to $60,000 have been under written."

46. Brochure in the T. Perceval Gerson Collection, box 13, Charles E. Young
Research Library, UCLA.

47. *Hollywood Weekly Citizen,* October 1, 1920. The story names W. A.

Kling and William A. Biby as "special organizers"; Biby is listed as a "publici-tyman" in the 1921 Los Angeles City Directory.

48. "Board of Directors for Community Park and Art Association Is Named by Leaders in Great Civic Project," *Hollywood Weekly Citizen*, October 22, 1920. The new board: George L. Eastman, G. G. Detzer, Dr. John R. Haynes, F. E. Keeler, A. C. Balch, Marco H. Hellman, Frank Keenan, William May Garland, H. Gale Atwater, Albert G. Bartlett, Anna George de Mille, Harry Chandler, Arthur Letts, Orra E. Monnette, A. Z. Taft, Jr., Frank Meline, Mrs. H. T. Wright, F. E. Woodley, Dr. William H. Snyder, Dr. Ernest C. Moore, A. M. Carter, G. G. Greenwood, C. E. Toberman, T. P. Gerson, Willsie Martin, DD., E. N. Martin, L. E. Behymer, Marie Rankin Clarke, Ray M. Gale, F. W. Blanchard, and Eleanor Brodie Jones.

49. Board of Directors, Hollywood Bowl Association, *A Brief History*, "'Symphonies under the Stars.'"

50. Jones, *Hollywood Bowl*, 58, reports that Mrs. Carter told the Hollywood businessmen's committee, "'I voted for your sewers when you wanted them; now, you vote for my symphonies!'"

51. Ibid., 33–34, 46. See also Brite, "Hollywood Bowl and the 'Symphonies under the Stars,'" 97–128. Neither the Hollywood Chamber of Commerce nor the directors of the CPAA endorsed the first season of Symphonies under the Stars. L. E. Behymer was ambivalent about the Bowl. He took part in the orga-nization of the TAA, hosting one of the preliminary meetings at his house, but he tended to be skeptical about such community-based enterprises, seeing them as money-losing propositions. The typescript memoir compiled by Minette Sparkes Behymer after his death in 1947 mentions the Bowl mainly in connec-tion with events in the later 1920s that lost money.

52. Jones, *Hollywood Bowl*, 51.

53. Ibid., 69, 71, 74. Marion Fairfax Marshall and A. J. Verheyn were the two others.

54. Koopal, *Miracle of Music*, 66–67.

55. Carter's statement was printed in full on page 1 of both the *Los Angeles Evening Express* and the *Los Angeles Evening Herald;* it also appeared in the *Times.* This version appeared in the *Los Angeles Examiner*, March 25, 1926.

56. Ibid., "a former high official of the Hollywood Bowl, who resigned year before last on account of asserted difficulties with Mrs. Carter."

57. Koopal, *Miracle of Music*, 38, 66, 67. Compare this especially with Koopal's handling of Frederick W. Blanchard's resignation over the same issue in 1923: "At this time President Blanchard suddenly resigned, midst newspaper rumors that dissension was rife in the Bowl organization" (65–66).

58. Jones, *Hollywood Bowl*, 110; *Los Angeles Evening Express*, Friday, March 26, 1926, 1, 10. The contemporary newspaper story contradicts some later accounts.

59. *Los Angeles Evening Herald*, March 25, 1926, A-11.

60. Charles E. Toberman is quoted in the *Los Angeles Evening Herald*, March 25, 1926, A-11: "I would suggest that she be given a year's leave of ab-

sence. She is not well, and is really overworked. I really don't know whether she intends to resign or not. She has so often resigned, you know, and later taken it back." This view is repeated in Koopal, *Miracle of Music*, 67.

61. Koopal, *Miracle of Music*, 105.

62. Letter, T. P. Gerson to Allan C. Balch, March 25, 1935, T. Perceval Gerson Collection, box 1, HL. At that time, Gerson was president of the Hollywood Bowl Association. The occasion of his initiative was probably the prospect of funding from the WPA for substantial improvements at the Bowl site, a prospect that did not materialize in any case.

63. Letter, Charles E. Toberman to Gerson, July 9, 1935, T. Perceval Gerson Collection, box 2, HL.

64. Alfred Hertz, typescript memoir, box 45, item 274, Alfred Hertz Collection, University of California, Berkeley, Music Library: "When Mr. Rothwell heard about Mrs. Carter's plans, he made a special trip to San Francisco to dissuade me from giving concerts in the Hollywood Bowl. His claim was that it was beneath my dignity and that it would be bad for the orchestra to play out of doors. . . . he never forgave me for starting these concerts" (91). The memoir appeared serially in the *San Francisco Chronicle*, May 3–July 14, 1942. Hertz had recommended Rothwell for his position with the Philharmonic.

65. For the first two seasons and occasionally thereafter, the Philharmonic's name was not used in connection with the Bowl's summer series.

66. The CPAA brochure from 1920 included this: "Do You Know . . . that Los Angeles has unconsciously drifted into a myriad of sets or groups that never can be bridged until a community spirit has been developed through the medium of a Community Park and Art Center?"

67. Interview, Ray C. B. Brown of the *San Francisco Chronicle*, quoted in the *Chicago Musical Leader*, September 30, 1922, Alfred Hertz Collection, box 44, item 223, typescript memoir, 190A, 196, University of California, Berkeley. The Hertz Collection includes a logbook listing 1,409 opera performances he conducted through April 1913. It must be added that Hertz was not a disinterested party in this statement; he always faced opposition in San Francisco, and he was paid $250 per concert in the Bowl's first season.

68. When Carter left and Brite was hired to replace her in 1926, Florence Atherton (Mrs. Leiland) Irish, a leader in the music club movement in LA, was appointed to the board of directors. When a second male manager, Glenn M. Tindall, was markedly unsuccessful during his term in the early 1930s, Irish succeeded him as the unpaid Bowl manager, remaining in that position until the late 1940s.

11. OLD COMPETITORS, NEW OPERA COMPANIES IN 1925

1. For the San Francisco Opera, see Arthur Bloomfield, *San Francisco Opera—1923–1961* (New York: Appleton-Century-Crofts, 1961). For Los Angeles, see Bishop, *The Los Angeles Grand Opera Association*. The competition

described in the following paragraph is from Sanders, "Los Angeles Grand Opera Association."

2. Album 153, "Biographies, Special Articles, Fugitive," Behymer Ephemera Collection, HL. The program for the grand opening of Olympic Auditorium (in the same collection), August 5, 1925, includes this statement from Harry M. Pollok, booking manager:

> The Olympic Auditorium can be used for as many purposes as Joseph's coat had colors.
>
> "Adaptability" is its slogan.
>
> For instance: Tonight a boxing or wrestling show with a seating capacity of 15,000; early in October a season of Grand opera,—six performances, by the California Grand Opera Company, showing the greatest stars of the operatic stage,—with seats for 6,000 music lovers; two weeks later a trade exposition,—the Home beautiful Show,—with a clear floor space of approximately 30,000 square feet.

3. This interpretation is certainly not contradicted by Swan in his discussion of monopolies by both eastern agents and Behymer (*Music in the Southwest*, 250–52). Swan fails to mention the 1924 or 1925 seasons of the Southern California Grand Opera Company in his discussion of the California Grand Opera Association (253).

4. Eleanor Barnes, "All Serene in Musicland with Impresarios: They Have Buried Hatchet," undated clipping, album 86, "Great Western Lyceum and Musical Bureau," Behymer Ephemera Collection, HL. The caption accompanying a photo of Behymer with Armitage reads, "L. E. Behymer, famed impresario, and his younger rival, Merle Armitage, who ended a 15-year battle of operas yesterday at the Biltmore by joining hands in an operetta venture, which will start on May 20 at Philharmonic Auditorium."

5. For another account of an early competition over the social role of opera, see Karen Ahlquist, *Democracy at the Opera: Music, Theater, and Culture in New York City, 1815–60* (Urbana: University of Illinois Press, 1997). Katherine K. Preston, *Opera on the Road: Traveling Opera Troupes in the United States, 1825–60* (Urbana: University of Illinois Press, 1993), chronicles the early ubiquity and importance of traveling opera companies in the early nineteenth century. In "Between the Cracks: The Performance of English-Language Opera in Late Nineteenth-Century America," *American Music* 21 (2003): 349–74, Preston carries her thesis forward for several more decades.

6. Martin M. Marks, *Music and the Silent Film: Contexts and Case Studies, 1895–1924* (New York: Oxford University Press, 1997), chapter 4, 109–66, and appendices 8–13, 198–217, are devoted to Breil's score. While most of the score was composed, there were also large interpolations by other composers.

7. From Keri Leigh, "Douglas Fairbanks," excerpted from the projected book *Stars of the Silent Cinema, 1900–1930* (1997) on www.fortunecity.com/lavender/wargames/154/bio.htm (accessed December 19, 2006): "The goal of UA was to provide independent distribution for artists who produced their own movies,

and to break the big studios' practice of 'block booking' pictures into theatres. Merit alone would determine a picture's success or failure. The idea was fresh, new, ambitious, and for once, on the side of the artist. It upset the balance in Hollywood, luring big name directors and stars away from major studio contracts to make their own pictures."

8. *The Fall of a Nation* (1916), a sequel to *The Birth of a Nation*, was advertised as "the first grand opera cinema." See Gillian B. Anderson, "The Presentation of Silent Films, or, Music as Anaesthesia," *Journal of Musicology* 5, no. 2 (1987): 257–95, 260. Anderson discusses the early connection between opera and film.

9. The short biography of Mortimer Wilson that is part of the finding aid to the collection of his music at UCLA reads:

> Wilson was born on Aug. 6, 1876 in Chariton, IA; studied in Chicago with Jacobsohn, Gleason, and Middelschulte (1894–1900); taught theory at University School of Music in Lincoln, NE (1901–7); spent 3 years in Leipzig, Germany, studying with Sitt and Reger; was at the Atlanta Conservatory in 1911 and conducted the Symphony Orchestra; taught at Brenau College, Gainesville, GA (1916–18); was consulting editor for the National Academy of Music in NY; wrote The Rhetoric of Music (1907); composed five symphonies, chamber music, and many songs and piano pieces; wrote music for silent films produced by Douglas Fairbanks, including The Thief of Bagdad (1924), Don Q. Son of Zorro (1925), and The Black Pirate (1926); died on Jan. 27, 1932, in New York.

Meredith Willson, one of his students, probably used Wilson as his model for his hero in *The Music Man*. I am grateful to Lance Bowling for showing me his draft of Mortimer Wilson's chronology and sharing the Mortimer Wilson scrapbook materials in his possession.

10. Smith and Richardson, *Mary Carr Moore, American Composer*, chapters 15 and 16, 136–61. For *Narcissa*, see chapter 9, 69–83, and chapter 20, 187–93, as indicated in chapter 9's notes.

11. Pauline Alderman, *We Build a School of Music: The Commissioned History of Music at the University of Southern California* (Los Angeles: Alderman Book Committee, 1989), 121, 154–57.

12. THE NEW NEGRO MOVEMENT IN LOS ANGELES

1. For example, see the *Times*, February 1, 1922, part I, 3, 2, "The World's News in Spanish," two columns of short dispatches in Spanish, prefaced by the following in English, then Spanish: "For the benefit of the many Spanish-speaking friends of the Times and the many students of that tongue in Los Angeles, The Times presents herewith a digest of the most important news of the day in Spanish. A working knowledge of correct everyday Spanish is an asset of immense value, especially in the Southwest, as is indicated by the fact that pub-

lic and private Spanish instructors have more than 18,000 pupils in Los Angeles alone."

2. Bagley, "History," *Overture* 4, no. 24 (April 1, 1925): 1.

3. A few weeks later, the Hungarian Ladies Orchestra (whose members' ethnicity and gender did not universally match its name) began a long engagement at the Palace Saloon, where they played seven nights a week from 7:30 to midnight, plus one matinee. As previously mentioned, one member, clarinetist Joseph N. Weber, became president of the fledgling American Federation of Musicians a few years later and held the job for thirty years.

4. Bagley, "History," *Overture* 7, no. 9 (January 1928): 4. The concerts took place in 1896–97.

5. Bagley, "History," *Overture* 8, no. 2 (June 1928): 7. Bagley's material on the diversity of music makers antedates that collected by such later figures as librarian Miriam Matthews and activist-author Bette Yarbrough Cox. Miriam Matthews, "The Negro in California from 1781–1910: An Annotated Bibliography," paper for library science course, University of Southern California, 1944; Miriam Matthews as interviewed by Eleanor Roberts, March 14, 16, 17, and 22, 1977, in *The Black Women Oral History Project: From the Arthur and Elizabeth Schlesinger Library on the History of Women in America, Radcliffe College*, edited by Ruth Edmonds Hill (Westport, CT: Meckler, 1991); "Miriam Matthews: West Coast Historian!" African American Registry, www.aaregistry.com/african_american_history/2006/Miriam_Matthews_west_coast_historian, accessed February 19, 2007; Bette Yarbrough Cox, *Central Avenue: Its Rise and Fall (1890–c. 1955) including the Musical Renaissance of Black Los Angeles* (Los Angeles: BEEM Publications, 1993).

6. Ethnic Mexicans are listed in the census with ethnic Europeans, and they are well down the list in terms of numbers. In 1920 the number of ethnic Germans was three times that of ethnic Mexicans; likewise, there were many more English, Canadians, and Irish than Mexicans and almost as many Russians and Swedes. This careful accounting by national origin, which ended in 1920, is a reflection of an older hierarchy of "whiteness," in which one's place in the hierarchy is governed by the number of generations spent in the United States and the part of Europe from which the individuals came. The farther east or south their country of origin, the farther down the hierarchical framework. See Matthew Frye Jacobson, *Whiteness of a Different Color: European Immigrants and the Alchemy of Race* (Cambridge, MA: Harvard University Press, 1998). The implications of these ethnic/cultural differences for music making have not been explored in this book, though they would make a topic of some interest for further study.

7. Regarding the Chinese, see Bagley, "History," *Overture* 5, no. 19 (January 15, 1926): 10. All of the four "colored" musicians and teachers of music listed in the 1890 Census were males. Of the twelve listed in the 1900 Census, two (both African American) were females.

8. See chapter 3. The various white ethnic minorities were often represented in La Fiesta de Los Angeles by floats and marchers who were members of those

minorities. By contrast, Asians were always represented in the programs by persons with Anglo names. Nothing in the programs suggests the participation of African Americans.

9. It should be pointed out that, while most of the white European ethnic groups were assimilated within a generation or two, a quiet but pervasive anti-Semitism persisted in Los Angeles, demonstrated most obviously in the parallel club structures for Jewish and white non-Jewish groups. For a survey of African American history in California, see Rudolph M. Lapp, *Afro-Americans in California*, 2nd ed. (San Francisco: Boyd & Fraser Publishing Company, 1987).

10. "Dr. Locke to Repeat Lecture for Negroes . . . ," *Los Angeles Evening Express*, Tuesday, February 11, 1913, 5. Charles Edward Locke was a nationally prominent, white Methodist minister. The location, the First Methodist Episcopal Church, predominantly white, was located at Sixth and South Hill, perhaps a half mile from the First AME Church, founded in 1871 by former slave Biddy Mason.

11. Koegel, "*Canciones del país*"; Koegel, "Calendar of Southern California Amusements"; Koegel, "Mexican and Mexican-American Musical Life in Southern California"; and Koegel, "Preserving the Sounds of the 'Old' Southwest." Examples from "Calendar" (139) are these references to music for 1887: January 29, an ad by Arévalo for a benefit performance at Armory Hall to help build a Catholic church in Wilmington; September 5–14, Zerega's Royal Spanish Troubadours at the Grand Opera House (three nights), San Bernardino Opera House (one night), San Diego (two nights), and Pomona (one night). For 1888 (149): April 29, the Great Zarzuela Spanish Opera Bouffe Company, Grand Opera House *(Boccaccio; Les Noces d'Olivette)*; May 12–18, the Hispano-Mexicano Opera Company *(El Reloj de Lucerna; El Sargento Federico)*.

12. G. Bromley Oxnam, director, Los Angeles City Survey, *The Mexican in Los Angeles: Los Angeles City Survey* (Los Angeles: Interchurch World Movement of North America, June 1920). See also Roberto R. Trevino, *Becoming Mexican American: The Spanish-Language Press and the Biculturation of California Elites, 1852–1870* (Stanford, CA: Stanford Center for Chicano Research, Working Paper Series, no. 27, 1989).

13. Douglas Monroy, "Making Mexico in Los Angeles," in Thomas Sitton and William Deverell, eds., *Metropolis in the Making: Los Angeles in the 1920s* (Berkeley and Los Angeles: University of California Press, 2001), 161–78.

14. Monroy (ibid., 163–65) calls that period a high point in such activity.

15. Luis Reyes and Peter Rubie, *Hispanics in Hollywood: An Encyclopedia of Film and Television* (New York: Garland Publishing, 1994), introduction.

16. The grand opening of a Chinese theater was reported in the *Los Angeles Times*, September 25, 1890, 1, col. 1. Guangming Li, "Music in the Chinese Community of Los Angeles: An Overview," *Musical Aesthetics and Multiculturalism in Los Angeles: Selected Reports in Ethnomusicology* 10 (1994): 105–21, mentions only "reports of some scattered records from the past" (105).

17. The white imitators were the Schoneman-Blanchard band, which had initially made its name by performing in blackface. Bagley, "History of the Band and Orchestra Business in Los Angeles," *Overture* 7, no. 9 (January 1928): 4.

18. Minako Waseda, "Japanese American Musical Culture in Southern California: Its Formation and Transformation in the 20th Century," PhD dissertation, University of California, Santa Barbara, 2000.

19. Caroline Reynolds, "Theaters," *Los Angeles Graphic* 37, no. 22 (October 26, 1912): 13. It's not known what music accompanied this play. The Mason Opera House opened in 1903.

20. Letter, Arna Bontemps to Verna Arvey, December 29, 1941, William Grant Still and Verna Arvey Papers, Special Collections, University of Arkansas, Fayetteville. "I am a product of neighborhoods in which relatively few Negroes lived and of schools in which we were always greatly in the minority. The same is true, I believe, of a good many Negroes who grew up in Los Angeles in those days. . . . My parents were always anxious to put the South (and the past) as far behind as possible. . . . A link with the past was established for me in spite of all efforts to the contrary."

21. Henry T. Sampson, *The Ghost Walks: A Chronological History of Blacks in Show Business, 1865–1910* (Metuchen: Scarecrow Press, 1988). The early companies that failed in Los Angeles, marooning H. C. Wyatt and Harley Hamilton at different times, were white troupes that played in blackface. White minstrel companies were always more numerous.

22. "Amusements," *Los Angeles Times*, December 24, 1889, 5.

23. For information on Jones, see John Graziano, "The Early Life and Career of the 'Black Patti': The Odyssey of an African American Singer in the Late Nineteenth Century," *Journal of the American Musicological Society* 53 (2000): 543–96. More generally, see Thomas L. Riis, "Concert Singers, Prima Donnas, and Entertainers: The Changing Status of Black Women Vocalists in Nineteenth-Century America," in Michael Saffle, ed., *Music and Culture in America, 1861–1918* (New York: Garland, 1998), 53–78; also Editorial Staff, "In Retrospect: Black Prima Donnas of the Nineteenth Century," *Black Perspective in Music* 7, no. 1 (Spring 1979): 95–106.

24. Behymer Ephemera Collection, album 60, HL (for the year 1896–97), 157, 158, two programs for the Original Nashville Students at the Music Hall, Tuesday evening, December 7, 1896. Patrons could purchase tickets in advance at Bartlett's Music House. Henry Sampson (see below) missed this appearance. In this case, Behymer was indeed the promoter. It is likely that, given the small size of the Music Hall, these performances were intended to appeal primarily to black audiences, who were consigned to the balcony benches in larger theaters.

25. A four-page flyer in the Museum of the City of New York, courtesy of John Graziano, lists the following California and Nevada dates for what is said to be the sixth "grand triumphal tour" itinerary for the Black Patti Troubadours. They take up the month of January 1902: San Francisco, 1–4; San Diego, 5–7; Santa Ana, 8; Riverside, 9; San Bernardino, 10; Pomona, 11; Los Angeles, 12–15; Pasadena, 16; Santa Barbara, 17; Ventura, 18.; open, 19; Bakersfield, 20; Tulare,

21; Visalia, 22; Fresno, 23; San Jose, 24; Stockton, 25; open, 26; Nevada City, 27; Grass Valley, 28; Virginia City (NV), 29; Reno, 30; travel east, 31. Dates in Utah and Colorado fill most of February.

26. Sampson, *The Ghost Walks,* 337, quoting a report in the *Los Angeles Times,* dates Jones's second visit between February 11 and February 22, 1905, and locates it at the Grand Opera House. He adds that Sissieretta Jones could still sing well. For more on Williams and Walker, see Thomas Riis, *Just before Jazz: Black Musical Theater in New York, 1890–1915* (Washington, DC: Smithsonian Institution Press, 1989). Bert Williams, a native of Antigua who spent several years in Riverside (near Los Angeles) before going to San Francisco, formed his partnership with George Walker in San Francisco in the 1890s. By 1898 they had brought the cakewalk to Broadway, achieving lasting stardom in the process. For the stereotype, see the *Times* report, quoted in Sampson: "Chief among the celebrants is John Rucker, a Negro so homely that a single look at his black face is enough to make one laugh. Rucker has great vivacity, an inexhaustible stock of facial contortions, and jokes, which—if not new—are told in a humor creating way" (337).

27. See chapter 6, n. 17.

28. *Lonesome Town* played on Broadway in New York for eleven weeks in 1908. In jarring contrast to Bontemps's affectionate reminiscences below, *Lonesome Town* plays on ethnic and racial stereotypes as well as regional ones for the "amusement" of distant white audiences, with songs such as "The Lanky, Yankee Boys in Blue," "Mission Bells," and "Big Chief Smoke." Description from Gerald M. Bordman, *American Musical Theatre: A Chronology,* 3rd ed. (New York: Oxford University Press, 2001), 239. Song titles from Richard C. Norton, *A Chronology of American Musical Theater,* 3 vols. (New York: Oxford University Press, 2002), 1: 883–84. C. William Kolb and Matt M. Dill were white actors who had made their careers in blackface, largely in the Far West; the comedy involves two tramps who find themselves in Watts and indulge in scams based on the (reported) death of an absentee landlord.

29. E. Frederick Anderson, *The Development of Leadership and Organization Building in the Black Community of Los Angeles from 1900 through World War II* (Saratoga, CA: Century Twenty-one Publishing, 1980). His goal was to describe "nontraditional indigenous organizations" (2). He also mentions the Woman's Republican Study Club (1929) and the Victory Club (1942). For Garvey's organization in Los Angeles, see Emory J. Tolbert, *The UNIA and Black Los Angeles: Ideology and Community in the American Garvey Movement* (Los Angeles: Center for Afro-American Studies, 1980).

30. The Pasadena papers, the *Star* and the *News* (later consolidated as the *Star-News*), report a range of lectures, weddings, and other events involving that city's small black population, albeit in small type on back pages. On the other hand, the *Los Angeles Times* simply ignored the city's African American citizens except for sensationalized reports of criminal activity. The more liberal *Los Angeles Evening Express* tried to do better, but its reports are often problematic.

31. Charlotta Bass, *Forty Years: Memoirs from the Pages of a Newspaper* (Los Angeles: n.p., 1960).

32. Delilah L. Beasley, *Negro Trail Blazers of California; a Compilation of Records from the California Archives in the Bancroft Library at the University of California, in Berkeley; and from the Diaries, Old Papers and Conversations of Old Pioneers in the State of California. It Is a True Record of Facts, as They Pertain to the History of the Pioneer and Present Day Negroes of California* (San Francisco, CA, 1919; reprint, R & E Research, 1968).

33. The census summaries provide analysis of occupations (including musicians and teachers of music) for "racial" minorities, that is, persons of African, Asian, and Native American descent, but not for "ethnic" minorities, including Latinos. At the same time, it lumps persons of Chinese and Japanese descent together as "Asians," thereby missing significant differences between these groups.

34. J. Max Bond, "The Negro in Los Angeles," PhD dissertation (sociology), University of Southern California, 1936. A table showing illiteracy among Negroes by age in 1910 demonstrates the much higher literacy rate among persons under age forty-five. For more on occupations through 1925, see Charles S. Johnson, director, *Industrial Survey of the Negro Population of Los Angeles* (Los Angeles: National Urban League, 1926). By comparison, the literacy rate among foreign-born whites was lower (91.5 percent) than it was for Los Angeles' urban black people.

35. In 1933 Wilkins sought advanced training in music composition, taking a class from Mary Carr Moore at California Christian College (predominantly white, now Chapman University and in another location) on Vermont Avenue. It is likely that he also wanted to observe her unusual gift for eliciting creative work from all of her students, even the shyest and least prepared. Mary Carr Moore, datebook entry, March 10, 1933, Mary Carr Moore Archive, Music Library, UCLA.

Her class was racially diverse; of the seven students whose compositions were performed that evening, Wilkins was African American and Sei-Hyung Kim was probably Korean American. Moore's datebook entry for that day reveals that it was the date of a major earthquake: "Found the main building unsafe, concert transferred to small hall. Audience kept arriving so it seemed best to go on with concert. *Four* heavy shocks during program. All very courageous. . . . we all repeated the Lord's Prayer together. So many colored people in audience owing to Mr. Wilkins' numbers—all very brave."

36. Jacqueline Cogdell DjeDje, "Los Angeles Composers of African American Gospel Music: The Early Generation," *American Music* 11 (1993): 412–57; Jacqueline Cogdell DjeDje, "California Black Gospel Tradition," in DjeDje and Eddie S. Meadows, eds., *California Soul: Music of African Americans in the West* (Berkeley and Los Angeles: University of California Press, 1998), 124–75; Bette Yarbrough Cox, *Central Avenue: Its Rise and Fall (1890–c. 1955) including the Musical Renaissance of Black Los Angeles* (Los Angeles: BEEM Publications, 1993), especially chapter 1, "The Move West," 5–22; also Bette

Yarbrough Cox, "The Evolution of Black Music in Los Angeles, 1890–1955," in Lawrence B. De Graaf, Kevin Mulroy, and Quintard Taylor, *Seeking El Dorado: African Americans in California* (Los Angeles: Autry Museum of Western Heritage, and Seattle: University of Washington Press, 2001), 249–78.

37. Sherrie Tucker, *Swing Shift: "All-Girl" Bands of the 1940s* (Durham, NC: Duke University Press, 2000), 38–39.

38. Arna Bontemps, *God Sends Sunday* (New York: Harcourt Brace, 1931; reprint, New York: AMS Press, 1972); Arna Bontemps and Jack Conroy, *Anyplace but Here* (New York: Hill and Wang, 1966); originally published (1945) as *They Seek a City*. The Fifty-first Street School, near Holmes Avenue, which opened in 1910, is said to have been the first school in this generally black neighborhood.

39. Bontemps and Conroy, *Anyplace but Here*, 5.

40. Ibid., 8–9.

41. Ibid., 10. Whetsol played in the band Duke Ellington organized in Washington, DC, and had taken to New York at an early stage in his career; the literature on Ellington has him returning to Howard University in Washington rather than going with Ellington on his second successful New York venture. There is no mention of Whetsol in the literature on early black Los Angeles musicians. If Bontemps is correct, he must have left Los Angeles very early in his career. Woody Strowe is probably Woody Strobe, who became a screen actor. Black achievers in public administration and politics, such as Ralph Bunche of the United Nations in its early years and Mayor Tom Bradley, emerged still later.

42. Samples of these and other newspapers from the 1920s and '30s exist in the George P. Johnson Negro Film Collection, MS 1042, Department of Special Collections, UCLA. It is doubtful that any of them published for a very long period of time.

43. The letterhead listed these names: Theodore Banks, Roy Johnson, William Middleton, Eardly Gauff, Harold Forsythe, Haven Johnson, David Floyd, Lawrence Johnson, Ronald Jefferson, Clifford Gantt, Marvin Johnson, and Lawrence Lassiter.

44. Several issues of *Flash* are at the Huntington Library. No complete run is known.

45. Forsythe's career is described in the chapter "An Unknown 'New Negro,'" in Catherine Parsons Smith, *William Grant Still: A Study in Contradictions* (Berkeley and Los Angeles: University of California Press, 2000), 94–113. Forsythe's account of Still's work, "William Grant Still: A Study in Contradictions" (typescript, c. 1932), appears on 274–303 in Smith. Forsythe's papers are at the Huntington Library.

46. For information on *Troubled Island*, see Tammy L. Kernodle, " 'Sons of Africa, Come Forth': Compositional Approaches of William Grant Still in the Opera *Troubled Island*," *American Music Research Center Journal* 13 (2003): 25–36; Gayle Murchison, "Was *Troubled Island* Seen by the Critics as a Protest Opera?" *AMRC Journal* 13 (2003): 37–60; Wayne D. Shirley, "Two Aspects of *Troubled Island*," *AMRC Journal* 13 (2003): 61–64; and Catherine Parsons

Smith, " 'Glory Is a Passing Thing': William Grant Still and Langston Hughes Collaborate on *Troubled Island*," *AMRC Journal* 13 (2003): 5–24. See Wayne D. Shirley, "William Grant Still's Choral Ballad *And They Lynched Him on a Tree*," *American Music* 12 (Winter 1994): 426–61.

47. See Smith, *William Grant Still: A Study in Contradictions*. Arvey is treated in the chapter "*they*, Verna and Billy," 152–81. Her early biography of Still is reprinted on 304–39.

48. Alain Locke, "The Negro Spirituals," in Locke, ed., *The New Negro* (New York: Albert Boni, 1925; reprint, New York: Atheneum; Toronto: Maxwell Macmillan Canada; New York: Maxwell Macmillan International, 1992), 209.

49. Even so perceptive a critic of musical modernism as Paul Rosenfeld assumed that the novelty of Still's new work came from its incorporation of jazz, writing that "the use of jazz motives in the last section of his work is more genuinely musical than any to which they have been put, by Milhaud, Gershwin, or any one else," quoted in William Grant Still, "Personal Notes" [c. 1932], in Smith, *William Grant Still: A Study in Contradictions*, 223.

50. Letter, Alain Locke to Verna Arvey, Still and Arvey Papers, Department of Special Collections, University of Arkansas, Fayetteville.

51. The manuscript is in the Forsythe Papers at HL.

52. Forsythe, "William Grant Still," in Smith, *William Grant Still: A Study in Contradictions*, 278–80.

53. Forsythe, untitled essay, written for the *California News*, Forsythe Papers, folder "Still and Johnson," HL. *Ofay* was a derogatory term for a white person.

54. Richard Bruce [Nugent], "Sahdji," in Alain Locke and Montgomery Gregory, eds., *Plays of Negro Life, a Source-Book of Native American Drama* (New York: Harper and Brothers, 1937; reprint, Westport, CT: Negro Universities Press, 1970), 389–400.

55. Forsythe, "Sahdji," typescript, Forsythe Papers, HL.

56. Hansonia L. Caldwell, "Music in the Lives of Blacks in California: The Beginnings," *Triangle of Mu Phi Epsilon* 82, no. 4 (1988): 10, 18, for example, describes it as "emulative."

57. For a telling account of this class difference and its relation to white concert culture (in this case opera) in Atlanta, Georgia, see Gavin James Campbell, "Music and the Making of a Jim Crow Culture, 1900–1925," PhD dissertation, University of North Carolina at Chapel Hill, 1999.

58. See Charles Mingus, *Beneath the Underdog: His World as Composed by Mingus*, edited by Nel King (New York: Knopf, 1971).

59. Henry T. Sampson, *Blacks in Black and White: A Source Book on Black Films* (Metuchen, NJ: Scarecrow Press, 1977), includes a chronology of black-produced films (8–17) in the United States and a listing of U.S. movie theaters that catered to African American audiences (18–24). The Lincoln Motion Picture Company was organized in Los Angeles in 1916 and incorporated the following year. In 1916, it produced *Realization of a Negro's Ambition* and *The Troopers of Company K*. Two years later, it produced a newsreel of the Tenth Black Cav-

alry at Fort Huachaca, Arizona; in addition, *Law of Nature* played in the East. Noble Johnson resigned from the company in that year. In 1921, the company produced its last film, *By Right of Birth*.

By 1921, 308 theaters nationwide played to the African American trade; 143 of these combined vaudeville acts with film. In 1916, J. W. Gordon, an African American, purchased the New Angelus Theatre, 1107 S. Central (different from the Los Angeles Theater). The Tivoli, farther out on South Central, opened in 1933. By 1937, four black theaters were operating in Los Angeles: the Florence Mills (capacity 700), the Lincoln (1,960), the Rosebud (800), and the Tivoli (763).

60. Tom Stoddard, *Jazz on the Barbary Coast* (Chigwell, Essex: Storyville, 1982), 127. For an account of Williams's and Walker's careers, see Riis, *Just before Jazz*. Irene Castle, supported by James Reese Europe's band, was the leading advocate of the new forms of ballroom dancing. In the *San Francisco Bulletin* (March 6, 1913, 16), the word *jazz* was first applied to the black dance music that had previously been known as ragtime. The style was probably somewhere between what we now think of as ragtime, as it had crystallized by 1895, and Dixieland, which emerged in the early 1920s. From the first, according to 1910 Census reports, a large proportion of the (relatively few) blacks listed as "professionals" in San Francisco were musicians and entertainers, an indication of the importance of these performance venues to the black community.

61. Most of the material on jazz in Los Angeles is drawn from Michael Bakan, "Way Out West on Central," in DjeDje and Meadows, eds., *California Soul*, 23–78.

62. Lawrence Gushee, *Pioneers of Jazz: The Story of the Creole Band* (New York: Oxford University Press, 2005), 51, 71.

63. For more on Morton, see Phil Pastras, *Dead Man Blues: Jelly Roll Morton Way Out West* (Berkeley and Los Angeles: University of California Press, 2001).

64. When Local 767 was formally chartered by the American Federation of Musicians is not clear. It celebrated its twenty-fifth anniversary, however, in 1945. By that time the federation was having doubts about its various segregated locals.

65. Bontemps, *God Sends Sunday*, 153.

66. Bontemps, *God Sends Sunday*, 160–61.

67. Jelly Roll Morton, as paraphrased by Alan Lomax in *Mister Jelly Roll: The Fortunes of Jelly Roll Morton, New Orleans Creole and "Inventor of Jazz,"* 2nd ed. (Berkeley and Los Angeles: University of California Press, 1973), 162–63; cited in Bakan, "Way Out West on Central," 37. The city of Watts, named after the developer who subdivided it, was incorporated in 1906, when the area acquired an interurban train station (still extant) and claimed fourteen hundred inhabitants. When it became clear in 1926 that soon a majority of its voters would be black, it was absorbed into the City of Los Angeles.

68. Marl Young (1917–), oral history, in Cox, *Central Avenue*, 317–23. In a private conversation, Young confirmed that Bagley opposed the merger. For a

more detailed account of this merger and its context, see Lowell Dwight Dickerson, "Central Avenue Meets Hollywood: The Amalgamation of the Black and White Musicians' Unions in Los Angeles," PhD dissertation, University of California, Los Angeles, 1998. A union account is also on the Web site of the American Federation of Musicians.

13. WELCOMING THE ULTRAMODERN

1. Moross, "Hollywood Music without Movies," 261. He added, "The concentration of important musical figures in America is at the moment very heavy in and around Hollywood." The composers listed are Igor Stravinsky, Arnold Schoenberg, Ernst Toch, Louis Gruenberg, George Antheil, Eugene Zador, Joseph Achron, and Mario Castelnuovo-Tedesco.

2. The first New Music Society concert, held in Los Angeles in October 1925, is described in some detail in Rita Mead, *Henry Cowell's New Music, 1925–1936: The Society, the Music Editions, and the Recordings* (Ann Arbor: UMI Research Press, 1981), 31–49.

3. Even Carol J. Oja, in *Making Music Modern: New York in the 1920s* (New York: Oxford University Press, 2000), does not attempt a definition of "modern music."

4. Seattle and San Francisco tended to level off in population growth after 1910, but not Los Angeles. In 1926, the *Pacific Coast Musician* estimated the population of the city proper at 1.25 million and reported Los Angeles County at 2,147,788, the first number possibly inflated, to judge from the census figures in appendix A.

5. The *B'nai B'rith Messenger* and *Rob Wagner's Script*, both with a somewhat more liberal bent, became factors only in the 1930s.

6. The Depression took a major toll on the press; *LA Saturday Night* folded in 1929; the old *LA Evening Express.* in 1931; and the *Hollywood Citizen-News*, a few years later, leaving Ussher among the unemployed until a slot was created for him in the Federal Music Project.

7. *Los Angeles County Culture and the Community* (Los Angeles: Civic Bureau of Music and Art of Los Angeles, 1927), 7.

8. Little evidence of these industrial orchestras survives outside the pamphlet. Barker Brothers had an auditorium in its store for many years and frequently sponsored afternoon concerts there, often using local musicians and music students. The house orchestra at the Grauman Theatre gave a concert of music by American composers as early as June 1920 and another of resident composers' music in July 1921. Both concerts were reported in the *PCMR*.

The pamphlet's description of music activity deals only with so-called art music activities. There is no mention of jazz or of nightclub entertainment. One page (of sixty-eight total) is devoted to the Hollywood film colony, which by then was making 85 percent of American films.

9. Sanders, "Los Angeles Grand Opera Association."

10. Joseph Zoellner and his children, Joseph, Jr., Amandus, and Antoinette,

were the members of this quartet. Their tours were reported in *Pacific Coast Musician* and *PCMR*.

11. For more on Elizabeth Sprague Coolidge (1864–1953), see Cyrilla Barr, *Elizabeth Sprague Coolidge: American Patron of Music* (New York: Schirmer Books; London: Prentice Hall International, 1998). See also Bertha McCord Knisely, "Chamber Music in Southern California," in Ussher, ed., *Who's Who in Music and Dance in Southern California*, 63–67.

12. José Rodríguez, "Music Mostly in the Air," in Ussher, ed., *Who's Who in Music and Dance in Southern California*, 120–21.

13. For USC, see Alderman, *We Build a School of Music*. The main campus of the University of California remained in Berkeley. The earliest ancestor of UCLA, founded in 1882 and located on the present site of the Los Angeles Public Library, was a state normal school, dedicated mainly to the training of teachers; it was a branch of San Jose State College, the original teacher training institution in the state. In 1914 it moved to 855 North Vermont Avenue, where it was presently taken over by the University of California and in 1918 became the Southern Branch of the university. In 1927 the present UCLA campus in Westwood first opened; eventually the old Southern Branch campus became the home of LA City College, a two-year school. In deference to the large music programs at USC and several other private colleges, UCLA did not offer a music major until the mid-1930s.

14. Suzanne Shelton, *Ruth St. Denis: A Biography of the Divine Dancer* (Austin: University of Texas Press, 1990); Jane Sherman, *The Drama of Denishawn Dance* (Middletown, CT: Wesleyan University Press, 1979); Christena L. Schlundt, *Into the Mystic with Miss Ruth* (New York: Dance Perspectives Foundation, 1971).

15. Photograph in Bessie Bartlett Frankel, *History of the California Federation of Music Clubs, 1918–1930*, 27 pp., pamphlet in box 1, Bessie Bartlett Frankel Papers, Department of Special Collections, Young Research Library, UCLA, also in *Musical America*, May 24, 1919, 9.

16. "At Dawning" (1906) was the most successful song. *Shanewis, or the Robin Woman* was produced by the Met in 1918 and revived in 1919. Nelle Richmond Eberhart was lyricist and librettist for both. See Harry D. Perison, "Charles Wakefield Cadman: His Life and Works," PhD dissertation, Eastman School of Music, University of Rochester, 1978; also Lulu Marion Sanford Tefft, *Little Intimate Stories of Charles Wakefield Cadman* (Hollywood, CA: D. G. Fischer, 1926).

17. For more on Grunn, see Catherine Parsons Smith, "Grunn, (John) Homer," in *Grove Music Online*, ed. L. Macy, www.grovemusic.com (accessed December 20, 2004); see also the Grunn Papers, Department of Special Collections, Young Library, UCLA; for more on Dillon, see Carol Neuls-Bates, "Dillon, Fannie Charles," *Grove Music Online*, ed. L. Macy, www.grovemusic.com (accessed December 20, 2004); see also the Dillon Papers, Department of Special Collections, Charles E. Young Research Library, UCLA.

18. Ussher, ed., *Who's Who in Music and Dance in Southern California*.

Bond, Frankel, and Jamison were still active. Homer Grunn was a Chicago-trained pianist and teacher whose work included a ballet, *Xochitl,* commissioned by Ruth St. Denis; several operas; and numerous piano pieces in either an Indianist or Viennese style. In addition to his own piano studio, he taught with Mary Carr Moore at California Christian College. His music and a typescript autobiography are in the Music Library, UCLA. Dillon studied with Thilo Becker, then in Germany with Godowsky; she toured as a pianist, produced a series of orchestral works as well as piano music, and later taught at Los Angeles High School. Two manuscript theory texts and several scores are in the Music Library, UCLA. For Mary Carr Moore, see Smith and Richardson, *Mary Carr Moore, American Composer.* The younger Elinor Remick Warren was born in Los Angeles and studied there and in New York, only much later studying with Nadia Boulanger. She, too, had a career as a pianist. She produced large orchestral works, songs, and piano pieces. Her manuscripts are at the Library of Congress. For Warren, see Virginia Bortin, *Elinor Remick Warren: Her Life and Her Music* (Metuchen, NJ: Scarecrow Press, 1987); Bortin, *Elinor Remick Warren: A Bio-bibliography* (Westport, CT: Greenwood Press, 1993); and Susan Pearl Finger, "The Los Angeles Heritage: Four Women Composers, 1918–1939," PhD dissertation, University of California, Los Angeles, 1986.

19. Newly arrived critic Bruno David Ussher claimed, "Our proportionate concert attendance is said to be eight times as large as that of New York City," *PCMR* 37, no. 3 (October 18, 1919): 3. For example, the Hollywood Bowl concerts drew a total audience of over 250,000 in their second season.

20. Smith, "Primary Documentation of California Composers."

21. The quotation and the figure for 1927 are from "The Music Program in Los Angeles," *Playground and Recreation* 24 (June 1930): 177. This article reports an intermediate figure of 112,714 participants for June 1928. The figure for 1929 comes from "Los Angeles Community Music," *Things Worth Knowing about Music and Art* 5, no. 6 (November–December 1929). Neither article is signed. The first periodical was published in New York; the second, in Los Angeles.

22. Music directors worked from cue sheets, distributed along with the silent films to accompany them. These were lists of scenes with timings and suggestions for music suitable to support the action. The quick shifts were demanding for the musicians. Much of the music came from what had become the "pops" repertoire (marches, opera overtures, familiar songs) and was familiar to the audiences. Only a few movies came with published scores and parts.

23. At first the Steeb school was at 4009½ West Sixth Street, then at 453 South Wilton Place. The Steebs lived at the Wilton Place address until their move to a house on Mulholland Drive in early 1933, a marker of the school's financial success. The complex at 3839 Wilshire Boulevard was occupied at about the same time. Smith and Richardson conducted numerous interviews with surviving students, family and friends. See *Mary Carr Moore, American Composer,* 113–16, for their sketch of Steeb's career. See also Jean Preston, "Olga Steeb: A Biography," senior paper, Music Resource Center Department of Music, California State University, Long Beach, 1979.

24. *Continental Times,* November 1909, clipping, Olga Steeb scrapbook, courtesy of Lillian Steeb French.

25. In three separate concerts over a two-week period, Steeb played the following: Beethoven, opp. 58, 73, nos. 4 and 5; Brahms, op. 15, no. 1; Grieg, op. 16; Liszt, no. 1 in E-flat; Mozart, K. 537; Scharwenka, op. 83; Schumann, op. 54; and Tchaikowsky, op. 23 in B-flat Minor.

26. The male students and teachers were drawn into World War II; some of the women probably also found jobs in the new war industries. Lillian Steuber, one of Steeb's most successful pupils, offered master classes for a time. Among the letters from Fannie Charles Dillon to Percy Grainger in the Grainger Museum, University of Melbourne, Australia, is an undated announcement, possibly from fall 1942, of classes at the Steeb school. Norma Steeb, Olga's sister, is listed as the school's director and Dillon as teacher of theory and composition. Norma Steeb presently found another teaching position; her papers, which would have documented the school, were dissipated at her death.

27. See Smith and Richardson, *Mary Carr Moore, American Composer,* 110–13, for more on Frankel.

28. Barnsdall, a member of the Bowl's board of directors, put up the prize of five thousand dollars offered in 1924 for the design of a new music shell for the Bowl by an American architect. In line with her interest in children's theater and her earlier stage productions of *Alice in Wonderland,* she contributed fifteen hundred dollars to pay for the extra rehearsals needed to produce Deems Taylor's *Through the Looking Glass Suite* (Karasick, *The Oilman's Daughter,* 91).

29. Karasick, *The Oilman's Daughter.* Information on Barnsdall's connection with Bel Geddes comes from the Norman Bel Geddes Collection, Harry Ransom Humanities Research Library, University of Texas at Austin; also Norman Bel Geddes, *Miracle in the Evening: An Autobiography* (Garden City, NY: Doubleday, 1960).

30. Dan Georgakas, "Mooney, Tom," in Mari Jo Buhle, Paul Buhle, and Dan Georgakas, eds., *Encyclopedia of the American Left,* 2nd ed., (New York: Oxford University Press, 1998). Found on www.english.uiuc.edu/maps/poets/m_r/ridge/mooney.htm (accessed August 23, 2006).

Thomas J. Mooney (1892–1942) was the central figure in the most notorious labor frame-up in the early half of the twentieth century. He and Warren K. Billings (1893–1972) served twenty-three years (1916–1939) in California prisons for the death of ten persons killed when a bomb exploded during the 1916 Preparedness Day Parade in San Francisco. Mooney's actual offense was that he had been de facto leader of the left wing of the California Federation of Labor and his activities had alarmed some of the most powerful forces in the state. . . . In less than a year, solid evidence began to surface that the testimony against Mooney and Billings had been perjured.

31. Barnsdall's correspondence with Wright and with Rudolf Schindler, the architect who oversaw much of the work on Hollyhock House, is at the Getty

Library, Los Angeles. Since Wright's theater design was incomplete (it was not built on the Olive Hill site), Barnsdall arranged for the production company to use the theater at the Egan Dramatic School. Personal reasons and the mentioned political issues caused Barnsdall to drop her interest in her Los Angeles little theater company for the next several years. For more on Hollyhock House, see Kathryn Smith, *Frank Lloyd Wright, Hollyhock House and Olive Hill: Buildings and Projects for Aline Barnsdall* (New York: Rizzoli, 1992); James Steele, *Barnsdall House: Frank Lloyd Wright* (London: Phaidon, 1992); and Robert McCarter, James Steele, and Brian Carter, *Frank Lloyd Wright: Unity Temple, Barnsdall (Hollyhock) House, Johnson Wax Administration Building and Research Tower* (London: Phaidon, 1999).

32.   She may have met Cowell in San Francisco or Carmel. Cowell's music was played there, and Barnsdall attended the Carmel summer festivals.

33.   *Salome* premiered in Dresden in 1905. The opera created something of a scandal because of Salome's provocative dance, first to King Herod and then to the head of John the Baptist. The slim Craft was the first singer to dance the part herself rather than defer to a dancer.

34.   Arthur Farwell, "Where Is Truth of Music?" *Pacific Coast Musician* 12, no. 1 (January 1923): 10. Farwell's two-column essay is a diatribe against the commercialization of concert music: "And at last we have what we have—a completely commercialized musical life (or is it death?)—which for the maintenance of its respectability trades on its *rapprochement* with Beethoven—who, if he were alive, would anathematize it—which palms off on us all the sickening musical degeneracy of a spiritually bankrupt Europe, and which is so bent on the maintenance of its fashionable appeal and its private profits that with all the good it still has to offer, it is withheld from ninety-seven per cent of the people in America and given to only three per cent."

35.   Dane Rudhyar, Oral History, ed. Rayner, California State University, Long Beach, Arts Archive. The scores for both the *Pilgrimage Play* and *Surge of Fire* are lost. Rudhyar's role in the aesthetic shift from modernism to high modernism is documented in chapter 14. For an overview of Rudhyar, see Carol J. Oja, "Rudhyar, Dane [Chennevière, Daniel]," *Grove Music Online*, ed. L. Macy, www.grovemusic.com (accessed December 20, 2004). Rudhyar's significance is demonstrated by his frequent appearances in Oja's seminal *Making Music Modern*. See also Oja, "Dane Rudhyar's Vision of American Dissonance," *American Music* 17 (1999): 129–45. A selected list of Rudhyar's writings on Theosophy and music is presented in chapter 14.

36.   The prolific and innovative Cowell (1897–1965) had already produced a draft of his remarkable *New Musical Resources* (not published until 1930), the first of his several books. His papers and those of the New Music Society are at the New York Public Library for the Performing Arts; most of his scores are at the Library of Congress. The best discussion of his early career is found in Michael Hicks, *Henry Cowell, Bohemian* (Urbana: University of Illinois Press, 2003). Cowell and Rudhyar had met at Halcyon, the Theosophist colony near Pismo Beach in Southern California.

37. "Musical Lectures Popular: Many Give Interpretive Recitals This Year," *Los Angeles Times,* October 22, 1922, sec. III, 30.

38. Bruno David Ussher, "Music" column, *Los Angeles Saturday Night* 3, no. 41 (December 9, 1922): 10.

39. The guarantors listed in the first program, in addition to Barnsdall, are Mrs. Alice [Pike] Barney, Mrs. Thompson Buchanan, Mrs. Henry Eichheim, Mr. James Taber Fitzgerald, Mr. Montague Glass, Mrs. William de Mille, Mrs. Irwin Muna, Mr. Robert Nelson, and Mrs. W. H. Rothwell.

40. Bruno David Ussher, "Music," *Los Angeles Saturday Night* 5, no. 51 (October 31, 1925): 10.

41. Bruno David Ussher, "Music," *Los Angeles Saturday Night* 6, no. 8 (January 2, 1926): 10:

> At the first exclusive Saturday Morning Musical of next week [January 9] at eleven, the Little Symphony will bring a composition for string piano by Henry Cowell, the modern Bach. Among the modern composers who are today experimenting not only with the form but the actual content of music, the California composer, Henry Cowell is recognized as an unique figure for, while the majority of the moderns have occupied themselves with what might be termed the subjective aspect of music, Cowell has ventured into its more objective qualities.
>
> Winifred Hooke has long been identified with the work of the ultra moderns and has worked with Cowell in the execution and technique of all his experiments. Several of his better known compositions have been inscribed to her. She will give the first hearings anywhere of Cowell's most recent work for string piano and small orchestra.
>
> It is said to be most sensational in its effects. The round, delicate tone of the piano strings with string quartet and three wood-winds. One can well believe it is most difficult to learn, equal to the tackling of a new instrument. The piano is played standing from the bend, another person operating the damper pedal while the pianist reaches in to the deepest and furthest parts of the beautiful instrument to pluck and sweep the strings. Miss Hooke has devised a way for identifying the strings and Cowell states that he will use it when he plays the work in New York in February and later on his European tour.

42. Bruno David Ussher, "Music," *Los Angeles Saturday Night* 6, no. 10 (January 16, 1926): 10.

43. Letter, Tandler to Cowell, September 20, 1927, folder 414, Henry Cowell Collection, New York Public Library for the Performing Arts. Tandler's group played Cowell's *Chapter in Seven Paragraphs* at a Chautauqua concert in Santa Monica; it planned to play three of the "Paragraphs" at the opening of the new Ebell clubhouse on Wilshire Boulevard on October 3. He reported that his

" 'California Night of Music' turned out to be a great success—risky and very hard-earned" and that he had no further plans yet for that season.

44. Mead, *Henry Cowell's New Music*, 48. The concert took place on November 20, 1927.

45. The note in the folder 217, New Music Society Collection, New York Public Library for the Performing Arts, on which the first conclusion is based, may have been added by Sidney Cowell later on. The Henry Cowell Collection, to which Mead did not have access, contains further correspondence from Barnsdall to Cowell, suggesting that she maintained her interest in Cowell's musical judgment, that they occasionally met, and that they maintained cordial relations.

Barnsdall's colorful correspondence with Wright documenting their long-running business relationship is at the Getty Museum.

46. Patterson Greene, "Extremes in Music Heard at Concert," *Los Angeles Examiner*, November 22, 1926, sec. I, 12.

47. Bruno David Ussher, "Music," *Los Angeles Saturday Night* 7, no. 4 (December 4, 1926): 10.

14. SECOND THOUGHTS

1. The announcement came in December 1926, in the same column in which Ussher took such a dim view of Ruggles's music. For more on Pro Musica, see Ronald V. Wiecki, "A Chronicle of Pro Musica in the United States (1920–1944): With a Biographical Sketch of Its Founder, E. Robert Schmitz," PhD dissertation, University of Wisconsin, 1992.

2. *Grove* prefers "Arma" as Weisshaus's given name, but in 1927 he seemed to be using "Imre."

3. Letter, Winifred Hooke to Henry Cowell, n.d., folder 236, Henry Cowell Collection, New York Public Library for the Performing Arts. It must be added that performances of the music of the eighteenth-century composer Vivaldi were extremely rare in Los Angeles (and elsewhere in the United States) at that time.

4. Bruno David Ussher, "Music," *Los Angeles Saturday Night* 8, no. 3 (November 26, 1927): 15–16.

5. *Eolian Review*, billed as the "official publication of the National Association of Harpists, Inc.," was edited by Carlos Salzedo, a harpist and cofounder (with Varèse) of the International Composers' Guild; Salzedo, an ultramodernist, was sympathetic to Rudhyar's mysticism. Some of Rudhyar's articles in that journal are "The Harp and the Music of the Soul," 1, no. 1 (December 1921): 12–15; "What Is an Octave?" 2, no. 1 (December 1922): 8–11; "Toward a Deeper Musicality," 2, no. 3 (June 1923): 11–15; "The Revolt of the Angels: Carl Ruggles and the Future of Dissonant Counterpoint," 3, no. 1 (November 1923): 12–16 (answered by Charles Seeger in the same issue; Rudhyar's rejoinder appears in 3, no. 2); "A Program of Musical Regeneration," 3, no. 3 (May 1924): 13–20; and "The Phonograph as a Basis for Instrumental Musical Education," 4, no. 1 (January 1925): 7–10.

Musical Quarterly, the first comprehensive musicological journal in the United States, was edited by Oscar Sonneck and published by G. Schirmer between 1915 and 1965. The first three of Rudhyar's articles for this journal appeared under the name Rudhyar D. Chennevière (closer to his birth name, Daniel Chennevière) and were translated by Frederick H. Martens: "The Two Trends of Modern Music in Stravinsky's Works," 5, no. 2 (1919): 169–74; "Eric Satie and the Music of Irony," 5, no. 4 (1919): 469–78; and "The Rise of the Musical Proletariat," 6, no. 4 (1920): 500–509. Two later ones appear under "Rudhyar" as his surname and were apparently written in English: "The Relativity of Our Musical Conceptions," 8, no. 1 (1922): 108–18; and "Creators and Public: Their Relationship," 10, no. 1 (1924): 120–30. Oja ("Dane Rudhyar's Vision of American Dissonance") lists these and several more articles by Rudhyar, especially in *Musical America,* but not the review quoted below in the *LA Times.* Rudhyar eventually abandoned music in favor of astrology.

6. Rudhyar, "Toward a Deeper Musicality," 12, 14.

7. This point is made for American composers in Smith, " 'A Distinguishing Virility.' "

8. Dane Rudhyar, "Imre Weisshaus Termed a New Revelation," review of Weisshaus concert on November 18, in *Los Angeles Times,* Sunday, November 20, 1927, sec. III, 19.

9. Ibid. Pál Kadosa (1903–88) passed most of his career in Budapest, becoming a teacher of composition at the conservatory through World War II and subsequent decades. The piano sonata was issued on Hungaroton Records in 1970.

10. Ibid. Weisshaus (1905–87) toured widely as a pianist, then settled in Paris before World War II; he was active in the post–World War II avant-garde there. Rudhyar, however, had not expressed this powerful misogyny in his earlier articles.

11. Artie Mason Carter, as president of the Pro Musica chapter, to Henry Cowell, n.d., folder 51, Henry Cowell Collection, New York Public Library for the Performing Arts. The letterhead named a technical board, made up of Blanche Rogers Lott, longtime chamber musician and accompanist, as chairman, along with Arthur Farwell, Arthur Alexander, Dane Rudhyar, and Bruno David Ussher. Carter cited organizational problems in her letter:

> Now about your own coming to us this season—as much as I personally want you and other members of the Board too, I fear it cannot be arranged this season.
>
> We are planning a very full program and until we secure new members, there is some doubt about our resources. However, I am not giving this as a definite answer, for if there is anyway possible to bring you, *I shall.* I am interested in your work and really want you.

12. Quotation from Bruno David Ussher, "Copland Concerto Amuses; Scriabine Stirs Bowl Public," *Los Angeles Evening Express,* n.d., clipping in scrapbook, Los Angeles Philharmonic Archive.

13. See, for example, Howard Pollack, *Aaron Copland: The Life and Work of*

an Uncommon Man (Urbana: University of Illinois Press, 1999), 157. Copland premiered the piano concerto with the Boston Symphony in 1927; Pollack incorrectly reports the Los Angeles performance as also occurring in 1927.

14. Isabel Morse Jones, *Los Angeles Times*, July 21, 1928, A7, clipping in scrapbook, Los Angeles Philharmonic Archives.

15. Ussher, "Copland Concerto Amuses; Scriabine Stirs Bowl Public."

16. Gregory Goss, *Los Angeles Examiner*, n.d., clipping in scrapbook, Los Angeles Philharmonic Archive.

17. Rube Borough, *Los Angeles Record*, July 21, 1928, n.p., clipping in scrapbook, Los Angeles Philharmonic Archive.

18. Letter, Raymond Brite to Henry Cowell, April 14, 1928, folder 35, Henry Cowell Collection, New York Public Library for the Performing Arts. Brite suggested that Cowell submit his scores to conductor Eugene Goossens for review; Cowell seems to have ignored the suggestion. Later in 1928, Goossens conducted the first local performance of Stravinsky's *Rite of Spring*, an event scheduled before the Copland brouhaha erupted; this apparently did not precipitate such a stormy reaction.

19. Nicolas Slonimsky, *Perfect Pitch: An Autobiography*, new ed., ed. Electra Slonimsky Yourke (New York: Schirmer Trade Books, 2002), chapter 11, "Disaster in Hollywood," 124–27, 248–50. Slonimsky had conducted the Philharmonic at its regular subscription concerts the previous winter; his performances of music by Roy Harris and Charles Ives was well enough received to elicit an invitation to return in the summer. Of the Bowl performances, John Weatherwax remarked in "On the Pacific Coast," *Modern Music* 11(1934): 106–9, that the Bowl performances reversed his earlier success: "Besides a less responsive audience, he had a decidedly unobliging orchestra."

20. See, for example, Paul Ditzel, "Classical Notes," *Westways* 76, February 1984, 71: "Los Angeles' Golden Age of Music started in 1934 when Schoenberg moved here from Europe."

21. These are the criteria laid out by Carol Oja, in *Making Music Modern*, to explain the success of the ultramodern in New York City in the early 1920s. Absent only is the presence of younger composers to pick up on the new ideas coming in from elsewhere; John Cage, for example, was still a high school student who had not yet committed to a career in music. Crawford, *Evenings On and Off the Roof*, is based on the hypothesis that the series "brought Los Angeles to musical maturity" (from inside front flap of book cover).

22. *Los Angeles County Culture and the Community* (Los Angeles: Civic Bureau of Music and Art of Los Angeles, 1927), 7; Rudhyar, "Toward a Deeper Musicality," 14.

23. Sexual orientation remains a subtext of American musical modernism, although it is not treated here. For example, Nadine Hubbs, *The Queer Composition of America's Sound: Gay Modernists, American Music, and National Identity* (Berkeley and Los Angeles: University of California Press, 2004), passim, proposes that by 1930 Copland, influenced by Virgil Thomson and (indirectly) Gertrude Stein, abandoned the obvious uses of jazz and other "orien-

talisms" in favor of a more direct speech that expressed his position as a homosexual without offending his audiences, and he did it so effectively that his music eventually became "America's sound."

Among prominent Los Angeles musicians, it should be pointed out that Cadman's homosexuality was well known in Southern California and was generally ignored. Cadman lived for many years with his mother and avoided open relationships. Discretion was necessary, however; an early associate of Cadman at Krotona, violinist Sol Cohen, who later taught in North Carolina and Illinois, told me in a telephone interview, "One of us had to leave."

24. Letter, Peter Yates to Peyton Houston, January 12, 1945, quoted in Crawford, *Evenings On and Off the Roof*, 69. Behymer's longstanding ability to command precious newspaper space was particularly galling to new entrants in the concert-presenting field.

25. Among other things, as previously mentioned, her friend Aline Barnsdall reacted by withdrawing her considerable financial support for the Bowl and removing her name from the original list of founders.

26. Letter, Ida Gregory Scott to Cowell, December 1, 1927, in New Music Society Collection, folder 217, Music Division, New York Public Library for the Performing Arts. Scott noted that for a concert just given by Weisshaus in San Francisco, "85 there including 16 MEN . . . and such an interested audience."

27. Los Angeles' largely female concert audience had long accepted Charles Wakefield Cadman (born in 1881), who they well understood was a gay man; Cadman had long earned his living by touring, mainly in the United States, and performing for music club audiences, mainly of women.

28. Michael Hicks has since found some in Cowell's case, but it belongs to the 1930s.

29. Smith, "'A Distinguishing Virility.'" Cowell attacked women as patrons of modernist composers in "Kept Music," *Panorama* 2 (December 1934), 6 (quoted in Hicks, *Henry Cowell, Bohemian*, 124), but apparently not earlier.

30. Certainly anti-Semitism is strongly suggested by the membership practices of many of the music clubs. Because he was a native-born, non-Jewish Californian, Cowell's homosexuality was forgiven, at least for a time. Copland's, associated with New York City and jazz, was not.

31. For an excellent account of Cage's early years, see Thomas S. Hines, "Then Not Yet 'Cage': The Los Angeles Years, 1912–1938," in Marjorie Perloff and Charles Junkerman, eds., *John Cage: Composed in America* (Chicago: University of Chicago Press, 1994), 65–99. Even there, when, late in life, he gave a more balanced account of his Los Angeles years, he downplayed the model his mother had provided him for his own self-promotion. In addition, he misrepresented his visit to the Mary Carr Moore Manuscript Club, documented in Catherine Parsons Smith, "Athena at the Manuscript Club: John Cage and Mary Carr Moore," *Musical Quarterly* 79, no. 2 (1995): 351–67, and documented also in an interview by myself and Lance Bowling with Harry Hay, August 1992.

32. Mead, *Henry Cowell's New Music*, xv, xvi.

33. Steve Wasserman, "Cultural Earthquake: Why LA Isn't Lotus-Land

Anymore," *Opera News* 68, no. 1 (July 2003): 18. This was one of several feature articles celebrating the opening of Disney Hall, the newest home of the Los Angeles Philharmonic.

34. Fanny Morris Smith, "The Work of Our Women's Musical Clubs," *Etude* (July 1909): 490. Morris writes: "Never in the history of music has this most spontaneous of all arts had so many devotees. . . . Where is music to be found? . . . We are obliged to turn to the music club as the one and only force to which music may look for nurture and development."

15. CALLING THE TUNE

1. *Report of the President: Fifty-seventh Annual Convention of the American Federation of Musicians,* June 1954, Milwaukee, WI, 30, Bagley Papers, box 5, Archival Research Center, University of Southern California. The number of musicians employed by the studios to make sound tracks using the new technology was always modest in comparison with these losses.

2. The close connection is seen in the carefully constructed balance between what became the Federal Music Project (FMP) and the Federal Theatre Project (FTP). The Music Project tried to avoid programs involving theatrical staging, leaving them to the FTP; the Los Angeles FMP opera productions were a major exception. Another of the Federal One agencies, the Southern California Writers' Project, produced a section on music for its *Los Angeles; A Guide to the City and Its Environs, Compiled by Workers of the Writers' Program of the Work Projects Administration in Southern California . . .* (New York: Hastings House, 1941). The Federal Writers' Project Papers for Los Angeles are in the Department of Special Collections, Charles E. Young Research Library, UCLA.

3. Modest Altschuler to Dr. Ussher, "Unit and Department Activities Report," March 4, 1936, *District Narrative Reports, Federal Music Projects, State of California, up to February 29, 1936,* NARA, RG 69.

Material on the pre-WPA public music programs is very spotty. Most of the information on these comes from the records of the Federal Theatre Project. These were consulted while they were on loan to George Mason University (from c. 1970 to 1995); they are now at the Library of Congress.

4. The models were New York State's TERA, Temporary Emergency Relief Administration, and the Emergency Work Bureau, which functioned in New York City as early as 1931, when, by no coincidence, Roosevelt was governor of New York State.

5. A short summary of the FMP's history is in *The U.S. Work Projects Administration Federal Music Project* (Washington, DC: Library of Congress, 1999), iv–v, a finding aid for FMP manuscript materials in the Library of Congress (http://hdl.loc.gov/loc.music/eadmus.mn2005.wp.0042, accessed January 17, 2007). Background on the Federal Music Project and its predecessors comes from Cornelius B. Canon, "The Federal Music Project of the Works Progress Administration," PhD dissertation, University of Minnesota, 1963; Jannelle Jedd Warren Findley, "Of Tears and Need: The Federal Music Project,

1935–1943," PhD dissertation (history), George Washington University, 1973; Victoria Jane O'Reilly, "Women's Participation in the Federal Music Project and Work Projects Administration Music Program," MA thesis, George Washington University, 1990; and William Francis McDonald, *Federal Relief Administration and the Arts: The Origins and Administrative History of the Arts Projects of the Works Progress Administration* (Columbus: Ohio State University Press, 1969).

6. *Rob Wagner's Script* 5, no. 127 (July 18, 1931): 13–14, reports the fourth of these. Leonard Walker was the conductor.

7. "RFC Music in Los Angeles," *Pacific Coast Musician* 23, no. 2 (January 13, 1934): 6. In this case, the program was administered by the Los Angeles County director of recreation.

8. *PCM* 23, no. 262 (June 30, 1934): 6.

9. Drama scrapbook of SERA Drama and Choral Division, assembled by J. Howard Miller, TOT 65, Miller box 5. I saw this photograph when the Federal Theatre Project Collection was housed at George Mason University. Since the removal of the collection to the Library of Congress, the photograph has not been located.

10. See Joanne Bentley, *Hallie Flanagan: A Life in the American Theatre* (New York: Knopf, distributed by Random House, 1988); also Hallie Flanagan, *Arena: The History of the Federal Theatre* (New York: Duell, Sloan and Pearce, 1940; reprint, New York: B. Blom, 1965). The FTP was shut down by Congress in 1939, several years before the other arts projects were closed. Opposition came largely from representatives of states without FTP units. Flanagan did not grasp the importance of separating the FTP's liberal orientation from Communist activists, making that Project an easier target. The 1990s movie *The Cradle Will Rock* (name taken from an opera by Marc Blitzstein famously closed down before it could open in a New York FTP production) gives an idea of the issues that swirled around the Federal Theatre Project.

11. Federal Theatre Project Collection, box 6 1.1.101 0 1.1.122, 1939, "Director's report" (mimeographed), January 1939, Library of Congress. In San Francisco, there were 254 people in drama, Jewish, and marionette units. The Southern California number included fifty people in a drama unit in San Diego.

12. The information on Sokoloff (1886–1965) is taken from www.clevelandorch.com/html/about/OrchestraHistory.asp, accessed July 10, 2004). Sokoloff's record of public involvement, his availability, and, conceivably, a suggestion from the Ohio congressional delegation (headed by Republican senator Robert A. Taft) because of his long residence in Cleveland made him seem a reasonable choice in terms of both "high standards of musicianship" and "educating the public."

13. Presidential Letter no. 5020, November 4, 1935, NARA, RG 69, WPA Central Files: State, California, 651.31; *Federal Music Project Manual: Preliminary Statement of Information*, 1935, 1, Library of Congress and NARA.

14. The conductors were Walter Damrosch (New York Philharmonic), Alfred Hertz (San Francisco Symphony), Hans Kindler (National Symphony),

Leopold Stokowski (Philadelphia Orchestra), and Frederick Stock (Chicago Symphony). Conservatory directors included Rudolph Ganz (Chicago Musical College), Wallace Goodrich (New England Conservatory), and Howard Hanson and William Earhart (both Eastman School of Music). Other music educators were Dorothy Gordon (exponent of Columbia "School of the Air") and Olga Samaroff Stokowski (Juilliard School of Music). Music clubs were represented by Mrs. John Alexander Jardine (National Federation of Music Clubs) and Mrs. Frederick Steinway (National Music League). Publishers included Carl Engel (G. Schirmer) and A. Walter Kramer (Galaxy Music). Joseph Weber was president of the American Federation of Musicians. George Gershwin and Paul Whiteman represented the popular music field. In addition, there were Olin Downes (music critic of the *New York Times*), Edward Johnson and Lawrence Tibbett (Metropolitan Opera), Carleton Sprague Smith (New York Public Library), John Powell (Folk Festival Authority), and Augustus D. Zansig (National Recreation Association). Damrosch, Gershwin, Kramer, and Powell were also listed as composers. The absence of African Americans is symptomatic of the racism of the time, as is the presence of Powell, whose White Top festivals were quite explicitly racist.

15. Kenneth J. Bindas, *All of This Music Belongs to the Nation* (Knoxville: University of Tennessee Press, 1996). Bindas claims erroneously that the Federal Music Project ended in 1938; in fact, it was reorganized and extended for several more years.

16. Samples of the folk music recorded through the WPA can be heard on the Library of Congress's American Memory Web site. Most derive from a project formulated by Charles Seeger that was rejected by the FMP under Sokoloff and funded for its first several years by another New Deal agency, the Farm Resettlement Administration. Other folk music collecting was supported by the FMP after Sokoloff departed. In California, Sydney Robertson (later Cowell) did much of the work of collecting.

In Los Angeles, a "folkloristic" unit was organized within the FMP early on but ordered closed in 1937. No record of its work has been located. A memo by Seeger, "The Importance to Cultural Understanding of Folk and Popular Music" (14 pp.), dated October 1939, after Sokoloff had left the project, is in NARA, RG 69, Hewes Correspondence, box 31. In addition, Seeger wrote *Music as Recreation* (Washington, DC: Federal Works Agency, Work Projects Administration, Division of Professional and Service Projects, 1940).

17. NARA, RG 69, WPA General Files, 211.1 AAAA. "Music Allotment to States" for six months starting November 23, 1935, provides for 16,000 musicians in forty state projects. In comparison with the 3,200 allotted to California, which was treated administratively as a single project, New York City had 2,300 musicians, and the remainder of New York State had 500. The numbers shrank steadily, so the project was perhaps half as large by 1941, its last full year of operation. By comparison, in 1937 the Federal Theatre Project employed 8,474, of whom 3,618 were in New York City and 1,594 in the entire state of California (Library of Congress, Federal Theatre Project Collection, box 2 1.1.25–1.1.41

[c.2] 1937–38, Educational Activities, 8/1937). These numbers are inconsistent; another report has 12,700 employees in the FTP in 1937 (box 5, 1.1.79–1.1.100 1938–39, summary of FTP activities to September 1938).

The initial numbers in the FMP compute to about 10 percent of the total number of musicians and teachers of music counted in the U.S. Censuses of 1930 and 1940 and to just about half of those counted as unemployed in the 1940 Census.

18. Typed list, U.S. Work Projects Administration Federal Music Project Collection, Library of Congress (Reports, California), Box 1.

19. A twelve-person banjo band in Glendale was disbanded in May 1936 (NARA, RG 69, 651.311). There was a protest in March 1938 regarding black units that were disbanded and not rehired (651.311). Carlyle Scott's highly successful colored chorus was abolished, along with the black radio unit in 1939; two years later, a sixty-piece black band was let go (box 0928, 651.3119 A–J).

20. See chapter 6, n. 48.

21. *Los Angeles Times,* October 21, 1936, A3.

22. Ussher, ed., *Who's Who in Music and Dance in Southern California,* 239.

23. NARA, RG 69, 651.311 California, Mar. 1, 1936. Also, *District Narrative Reports, Federal Music Projects, State of California, up to February 29, 1936,* NARA, RG 69. Reports of many individual units are dated March, in spite of the date in the report's title.

24. Ussher to Sokoloff, July 9, 1936: "I FEEL I CAN GET SUPPORT FOR A COMPANY IN WHICH THE BEST TALENT HERE IS IMPLODE *[sic] ARTISTICALLY,* where people are not given second and third rate so-called stars, but an ensemble. . . . The repertoire should be suited to the company and not people imported to suit a repertoire." NARA, RG 69, 651.311 California, July 1936.

25. Vernice Brand, James McGarrigle, Monte Carter, McKinley of Personnel, "and others" are mentioned in Alexander Stewart's summary of this phase of the production, dated October 30, 1936. This summary, along with all the telegrams, reports, and communications mentioned in the remainder of this discussion, is contained in NARA, RG 69, 651.311, California, October 1936. Stewart, long a choral director at the University of Southern California, was demoted from county director of the FMP to supervisor of Musical Activities in the course of this controversy. Lorne S. Greene replaced him as county director.

26. Five weeks after he was appointed as a conductor in the opera production department, Richard Lert, the widely respected conductor of the Pasadena Symphony and a participant in those organizational meetings, withdrew from the projected production of *La Traviata* "on account of artistic reasons," that is, in protest. Concerning those who were not on the payroll when they expected to be, see NARA, RG 69, 651.311 California, November 1936.

27. Letter, Harry E. Claiborne and other band members to the FMP in Washington, October 22, 1936, NARA, RG 69, 651.311, California, October 1936.

28. *Los Angeles Times,* October 28, 1936, clipping in NARA, RG 69, 651.311,

California, October 1936. Not found in microfilmed or *Proquest Historical Newspapers*. A similarly favorable review by F. Law, "Philharmonic Opera Pleases Large Audience," appeared in the *Los Angeles Examiner*, October 28, 1936, A12.

29. "Opera Venture Draws Fire; Large Percentage in Federal Project Declared Not on Relief," *Los Angeles Times*, October 28, 1936, A3. A follow-up story appeared two days later.

30. "Relief and Non-relief," *Los Angeles Times*, October 30, 1936, A4.

31. Ussher wrote, "The decision . . . has been weighed carefully in the interest of the project, of the administration and of yourself, of course. It has been carefully analyzed with and by Mr. Clayton Triggs, Regional Director Women's and Professional Projects. It is also in accord with the opinion of leading advisory board members." Alexander Stewart concluded his report, also dated October 30, by repeating the recommendations of Loren Greene (newly appointed the local project's business administrator), Jervis, and Ussher:

> I do not think that with the type of opera performance and the method of preparation which culminated in the performance of La Traviata, conform at all to the idea of grand opera which we were given to understand was recommended by those who formulate the policies of the Federal Music Project.
>
> Considering all the facts set forth above, I am of the opinion that Mr. Rabinoff's continuation as member of the Los Angeles Federal Music Project would be most undesirable.
>
> I, therefore, recommend that his services be discontinued with the present performance of La Traviata.

Longstanding politics related to the local art scene as well as administrative breakdowns played into this decision. Behymer may have been among those who leaked information about the 10 percent rule to the press.

32. Report from Loren S. Greene to Harlé Jervis, forwarded to Sokoloff with a memo from Jervis, November 9, 1936, NARA, RG 69, 651.311, California, November 1936.

33. Information on Jervis, who was roundly attacked for firing Ernst Bacon as director of the San Francisco project (not discussed here), has been difficult to obtain, partly because her birth name, Hortense Gerv(w)itz, was long unknown to me. Born in New York between 1898 and 1902, she eventually studied piano and composition in France with Isador Philipp and Nadia Boulanger. She was associated with dancers, including Martha Graham, as a pianist and may have earned a master's degree in physical education at UCLA. After World War II she served as a cultural attaché in Paris, where she was involved with the Aix-en-Provence Music Festival. She died in London in 1997, before her godson, Peter-Gabriel de Loriol, discovered my interest in her. She spent the last several years of her life in de Loriol's household. I am grateful to him for most of this information; he adds that despite her brilliance she had an "uncontrolled temper" and "hated Arabs and Jews," though he remembers her with fondness

and admiration. How she came to secure the position as California state director remains unknown.

34. Letter from Sokoloff to Jervis, July 24, 1937, NARA, RG 69, 651.311, California, July 16–31, 1937. Permission for restoration was granted on these two conditions: 1. A cooperating sponsor had to pay for scenery, costumes, properties, stage hands, et cetera. 2. They could give operas in concert form. Revenues from concert productions of opera could be used toward stage productions but not for extra personnel or "stage paraphernalia."

35. Earl V. Moore, "The WPA Music Program," *Who Is Who in Music: A Complete Presentation of the Contemporary Music Scene* (Chicago: Lee Stern Press, 1940), 388–90. Moore eventually became dean of the University of Michigan School of Music.

36. Barbara Zuck, *A History of Musical Americanism* (Ann Arbor: UMI Research Press, 1980), includes a fine account of the incidents that led to the closing of the FTP.

37. Florence Lawrence, "U.S. Cash Spent on Alien Art," *Los Angeles Examiner,* November 1, 1936.

38. The American Composers Index, a card file in the Music Division, Library of Congress, lists the works performed and cites local music critics' reporting of them, alphabetically by composer.

39. National Federation of Music Clubs, *Title List of American Music for Program Planning: Supplementary List, to Be Used with the Parade of American Music* (New York, NY: NFMC Information Service, American Music Center, [195–?]). The *Parade* probably appeared initially as a part of the NFMC *Bulletin.* See also *A List of Compositions by Residents of California for Violin, Piano and Vocal Solos, Prepared under the Auspices of The California Federation of Music Clubs as a Guide to Contestants in the Young Professional Contests* (California Federation of Music Clubs, 1919), pamphlet in California State Library.

40. The gender issue appeared repeatedly. Harold Bruce Forsythe lampooned it in "Frailest Leaves" typescript, Forsythe Papers, HL. See also Smith, "'A Distinguishing Virility.'"

41. Mary Carr Moore, "New Composers Group Formed," *Music and Musicians,* August 1936.

42. Richard Drake Saunders, "California Composers Organize," *Educator,* 1936, 12. Grunn was announced as president and Charles E. Pemberton, head of Composition and Theory at the School of Music, University of Southern California, as vice president. Moore became secretary. Saunders was then critic for the *Hollywood Citizen-News.*

43. Only four women were included in this group: Moore, Frances Marion Ralston, Elinor Remick Warren, and Mabel Woodworth, indicating how few of the city's many women composers could offer orchestral or instrumental chamber compositions. Mostly they composed songs and teaching pieces for piano, works for which performance opportunities were more likely to be available. (Fannie Charles Dillon, an equally conservative composer, best known now as

an early teacher of John Cage, who seems to have remained aloof from the music club scene, is conspicuous by her absence here.)

44. Evenings on the Roof, the long-lived series devoted to "new" music (not necessarily American), got started in 1939. See Crawford, *Evenings On and Off the Roof.*

45. Ives's reservations about the Native American Composers are expressed in a letter to Henri Lloyd Clement (aka Ethel Dofflemeyer), March 1943, Charles Ives Collection, Music Library, Yale University, and other correspondence in the Ives Collection from Morris Browda and Mary Carr Moore.

46. Richard Drake Saunders, "New Group to Back Music of Americans," unidentified clipping (probably from the *Hollywood Citizen-News*), in Scrapbook no. 13, Mary Carr Moore Archive, Music Library, University of California at Los Angeles.

47. Bruno David Ussher, *Pasadena Star-News,* October 26, 1940, 19, reviewing the first of the season of FMP symphony concerts "sponsored" by the Society of Native American Composers. Ussher's bitterness was probably fanned by the nationalist politics that had swirled around the WPA and Federal One even when he had been a regional director of the Music Project; the demise of the FTP, a casualty of these politics, was still fresh.

48. The film composers organized the American Society of Music Arrangers and Composers, which became a much more successful and long-lasting organization. See www.asmac.org, especially the "About ASMAC" section, accessed December 25, 2006.

49. Lionel Barrymore was famous as an actor; Barber was a younger American composer of concert music; Korngold and Zador were émigrés who were already active in the film colony.

50. Moross, "Hollywood Music without Movies."

Bibliography

I. NEWSPAPERS AND JOURNALS
WITH LOS ANGELES MATERIAL

B'nai B'rith Messenger
California Eagle
California Outlook
Eolian Review
Etude
Flash
Hazard's Pavilion
Hollywood Citizen-News (ultimate name)
   Hollywood Weekly Citizen (original name)
   Hollywood Daily News (intermediate name)
Illustrated Daily News
Inter-American Musical Review
Los Angeles Capital
Los Angeles Evening Express
Los Angeles Evening Herald
Los Angeles Examiner
Los Angeles Graphic
Los Angeles Municipal News
Los Angeles Record
Los Angeles Saturday Night
Los Angeles Saturday Post: A Family Story Paper
Los Angeles Times
Los Angeles Tribune
Los Angeles World
Modern Music
Musical America
Musical Quarterly

Music and Musicians
The Overture (of the Los Angeles Musicians Mutual Protections Association)
Pacific Coast Musical Review (PCMR)
Pacific Coast Musician (PCM)
Pasadena Star-News
Playground and Recreation
Rob Wagner's Script
Santa Monica Outlook
Theosophical Path (Pismo Beach, CA)
Things Worth Knowing about Music and Art
Western Graphic

II. ARCHIVAL COLLECTIONS

California State Library, Sacramento
California State University, Long Beach, Arts Archive: Rudhyar, Oral History
Cambria Master Recordings and Archives, Lomita, California
Claremont College, Honnold Library, Claremont, CA
Getty Library, Los Angeles: Aline Barnsdall correspondence, Frank Lloyd Wright correspondence
Hollywood Bowl Museum
The Huntington Library (HL): Behymer Ephemera Collection; Behymer Manuscript Collection; Clara Bradley Burdette Collection, Harold Bruce Forsythe Papers, Foy Family Papers (FFP), Friday Morning Club Collection, T. Perceval Gerson Collection, Harriet Williams (Russell) Strong
Library of Congress: Federal Theatre Project Collection; Music Division, Theodore Thomas Collection; Work Projects Administration (WPA) Central Files
Los Angeles City Archives, Los Angeles City Clerk's Office, Records Management Division
Los Angeles Philharmonic Archives
Los Angeles Public Library: music files
National Archives and Records Administration (NARA), Record Group (RG) 69
New York Public Library for the Performing Arts: Henry Cowell Collection, New Music Society Collection, Elinor Remick Warren Papers
San Francisco Public Library: Alfred Hertz Papers
Southwest Museum, Los Angeles: Lummis Collection
Syracuse University, Arents Research Library: H. H. Noyes Collection
University of Arkansas, Fayetteville, Library: William Grant Still and Verna Arvey Papers
University of California, Berkeley, Music Library, Bancroft Library: Alfred Hertz Collection
University of California, Los Angeles (UCLA):
    Charles E. Young Research Library: Dillon Papers; Federal Writers' Project Papers; Bessie Bartlett Frankel Papers; T. Perceval Gerson Collection; George P. Johnson Negro Film Collection; Katherine Philips Edson Papers

Music Library: Mrs. Albert Atwood Collection; Homer Grunn Papers; Mary Carr Moore Archive

University of Melbourne, Grainger Museum: Dillon–Grainger correspondence

University of Southern California, Archival Research Center: Bagley Collection

University of Texas, Austin, Harry Ransom Humanities Research Library: Armitage, Norman Bel Geddes Collections

Yale University, Beinecke Library: Horatio Parker Papers; Music Library: Charles Ives Collection

III. BOOKS, ARTICLES, DISSERTATIONS, AND THESES

Ahlquist, Karen. *Democracy at the Opera: Music, Theater, and Culture in New York City, 1815–60.* Urbana: University of Illinois Press, 1997.

Alderman, Pauline. *We Build a School of Music: The Commissioned History of Music at the University of Southern California.* Los Angeles: Alderman Book Committee, 1989.

Almaguer, Tomás. *Racial Fault Lines: The Historical Origins of White Supremacy in California.* Berkeley and Los Angeles: University of California Press, 1994.

Ammer, Christine. *Unsung: A History of Women in American Music.* 2nd ed. Portland, OR: Amadeus, 2001.

Anderson, E. Frederick. *The Development of Leadership and Organization Building in the Black Community of Los Angeles from 1900 through World War II.* Saratoga, CA: Century Twenty-one Publishing, 1980.

Apostal, Jane. "Mary Emily Foy: 'Miss Los Angeles Herself.'" *Southern California Quarterly* 78, no. 2 (Summer 1996): 109–38.

———. "They Said It with Flowers: The Los Angeles Flower Festival Society." *Southern California Quarterly* 64, no. 1 (Spring 1980): 67–76.

Art and Music in California. Reprinted from *News Notes of California Libraries* 3, no. 1 (January 1908). Sacramento: W. W. Shannon, Superintendent State Printing, 1908.

Bagley, Charles Leland. "History of the Band and Orchestra Business in Los Angeles." Published serially in *The Overture* 4, nos. 15 (October 1, 1924) through 16, no. 12 (April 1937).

Bakan, Michael. "Way Out West on Central." In Jacqueline DjeDje and Eddie Meadows, eds., *California Soul: Music of African Americans in the West,* 23–78. Berkeley and Los Angeles: University of California Press, 1998.

Barr, Cyrilla. *Elizabeth Sprague Coolidge: American Patron of Music.* New York: Schirmer Books; London: Prentice Hall International, 1998.

Bass, Charlotta. *Forty Years: Memoirs from the Pages of a Newspaper.* Los Angeles: author, 1960.

Baur, John E. *The Health Seekers of Southern California, 1870–1900.* San Marino, CA: Huntington Library, 1959.

Baxter, Francis Hill. "A History of Music Education in the Los Angeles City Schools." DMA dissertation, University of Southern California, 1960.

Beasley, Delilah L. *Negro Trail Blazers of California; a Compilation of Records from the California Archives in the Bancroft Library at the University of California, in Berkeley; and from the Diaries, Old Papers and Conversations of Old Pioneers in the State of California. It Is a True Record of Facts, as They Pertain to the History of the Pioneer and Present Day Negroes of California.* San Francisco, CA, 1919; reprint, R & E Research, 1968.

Beck, William. "The Ellis-Orpheus Men's Chorus: The Story of Its First Century." *Hazard's Pavilion* 5 (1988): 1–33.

Bel Geddes, Norman. *Miracle in the Evening: An Autobiography.* Garden City, NY: Doubleday, 1960.

Bentley, Joanne. *Hallie Flanagan: A Life in the American Theatre.* New York: Knopf, distributed by Random House, 1988.

Bindas, Kenneth J. *All of This Music Belongs to the Nation.* Knoxville: University of Tennessee Press, 1996.

Bishop, Cardell. *The Los Angeles Grand Opera Association—1924–1934: A Short Career in a Big City.* Santa Monica: Bishop, 1979.

Blair, Karen. *The Clubwoman as Feminist: True Womanhood Redefined, 1868–1914.* New York: Holmes and Meier Publishers, 1980.

———. *The Torchbearers: Women and Their Amateur Arts Associations in America, 1890–1930.* Bloomington: Indiana University Press, 1994.

Block, Adrienne Fried. "New York's Orchestras and the 'American' Composer: A Nineteenth-Century View." In John Graziano, ed., *European Music and Musicians in New York, 1840–1890,* 114–34. Rochester, NY: University of Rochester Press, 2006.

Bloomfield, Arthur. *San Francisco Opera—1923–1961.* New York: Appleton-Century-Crofts, 1961.

Board of Directors, Hollywood Bowl Association. *A Brief History of Hollywood Bowl: Authorized and Approved by the Board of Directors of the Hollywood Bowl Association.* June 11, 1926, unpaginated pamphlet; reprinted in Bruno David Ussher, *Who's Who in Music and Dance in Southern California* (Hollywood: Bureau of Musical Research, 1933), 29–34.

Bond, J. Max. "The Negro in Los Angeles." PhD dissertation, University of Southern California, 1936.

Bontemps, Arna. *God Sends Sunday.* New York: Harcourt Brace, 1931; reprint, New York: AMS Press, 1972.

Bontemps, Arna, and Jack Conroy. *Anyplace but Here.* New York: Hill and Wang, 1966; originally published (1945) as *They Seek a City.*

Bordman, Gerald M. *American Musical Theatre: A Chronology.* 3rd ed. New York: Oxford University Press, 2001.

Bortin, Virginia. *Elinor Remick Warren: A Bio-bibliography.* Westport, CT: Greenwood Press, 1993.

———. *Elinor Remick Warren: Her Life and Her Music.* Metuchen, NJ: Scarecrow Press, 1987.

Bragdon, Claude. *More Lives Than One.* New York: Alfred A. Knopf, 1938.

Braitman, Jacqueline R. "A California Stateswoman: The Public Career of

Katherine Philips Edson." *California History: The Magazine of the California Historical Society* 65 (1986): 82–95.

Brite, Raymond. "Hollywood Bowl and the 'Symphonies under the Stars.'" In Caroline Estes Smith, *The Philharmonic Orchestra of Los Angeles: The First Decade, 1919–1929.* Los Angeles: United Printing Company, 1930.

Brookwell, George. *Saturdays in the Hollywood Bowl.* Hollywood: Sutton-house Publishers, 1940.

Brothers, Thomas. Review of Gushee, *Pioneers of Jazz. Journal of the American Musicological Society* 59, no. 3 (Fall 2006): 747–55.

Broyles, Michael. "Art Music from 1860 to 1920." In David Nicholls, ed., *The Cambridge History of American Music,* 214–54. Cambridge: Cambridge University Press, 1998.

———. "Music and Class Structure in Antebellum Boston." *Journal of the American Musicological Society* 44 (1991): 451–93.

Bruce [Nugent], Richard. "Sahdji." In Alain Locke and Montgomery Gregory, eds., *Plays of Negro Life, a Source-Book of Native American Drama,* 389–400. New York: Harper and Brothers, 1937; reprint, Westport, CT: Negro Universities Press, 1970.

Bryant, Clora, ed. *Central Avenue Sounds: Jazz in Los Angeles.* Berkeley and Los Angeles: University of California Press, 1998.

Buckland, Michael, and John Henken, eds. *The Hollywood Bowl: Tales of Summer Nights.* Los Angeles: Balcony Press, 1996.

Burdette, Clara B. *The Rainbow and the Pot of Gold.* Pasadena: Clara Vista Press, 1907.

Caldwell, Hansonia L. "Music in the Lives of Blacks in California: The Beginnings." *Triangle of Mu Phi Epsilon* 82, no. 4 (1988): 10, 18.

California Federation of Music Clubs. *A List of Compositions by Residents of California for Violin, Piano and Vocal Solos, Prepared under the Auspices of the California Federation of Music Clubs as a Guide to Contestants in the Young Professional Contests.* Los Angeles: California Federation of Music Clubs, 1919.

Campbell, Gavin James. "Music and the Making of a Jim Crow Culture, 1900–1925." PhD dissertation, University of North Carolina at Chapel Hill, 1999.

———. *Music and the Making of a New South.* Chapel Hill: University of North Carolina Press, 2004.

Cannon, Marian G. "His Music Left an Echo: A Biography of Harley Hamilton, 1861–1933." *The Californians* (May/June 1983): 31–34.

Canon, Cornelius B. "The Federal Music Project of the Works Progress Administration." PhD dissertation, University of Minnesota, 1963.

Carter, Marva Griffin. "The Life and Music of Will Marion Cook." PhD dissertation, University of Illinois, 1988.

Chase, Gilbert. *America's Music, from the Pilgrims to the Present.* 3rd ed. New York: McGraw-Hill, 1955; rev. eds., New York: McGraw-Hill, 1966, and Urbana: University of Illinois Press, 1987.

Chatfield-Taylor, Joan. *San Francisco Opera: The First Seventy-five Years.* San Francisco: Chronicle Books, 1997.

Chennevière, Rudhyar D. [Dane Rudhyar]. "Eric Satie and the Music of Irony," trans. Frederick H. Martens. *Musical Quarterly* 5, no. 4 (1919): 469–78.

———. "The Rise of the Musical Proletariat," trans. Frederick H. Martens. *Musical Quarterly* 6, no. 4 (1920): 500–509.

———. "The Two Trends of Modern Music in Stravinsky's Works," trans. Frederick H. Martens. *Musical Quarterly* 5, no. 2 (1919): 169–74.

Collette, Buddy. *Jazz Generations: A Life in American Music and Society.* With Steven Isoardi. London: Continuum, 2000.

Cox, Bette Yarbrough. *Central Avenue: Its Rise and Fall (1890–c. 1955) Including the Musical Renaissance of Black Los Angeles.* Los Angeles: BEEM Publications, 1993.

———. "The Evolution of Black Music in Los Angeles, 1890–1955." In Lawrence B. De Graaf, Kevin Mulroy, and Quintard Taylor, *Seeking El Dorado: African Americans in California,* 249–78. Los Angeles: Autry Museum of Western Heritage, and Seattle: University of Washington Press, 2001.

Crawford, Dorothy Lamb. *Evenings On and Off the Roof: Pioneering Concerts in Los Angeles, 1939–1971.* Berkeley and Los Angeles: University of California Press, 1995.

Crawford, Richard. *America's Musical Life: A History.* New York: Norton, 2001.

Culbertson, Evelyn Davis. *He Heard America Singing: Arthur Farwell, Composer and Crusading Music Educator.* Metuchen, NJ: Scarecrow Press, 1992.

De Graaf, Lawrence B., Kevin Mulroy, and Quintard Taylor. *Seeking El Dorado: African Americans in California.* Los Angeles: Autry Museum of Western Heritage; and Seattle: University of Washington Press, 2001.

de Lange, Daniel. "Thoughts on Music." *Theosophical Path* 11 (July–December 1916): 553.

———. "Thoughts on Music, Part IV." *Theosophical Path* 13 (July–December 1913): 117.

Deverell, William. *California Progressivism Revisited.* Berkeley and Los Angeles: University of California Press, 1994.

———. *Whitewashed Adobe: The Rise of Los Angeles and the Remaking of Its Mexican Past.* Berkeley and Los Angeles: University of California Press, 2004.

Dickerson, Lowell Dwight. "Central Avenue Meets Hollywood: The Amalgamation of the Black and White Musicians' Unions in Los Angeles." PhD dissertation, University of California, Los Angeles, 1998.

Ditzel, Paul. "Classical Notes." *Westways* 76, February 1984, 71.

DjeDje, Jacqueline Cogdell. "California Black Gospel Tradition." In Jacqueline Cogdell DjeDje and Eddie S. Meadows, eds., *California Soul: Music of African Americans in the West,* 124–75. Berkeley and Los Angeles: University of California Press, 1998.

———. "Los Angeles Composers of African American Gospel Music: The Early Generation." *American Music* 11 (1993): 412–57.

DjeDje, Jacqueline Cogdell, and Eddie S. Meadows, eds. *California Soul: Music of African Americans in the West.* Berkeley and Los Angeles: University of California Press, 1998.

Dwight's Journal of Music. Boston, 1852–81; reprinted in multivolume set, New York: Johnson Reprint Corporation, 1968.

Earnest, Sue Wolfer. "An Historical Study of the Growth of the Theatre in Southern California." PhD dissertation, University of Southern California, 1947.

Eckler, A. Ross. *The Bureau of the Census.* New York: Praeger, 1972.

Editorial Staff. "In Retrospect: Black Prima Donnas of the Nineteenth Century." *Black Perspective in Music* 7, no. 1 (Spring 1979): 95–106.

Edson, Charles Farwell. *The Stranger.* Los Angeles: Braxton Press, 1930.

Edson, Charles Farwell, Jr., and Katharane Edson Mershon. *Katherine Philips Edson Remembered.* Jacqueline R. Braitman, interviewer. Oral History Program, University of California, Los Angeles, copyright 1987.

Elson, Louis C. *The History of American Music.* New York: Macmillan, 1904; rev. ed., 1915.

Engh, Michael E. *Frontier Faiths: Church, Temple, and Synagogue in Los Angeles, 1846–1888.* Albuquerque: University of New Mexico Press, 1992.

Epstein, Dena. "From Sherburne, N.Y., to the Library of Congress: The Progress of a Musical American Family." In Carol June Bradley and James B. Coover, eds., *Richard S. Hill: Tributes from Friends,* 211–20. Detroit: Information Coordinators, 1987.

Farwell, Arthur. *"Wanderjahre of a Revolutionist" and Other Essays on American Music.* Edited by Thomas Stoner. Rochester, NY: University of Rochester Press, 1995.

———. "Where Is Truth of Music?" *Pacific Coast Musician* 12, no. 1 (January 1923): 10.

Federal Writers' Project; Southern California Writers Project. *Los Angeles; a Guide to the City and Its Environs, Compiled by Workers of the Writers' Program of the Work Projects Administration in Southern California.* New York: Hastings House, 1941; 2nd ed., 1951.

Fetterley, Judith. *Writing out of Place: Regionalism, Women, and American Literary Culture.* Urbana: University of Illinois Press, 2003.

Findley, Jannelle Jedd Warren. "Of Tears and Need: The Federal Music Project, 1935–1943." PhD dissertation, George Washington University, 1973.

Finger, Susan Pearl. "The Los Angeles Heritage: Four Women Composers, 1918–1939." PhD dissertation, University of California, Los Angeles, 1986.

Flanagan, Hallie. *Arena: The History of the Federal Theatre.* New York: Duell, Sloan and Pearce, 1940; reprint, New York: B. Blom, 1965.

Fogarty, Robert S. *All Things New: American Communes and Utopian Movements, 1860–1914.* Chicago: University of Chicago Press, 1990.

———, ed. *Desire and Duty at Oneida: Tirzah Miller's Intimate Memoir.* Bloomington: Indiana University Press, 2000.

Forsythe, Harold Bruce. "William Grant Still: A Study in Contradictions." Typescript, c. 1932. Published in Catherine Parsons Smith, *William Grant Still: A Study in Contradictions*, 278–80. Berkeley and Los Angeles: University of California Press, 2000.

Foy, Janice Ann. "Croatian Sacred Musical Tradition in Los Angeles: History, Style, and Meaning." PhD dissertation, University of California, Los Angeles, 1990.

Fredericks, Jessica M., comp. *California Composers: Biographical Notes.* San Francisco: California Federation of Music Clubs, 1934.

Fry, Stephen, ed. *California's Musical Wealth: Sources for the Study of Music in California.* Glendale, CA: Music Library Association, Southern California Chapter, 1988.

Gates, W. Francis, ed. *Who's Who in Music in California.* Los Angeles: "The Pacific Coast Musician," Colby and Pryibil, Publishers, 1920.

Geddes, Norman Bel. *Miracle in the Evening: An Autobiography.* Garden City, NY: Doubleday, 1960.

Geoffrion, Victor O. "The Outlook in the South." *Musical and Theatrical News* 1 no. 1 (January 15, 1920): 1, 10.

Georgakas, Dan. "Mooney, Tom." In Mari Jo Buhle, Paul Buhle, and Dan Georgakas, eds., *Encyclopedia of the American Left.* 2nd ed. New York: Oxford University Press, 1998. www.english.uiuc.edu/maps/poets/m_r/ridge/mooney.htm.

Glassberg, David. *American Historical Pageantry: The Uses of Tradition in the Early Twentieth Century.* Chapel Hill: University of North Carolina Press, 1990.

Grau, Robert. *The Business Man in the Amusement World: A Volume of Progress in the Field of the Theatre.* New York: Broadway Publishing Company, 1910.

Graziano, John. "The Early Life and Career of the 'Black Patti': The Odyssey of an African American Singer in the Late Nineteenth Century." *Journal of the American Musicological Society* 53 (2000): 543–96.

Greene, Patterson. "Extremes in Music Heard at Concert." *Los Angeles Examiner*, November 22, 1926, sec. I, 12.

Griswold Del Castillo, Richard. *The Los Angeles Barrio 1850–1950: A Social History.* Berkeley and Los Angeles: University of California Press, 1979.

Gushee, Lawrence. *Pioneers of Jazz: The Story of the Creole Band.* New York: Oxford University Press, 2005.

Haas, Lisbeth. *Conquests and Historical Identities in California, 1769–1936.* Berkeley and Los Angeles: University of California Press, 1995.

Hamm, Charles. *Music in the New World.* New York: Norton, 1983.

Harris, Henry J. "The Occupation of Musician in the United States." *Musical Quarterly* 1, no. 2 (April 1915): 299–311.

Haynes, Bruce. "Pitch," I.2.vii. In Stanley Sadie, ed., *Revised New Grove Dictionary of Music and Musicians*, vol. 19, 800. London: Macmillan Press, 2000.

Hicks, Michael. *Henry Cowell, Bohemian.* Urbana: University of Illinois Press, 2003.

Hill, Joseph A. *Women in Gainful Occupations: 1870 to 1920.* Census Monographs 9. Washington, DC: U.S. Department of Commerce, 1929.

Hine, Robert V. *California's Utopian Colonies.* San Marino: Huntington Library, 1953.

Hines, Thomas S. "Then Not Yet 'Cage': The Los Angeles Years, 1912–1938." In Marjorie Perloff and Charles Junkerman, eds., *John Cage: Composed in America,* 65–99. Chicago: University of Chicago Press, 1994.

Hipsher, Edward E. *American Opera and Its Composers.* Philadelphia: Theodore Presser Co., 1934; reprint, New York: Da Capo, 1978.

Hitchcock, H. Wiley. *Music in the United States: A Historical Introduction.* Englewood Cliffs, NJ: Prentice-Hall, 1969, rev. 1974, 1988, and 2000.

Hobsbawm, Eric. "Introduction: Inventing Traditions." In Eric Hobsbawm and Terence Ranger, eds., *The Invention of Tradition,* 1–14. Cambridge: Cambridge University Press, 1983.

———. "Mass-Producing Traditions: Europe, 1870–1914." In Eric Hobsbawm and Terence Ranger, eds., *The Invention of Tradition,* 263–307. Cambridge: Cambridge University Press, 1983.

Hobsbawm, Eric, and Terence Ranger, eds. *The Invention of Tradition.* Cambridge: Cambridge University Press, 1983.

Howard, John Tasker. *Our American Music: Three Hundred Years of It.* New York: Thomas Y. Crowell Co., 1931, rev. 1939, 1946, and 1954.

Hubbell, Thelma Lee, and Gloria Ricci Lothrop. "The Friday Morning Club: A Los Angeles Legacy." *Southern California Quarterly* 50, no. 1 (Spring 1968): 59–90.

Hubbs, Nadine. *The Queer Composition of America's Sound: Gay Modernists, American Music, and National Identity.* Berkeley and Los Angeles: University of California Press, 2004.

Hunter, A. D., comp. Southern California [Los Angeles] Music Teachers Association (SCMTA), minutes. Typescript, in possession of Helen Nash.

Hyde Heritage, 1880s to 1977. Highmore, SD: Hyde County Historical and Genealogical Society, 1977.

Isoardi, Steven L. *The Dark Tree: Jazz and the Community Arts in Los Angeles.* With an appendix by Roberto Miranda. Berkeley and Los Angeles: University of California Press, 2006.

Jacobson, Matthew Frye. *Whiteness of a Different Color: European Immigrants and the Alchemy of Race.* Cambridge, MA: Harvard University Press, 1998.

Jensen, Joan. "After Slavery: Caroline Severance in Los Angeles." *Quarterly of the Historical Society of Southern California* 48, no. 2 (June 1966): 175–86.

Johnson, Charles S. *Industrial Survey of the Negro Population of Los Angeles.* Los Angeles: National Urban League, 1926.

Johnson, Julian. "Music and Musicians." *Los Angeles Times,* June 6, 1909, sec. III, 2.

———. "Music in Los Angeles." *Pacific Coast Musical Review* 19, no. 16 (January 7, 1911): 5.

Jones, Isabel Morse. *Hollywood Bowl.* New York: G. Schirmer, 1936.

———. "Words and Music" column. *Los Angeles Times,* passim.

Karasick, Norman M. and Dorothy K. *The Oilman's Daughter: A Biography of Aline Barnsdall.* Encino, CA: Carleston Publishing, 1993.

Karson, Burton Lewis. "Music Criticism in Los Angeles, 1895–1910." DMA dissertation, University of Southern California, 1964.

Kern, Louis J. *An Ordered Love: Sex Roles and Sexuality in Victorian Utopias: The Shakers, the Mormons, and the Oneida Community.* Chapel Hill: University of North Carolina Press, 1981.

Kernodle, Tammy L. "'Sons of Africa, Come Forth': Compositional Approaches of William Grant Still in the Opera *Troubled Island.*" *American Music Research Center Journal* 13 (2003): 25–36.

Knisely, Bertha McCord. "Chamber Music in Southern California." In Bruno David Ussher, ed., *Who's Who in Music and Dance in Southern California,* 63–67. Hollywood: Bureau of Musical Research, 1933.

Koegel, John. "Bibliography and Research Guide to California Music." Unpublished typescript, October 2003.

———. "Calendar of Southern California Amusements 1852–1897; Designed for the Spanish-Speaking Public." *Inter-American Music Review* 13, no. 2 (1993): 115–43.

———. "*Canciones del país:* Mexican Musical Life in California after the Gold Rush." *California History* 78, no. 3 (1999): 160–87, 215–19.

———. "Mexican American Music in Nineteenth-Century Southern California: The Lummis Wax Cylinder Collection at the Southwest Museum, Los Angeles." PhD dissertation, Claremont Graduate University, 1994.

———. "Mexican and Mexican-American Musical Life in Southern California, 1850–1900." *Inter-American Music Review* 13, no. 2 (1993): 111–14.

———. "Mexican Musicians in California and the United States, 1910–50." *California History* 84, no. 1 (Fall 2006): 6–29.

———. "Preserving the Sounds of the 'Old' Southwest: Charles Lummis and His Cylinder Collection of Mexican American and Indian Music." *Association for Recorded Sound Collections Journal* 29 (1998): 1–29.

Koopal, Grace G. *Miracle of Music.* Los Angeles: Charles E. Toberman, 1972.

Kraft, James P. *Stage to Studio: Musicians and the Sound Revolutions, 1890–1950.* Baltimore: Johns Hopkins University Press, 1996.

Kropp, Phoebe S. *California Vieja: Culture and Memory in a Modern American Place.* Berkeley and Los Angeles: University of California Press, 2006.

Kyle, Julian. "Sounding the City: Jazz, African American Nightlife, and the Articulation of Race in 1940s Los Angeles." PhD dissertation, University of California, Irvine, 2000.

Lapp, Rudolph M. *Afro-Americans in California.* 2nd ed. San Francisco: Boyd and Fraser Publishing, 1987.

Lears, T. J. Jackson. *No Place of Grace: Antimodernism and the Transformation of American Culture, 1880–1920*. New York: Pantheon, 1981.

Leavitt, M. B. *Fifty Years in Theatrical Management*. New York: Broadway Publishing Company, 1912.

Leigh, Keri. "Douglas Fairbanks." www.fortunecity.com/lavender/wargames/ 154/bio.htm. Accessed December 19, 2006.

Levine, Lawrence. *Highbrow/Lowbrow: The Emergence of Cultural Hierarchy in America*. Cambridge, MA: Harvard University Press, 1988.

Lewis, Robert M., ed. *From Traveling Show to Vaudeville: Theatrical Spectacle in America, 1830–1910*. Baltimore: Johns Hopkins University Press, 2003.

Li, Guangming. "Music in the Chinese Community of Los Angeles: An Overview." *Musical Aesthetics and Multiculturalism in Los Angeles: Selected Reports in Ethnomusicology* 10 (1994): 105–21.

Locke, Alain. "The Negro Spirituals." In Locke, ed., *The New Negro*. New York: Albert Boni, 1925; reprint, New York: Atheneum; Toronto: Maxwell Macmillan Canada; New York: Maxwell Macmillan International, 1992.

Locke, Ralph P., and Cyrilla Barr. *Cultivating Music in America: Women Patrons and Activists since 1860*. Berkeley and Los Angeles: University of California Press, 1997.

Lomax, Alan. *Mister Jelly Roll: The Fortunes of Jelly Roll Morton, New Orleans Creole and "Inventor of Jazz."* 2nd ed. Berkeley and Los Angeles: University of California Press, 1973.

Los Angeles County Culture and the Community. Los Angeles: Civic Bureau of Music and Art of Los Angeles, 1927.

Lothrop, Gloria Ricci. "Strength Made Stronger: The Role of Women in Southern California Philanthropy." *Southern California Quarterly* 71, no. 2 (Summer 1989): 143–94.

Loza, Steven Joseph. *Barrio Rhythm: Mexican American Music in Los Angeles*. Urbana: University of Illinois Press, 1993.

Lummis, Charles F. *The Land of Poco Tiempo*. New York: C. Scribner's Sons, 1921.

———. *The Spanish Pioneers*. Chicago: A. C. McClurg, 1893.

Lummis, Charles F., collector and translator; Arthur Farwell, piano accompaniments. *Spanish Songs of Old California*. Reprint, ed. Michael Heisley. 1st ed., 1923; Los Angeles: Historical Society of Southern California, 1987.

Mangram, William D. *The Clarks: An American Phenomenon*. New York: Silver Bow Press, 1941.

Marcus, Kenneth. *Musical Metropolis: Los Angeles and the Creation of a Music Culture, 1880–1940*. London: Palgrave Macmillan, 2004.

Marks, Martin M. *Music and the Silent Film: Contexts and Case Studies, 1895–1924*. New York: Oxford University Press, 1997.

Martin, George R. *The Clarke Story: Chauncey Dwight Clarke, Marie Rankin Clarke and the Claremont Colleges*. 3rd ed. Claremont, CA: Claremont Graduate School and University Center, 1964.

Martin, Theodora Penny. *The Sound of Our Own Voices: Women's Study Clubs, 1860–1910*. Boston: Beacon Press, 1987.

Mason, Mrs. Dean. "The Los Angeles Symphony Orchestra." In Caroline Estes Smith, *The Philharmonic Orchestra of Los Angeles: The First Decade, 1919–1929*, 27–38. Los Angeles: Press of United Printing Company, 1930.

Matthews, Miriam. "The Negro in California from 1781–1910: An Annotated Bibliography." Paper for library science course, University of Southern California, 1944.

———. Interviews by Eleanor Roberts, March 14, 16, 17, and 22, 1977. In *The Black Women Oral History Project: From the Arthur and Elizabeth Schlesinger Library on the History of Women in America, Radcliffe College*, edited by Ruth Edmonds Hill. Westport, CT: Meckler, 1991.

May, Lary L. *The Big Tomorrow: Hollywood and the Politics of the American Way*. Chicago: University of Chicago Press, 2000.

———. *Screening Out the Past: The Birth of Mass Culture and the Motion Picture Industry*. New York: Oxford University Press, 1980.

McCarter, Robert, James Steele, and Brian Carter. *Frank Lloyd Wright: Unity Temple, Barnsdall (Hollyhock) House, Johnson Wax Administration Building and Research Tower*. London: Phaidon, 1999.

McDonald, William Francis. *Federal Relief Administration and the Arts: The Origins and Administrative History of the Arts Projects of the Works Progress Administration*. Columbus: Ohio State University Press, 1969.

McDougal, Dennis. *Privileged Son: Otis Chandler and the Rise and Fall of the L.A. Times Dynasty*. Cambridge, MA: Perseus Publishing, 2001.

McWilliams, Carey. *Southern California Country: An Island on the Land*. New York: Duell, Sloan and Pearce, 1946.

Mead, Rita. *Henry Cowell's New Music, 1925–1936: The Society, the Music Editions, and the Recordings*. Ann Arbor: UMI Research Press, 1981.

Miller, Dorothy Grace. "Within the Bounds of Propriety: Clara Burdette and the Women's Movement." PhD dissertation, University of California, Riverside, 1984.

Mingus, Charles. *Beneath the Underdog: His World as Composed by Mingus*. Edited by Nel King. New York: Knopf, 1971.

"Miriam Matthews: West Coast Historian!" African American Registry. www.aaregistry.com/african_american_history/2006/Miriam_Matthews _west_coast_historian. Accessed February 19, 2007.

Monroy, Douglas. "Making Mexico in Los Angeles." In Thomas Sitton and William Deverell, eds., *Metropolis in the Making: Los Angeles in the 1920s*, 161–78. Berkeley and Los Angeles: University of California Press, 2001.

———. *Rebirth: Mexican Los Angeles from the Great Migration to the Great Depression*. Berkeley and Los Angeles: University of California Press, 1999.

———. *Thrown among Strangers: The Making of Mexican Culture in Frontier California*. Berkeley and Los Angeles: University of California Press, 1990.

Moore, Earl V. "The WPA Music Program." *Who Is Who in Music: A Complete Presentation of the Contemporary Music Scene*, 388–90. Chicago: Lee Stern Press, 1940.

Moore, Mary Carr. "New Composers Group Formed." *Music and Musicians,* August 1936.

Morgan, Thomas L. "Will Marion Cook." www.jass.com/wcook.tml. n.d.

Moross, Jerome. "Hollywood Music without Movies." *Modern Music* 18 (1941): 261.

Murchison, Gayle. "Was *Troubled Island* Seen by the Critics as a Protest Opera?" *AMRC Journal* 13 (2003): 37–60.

Musicians of Los Angeles: Embracing 150 Singers, Instrumentalists and Teachers, and including the Choirs of 21 Churches as Constituted at the Time of Writing. Los Angeles: Los Angeles Evening Express, 1904–5.

National Federation of Music Clubs. *Title List of American Music for Program Planning: Supplementary List, to Be Used with the Parade of American Music.* New York: NFMC Information Service, American Music Center [195–?].

Naylor, Blanche. *The Anthology of the Fadettes.* n.p., n.d.

———. Untitled article. *Women in Music,* February 1936.

Nelson, Beverly Blanchard, and Pamela T. Lundquist. *F. W. Blanchard: First President of the Hollywood Bowl.* Victoria, BC: Trafford Publishing Co., 2006.

Nicholls, David, ed. *The Cambridge History of American Music.* Cambridge: Cambridge University Press, 1998.

Nordskog, Andrae Arne. "The Earliest Musical History in the Hollywood Bowl: 1920 and 1921." Typescript, copyright 1957.

Northcutt, John Orlando. *Magic Valley: The Story of Hollywood Bowl.* Los Angeles: Osherenko, 1967.

———. "The Philharmonic and the Bowl." In Jose Rodriguez, ed., *Music and Dance in California.* Hollywood: Bureau of Musical Research, 1940.

———. *Symphony: The Story of the Los Angeles Philharmonic Orchestra.* Los Angeles: Southern California Symphony Association, 1963.

Norton, Richard C. *A Chronology of American Musical Theater.* 3 vols. New York: Oxford University Press, 2002.

Nouryeh, Andrea J. "When the Lord Was a Black Man: A Fresh Look at the Life of Richard Berry Harrison." *Black American Literature Forum* 16, no. 4 (Winter 1982): 142–46.

Odell, George C. D. *Annals of the New York Stage.* New York: Columbia University Press, 1927–49.

O'Gorman, Ella F. "Foy and Allied Families." *Americana Illustrated* 25 (April 1931): 220–301.

Oja, Carol J. "Dane Rudhyar's Vision of American Dissonance." *American Music* 17 (1999): 129–45.

———. *Making Music Modern: New York in the 1920s.* New York: Oxford University Press, 2000.

———. "Rudhyar, Dane [Chennevière, Daniel]." In *Grove Music Online,* ed. L. Macy, www.grovemusic.com (accessed December 20, 2004).

O'Reilly, Victoria Jane. "Women's Participation in the Federal Music Project and Work Projects Administration Music Program." MA thesis, George Washington University, 1990.

Oxnam, G. Bromley. *The Mexican in Los Angeles: Los Angeles City Survey*. Los Angeles: Interchurch World Movement of North America, June 1920.

Palmer, Edwin O. *History of Hollywood*. Hollywood: Arthur H. Cawston, 1937.

Pastras, Phil. *Dead Man Blues: Jelly Roll Morton Way Out West*. Berkeley and Los Angeles: University of California Press, 2001.

Peiss, Kathy Lee. *Cheap Amusements: Working Women and Leisure in Turn-of-the-Century New York*. Philadelphia: Temple University Press, 1986.

Peress, Maurice. *Dvořák to Duke Ellington*. Oxford: Oxford University Press, 2004.

Perison, Harry D. "Charles Wakefield Cadman: His Life and Works." PhD dissertation, Eastman School of Music, University of Rochester, 1978.

Pico, Pio. *Don Pio Pico's Historical Narrative* (July 1848). Translated by Arthur P. Botello, edited by Martin Cole and Henry Welcome. Glendale, CA: A. H. Clark, 1973.

Pitt, Leonard. *The Decline of the Californios: A Social History of the Spanish-Speaking Californians, 1846–1890*. Berkeley and Los Angeles: University of California Press, 1966.

Pollack, Howard. *Aaron Copland: The Life and Work of an Uncommon Man*. Urbana: University of Illinois Press, 1999.

Pond, Major James B. *Eccentricities of Genius: Memories of Famous Men and Women of the Platform and Stage*. New York: G. W. Dillingham Company, 1900.

Pool, Jeannie G. "Music in Los Angeles, 1860–1900." MA thesis, California State University, Northridge, 1987.

Pratt, Mary Louise. *Imperial Eyes: Travel Writing and Transculturation*. London: Routledge, 1992.

Preston, Jean. "Olga Steeb: A Biography." Senior paper, Music Resource Center Department of Music, California State University, Long Beach, 1979.

Preston, Katherine K. "Between the Cracks: The Performance of English-Language Opera in Late Nineteenth-Century America." *American Music* 21 (2003): 349–74.

———. *Opera on the Road: Traveling Opera Troupes in the United States, 1825–60*. Urbana: University of Illinois Press, 1993.

Prevots-Wallen, Naima. "Art and Democracy." In *A Vision for Music*, ed. Carol Merrill-Mirsky. Los Angeles: Hollywood Bowl Museum, 1985.

———. "The Hollywood Bowl and Los Angeles Dance, 1926–1941: Performance Theory and Practice." PhD dissertation, University of Southern California, 1983.

Reese, Carol. "The Hollywood Bowl 1919–1989: The Land, the People, and the Music." Published serially in *Performing Arts* (Los Angeles), July 1989: 17–34; August 1989: 9–25; and September 1989: 25–32.

Report of the State Recreational Inquiry Committee, September 28, 1914. Sacramento: California State Printing Office, 1914.

Reyes, Luis, and Peter Rubie. *Hispanics in Hollywood: An Encyclopedia of Film and Television.* New York: Garland Publishing, 1994.

Reynolds, Caroline. "Theaters" column. *Los Angeles Graphic,* passim.

Riis, Thomas L. "Concert Singers, Prima Donnas, and Entertainers: The Changing Status of Black Women Vocalists in Nineteenth-Century America." In Michael Saffle, ed., *Music and Culture in America, 1861–1918,* 53–78. New York: Garland, 1998.

———. *Just before Jazz: Black Musical Theater in New York, 1890–1915.* Washington, DC: Smithsonian Institution Press, 1989.

Ríos-Bustamante, Antonio, and Pedro Castillo. *An Illustrated History of Mexican Los Angeles 1781–1985.* Los Angeles: University of California, Los Angeles, Chicano Studies Research Center, 1986.

Roberts, John Storm. *The Latin Tinge: The Impact of Latin American Music on the United States,* 2nd ed. New York: Oxford University Press, 1999.

Rodriguez, Jose, ed. *Music and Dance in California.* Hollywood: Bureau of Musical Research, 1940.

———. "Music Mostly in the Air." In Bruno David Ussher, ed., *Who's Who in Music and Dance in Southern California,* 20–21. Hollywood: Bureau of Musical Research, 1933.

Romo, Ricardo. *East Los Angeles: History of a Barrio.* Austin: University of Texas Press, 1983.

Rosenzweig, Roy. *Eight Hours for What We Will: Workers and Leisure in an Industrial City, 1870–1920.* Cambridge: Cambridge University Press, 1983.

Ross, Joseph E. *Krotona of Old Hollywood.* Montecito, CA: El Montecito Oaks Press, 1989.

Rubin, Emanuel. "Jeannette Meyer Thurber (1850–1946): Music for a Democracy." In Ralph P. Locke and Cyrilla Barr, eds., *Cultivating Music in America: Women Patrons and Activists since 1860,* 134–63. Berkeley and Los Angeles: University of California Press, 1997.

Ruddy, Ella Giles, ed. *The Mother of Clubs: Caroline M. Severance, an Estimate and an Appreciation.* Los Angeles: Baumgardt Publishing Company, 1906.

Rudhyar, Dane. "Creators and Public: Their Relationship." *Musical Quarterly* 10, no. 1 (1924): 120–30.

———. "The Harp and the Music of the Soul." *Eolian Review* 1, no. 1 (December 1921): 12–15.

———. "Imre Weisshaus Termed a New Revelation." *Los Angeles Times,* Sunday, November 20, 1927, sec. III, 19.

———. "The Phonograph as a Basis for Instrumental Musical Education." *Eolian Review* 4, no. 1 (January 1925): 7–10.

———. "A Program of Musical Regeneration." *Eolian Review* 3, no. 3 (May 1924): 13–20.

———. "The Relativity of Our Musical Conceptions." *Musical Quarterly* 8, no. 1 (1922): 108–18.

———. "The Revolt of the Angels: Carl Ruggles and the Future of Dissonant Counterpoint." *Eolian Review* 3, no. 1 (November 1923): 12–16.

———. "Toward a Deeper Musicality." *Eolian Review* 2, no. 3 (June 1923): 11–15.

———. "What Is an Octave?" *Eolian Review* 2, no. 1 (December 1922): 8–11.

Sampson, Henry T. *Blacks in Black and White: A Source Book on Black Films.* Metuchen, NJ: Scarecrow Press, 1977.

———. *The Ghost Walks: A Chronological History of Blacks in Show Business, 1865–1910.* Metuchen, NJ: Scarecrow Press, 1988.

Sanders, John. "Los Angeles Grand Opera Association: The Formative Years, 1924–26." *Southern California Quarterly* 55, no. 3 (Fall 1973): 261–302.

Sanford, Maria L. "The Influence of Good Art and Literature on Character." *California Outlook* 14, no. 14 (March 29, 1913): 15.

Saunders, Ann Wardell. "Hollywood–Los Angeles." In Richard Drake Saunders, ed., *Music and Dance in California and the West,* 153, 282–83. Hollywood: Bureau of Musical Research, 1948.

Saunders, Richard Drake. "California Composers Organize." *Educator,* 1936, 12.

———, ed. *Music and Dance in California and the West.* Hollywood: Bureau of Musical Research, 1948.

Schabas, Ezra. "Thomas, Theodore." In H. Wiley Hitchcock and S. Sadie, eds., *Grove Dictionary of American Music,* vol. 3, 381. London: Macmillan, 1896.

Schlundt, Christena L. *Into the Mystic with Miss Ruth.* New York: Dance Perspectives Foundation, 1971.

Searight, Frank T. "Schumann-Heink—Isn't She on at the Orpheum?" *Los Angeles Record,* March 29, 1905.

Shaffer, Ralph E. *"Crazy Shaw": Frederick M. Shaw, Southern California's Forgotten Dreamer.* Pomona, CA: author, 2007.

———. *Letters from the People: The Los Angeles Times Letters Column, 1881–1889.* www.intranet.csupomona.edu/~reshaffer/copyrtx.htm. 1999.

Shelton, Suzanne. *Ruth St. Denis: A Biography of the Divine Dancer.* Austin: University of Texas, 1990.

Sherman, Jane. *The Drama of Denishawn Dance.* Middletown, CT: Wesleyan University Press, 1979.

Shirley, Wayne D. "Two Aspects of *Troubled Island.*" *AMRC Journal* 13 (2003): 61–64.

———. "William Grant Still's Choral Ballad *And They Lynched Him on a Tree.*" *American Music* 12 (Winter 1994): 426–61.

Slonimsky, Nicolas. *Perfect Pitch: An Autobiography.* Edited by Electra Slonimsky Yourke. New York: Schirmer Trade Books, 2002.

Small, Christopher. *Musicking: The Meanings of Performing and Listening.* Hanover, NH: University Press of New England, 1998.

Smith, Caroline Estes. *The Philharmonic Orchestra of Los Angeles: The First Decade, 1919–1929.* Los Angeles: Press of United Printing Company, 1930.

Smith, Catherine Parsons. "Athena at the Manuscript Club: John Cage and Mary Carr Moore." *Musical Quarterly* 79, no. 2 (1995): 351–67.

———. "'A Distinguishing Virility': On Feminism and Modernism in American Art Music." In S. Cook and J. Tsou, eds., *Cecilia Reclaimed: Perspectives on Gender and Music,* 90–106. Urbana: University of Illinois Press, 1994.

———. "Founding the Hollywood Bowl." *American Music* 11 (1993): 206–43.

———. "'Glory Is a Passing Thing': William Grant Still and Langston Hughes Collaborate on *Troubled Island*." *American Musical Research Center Journal* 13 (2003): 5–24.

———. "Grunn, (John) Homer." In *Grove Music Online*, ed. L. Macy. www.grovemusic.com (accessed December 20, 2004).

———. "Inventing Tradition: Symphony and Opera in Progressive-Era Los Angeles." In Michael Saffle, ed., *Music and Culture in America, 1861–1918*, 299–322. New York: Garland Publishing, 1998.

———. "An Operatic Skeleton on the Western Frontier: Zitkala Sa, William F. Hanson, and *The Sun Dance Opera*." *Women & Music: A Journal of Gender and Culture* 5 (2001): 1–30.

———. "'Popular Prices Will Prevail': Setting the Social Role of European-Based Concert Music." *Selected Reports in Ethnomusicology* (Los Angeles issue) 10 (1994): 206–21.

———. "Primary Documentation of California Composers." In Stephen Fry, ed., *California's Musical Wealth*, 1–8. Los Angeles: Southern California Music Library Association, 1988.

———. "'Something of Good for the Future': The People's Orchestra of Los Angeles, 1912–1913." *Nineteenth-Century Music* 16 (1992): 147–61.

———. *William Grant Still*. Urbana: University of Illinois Press, forthcoming.

———. *William Grant Still: A Study in Contradictions*. Berkeley and Los Angeles: University of California Press, 2000.

Smith, Catherine Parsons, and Cynthia S. Richardson. *Mary Carr Moore, American Composer*. Ann Arbor: University of Michigan Press, 1987.

Smith, Fanny Morris. "The Work of Our Women's Musical Clubs." *Etude* (July 1909): 490.

Smith, Kathryn. *Frank Lloyd Wright, Hollyhock House and Olive Hill: Buildings and Projects for Aline Barnsdall*. New York: Rizzoli, 1992.

Southern California Writers Project. *Los Angeles: A Guide to the City and Its Environs*. New York: Hastings House, 1941, 1951.

Splitter, Henry Winfred. "Music in Los Angeles." *Historical Society of Southern California Quarterly* (December 1956): 307–44.

———. "Newspapers of Los Angeles: The First Fifty Years, 1851–1900." *Journal of the West* 2 (1963): 435–58.

Stanton, Jeffrey. *Venice, California: Coney Island of the Pacific*. Los Angeles: Donahue Publishing, 1993.

Starr, Kevin. *The Dream Endures: California Enters the 1940s*. New York: Oxford University Press, 1997.

———. *Endangered Dreams: The Great Depression in California*. New York: Oxford University Press, 1996.

———. *Inventing the Dream: California through the Progressive Era*. New York: Oxford University Press, 1985.

———. *Material Dreams: Southern California through the 1920s*. New York: Oxford University Press, 1990.

Steele, James. *Barnsdall House: Frank Lloyd Wright.* London: Phaidon, 1992.

Stein, Louise K. "Before the Latin Tinge: Spanish Music and the 'Spanish Idiom' in the United States, 1778–1940." In Richard L. Kagan, ed., *Spain in America: The Origins of Hispanism in the United States,* 193–246. Urbana: University of Illinois Press, 1990.

Stern, Charles W. *American Vaudeville.* New York: Da Capo Press, 1984.

Stevenson, Robert Murrell. "Carreño's 1875 California Appearances." *Inter-American Music Review* 5, no. 2 (1983): 9–15.

———. "The Latin Tinge, 1800–1900." *Inter-American Music Review* 2, no. 2 (Spring–Summer 1980): 73–101.

———. "Los Angeles." In H. Wiley Hitchcock and Stanley Sadie, eds., *The New Grove Dictionary of American Music,* vol. 3, 107–15. London: Macmillan Press, 1986.

———. "Los Angeles." In Stanley Sadie, ed., *The New Grove Dictionary of Opera,* vol. 3, 51–52. London: Macmillan Press Limited and New York: Grove's Dictionaries of Music, Inc., 1992.

———. "Music in Southern California: A Tale of Two Cities." *Inter-American Music Review* 10, no. 1 (1988): 51–111.

Stevenson, Robert Murrell, and William E. Conway. *William Andrews Clark, Jr., His Cultural Legacy; Papers Read at a Clark Library Seminar, 7 November 1981.* Los Angeles: William Andrews Clark Memorial Library, 1985.

Still, William Grant. "Personal Notes" [c. 1932]. Published in Catherine Parsons Smith, *William Grant Still: A Study in Contradictions,* 215–34. Berkeley and Los Angeles: University of California Press, 2000.

Stoddard, Tom. *Jazz on the Barbary Coast.* Chigwell, Essex: Storyville, 1982.

Sutherland, Henry A. "Requiem for the Los Angeles Philharmonic Auditorium." *Southern California Quarterly* (September 1965): 303–31.

Swan, Howard. *Music in the Southwest.* San Marino, CA: Huntington Library, 1952.

Teeple, John B. *The Oneida Family: Genealogy of a 19th Century Perfectionist Commune.* Cazenovia, NY: Gleaner Press, 1985.

Tefft, Lulu Marion Sanford. *Little Intimate Stories of Charles Wakefield Cadman.* Hollywood, CA: D. G. Fischer, 1926.

Thomas, Rose Fay, ed. *Memoirs of Theodore Thomas.* 1911; reprint, Freeport, NY: Books for Libraries Press, 1971.

Tibbetts, John C., ed. *Dvořák in America, 1892–95.* Portland, OR: Amadeus Press, 1993.

Tick, Judith. "Passed Away Is the Piano Girl." In Jane Bowers and Judith Tick, eds., *Women Making Music: The Western Art Tradition, 1150–1950,* 325–48. Urbana: University of Illinois Press, 1986.

———. "Ruth Crawford's 'Spiritual Concept': The Sound-Ideals of an Early American Modernist." *Journal of the American Musicological Society* 44, no. 2 (Summer 1991): 221–61.

Tindall, Glenn M. "Symphonies under the Stars: Concerts in the Hills of Hollywood." In Bruno David Ussher, ed., *Who's Who in Music and Dance in Southern California*, 27–28. Hollywood: Bureau of Musical Research, 1933.

Tolbert, Emory J. *The UNIA and Black Los Angeles: Ideology and Community in the American Garvey Movement*. Los Angeles: Center for Afro-American Studies, 1980.

Trevino, Roberto R. *Becoming Mexican American: The Spanish-Language Press and the Biculturation of California Elites, 1852–1870*. Stanford, CA: Stanford Center for Chicano Research, Working Paper Series, no. 27, 1989.

Tucker, Sherrie. *Swing Shift: "All-Girl" Bands of the 1940s*. Durham, NC: Duke University Press, 2000.

U.S. Bureau of the Census. *Occupations of the Twelfth Census*. Washington, DC: Government Printing Office, 1904.

———. *Statistical Abstracts of the United States*. Washington, DC: Government Printing Office, 1934, 1943.

———. *Tenth Census of the United States, 1880*, vol. 19. Washington, DC: Government Printing Office, 1883.

———. *United States Census*. Summary volumes of decennial censuses. Washington, DC: Government Printing Office, Department of Commerce, 1870–1940.

Ussher, Bruno David. "Music" column. *Los Angeles Saturday Night*, passim.

———, ed. *Who's Who in Music and Dance in Southern California*. Hollywood: Bureau of Musical Research, 1933.

Vaillant, Derek. *Sounds of Reform: Progressivism and Music in Chicago, 1873–1935*. Chapel Hill: University of North Carolina Press, 2003.

Walls, Brian Scott. "Chamber Music in Los Angeles, 1922–1954: A History of Concert Series, Ensembles, and Repertoire." MA thesis, California State University, Long Beach, 1980.

Waseda, Minako. "Japanese American Musical Culture in Southern California: Its Formation and Transformation in the 20th Century." PhD dissertation, University of California, Santa Barbara, 2000.

Wasserman, Steve. "Cultural Earthquake: Why LA Isn't Lotus-Land Anymore." *Opera News* 68, no. 1 (July 2003): 18.

Weatherwax, John. "On the Pacific Coast." *Modern Music* 11(1934): 106–9.

Who's Who in the Pacific Southwest: A Compilation of Authentic Biographical Sketches of Citizens of Southern California and Arizona. Los Angeles: Times-Mirror Printing and Binding House, 1913.

Wiecki, Ronald V. "A Chronicle of Pro Musica in the United States (1920–1944): With a Biographical Sketch of Its Founder, E. Robert Schmitz." PhD dissertation, University of Wisconsin, 1992.

Willhartitz, Adolph. *Some Facts about Woman in Music*. Los Angeles: Press of Out West Company, 1902.

———. "Woman in Music." *Musical Courier* 37, no. 9 (August 31, 1898): 29.

Williamson, Mrs. Burton M., ed. *Ladies Clubs and Societies in Los Angeles in 1892*. Los Angeles: Elmer King, 1925.

Winter, Robert. *Coleman: Musicmaker.* Los Angeles: Balcony Press, 2000.

Yeoman, Sharyn Wiley. "Messages from the Promised Land: Bohemian Los Angeles, 1880–1920." PhD dissertation, University of Colorado at Boulder, 2003.

Zuck, Barbara. *A History of Musical Americanism.* Ann Arbor: UMI Research Press, 1980.

Index

Page numbers in italics indicate figures.

Text:	10/13 Aldus
Display:	Aldus
Compositor:	Binghamton Valley Composition, LLC
Printer and Binder:	Maple-Vail Manufacturing Group